Mathematical Foundations of

Trustworthy AI

Theory, Algorithms, and Engineering Principles

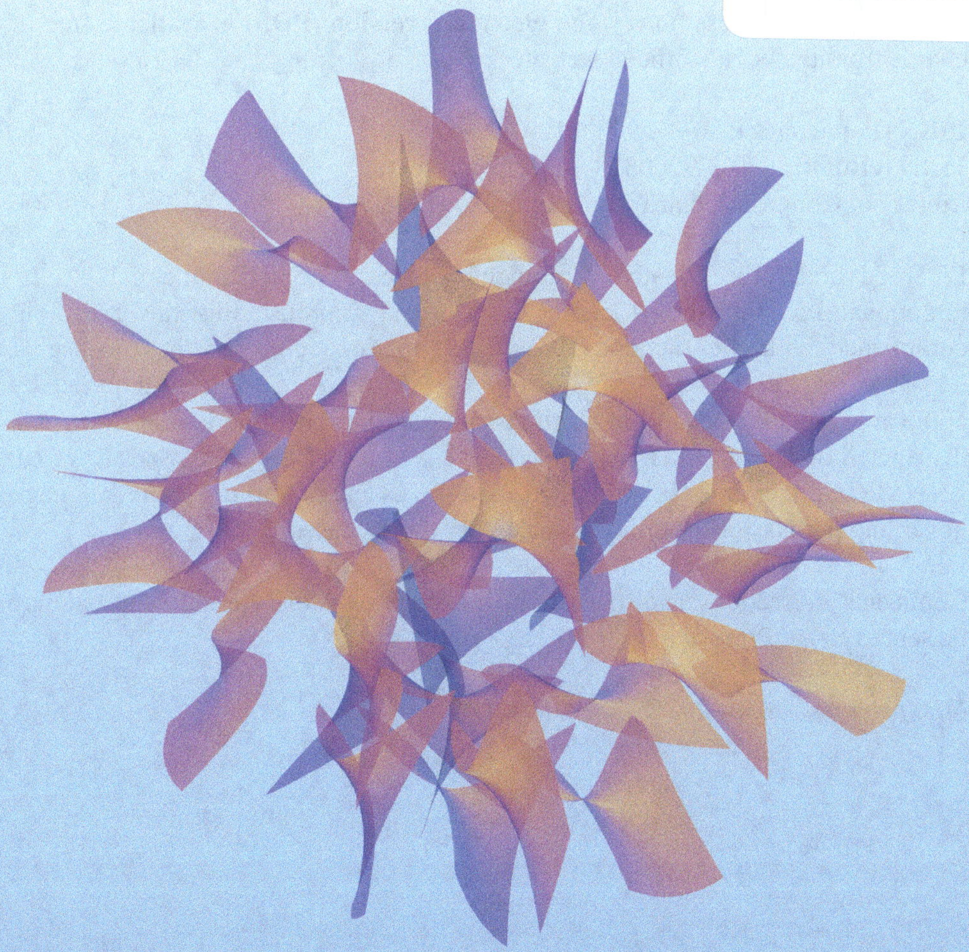

Aizierjiang Aiersilan

MATHEMATICAL FOUNDATIONS OF TRUSTWORTHY AI
Theory, Algorithms, and Engineering Principles

FIRST EDITION

Ezhar Press

This is an open-access book. The electronic version (PDF) is available free of charge from the book's official website: ezharjan.github.io/TAIBook.

ISBN (Paperback): 979-8-9960818-0-6
ISBN (eBook): 979-8-9960818-1-3 (Open Access)
Library of Congress Control Number: 2026913060

Comments, corrections, and suggestions for future revisions are welcome and may be sent to Ezhar Press at ezhar.press@gmail.com.

First printing, August 2026.

To the students, researchers, and practitioners working to make AI safer, fairer, and more trustworthy.

Preface

This book grew out of notes I compiled during the early phase of my self-study in Trustworthy AI. At the time, I found that while the research literature was rich and rapidly expanding, there were few systematic treatments that presented the mathematical foundations of this field in a unified, textbook-style manner. The notes were my attempt to fill that gap for my own learning; this book is an attempt to make them useful to others.

To the best of my knowledge, this is among the first books to offer a systematic mathematical foundation for Trustworthy AI. It brings together, under a single cover, the core theoretical results from constrained optimization, statistical learning theory, and differential geometry that underpin robustness, fairness, privacy, explainability, causality, and safety in machine learning systems. I make this claim with the caveat that the field is young and evolving quickly; other valuable perspectives certainly exist, and I welcome any work that advances this important area.

The material is intended for graduate students, researchers, and practitioners who seek precise mathematical statements, rigorous proofs, and concrete examples. Each chapter includes worked problems and exercises. Where a proof is only sketched, references to the full argument are provided.

Organization. The book has five parts and several appendices.

Part I (Foundations) introduces notation (Chapter 1), motivates the trust agenda (Chapter 2), and develops statistical learning theory (Chapter 3): concentration inequalities, VC dimension, Rademacher complexity, PAC learning, and uniform convergence.

Part II (Robustness, Fairness, Privacy) covers adversarial attacks and certified defenses (Chapter 4), impossibility theorems in algorithmic fairness (Chapter 5), and differential privacy with composition and accounting (Chapter 6).

Part III (Interpretability, Causality) develops Shapley values, LIME, integrated gradients (Chapter 7), structural causal models, the do-calculus, and counterfactual reasoning (Chapter 8).

Part IV (Distributed Learning, Decision Making) treats federated learning convergence and Byzantine robustness (Chapter 9), safe reinforcement learning with constraints and value alignment (Chapter 10), and out-of-distribution detection with conformal prediction (Chapter 11).

Part V (Engineering, Governance, Frontiers) addresses formal verification of neural networks and AI governance (Chapter 12), advanced techniques such as Lipschitz networks, robust statistics, and shuffle-model privacy (Chapter 13), and trustworthy agentic AI together with open research directions (Chapter 14).

Appendices provide mathematical prerequisites (Appendix A), extended proofs (Appendix B), Python implementations (Appendix C), evaluation metrics (Appendix D), and a glossary of key terms (Appendix E). All mathematical notation used throughout the book is collected, organized thematically by sub-discipline, in the dedicated notation chapter at the front of the book (Chapter 1), which serves as the single, authoritative reference for every symbol.

Figure 1 visualizes how these parts fit together as a single mathematical pipeline, beginning with foundational theory, ascending through the five trust dimensions, culminating in engineering and governance, and supported throughout by appendix material.

Insights for the reader. A few editorial principles shaped this book and may be useful to keep in mind while reading. First, *trust is treated as a quantifiable property, not a slogan*: every chapter reduces an informal desideratum (robustness, fairness, privacy, explainability, causality, safety) to one or more mathematical objects with explicit guarantees, sample complexities, or impossibility results. Second, the chapters are designed to be *compositional*: the concentration inequalities and complexity measures of Part I reappear as the privacy accountant in Part II, the generalization bound on counterfactual estimators in Part III, the convergence proof of FedAvg in Part IV, and the certified-training bounds in Part V. Third, the book deliberately pairs *positive results with their limits*; impossibility theorems (Kleinberg–Chouldechova in fairness, Dinur–Nissim in privacy, no-free-lunch in OOD) are presented as first-class citizens rather than footnotes, because honest trustworthy AI is as much about knowing what cannot be done as about engineering what can. Finally, although the treatment is mathematical, every theoretical result in the book is accompanied either by a worked example, a reference Python implementation in Appendix C, or an evaluation protocol in Appendix D, so that the chain from theorem to deployable algorithm is never left implicit.

Scope and limitations. Impossibility results are stated where they apply. Where theory lags behind practice, I note the gap. This field moves quickly; some results will be superseded. I have aimed for accuracy, but errors may remain.

Access. The electronic edition of this book is Open Access and freely available online; a paperback edition is also available.

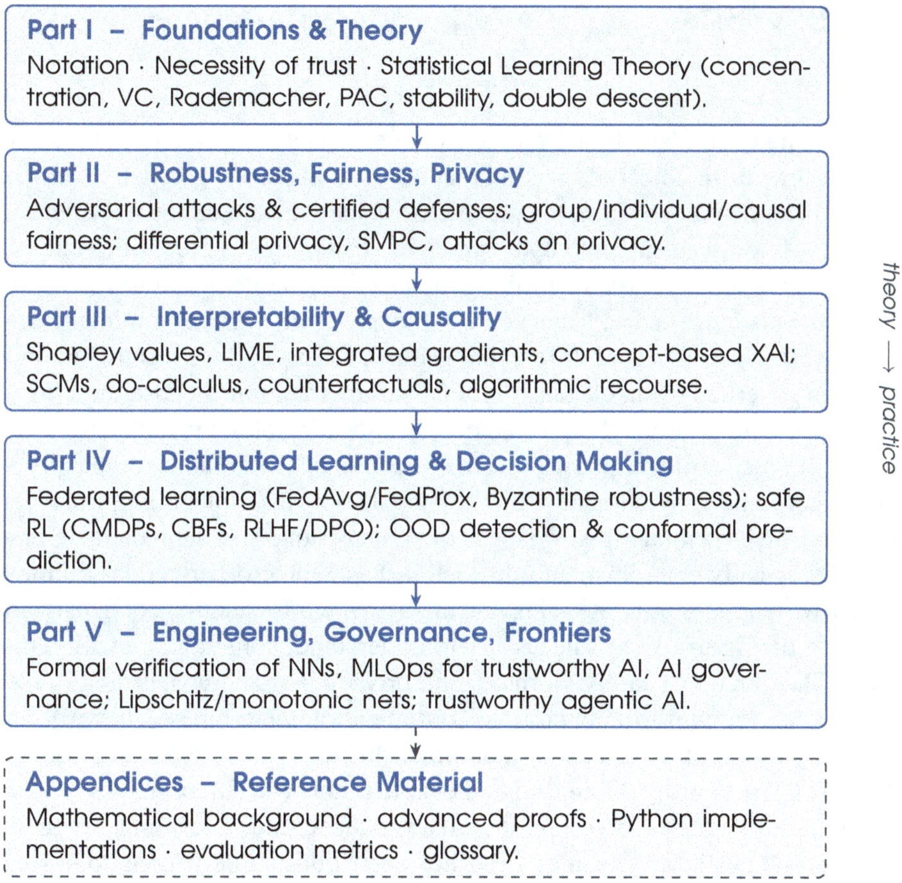

Figure 1: Structure of the book. The five Parts are arranged as a vertical pipeline: foundational theory (Part I) feeds into the three core trust properties (Part II), interpretability and causality (Part III), distributed and sequential decision-making (Part IV), and finally verification, deployment, and frontier topics (Part V). The appendices (dashed) provide cross-cutting reference material used throughout.

Read the e-book online

Scan the QR code with your phone, or open the link below in any modern browser:

ezharjan.github.io/TAIBook

Open Access · Free to read, share, and cite.

A note on the cover. The figure on the front cover is a cross-section of a Calabi–Yau-type surface, an object of the kind that arises in algebraic geometry and string theory. It is rendered here from the parametric equations that define it. Its intricate, self-similar folds are generated by a handful of trigonometric identities and complex phase rotations, yet the resulting geometry is rich enough to have occupied mathematicians for decades. The back cover depicts the Enneper minimal surface, one of the classical objects of differential geometry. This surface locally minimizes area and is governed by an elegantly simple parametrization. I chose these figures because they embody something I find deeply appealing about mathematics: that a small set of precise rules can give rise to structures of remarkable complexity and beauty. That same conviction animates this book. The invisible, high-dimensional spaces navigated by modern AI systems are often opaque and unpredictable, much like a topologically complex manifold. Yet, just as geometric principles illuminate the order within these intricate folds, the mathematical foundations of Trustworthy AI provide the rigorous tools necessary to understand, constrain, and align these models. The pursuit of safety, fairness, and privacy in machine learning is essentially a search for equilibria in complex optimization landscapes. This process is mirrored by the elegant balance of a minimal surface. I believe the consequential problems of Trustworthy AI are fully amenable to this careful, principled analysis. If the cover art suggests anything, it is that provably safe algorithms, mathematical rigor, and aesthetic elegance need not be at odds. The source code for all cover artwork, chapter headers, and visual design elements is publicly available at https://github.com/Ezharjan/TAIBookUI.

Aizierjiang Aiersilan

August 2026

Contents

III Interpretability and Causality

IV Distributed Learning and Decision Making

List of Tables

Foundations and Theory

Contents of This Part

Chapter 1
Notation and Conventions

Throughout this book, we use consistent mathematical notation. This chapter is the **single, authoritative reference** for every symbol used in the text and should be the reader's first point of consultation when a symbol is unfamiliar. Core symbols are grouped by topic in Tables 1.1–1.4; fairness, calibration, conformal-prediction, and out-of-distribution detection symbols appear in Tables 1.5–1.6; typographic conventions are summarized in Table 1.7; and the notation specific to agentic AI appears in Table 1.8. A small number of symbols (notably the Greek letters $\alpha, \beta, \gamma, \ldots$ and several calligraphic capitals) are necessarily *overloaded* across sub-disciplines; Tables 1.9 and 1.10 list every such symbol together with the context in which each meaning applies. The intended reading is always unambiguous from the surrounding text, and each symbol is also redefined at its first use in the chapter where it appears.

Table 1.1: Core mathematical notation: spaces, probability, norms, and distances.

Symbol	Description
Spaces and Data	
$\mathcal{X} \subseteq \mathbb{R}^d$	Input (feature) space
$\mathcal{Y}$	Output (label) space
$\mathcal{H} \subseteq \{f : \mathcal{X} \to \mathcal{Y}\}$	Hypothesis class
$\mathcal{D} = \{(x_i, y_i)\}_{i=1}^n$	Training dataset of n i.i.d. samples
$\mathcal{P}$	Joint distribution over $\mathcal{X} \times \mathcal{Y}$
Δ^{K-1}	$(K-1)$-dimensional probability simplex
Probability and Statistics	
$P(\cdot)$	Probability measure
$\mathbb{E}[\cdot]$	Expectation
$\mathrm{Var}[\cdot]$, $\mathrm{Cov}[\cdot,\cdot]$	Variance and covariance
$X \perp Y \mid Z$	Conditional independence of X and Y given Z
$\mathcal{N}(\mu, \sigma^2)$	Univariate Gaussian distribution with mean μ and variance σ^2
$\mathrm{Lap}(b)$	Laplace distribution with scale b (location 0)
$\mathrm{Dir}(\alpha)$	Dirichlet distribution with concentration parameter α
$H(X) = -\mathbb{E}[\log P(X)]$	Shannon entropy of X
$I(X;Y) = H(X) - H(X \mid Y)$	Mutual information between X and Y
$D_{\mathrm{KL}}(P\|Q) = \mathbb{E}_P\left[\log \frac{dP}{dQ}\right]$	Kullback–Leibler divergence (relative entropy of P w.r.t. Q)
$D_\alpha(P\|Q) = \frac{1}{\alpha-1} \log \mathbb{E}_Q\left[\left(\frac{dP}{dQ}\right)^\alpha\right]$	Rényi divergence of order $\alpha > 1$
$D_f(P\|Q) = \mathbb{E}_Q\left[f\left(\frac{dP}{dQ}\right)\right]$	f-divergence with convex generator f (with $f(1) = 0$)
$W_p(P,Q)$	Wasserstein-p distance between P and Q
Norms and Distances	
$\|x\|_p = \left(\sum_i \|x_i\|^p\right)^{1/p}$	L_p (vector) norm, $p \geq 1$
$\|x\|_1 = \sum_i \|x_i\|$	L_1 norm (Manhattan distance)
$\|x\|_2 = \sqrt{\sum_i x_i^2}$	L_2 norm (Euclidean distance)
$\|x\|_\infty = \max_i \|x_i\|$	L_∞ norm (Chebyshev distance)
$\|W\|_{\mathrm{op}} = \sup_{\|x\|_2=1} \|Wx\|_2$	Spectral norm (largest singular value)
$d(\cdot,\cdot)$	A metric or distance function
$\mathcal{B}_\varepsilon(x) = \{x' : \|x' - x\|_p \leq \varepsilon\}$	ℓ_p-ball of radius ε centered at x
$\Pi_C(\cdot)$	Euclidean projection onto a closed convex set C

Table 1.2: Core mathematical notation: functions, operators, and learning parameters.

Symbol	Description
Functions and Operators	
$\ell(\hat{y}, y)$	Loss function
$\mathscr{R}(f) = \mathbb{E}_{(x,y)\sim\mathscr{P}}[\ell(f(x), y)]$	Expected (population) risk
$\hat{\mathscr{R}}_n(f) = \frac{1}{n}\sum_{i=1}^{n} \ell(f(x_i), y_i)$	Empirical risk over n samples
∇f, $\nabla_x f$	Gradient of f (with respect to x)
arg min, arg max	Minimizing and maximizing arguments
$\mathbb{I}(\cdot)$	Indicator function (1 if true, 0 otherwise)
$\sigma(\cdot)$	Activation function (e.g., ReLU, sigmoid) unless stated otherwise
$\mathrm{sign}(x) \in \{-1, 0, +1\}$	Sign function (element-wise)
$\odot$	Element-wise (Hadamard) multiplication
$\mathrm{diag}(\cdot)$	Diagonal-matrix constructor / extraction of diagonal
$\mathrm{Top}_k(\cdot)$	Top-k sparsification operator (keeps the k largest magnitudes)
$\mathrm{Quantile}_p(\cdot)$	p-th empirical quantile
$f_\theta : \mathscr{X} \to \mathscr{Y}$	Parametric model with parameters θ
$d_{VC}(\mathscr{H})$	VC dimension of hypothesis class $\mathscr{H}$
$\mathfrak{R}_n(\mathscr{H})$	Rademacher complexity of $\mathscr{H}$ on n samples
Learning Parameters	
η	Learning rate
λ	Regularization strength or Lagrange multiplier (context-dependent)
ε	Perturbation budget (robustness), privacy budget (DP), or error tolerance (PAC)
δ	Failure probability or privacy failure parameter
T	Number of training rounds or time steps
Subscript $_t$	Round or time step
Superscript *	Optimal value
$\hat{\cdot}$	Empirical estimate

Table 1.3: Domain-specific notation: differential privacy and causal inference.

Symbol	Description
Differential Privacy	
$\mathscr{M}$	A randomized mechanism
$\Delta_1 f = \max_{D,D'} \|f(D) - f(D')\|_1$	ℓ_1-sensitivity of f over neighboring datasets
$\Delta_2 f = \max_{D,D'} \|f(D) - f(D')\|_2$	ℓ_2-sensitivity of f over neighboring datasets
(ε, δ)-DP	Mechanism satisfies (ε, δ)-differential privacy
q	Subsampling rate (fraction of data used per step)
$Z = \log\left[\frac{P(\mathscr{M}(D)=o)}{P(\mathscr{M}(D')=o)}\right]$	Privacy-loss random variable for output o on neighboring D, D'
$\alpha_{\mathscr{M}}(\lambda) = \log \mathbb{E}[e^{\lambda Z}]$	Log-moment generating function of the privacy loss (moments accountant)
n_c	Vote count for class c in the PATE aggregator
C	Gradient clipping threshold (DP-SGD)
Causal Inference	
$\mathscr{G} = (\mathscr{V}, \mathscr{E})$	Directed acyclic graph (DAG)
$\mathrm{Pa}(X)$, Pa_i	Parent nodes of X (resp. of V_i) in $\mathscr{G}$
V_i, U_i	Endogenous (observed) and exogenous (latent) variables
$f_i : V_i = f_i(\mathrm{Pa}(V_i), U_i)$	Structural equation for variable V_i
$\mathscr{F} = \{f_1, \ldots, f_n\}$	Collection of structural equations of an SCM
$\mathrm{do}(X = x)$	Intervention setting X to x
$Y_{x'}$	Counterfactual value of Y under $\mathrm{do}(X = x')$
$G_{\bar{X}}$	Graph with incoming edges to X removed
$G_{\underline{X}}$	Graph with outgoing edges from X removed
$G_{\bar{X}\underline{Z}}$	Graph with arrows into X and out of Z removed
$G_{\bar{X}\bar{Z}(W)}$	Graph with arrows into X and into the W-ancestors of Z removed
$x'_{\text{actionable}}$, $x'_{\text{downstream}}$	Actionable and downstream features for algorithmic recourse
$\mathscr{I}$	Set of immutable or monotonic features in actionable recourse

Table 1.4: Domain-specific notation: explainability, reinforcement learning, and federated learning.

Symbol	Description
Explainability	
$\phi_i(f,x)$	Shapley value of feature i for model f at input x
$f_x(S)$	Prediction of f with feature subset $S \subseteq [d]$ (with the rest marginalized)
$g^*(x)$	Locally fitted interpretable surrogate model (e.g., LIME)
Reinforcement Learning	
$\mathscr{S}, \mathscr{A}$	State and action spaces
$\pi(a \mid s)$	Policy (stochastic, conditional on state)
$V^\pi(s) = \mathbb{E}^\pi\left[\sum_{t=0}^{\infty} \gamma^t r_t \mid s_0 = s\right]$	State-value function under policy π
$Q^\pi(s,a)$	State-action value function
$A^\pi(s,a) = Q^\pi(s,a) - V^\pi(s)$	Advantage function under policy π
$J(\pi) = \mathbb{E}^\pi\left[\sum_t \gamma^t r_t\right]$	Expected discounted return
$J_R(\pi), J_C(\pi)$	Expected return and expected cost of π (CMDP)
$C_i(\pi)$	Expected cost for constraint i in constrained MDPs
$L_{\pi_k}(\pi)$	Surrogate objective at iterate π_k (CPO/TRPO)
$\bar{D}_{\mathrm{KL}}(\pi_k \\| \pi)$	State-averaged KL divergence between policies (old policy π_k first)
$\gamma \in [0,1)$	Discount factor
$h(s)$	Control barrier function
$V_L(s)$	Lyapunov function
$F : r' = r + F(s,a,s')$	Potential-based reward-shaping function
$\mathscr{L}_{\mathrm{RM}}, \mathscr{L}_{\mathrm{DPO}}$	Reward-model and Direct-Preference-Optimization losses
π_{ref}	Reference policy used in RLHF / DPO
Federated Learning	
K	Number of clients
E	Number of local epochs per round
$p_k = n_k/n$	Aggregation weight of client k (proportional to local data size)
$F_k(\mathbf{w})$	Local objective of client k
$S_t \subseteq [K]$	Set of clients selected at round t
σ_k^2, σ_g^2	Local-gradient variance bound and inter-client heterogeneity bound
$Q(g)$	Quantized version of gradient g
$U,V\,;r$	Low-rank factor matrices and the rank used in compression
ϕ, ψ_k	Shared (global) and personal layer parameters
x^*, y^*	Reconstructed input and label from a gradient-leakage attack

Table 1.5: Domain-specific notation: algorithmic fairness.

Symbol	Description
Algorithmic Fairness	
A	Sensitive (protected) attribute (e.g., gender, race)
$Y, \hat{Y}$	True label and predicted label
$\mathrm{TPR}_a = P(\hat{Y}=1 \mid Y=1, A=a)$	Group-conditional true-positive rate
$\mathrm{FPR}_a = P(\hat{Y}=1 \mid Y=0, A=a)$	Group-conditional false-positive rate
DPD	Demographic-parity difference: $\lvert P(\hat{Y}=1 \mid A=0) - P(\hat{Y}=1 \mid A=1) \rvert$
EOD	Equalized-odds difference: $\frac{1}{2}\left(\lvert \mathrm{TPR}_0 - \mathrm{TPR}_1 \rvert + \lvert \mathrm{FPR}_0 - \mathrm{FPR}_1 \rvert\right)$
$\hat{Y} \perp A$	Statistical (demographic) parity
$\hat{Y} \perp A \mid Y$	Equalized odds (separation)

Table 1.6: Domain-specific notation: calibration, conformal prediction, and out-of-distribution (OOD) detection.

Symbol	Description
Calibration	
B_b	The b-th calibration bin (used in ECE / reliability diagrams)
$\mathrm{acc}(B_b)$, $\mathrm{conf}(B_b)$	Accuracy and average confidence inside bin B_b
$\mathrm{ECE} = \sum_b \frac{\lvert B_b \rvert}{n} \lvert \mathrm{acc}(B_b) - \mathrm{conf}(B_b) \rvert$	Expected calibration error
$T^\star$	Optimal temperature (temperature scaling)
Conformal Prediction & Selective Classification	
$s(x,y)$	(Non-)conformity score
$\hat{q}_{1-\alpha}$	Conformal quantile at miscoverage α
$C(x) \subseteq \mathscr{Y}$	Prediction set at input x
$\kappa(x)$	Confidence (rejection) function in selective prediction
$R(\tau)$	Selective risk at threshold τ
$S_{\mathrm{MSP}}(x) = \max_c \hat{p}(y=c \mid x)$	Maximum-softmax-probability score
$S_{C,k}$	Concept-sensitivity score for concept k
OOD Detection	
$P_{\mathrm{train}}, P_{\mathrm{test}}$	Training (in-distribution) and test / deployment distributions
$\tilde{x}$	Perturbed or OOD input
$E(x) = -\log \sum_c e^{f_c(x)}$	Energy-based OOD score (negative log-sum-exp of logits)
q_ϕ	Variational posterior with parameters ϕ (BNN / VI)
$\mathbf{w}$, $\mathbf{z}$	Bayesian-NN weights and Monte-Carlo dropout masks

Table 1.7: Typographic conventions.

Convention	Description
Boldface ($\mathbf{w}$, $\mathbf{x}$)	Vectors or matrices
Calligraphic ($\mathscr{X}$, $\mathscr{H}$)	Sets, spaces, or hypothesis classes
Blackboard bold ($\mathbb{R}$, $\mathbb{N}$, $\mathbb{E}$)	Number fields and expectation
$[K] = \{1, 2, \ldots, K\}$	Index set
Subscript $_k$	Client index in federated settings
Primed symbols (x', D')	Perturbed or alternative versions
log / ln	Natural logarithm (used interchangeably unless a base is stated)

Table 1.8: Domain-specific notation: agentic AI and multi-agent systems.

Symbol	Description
Tools and Action Spaces	
$\mathscr{T} = \{t_1, \ldots, t_m\}$	Tool set available to the agent
$t_i : \mathscr{D}_i \to \mathscr{R}_i$	Tool i mapping its input domain $\mathscr{D}_i$ to its output range $\mathscr{R}_i$
$\mathscr{A}_{\text{text}}$	Natural-language action space
$\mathscr{A}_{t_i}$	Tool-invocation action space for tool t_i
$\mathscr{A}_{\text{safe}}$	Safe action subset
$\mathscr{A}_{\text{corr}}$	Correction actions (e.g., shutdown, ask-for-help)
Pre_i, Post_i	Tool precondition / postcondition
σ	Action shield function (filters unsafe actions)
Dynamics and Trajectories	
P_{env}	Environment transition-observation dynamics
$\tau = (s_0, o_0, a_0, s_1, o_1, a_1, \ldots, s_T, o_T)$	Agent trajectory
$P_\pi(\tau)$	Trajectory distribution induced by policy π
δ_k	Per-step failure probability at step k
Multi-Agent and Welfare	
N	Number of agents (Markov games)
$\boldsymbol{\pi} = (\pi_1, \ldots, \pi_N)$	Joint policy across N agents
$V_i^{\boldsymbol{\pi}}(s)$	Value function of agent i under joint policy $\boldsymbol{\pi}$
$W(\boldsymbol{\pi})$	Social welfare of joint policy $\boldsymbol{\pi}$
NE	Set of Nash equilibria
PoA	Price of anarchy
U_H	Human principal's utility function
Trust and Evaluation	
TCR	Task completion rate
SVR	Safety violation rate
$\text{Trust}(\tau)$	Trajectory-level trust score

Table 1.9: Context-dependent meanings of recurring Greek-letter symbols.

Symbol	Contextual meanings
α	class-$\mathscr{K}$ function parameter (CBF); significance level (conformal prediction; fairness confidence intervals); interpolation parameter (integrated gradients); inner-loop learning rate (MAML); order parameter (Rényi divergence / RDP)
β	trade-off coefficient (TRADES); KL coefficient (RLHF/DPO); regularizer strength (IRM)
γ	MDP discount factor; classification margin (statistical learning theory); integration path $\gamma(\alpha)$ (integrated gradients)
δ	trust-region size (CPO); failure probability (DP, PAC); additive perturbation (adversarial); dual variable (CPO)
η	gradient step / learning rate; additive perturbation (linearity hypothesis)
θ	model parameters; policy parameters (RL)
κ	confidence parameter (Carlini–Wagner attack); confidence function (selective prediction); condition number L/μ (convex optimization)
λ	Lagrange multiplier; regularization weight; moment order (moments accountant); DiCE hyperparameter
μ	proximal coefficient (FedProx); zeroth-order step size; class mean (Mahalanobis distance)
ν	dual variable (CPO)
ξ	random binary vector (stochastic quantization); LIME objective
π	policy (RL); mixing coefficients (mixtures of experts); proximity kernel (LIME)
ρ	uncertainty-set radius (DRO)
σ	activation function (general); Gaussian-mechanism noise scale; Gaussian noise standard deviation; action shield (agentic AI)
τ	threshold (selective prediction); temperature (temperature scaling); trajectory (RL, agentic AI)
ϕ	coverage (selective prediction); shared layers (personalized FL); Shapley value; property specification (formal verification)
Φ	potential function (reward shaping); standard-normal inverse CDF (randomized smoothing)
χ	chi-squared divergence (DRO)
ψ	personal layers (personalized FL)

Table 1.10: Context-dependent meanings of recurring calligraphic symbols.

Symbol	Contextual meanings
$\mathscr{A}$	adversary (security); action space (MDP); action set (agentic AI)
$\mathscr{B}$	uncertainty set (robust recourse); calibration bins (ECE)
$\mathscr{C}$	safe set (CBF); prediction set (conformal prediction)
$\mathscr{E}$	edge set (causal DAG); training environments (IRM)
$\mathscr{F}$	structural-equation collection (SCM)
$\mathscr{G}$	directed acyclic graph (causal inference); manipulated graph variants (e.g. $G_{\bar{X}}$)
$\mathscr{I}$	immutable or monotonic features (actionable recourse)
$\mathscr{M}$	randomized mechanism (DP); structural causal model
$\mathscr{P}$	probability distribution; protocol (MPC)
$\mathscr{R}$	risk functional; output space (DP)
$\mathscr{S}$	state space (MDP); perturbation set; unsafe-state set
$\mathscr{T}$	tool set (agentic AI)
$\mathscr{U}$	uncertainty set (DRO); unsafe-state set
$\mathscr{Z}$	latent space; exogenous variables (SCM)

Chapter 2

Introduction: The Necessity of Trust

The rapid and pervasive integration of Artificial Intelligence (AI) into the fabric of modern society has fundamentally altered the landscape of decision-making in critical sectors such as healthcare, epidemiological modeling, medical imaging, and mathematical theorem proving. While the empirical performance of these systems, measured by aggregate metrics like accuracy or F1-score on static test sets, has reached superhuman levels on specific benchmarks, this superficial success often masks deep-seated vulnerabilities. The deployment of AI in high-stakes environments has precipitated a crisis of trust. This crisis is driven by high-profile failures where systems have exhibited brittleness in the face of adversarial manipulation, displayed unintended disparities in data subpopulations, leaked sensitive personal information, or operated as inscrutable black boxes whose reasoning cannot be audited. Trustworthy AI, therefore, is not merely a collection of ethical guidelines or policy desiderata; it is a rigorous technical discipline that demands a foundational reimagining of how we design, train, and verify machine learning systems. It requires moving beyond the paradigm of average-case performance maximization to a regime of worst-case robustness, causal validity, and provable constraints.

We posit that the nebulous concept of "trust" can be decomposed into a set of mathematically precise, verifiable properties. Rather than relying on intuition, we define these properties through the lens of constrained optimization, statistical learning theory, and differential geometry. **Robustness** is formalized as the invariance of the model's output under bounded perturbations of the input, requiring Lipschitz continuity or specific geometric margins. **Fairness** is articulated as statistical independence between model predictions and sensitive attributes, or as the equality of error rates across demographic groups, often invoking impossibility theorems that delineate the trade-offs between different ethical ideals. **Privacy** is rigorously defined via Differential Privacy, which quantifies the stability of the algorithm's output distribution with respect to the presence or absence of any single individual's data. **Explainability** seeks to provide faithful, interpretable surrogates or attribution maps that elucidate the decision boundary. **Causality** ensures that the model captures the structural equations governing the data-generating process, rather than merely exploiting spurious correlations. This book is intended to serve as a comprehensive mathematical and technical reference for Trustworthy AI. Table 2.1 summarizes the five dimensions developed in this book together with the mathematical formalisms used to make them precise.

Table 2.1: Dimensions of Trustworthy AI and their Mathematical Formalizations

Dimension	Core Concept	Mathematical Formalism
Robustness	Stability under perturbation	Lipschitz continuity, Dual norms, Min-max optimization
Fairness	Independence from sensitive traits	Statistical Parity ($\hat{Y} \perp A$), Equalized Odds ($\hat{Y} \perp A \mid Y$)
Privacy	Indistinguishability of datasets	Differential Privacy ((ε, δ)-DP), Rényi Divergence
Explainability	Interpretability of decisions	Shapley values, Local linear approximations, Saliency maps
Causality	Structural validity	Structural Causal Models (SCMs), Do-calculus, Interventions

Note: In this table, $\hat{Y}$ denotes the model prediction, A represents the sensitive attribute, Y is the true label, $\perp$ indicates statistical independence, and ε, δ are privacy budget parameters.

Chapter 3

Statistical Learning Theory and Generalization

This chapter establishes the mathematical foundations of statistical learning theory [55, 69], which provides the theoretical framework for understanding when and why machine learning algorithms work. We develop the core concepts rigorously, with complete proofs and detailed explanations that connect the mathematical formalism to practical implications for Trustworthy AI.

3.1 The Learning Problem Formulation

3.1.1 Mathematical Setup

The fundamental goal of supervised machine learning is to construct a predictive mapping $f : \mathscr{X} \to \mathscr{Y}$ that generalizes well to unseen data. Let $\mathscr{X} \subseteq \mathbb{R}^d$ denote the input space and $\mathscr{Y}$ the output space. We assume the existence of a joint probability distribution $\mathscr{P}$ over $\mathscr{X} \times \mathscr{Y}$. The learner is provided with a training dataset $\mathscr{D} = \{(x_i, y_i)\}_{i=1}^n$, where each sample is drawn independently and identically distributed (i.i.d.) from $\mathscr{P}$.

Definition 3.1.1 — Statistical Learning Problem. A statistical learning problem is specified by a tuple $(\mathscr{X}, \mathscr{Y}, \mathscr{P}, \mathscr{H}, \ell)$ where:

- $\mathscr{X} \subseteq \mathbb{R}^d$ is the **input space** (feature space)
- $\mathscr{Y}$ is the **output space** (label space)
- $\mathscr{P}$ is an unknown probability distribution over $\mathscr{X} \times \mathscr{Y}$
- $\mathscr{H} \subseteq \{f : \mathscr{X} \to \mathscr{Y}\}$ is the **hypothesis class**
- $\ell : \mathscr{Y} \times \mathscr{Y} \to \mathbb{R}_{\geq 0}$ is the **loss function**

The assumption of i.i.d. sampling is central to classical learning theory, allowing us to apply the Law of Large Numbers and concentration inequalities to bound the difference between empirical observations and true population statistics. However, in the context of Trustworthy AI, this assumption is often violated; adversaries may shift the distribution, or the deployment environment may differ from the training environment (distribution shift).

3.1.2 Common Output Spaces and Loss Functions

For **binary classification**, $\mathcal{Y} = \{-1,+1\}$ or $\{0,1\}$. Common loss functions include:

- **0-1 Loss**: $\ell_{0-1}(\hat{y},y) = \mathbb{I}(\hat{y} \neq y)$
- **Hinge Loss**: $\ell_{\text{hinge}}(\hat{y},y) = \max(0, 1 - y\hat{y})$ (used in SVMs; requires $y \in \{-1,+1\}$)
- **Logistic Loss**: $\ell_{\log}(\hat{y},y) = \log(1+e^{-y\hat{y}})$ (used in logistic regression; requires $y \in \{-1,+1\}$)
- **Exponential Loss**: $\ell_{\exp}(\hat{y},y) = e^{-y\hat{y}}$ (used in AdaBoost; requires $y \in \{-1,+1\}$)

For **multi-class classification**, $\mathcal{Y} = \{1,2,\ldots,K\}$. The cross-entropy loss is:

$$\ell_{\text{CE}}(\hat{p},y) = -\sum_{k=1}^{K} \mathbb{I}(y=k)\log \hat{p}_k = -\log \hat{p}_y \tag{3.1}$$

where $\hat{p} \in \Delta^{K-1}$ is a probability distribution over classes, $\hat{p}_k$ is the predicted probability for class k, $y \in \{1,\ldots,K\}$ is the true class label, and $\mathbb{I}(\cdot)$ is the indicator function which is 1 if the argument is true and 0 otherwise. Concretely, $\Delta^{K-1} = \{p \in \mathbb{R}^K : p_k \geq 0,\ \sum_k p_k = 1\}$ is the $(K-1)$-dimensional probability simplex (the set of all K-class probability vectors); $\hat{p}$ is just the model's confidence vector. The right-hand identity holds because exactly one indicator $\mathbb{I}(y=k)$ equals 1 (for the true class), so the sum collapses to the negative log-probability that the model assigns to the correct class.

For **regression**, $\mathcal{Y} = \mathbb{R}$ or $\mathcal{Y} = \mathbb{R}^m$. Common loss functions include:

- **Squared Loss**: $\ell_2(\hat{y},y) = (y-\hat{y})^2$
- **Absolute Loss**: $\ell_1(\hat{y},y) = |y-\hat{y}|$
- **Huber Loss**: $\ell_\delta(\hat{y},y) = \begin{cases} \frac{1}{2}(y-\hat{y})^2 & |y-\hat{y}| \leq \delta \\ \delta(|y-\hat{y}| - \frac{\delta}{2}) & \text{otherwise} \end{cases}$ where $\delta > 0$ is a threshold parameter controlling the transition from quadratic to linear behavior.
- **Quantile Loss**: $\ell_\tau(\hat{y},y) = \max(\tau(y-\hat{y}), (\tau-1)(y-\hat{y}))$ for $\tau \in (0,1)$, where τ represents the target quantile (e.g., $\tau = 0.5$ for median regression).

Table 3.1 collects these classification and regression loss functions together with their formulas, applicable settings, and label conventions.

3.1.3 Risk and Empirical Risk

The quality of a predictor f is measured by a loss function $\ell : \mathcal{Y} \times \mathcal{Y} \to \mathbb{R}_{\geq 0}$. The true objective is to minimize the *expected risk* (also called *population risk* or *true risk*), which represents the average loss over the entire data distribution:

Table 3.1: Summary of common loss functions.

Loss Function	Formula	Setting	Label Convention
0-1 Loss	$\mathbb{I}(\hat{y} \neq y)$	Binary classif.	$y \in \{0,1\}$ or $\{-1,+1\}$
Hinge Loss	$\max(0, 1 - y\hat{y})$	Binary (SVM)	$y \in \{-1,+1\}$
Logistic Loss	$\log(1 + e^{-y\hat{y}})$	Binary (logistic)	$y \in \{-1,+1\}$
Exponential	$e^{-y\hat{y}}$	Binary (AdaBoost)	$y \in \{-1,+1\}$
Cross-Entropy	$-\log \hat{p}_y$	Multi-class	$y \in \{1,\ldots,K\}$
Squared Loss	$(y - \hat{y})^2$	Regression	$y \in \mathbb{R}$
Absolute Loss	$\lvert y - \hat{y} \rvert$	Regression	$y \in \mathbb{R}$
Huber Loss	Quadratic if $\lvert y - \hat{y} \rvert \leq \delta$, linear o/w	Regression	$y \in \mathbb{R}$
Quantile Loss	$\max(\tau(y - \hat{y}), (\tau - 1)(y - \hat{y}))$	Regression	$y \in \mathbb{R}$

Definition 3.1.2 — Expected Risk. The expected risk of a hypothesis $f \in \mathscr{H}$ is:

$$\begin{aligned} \mathscr{R}(f) &:= \mathbb{E}_{(x,y) \sim \mathscr{P}}[\ell(f(x), y)] \\ &= \int_{\mathscr{X} \times \mathscr{Y}} \ell(f(x), y) \, d\mathscr{P}(x, y) \end{aligned} \tag{3.2}$$

where $\mathbb{E}$ denotes the expectation operator with respect to the joint distribution $\mathscr{P}$, and ℓ is the loss function.

Definition 3.1.3 — Bayes Optimal Predictor. The Bayes optimal predictor f^* minimizes the expected risk over all measurable functions:

$$f^* := \underset{f: \mathscr{X} \to \mathscr{Y}}{\arg\min} \, \mathscr{R}(f) \tag{3.3}$$

where the minimization is taken over the space of all measurable functions from $\mathscr{X}$ to $\mathscr{Y}$. The corresponding minimum risk $\mathscr{R}^* := \mathscr{R}(f^*)$ is called the **Bayes risk.**

Proposition 3.1.1 — Bayes Optimal Predictors. For common loss functions, the Bayes optimal predictor has closed form:

1. For squared loss: $f^*(x) = \mathbb{E}[Y|X = x]$ (conditional mean)
2. For absolute loss: $f^*(x) = \text{median}(Y|X = x)$ (conditional median)
3. For 0-1 loss: $f^*(x) = \arg\max_y P(Y = y|X = x)$ (MAP estimate)

Proof. In each case we apply the *tower property* (law of total expectation) to rewrite the risk as an outer expectation over X of an inner conditional expectation, and then minimize the inner expression pointwise in x. Since the inner minimization is unconstrained, the pointwise minimizer is also the global minimizer.

Case 1 (Squared Loss). By the tower property,

$$\mathscr{R}(f) = \mathbb{E}\big[(Y-f(X))^2\big] = \mathbb{E}_X\big[\mathbb{E}_{Y|X}\big[(Y-f(X))^2\,|\,X\big]\big]. \tag{3.4}$$

Because $f(X)$ is $\sigma(X)$-measurable, conditional on $X=x$ the value $f(x)$ is a deterministic constant; writing $c := f(x)$ and $\mu(x) := \mathbb{E}[Y \mid X=x]$, the inner expectation expands as

$$\mathbb{E}\big[(Y-c)^2\,|\,X=x\big] = \mathbb{E}[Y^2 \mid X=x] - 2c\,\mu(x) + c^2, \tag{3.5}$$

which is a strictly convex quadratic in c. Setting its derivative to zero,

$$\frac{d}{dc}\,\mathbb{E}\big[(Y-c)^2\,|\,X=x\big] = -2\mu(x)+2c = 0 \quad\Longrightarrow\quad c^\star = \mu(x). \tag{3.6}$$

Doing this for every x yields $f^*(x) = \mathbb{E}[Y \mid X=x]$, the conditional mean.

Case 2 (Absolute Loss). Again by the tower property,

$$\mathscr{R}(f) = \mathbb{E}[|Y-f(X)|] = \mathbb{E}_X\big[\mathbb{E}_{Y|X}[|Y-f(X)|\,|X]\big]. \tag{3.7}$$

Fix x and write $g(c) := \mathbb{E}[\,|Y-c|\,\,|\,X=x]$. The classical result is that g is minimized at any *conditional median* of Y given $X=x$. Although $|Y-c|$ is not differentiable at the single point $Y=c$, that exception has measure zero, so the derivative $\mathrm{sign}(c-Y)$ holds almost surely and a standard dominated-convergence argument lets us interchange derivative and expectation. We therefore get

$$g'(c) = \mathbb{E}[\mathrm{sign}(c-Y)\,|\,X=x] = P(Y<c \mid X=x) - P(Y>c \mid X=x), \tag{3.8}$$

which equals zero exactly when $P(Y<c \mid X=x) = P(Y>c \mid X=x)$. For continuous Y this forces each probability to equal $\frac{1}{2}$, so c splits the conditional mass of Y into two equal halves, which is the definition of the conditional median. (For distributions with point masses the median is any c satisfying $P(Y \le c) \ge \frac{1}{2}$ and $P(Y \ge c) \ge \frac{1}{2}$.) Hence $f^*(x) = \mathrm{median}(Y \mid X=x)$.

Case 3 (0-1 Loss). For 0-1 loss in classification,

$$\mathscr{R}(f) = \mathbb{E}[\mathbb{I}(f(X) \neq Y)] = \mathbb{E}_X[P(Y \neq f(X) \mid X)] \tag{3.9}$$

$$= \mathbb{E}_X[1 - P(Y = f(X) \mid X)]. \tag{3.10}$$

For each x, minimizing the inner term is equivalent to *maximizing* $P(Y=c \mid X=x)$ over $c \in \mathscr{Y}$. This is achieved by the maximum-a-posteriori (MAP) estimate

$$f^*(x) = \arg\max_{y\in\mathscr{Y}} P(Y=y \mid X=x). \tag{3.11}$$

■

Since $\mathscr{P}$ is unknown, we cannot compute $\mathscr{R}(f)$ directly. Instead, we employ the *Empirical Risk Minimization* (ERM) principle, which minimizes the empirical average of the loss on the training set:

Definition 3.1.4 — Empirical Risk. Given a dataset $\mathcal{D} = \{(x_i, y_i)\}_{i=1}^n$, the empirical risk is:

$$\hat{\mathcal{R}}_{\mathcal{D}}(f) := \frac{1}{n}\sum_{i=1}^{n}\ell(f(x_i), y_i) \tag{3.12}$$

where n is the number of training samples and (x_i, y_i) is the i-th input-output pair. When the training set is drawn as an i.i.d. sample $S = \{(x_i, y_i)\}_{i=1}^n \sim \mathcal{P}^n$, we also write $\hat{\mathcal{R}}_S(f)$ interchangeably with $\hat{\mathcal{R}}_{\mathcal{D}}(f)$.

Definition 3.1.5 — Empirical Risk Minimization. The ERM principle selects the hypothesis that minimizes empirical risk:

$$\hat{f}_{\text{ERM}} := \arg\min_{f\in\mathcal{H}} \hat{\mathcal{R}}_{\mathcal{D}}(f) \tag{3.13}$$

The central question of learning theory is: under what conditions does minimizing the empirical risk $\hat{\mathcal{R}}(f)$ lead to a small expected risk $\mathcal{R}(f)$? This convergence is governed by the complexity of the hypothesis class $\mathcal{H}$ from which f is chosen. If $\mathcal{H}$ is too complex, we may find a function that fits the training data perfectly (memorization) but fails to generalize. Conversely, if it is too simple, we may fail to capture the underlying patterns (underfitting).

3.1.4 Decomposition of Excess Risk

A key insight is to decompose the excess risk of ERM into interpretable components:

Theorem 3.1.2 — Excess Risk Decomposition. Let $f^* = \arg\min_f \mathcal{R}(f)$ be the Bayes optimal predictor, $f^*_{\mathcal{H}} = \arg\min_{f\in\mathcal{H}} \mathcal{R}(f)$ be the best-in-class predictor, and $\hat{f} = \arg\min_{f\in\mathcal{H}} \hat{\mathcal{R}}(f)$ be the ERM solution. Then:

$$\underbrace{\mathcal{R}(\hat{f}) - \mathcal{R}(f^*)}_{\text{Excess Risk}} = \underbrace{\mathcal{R}(f^*_{\mathcal{H}}) - \mathcal{R}(f^*)}_{\text{Approximation Error}} + \underbrace{\mathcal{R}(\hat{f}) - \mathcal{R}(f^*_{\mathcal{H}})}_{\text{Estimation Error}} \tag{3.14}$$

where $\mathcal{R}(\cdot)$ denotes the expected risk.

The **approximation error** measures the expressiveness of $\mathcal{H}$: how well the best function in our hypothesis class can approximate the true optimal function. This error decreases as $\mathcal{H}$ becomes richer.

The **estimation error** measures the statistical difficulty of finding the best function in $\mathcal{H}$ from finite samples. This error increases with the complexity of $\mathcal{H}$ and decreases with more data.

This decomposition reveals a fundamental trade-off: richer hypothesis classes reduce approximation error but increase estimation error. Trustworthy AI adds additional constraints to $\mathcal{H}$, such as Lipschitz bounds for robustness or independence constraints for fairness, which effectively restrict the hypothesis class and may therefore increase approximation error. However, these constraints provide crucial safety guarantees that are necessary for deployment in high-stakes settings.

3.2 Bias-Variance Decomposition

To understand the sources of error in a learning algorithm, we can decompose the expected risk into interpretable components. Consider the squared error loss $\ell(y,\hat{y}) = (y-\hat{y})^2$ in a regression setting. Let the true relationship be $y = g(x) + \varepsilon$, where $\varepsilon \sim \mathcal{N}(0,\sigma^2)$ is irreducible noise with zero mean and variance σ^2. Let $\hat{f}_D(x)$ be the predictor learned from a specific dataset D. We are interested in the expected error of the algorithm at a point x, averaged over all possible realizations of the training dataset D.

Theorem 3.2.1 — Bias-Variance Decomposition. For squared loss and $y = g(x) + \varepsilon$ with ε independent of x and D, $\mathbb{E}[\varepsilon] = 0$, and $\mathrm{Var}[\varepsilon] = \sigma^2$:

$$\mathbb{E}_D\mathbb{E}_\varepsilon[(y-\hat{f}_D(x))^2] = \sigma^2 + (g(x)-\bar{f}(x))^2 + \mathbb{E}_D[(\hat{f}_D(x)-\bar{f}(x))^2] \quad (3.15)$$

where $\bar{f}(x) = \mathbb{E}_D[\hat{f}_D(x)]$ is the average prediction over all possible training sets D, $\mathbb{E}_D$ denotes expectation over the random choice of training set, and $\mathbb{E}_\varepsilon$ denotes expectation over the noise in the test point.

Proof. We begin by expanding the expected squared error:

$$\mathbb{E}_D\mathbb{E}_\varepsilon[(y-\hat{f}_D(x))^2] = \mathbb{E}_D\mathbb{E}_\varepsilon[(g(x)+\varepsilon-\hat{f}_D(x))^2] \quad (3.16)$$

Expanding the square and using linearity of expectation:

$$= \mathbb{E}_D\mathbb{E}_\varepsilon[(g(x)-\hat{f}_D(x))^2 + \varepsilon^2 + 2\varepsilon(g(x)-\hat{f}_D(x))] \quad (3.17)$$

Since ε is independent of D and has mean zero, the cross-term vanishes ($\mathbb{E}_\varepsilon[\varepsilon] = 0$). Also, $\mathbb{E}_\varepsilon[\varepsilon^2] = \sigma^2$:

$$= \mathbb{E}_D[(g(x)-\hat{f}_D(x))^2] + \sigma^2 \quad (3.18)$$

Now we analyze the term $\mathbb{E}_D[(g(x)-\hat{f}_D(x))^2]$. Let $\bar{f}(x) = \mathbb{E}_D[\hat{f}_D(x)]$ be the average prediction. We add and subtract $\bar{f}(x)$:

$$\mathbb{E}_D[(g(x)-\hat{f}_D(x))^2] = \mathbb{E}_D[(g(x)-\bar{f}(x)+\bar{f}(x)-\hat{f}_D(x))^2] \quad (3.19)$$

Let $a = g(x) - \bar{f}(x)$ (a constant with respect to D) and $b = \bar{f}(x) - \hat{f}_D(x)$. Then:

$$\mathbb{E}_D[(a+b)^2] = a^2 + \mathbb{E}_D[b^2] + 2a\,\mathbb{E}_D[b] \tag{3.20}$$

$$= (g(x) - \bar{f}(x))^2 + \mathbb{E}_D[(\hat{f}_D(x) - \bar{f}(x))^2] + 2(g(x) - \bar{f}(x))\,\mathbb{E}_D[\bar{f}(x) - \hat{f}_D(x)] \tag{3.21}$$

The cross term is zero because $\mathbb{E}_D[\hat{f}_D(x)] = \bar{f}(x)$ by definition, so $\mathbb{E}_D[\bar{f}(x) - \hat{f}_D(x)] = 0$.

Thus, we arrive at the classic decomposition:

$$\text{Error} = \underbrace{\sigma^2}_{\text{Irreducible}} + \underbrace{(g(x) - \bar{f}(x))^2}_{\text{Bias}^2} + \underbrace{\mathbb{E}_D[(\hat{f}_D(x) - \bar{f}(x))^2]}_{\text{Variance}} \tag{3.22}$$

■

Ⓡ [Interpretation of Terms]

- The **Bias** term measures the systematic error introduced by the simplifying assumptions of the model class (e.g., approximating a nonlinear function with a linear model). It represents the error incurred even with infinite data, due to fundamental limitations of the hypothesis space.
- The **Variance** term measures the sensitivity of the model to the specific realization of the training data, quantifying how much predictions fluctuate across different datasets of the same size.
- The **Irreducible Error** (σ^2) represents noise inherent in the data-generating process that no model can eliminate.

In the context of Trustworthy AI, we often introduce constraints (such as fairness or robustness) that restrict the hypothesis space $\mathcal{H}$. This inevitably increases the bias of the model (as we may exclude the "true" unconstrained minimizer) but can potentially reduce variance or ensure safety properties that are critical for deployment. Understanding this trade-off is essential for designing trustworthy systems where perfect accuracy is sacrificed for guaranteed safety or fairness.

3.3 Concentration Inequalities: Hoeffding's Inequality

Before analyzing the convergence of empirical risk to true risk, we establish a fundamental concentration inequality that bounds the deviation of sample means from their true expectation. Hoeffding's inequality is the workhorse of learning theory, providing distribution-free bounds for bounded random variables.

Theorem 3.3.1 — Hoeffding's Inequality. Let $X_1, X_2, \ldots, X_n$ be n independent random variables such that $a_i \leq X_i \leq b_i$ almost surely for each i. Let $S_n = \sum_{i=1}^n X_i$ be their sum, and let $\mu = \mathbb{E}[S_n]$. Then for any $t > 0$:

$$P(S_n - \mu \geq t) \leq \exp\left(-\frac{2t^2}{\sum_{i=1}^n (b_i - a_i)^2}\right) \tag{3.23}$$

and similarly:

$$P(|S_n - \mu| \geq t) \leq 2\exp\left(-\frac{2t^2}{\sum_{i=1}^n (b_i - a_i)^2}\right) \tag{3.24}$$

The bound is distribution-free and depends only on the range of each variable, not on the underlying distribution.

Proof. The proof uses the moment generating function (MGF) and Markov's inequality. For any $\lambda > 0$:

$$P(S_n - \mu \geq t) = P(e^{\lambda(S_n - \mu)} \geq e^{\lambda t}) \tag{3.25}$$

$$\leq \frac{\mathbb{E}[e^{\lambda(S_n - \mu)}]}{e^{\lambda t}} \quad \text{(by Markov's inequality)} \tag{3.26}$$

Since $S_n - \mu = \sum_{i=1}^n (X_i - \mathbb{E}[X_i])$, we have:

$$\mathbb{E}[e^{\lambda(S_n - \mu)}] = \mathbb{E}[e^{\lambda \sum_{i=1}^n (X_i - \mathbb{E}[X_i])}] = \prod_{i=1}^n \mathbb{E}[e^{\lambda(X_i - \mathbb{E}[X_i])}] \tag{3.27}$$

where the last equality follows from independence of the X_i.

For each term, let $Y_i = X_i - \mathbb{E}[X_i]$, so $a_i - \mathbb{E}[X_i] \leq Y_i \leq b_i - \mathbb{E}[X_i]$. We now invoke the following auxiliary result.

Lemma 3.3.2 — Hoeffding's Lemma. Let Y be a random variable satisfying $a \leq Y \leq b$ almost surely and $\mathbb{E}[Y] = 0$. Then for any $\lambda \in \mathbb{R}$,

$$\mathbb{E}[e^{\lambda Y}] \leq \exp\left(\frac{\lambda^2 (b-a)^2}{8}\right). \tag{3.28}$$

Proof. Since $a \leq Y \leq b$, we may write Y as a convex combination of a and b:

$$Y = \frac{b - Y}{b - a} a + \frac{Y - a}{b - a} b. \tag{3.29}$$

By the convexity of $y \mapsto e^{\lambda y}$,

$$e^{\lambda Y} \leq \frac{b-Y}{b-a} e^{\lambda a} + \frac{Y-a}{b-a} e^{\lambda b}. \tag{3.30}$$

Taking expectations and using $\mathbb{E}[Y] = 0$,

$$\mathbb{E}[e^{\lambda Y}] \leq \frac{b}{b-a} e^{\lambda a} - \frac{a}{b-a} e^{\lambda b}. \tag{3.31}$$

Define $p := -a/(b-a) \in [0,1]$ (so $1-p = b/(b-a)$) and $h := \lambda(b-a)$. Then

$$\mathbb{E}[e^{\lambda Y}] \leq (1-p)e^{\lambda a} + pe^{\lambda b} = e^{\lambda a}\big(1-p+pe^h\big) = e^{-ph}\big(1-p+pe^h\big), \tag{3.32}$$

where the last identity uses $\lambda a = -ph$. Taking logarithms, define

$$L(h) := -ph + \ln\big(1-p+pe^h\big). \tag{3.33}$$

We claim $L(h) \leq h^2/8$ for all $h \in \mathbb{R}$. Direct computation gives

$$L(0) = 0, \qquad L'(h) = -p + \frac{pe^h}{1-p+pe^h}, \qquad L'(0) = -p+p = 0, \tag{3.34}$$

and

$$L''(h) = \frac{p(1-p)e^h}{\big(1-p+pe^h\big)^2}. \tag{3.35}$$

Setting $u := pe^h$ and $v := 1-p$, we have $L''(h) = uv/(u+v)^2$. The arithmetic–geometric mean inequality says that for any positive u, v, $(u-v)^2 \geq 0$, which rearranges to $(u+v)^2 \geq 4uv$, i.e. $uv/(u+v)^2 \leq 1/4$. Equality is attained when $u = v$, so the bound is tight. Hence $L''(h) \leq 1/4$ uniformly in h (and uniformly in $p \in [0,1]$). Taylor's theorem with the Lagrange remainder then yields, for some $h^* \in (0,h)$ (or $(h,0)$),

$$L(h) = L(0) + L'(0)h + \tfrac{1}{2}L''(h^*)h^2 \leq \tfrac{1}{8}h^2 = \tfrac{1}{8}\lambda^2(b-a)^2. \tag{3.36}$$

Exponentiating gives $\mathbb{E}[e^{\lambda Y}] \leq \exp\big(\lambda^2(b-a)^2/8\big)$, as required. ■

Applying Hoeffding's Lemma (Lemma 3.3.2) to each $Y_i = X_i - \mathbb{E}[X_i]$ (which has range $b_i - a_i$ and expectation zero):

$$\mathbb{E}[e^{\lambda(X_i - \mathbb{E}[X_i])}] \leq e^{\lambda^2(b_i-a_i)^2/8} \tag{3.37}$$

Therefore:

$$\mathbb{E}[e^{\lambda(S_n-\mu)}] \leq \prod_{i=1}^{n} e^{\lambda^2(b_i-a_i)^2/8} = \exp\left(\frac{\lambda^2}{8}\sum_{i=1}^{n}(b_i-a_i)^2\right) \tag{3.38}$$

Combining with Markov's inequality:

$$P(S_n - \mu \geq t) \leq \min_{\lambda>0} \frac{\exp\left(\frac{\lambda^2}{8}\sum_{i=1}^{n}(b_i - a_i)^2\right)}{e^{\lambda t}} \tag{3.39}$$

To optimize over λ, we take the derivative of the exponent with respect to λ and set it to zero:

$$\frac{d}{d\lambda}\left(\frac{\lambda^2}{8}\sum_{i=1}^{n}(b_i - a_i)^2 - \lambda t\right) = \frac{\lambda}{4}\sum_{i=1}^{n}(b_i - a_i)^2 - t = 0 \tag{3.40}$$

This gives $\lambda^* = \frac{4t}{\sum_{i=1}^{n}(b_i-a_i)^2}$. Substituting back:

$$P(S_n - \mu \geq t) \leq \exp\left(\frac{(\lambda^*)^2}{8}\sum_{i=1}^{n}(b_i - a_i)^2 - \lambda^* t\right) \tag{3.41}$$

$$= \exp\left(\frac{1}{8} \cdot \frac{16t^2}{(\sum(b_i - a_i)^2)^2} \cdot \sum(b_i - a_i)^2 - \frac{4t}{\sum(b_i - a_i)^2} \cdot t\right) \tag{3.42}$$

$$= \exp\left(\frac{2t^2}{\sum(b_i - a_i)^2} - \frac{4t^2}{\sum(b_i - a_i)^2}\right) \tag{3.43}$$

$$= \exp\left(-\frac{2t^2}{\sum_{i=1}^{n}(b_i - a_i)^2}\right) \tag{3.44}$$

The symmetric bound for $|S_n - \mu| \geq t$ follows by applying the above result to both $S_n - \mu$ and $\mu - S_n$:

$$P(|S_n - \mu| \geq t) \leq P(S_n - \mu \geq t) + P(\mu - S_n \geq t) \leq 2\exp\left(-\frac{2t^2}{\sum_{i=1}^{n}(b_i - a_i)^2}\right) \tag{3.45}$$

■

Corollary 3.3.3 — Hoeffding's Inequality for Sample Mean. Let $X_1, \ldots, X_n$ be independent random variables with $X_i \in [a, b]$ almost surely. Let $\bar{X} = \frac{1}{n}\sum_{i=1}^{n} X_i$ be the sample mean and $\mu = \mathbb{E}[\bar{X}]$. Then for any $\varepsilon > 0$:

$$P(|\bar{X} - \mu| \geq \varepsilon) \leq 2\exp(-2n\varepsilon^2/(b-a)^2) \tag{3.46}$$

Proof. Apply the main theorem to $S_n = \sum_{i=1}^{n} X_i$ with $a_i = a$ and $b_i = b$ for all i. Then $\bar{X} = S_n/n$, $\mu = \mathbb{E}[S_n]/n$, and $\sum_{i=1}^{n}(b_i - a_i)^2 = n(b-a)^2$. Since $\bar{X} = S_n/n$, the event $|\bar{X} - \mu| \geq \varepsilon$ is identical to $|S_n - n\mu| \geq n\varepsilon$, so substituting $t = n\varepsilon$ in the main theorem converts the bound on S_n into one on the sample mean: the exponent becomes $2(n\varepsilon)^2/(n(b-a)^2) = 2n\varepsilon^2/(b-a)^2$, yielding the stated rate. ■

This corollary is particularly useful in learning theory, where we apply it to the empirical risk, treating $\ell(f(X_i), Y_i) \in [0,1]$ as the bounded random variable.

(R) [Tightness of Hoeffding's Inequality] Hoeffding's inequality is optimal up to constant factors for the distribution-free setting. It depends only on the range of the variables and not on their variance, making it very general but sometimes loose when the variance is much smaller than the range. In such cases, Bernstein's inequality, which incorporates variance information, can provide tighter bounds.

3.4 Uniform Convergence and VC Dimension

To guarantee generalization, we require that the empirical risk converges to the true risk uniformly over the hypothesis class $\mathscr{H}$. If the convergence is not uniform, the learning algorithm might select a "bad" hypothesis that happens to perform well on the training set due to random chance.

Definition 3.4.1 — Uniform Convergence. A hypothesis class $\mathscr{H}$ has the uniform convergence property if for every $\varepsilon > 0$ and $\delta > 0$, there exists a sample size $n_0(\varepsilon, \delta)$ such that for all $n \geq n_0(\varepsilon, \delta)$:

$$P\left(\sup_{f\in\mathscr{H}} |\mathscr{R}(f) - \hat{\mathscr{R}}(f)| > \varepsilon\right) < \delta \tag{3.47}$$

where P denotes the probability over the random draw of the training set of size n.

The Vapnik–Chervonenkis (VC) dimension provides a combinatorial measure of the complexity of $\mathscr{H}$ for binary classification. It is defined as the size of the largest set of points that can be "shattered" by $\mathscr{H}$, meaning that the hypothesis class can realize all possible labelings of those points.

■ **Example 3.1 — VC Dimension of Linear Classifiers in $\mathbb{R}^2$.** Consider $\mathscr{H}$ as the set of all linear classifiers (lines) in $\mathbb{R}^2$. Given three non-collinear points, say $(0,0)$, $(1,0)$, and $(0,1)$, we can find a line that separates any of the $2^3 = 8$ possible labelings (e.g., to label only $(0,0)$ as $+1$, we draw a line close to the origin separating it from the other two). However, for four points in convex position (i.e., forming a convex quadrilateral), there always exists a labeling that no line can separate, specifically the "XOR" pattern where diagonally opposite points share the same label. Therefore, $d_{VC}(\text{linear classifiers in } \mathbb{R}^2) = 3$. In general,

d_{VC}(linear classifiers in $\mathbb{R}^d$) $= d+1$. For instance, in a medical imaging application where each image is represented by $d = 100$ features (e.g., pixel intensities or extracted measurements), a linear classifier has VC dimension 101, meaning the standard VC bound requires roughly $n = O\big((d_{VC}\log(d_{VC}/\varepsilon)+\log(1/\delta))/\varepsilon^2\big)$ training images to guarantee generalization with error at most ε. ■

3.4.1 Sauer's Lemma

The fundamental combinatorial result that connects VC dimension to the growth function is Sauer's Lemma. The growth function $\Pi_{\mathscr{H}}(n)$ counts the maximum number of distinct dichotomies (labelings) that a hypothesis class $\mathscr{H}$ can produce on any set of n points. For an unrestricted binary concept class, $\Pi_{\mathscr{H}}(n) = 2^n$ (all possible labelings are realizable). However, if $\mathscr{H}$ has finite VC dimension $d_{VC} = d$, Sauer's Lemma bounds the growth function by a polynomial in n of degree d.

Definition 3.4.2 — Growth Function. For a hypothesis class $\mathscr{H}$ and sample size n, the growth function is:

$$\Pi_{\mathscr{H}}(n) := \max_{x_1,\ldots,x_n\in\mathscr{X}} |\{(h(x_1),\ldots,h(x_n)) : h \in \mathscr{H}\}| \tag{3.48}$$

which counts the maximum number of distinct binary labelings of any n points that can be realized by hypotheses in $\mathscr{H}$.

Lemma 3.4.1 — Sauer's Lemma. If a hypothesis class $\mathscr{H}$ has VC dimension $d_{VC} = d < \infty$, then for any $n \geq d$:

$$\Pi_{\mathscr{H}}(n) \leq \sum_{i=0}^{d} \binom{n}{i} \tag{3.49}$$

Moreover, $\sum_{i=0}^{d}\binom{n}{i} \leq \left(\frac{en}{d}\right)^d$ for $n \geq d$.

Proof. We prove by induction on n that $\Pi_{\mathscr{H}}(n) \leq \sum_{i=0}^{d}\binom{n}{i}$ whenever $d_{VC}(\mathscr{H}) = d$.

Base case: For $n \leq d$, a set of n points can have at most 2^n dichotomies, and $\sum_{i=0}^{d}\binom{n}{i} = \sum_{i=0}^{n}\binom{n}{i} = 2^n$, where the first equality holds because $\binom{n}{i} = 0$ for $i > n$. Thus the bound holds trivially.

Inductive step: Assume the result holds for $n-1$ points. Consider n points $x_1,\ldots,x_n$. Let $\mathscr{H}_{|x_1\ldots x_{n-1}}$ be the set of dichotomies of the first $n-1$ points induced by hypotheses in $\mathscr{H}$. By the induction hypothesis:

$$|\mathscr{H}_{|x_1\ldots x_{n-1}}| \leq \sum_{i=0}^{d}\binom{n-1}{i} \tag{3.50}$$

Now, for the n points, we partition the possible dichotomies based on how $h(x_n)$ extends a dichotomy on the first $n-1$ points:

- **Dichotomies that can be extended in both ways:** These are dichotomies $y_1,\dots,y_{n-1}$ such that both $(y_1,\dots,y_{n-1},0)$ and $(y_1,\dots,y_{n-1},1)$ can be realized by some hypotheses in $\mathscr{H}$. Let there be Δ such dichotomies.
- **Dichotomies that can be extended in one way only:** These can be extended either with $h(x_n)=0$ or $h(x_n)=1$, but not both. There are $|\mathscr{H}_{|x_1\dots x_{n-1}}|-\Delta$ such dichotomies.

The total number of n-point dichotomies is:

$$\Pi_{\mathscr{H}}(n) \le 2\Delta + (|\mathscr{H}_{|x_1\dots x_{n-1}}| - \Delta) = \Delta + |\mathscr{H}_{|x_1\dots x_{n-1}}| \tag{3.51}$$

Now, the key observation is that the Δ dichotomies on $x_1,\dots,x_{n-1}$ that can be extended in both ways form precisely the set of dichotomies realizable by the *difference class* $\mathscr{H}_{x_n}^{\pm}$. This class is defined as the set of hypotheses h restricted to $x_1,\dots,x_{n-1}$ for which there exist $h',h''\in\mathscr{H}$ agreeing with h on $x_1,\dots,x_{n-1}$ but with $h'(x_n)=0$ and $h''(x_n)=1$. Crucially, $d_{VC}(\mathscr{H}_{x_n}^{\pm})\le d-1$. To see this, suppose $\mathscr{H}_{x_n}^{\pm}$ shatters some set T of d points among $x_1,\dots,x_{n-1}$. Then $T\cup\{x_n\}$ would be shattered by $\mathscr{H}$ (since every labeling of T can be paired with both labels for x_n), contradicting $d_{VC}(\mathscr{H})=d$. Applying the induction hypothesis to this difference class gives:

$$\Delta \le \sum_{i=0}^{d-1}\binom{n-1}{i} \tag{3.52}$$

Combining these bounds:

$$\begin{aligned}\Pi_{\mathscr{H}}(n) &\le \Delta + |\mathscr{H}_{|x_1\dots x_{n-1}}| &(3.53)\\ &\le \sum_{i=0}^{d-1}\binom{n-1}{i} + \sum_{i=0}^{d}\binom{n-1}{i} &(3.54)\end{aligned}$$

By Pascal's identity $\binom{n-1}{i}+\binom{n-1}{i-1}=\binom{n}{i}$, we can pair terms: the second sum contributes $\binom{n-1}{i}$ for $i=0,\dots,d$ and the first sum contributes $\binom{n-1}{i}$ for $i=0,\dots,d-1$, which serves as $\binom{n-1}{i-1}$ shifted by one index. Thus:

$$\begin{aligned}\sum_{i=0}^{d-1}\binom{n-1}{i} + \sum_{i=0}^{d}\binom{n-1}{i} &= \binom{n-1}{0} + \sum_{i=1}^{d}\left[\binom{n-1}{i}+\binom{n-1}{i-1}\right]\\ &= \sum_{i=0}^{d}\binom{n}{i}\end{aligned} \tag{3.55}$$

where we used $\binom{n-1}{0}=\binom{n}{0}=1$ and Pascal's identity for $i=1,\dots,d$.

For the second inequality, we prove that for $n \geq d \geq 1$,

$$\sum_{i=0}^{d} \binom{n}{i} \leq \left(\frac{en}{d}\right)^d. \tag{3.56}$$

Since $n/d \geq 1$, we have $(n/d)^{d-i} \geq 1$ for each $i \in \{0,1,\dots,d\}$. Multiplying each term on the left by $(n/d)^{d-i}$ can only increase it:

$$\sum_{i=0}^{d} \binom{n}{i} \leq \sum_{i=0}^{d} \binom{n}{i} (n/d)^{d-i} \tag{3.57}$$

$$\leq \sum_{i=0}^{n} \binom{n}{i} (d/n)^i (n/d)^d = (n/d)^d \sum_{i=0}^{n} \binom{n}{i} (d/n)^i \tag{3.58}$$

$$= (n/d)^d (1+d/n)^n \leq (n/d)^d e^d, \tag{3.59}$$

where the penultimate equality is the binomial theorem and the last inequality uses $(1+x)^n \leq e^{nx}$ with $x = d/n$. Hence $\sum_{i=0}^{d} \binom{n}{i} \leq (en/d)^d$. ■

Ⓡ [Significance of Sauer's Lemma] Sauer's Lemma is the bridge between the combinatorial property of VC dimension and the statistical property of uniform convergence. The polynomial bound $\Pi_{\mathscr{H}}(n) = O(n^d)$ (as opposed to exponential 2^n) is what makes it possible to apply a union bound over all dichotomies and still achieve uniform convergence using concentration inequalities like Hoeffding's.

Theorem 3.4.2 — Vapnik–Chervonenkis Bound. For a binary classification problem with 0-1 loss, if $\mathscr{H}$ has finite VC dimension d_{VC}, then with probability at least $1-\delta$, for any $f \in \mathscr{H}$:

$$\mathscr{R}(f) \leq \hat{\mathscr{R}}(f) + \sqrt{\frac{8 d_{VC} \ln(2n) + 8\ln(4/\delta)}{n}} \tag{3.60}$$

where n is the number of samples, ln is the natural logarithm, and the probability is taken over the random draw of the training set.

Proof. The proof combines Sauer's Lemma, a symmetrization argument, and Hoeffding's inequality. We assume the loss takes values in $[0,1]$ and that $d_{VC}(\mathscr{H}) = d$. Throughout, the function class effectively involved is the loss class $\ell \circ \mathscr{H} := \{(x,y) \mapsto \ell(f(x),y) : f \in \mathscr{H}\}$; with 0–1 loss, the projection of $\ell \circ \mathscr{H}$ onto any sample of size m has at most $\Pi_{\mathscr{H}}(m)$ distinct vectors, so Sauer's Lemma applies directly to $\ell \circ \mathscr{H}$.

Step 1: Symmetrization with a ghost sample. Let $S = \{z_i\}_{i=1}^n$ with $z_i = (x_i, y_i)$ be the training sample drawn i.i.d. from $\mathscr{P}$, and let $S' = \{z_i'\}_{i=1}^n$ be an independent ghost sample from the same distribution. Define

$$G(S) := \sup_{f\in\mathscr{H}} \big(\mathscr{R}(f) - \hat{\mathscr{R}}_S(f)\big). \tag{3.61}$$

A standard symmetrization inequality (see, e.g., [55]) states that for any $\varepsilon > 0$ such that $n\varepsilon^2 \geq 2$,

$$P_S\big(G(S) > \varepsilon\big) \leq 2P_{S,S'}\Big(\sup_{f\in\mathscr{H}} \big(\hat{\mathscr{R}}_{S'}(f) - \hat{\mathscr{R}}_S(f)\big) > \varepsilon/2\Big). \tag{3.62}$$

The factor 2 and the $\varepsilon/2$ on the right come from a standard *symmetrization lemma*, which transfers the deviation from the original sample to the ghost sample via Chebyshev's inequality. Intuitively, if the empirical risk on S already deviates from the true risk by more than ε for some f, then with probability at least $1/2$ the empirical risk on the independent ghost sample S' stays within $\varepsilon/2$ of the true risk, which forces $\hat{\mathscr{R}}_{S'}(f) - \hat{\mathscr{R}}_S(f) > \varepsilon/2$. The factor 2 is the cost of replacing the unknown true risk with the easier-to-bound empirical risk on S'.

Step 2: Reducing to a finite class on the doubled sample. On the joint sample $S \cup S'$ of size $2n$, the loss class $\ell \circ \mathscr{H}$ realizes at most $\Pi_{\mathscr{H}}(2n)$ distinct labelings (using $\{0,1\}$-valued losses; for general bounded losses the same bound applies because the only quantities that matter for $\hat{\mathscr{R}}_S(f) - \hat{\mathscr{R}}_{S'}(f)$ are the values of $\ell(f(\cdot),\cdot)$ on the $2n$ points, which determine an effective hypothesis class of size at most $\Pi_{\mathscr{H}}(2n)$ [80]). Thus, by the union bound,

$$\begin{aligned} &P_{S,S'}\Big(\sup_{f\in\mathscr{H}} \big(\hat{\mathscr{R}}_{S'}(f) - \hat{\mathscr{R}}_S(f)\big) > \varepsilon/2\Big) \\ &\quad\leq \Pi_{\mathscr{H}}(2n) \sup_{f\in\mathscr{H}} P_{S,S'}\Big(\hat{\mathscr{R}}_{S'}(f) - \hat{\mathscr{R}}_S(f) > \varepsilon/2\Big). \end{aligned} \tag{3.63}$$

Step 3: Hoeffding on the doubled sample. Fix $f \in \mathscr{H}$. Write $\hat{\mathscr{R}}_{S'}(f) - \hat{\mathscr{R}}_S(f) = \sum_{i=1}^n \frac{1}{n}\ell(f(x_i'), y_i') - \sum_{i=1}^n \frac{1}{n}\ell(f(x_i), y_i)$, a sum of $2n$ independent random variables: the ghost-sample summands lie in $[0, 1/n]$ and the original-sample summands lie in $[-1/n, 0]$. Each summand has range width $1/n$, and the sum has expectation zero. By Hoeffding's inequality applied to these $2n$ summands,

$$P_{S,S'}\Big(\hat{\mathscr{R}}_{S'}(f) - \hat{\mathscr{R}}_S(f) > \varepsilon/2\Big) \leq \exp\bigg(-\frac{2(\varepsilon/2)^2}{2n\cdot(1/n)^2}\bigg) = \exp\bigg(-\frac{n\varepsilon^2}{4}\bigg). \tag{3.64}$$

Step 4: Combining the bounds. Combining (3.62) with the previous two displays gives:

$$P_S\big(G(S) > \varepsilon\big) \leq 2\Pi_{\mathscr{H}}(2n) \exp\bigg(-\frac{n\varepsilon^2}{4}\bigg). \tag{3.65}$$

By Sauer's Lemma (Lemma 3.4.1), $\Pi_{\mathscr{H}}(2n) \le (2en/d)^d$ for $2n \ge d$. Setting the right-hand side equal to δ and solving for ε gives:

$$\varepsilon = \sqrt{\frac{4\left(\ln \Pi_{\mathscr{H}}(2n) + \ln(2/\delta)\right)}{n}} \le \sqrt{\frac{4\left(d\ln(2en/d) + \ln(2/\delta)\right)}{n}}. \tag{3.66}$$

Using the elementary bound $d\ln(2en/d) \le 2d\ln(2n)$ for $n \ge d$, and absorbing constants by replacing $\ln(2/\delta)$ with the slightly larger $2\ln(4/\delta)$, we obtain:

$$\varepsilon \le \sqrt{\frac{8d\ln(2n) + 8\ln(4/\delta)}{n}}. \tag{3.67}$$

Hence with probability at least $1-\delta$, simultaneously for every $f \in \mathscr{H}$:

$$\mathscr{R}(f) \le \hat{\mathscr{R}}(f) + \sqrt{\frac{8d_{VC}\ln(2n) + 8\ln(4/\delta)}{n}}, \tag{3.68}$$

which is the stated bound. ■

This bound is fundamental because it is distribution-free; it holds for any data distribution $\mathscr{P}$. However, this universality comes at a cost: the bound is often loose for practical applications. For modern neural networks, the VC dimension is roughly proportional to the number of parameters, which can be in the billions. The VC bound would suggest that we need billions of samples to generalize. Yet, these networks generalize well with far fewer samples. This discrepancy motivates the study of data-dependent complexity measures.

3.5 Rademacher Complexity

Rademacher Complexity [10] measures the expected supremum of the correlation between the hypothesis class and random label noise. Unlike VC dimension, which is a purely combinatorial quantity, Rademacher complexity depends on both the hypothesis class and the data distribution, making it a data-dependent complexity measure.

Definition 3.5.1 — Empirical Rademacher Complexity. Let $\sigma = (\sigma_1, \ldots, \sigma_n)$ be independent Rademacher variables where $P(\sigma_i = 1) = P(\sigma_i = -1) = 1/2$. The empirical Rademacher complexity of $\mathscr{H}$ on a dataset $S = \{x_1, \ldots, x_n\}$ is:

$$\hat{\mathfrak{R}}_S(\mathscr{H}) := \mathbb{E}_\sigma\left[\sup_{f\in\mathscr{H}} \frac{1}{n}\sum_{i=1}^{n} \sigma_i f(x_i)\right] \tag{3.69}$$

where $\mathbb{E}_\sigma$ denotes the expectation over the random variables σ.

Definition 3.5.2 — Rademacher Complexity. The Rademacher complexity of $\mathscr{H}$ for sample size n is the expected value of the empirical Rademacher complexity over random samples of size n:

$$\mathfrak{R}_n(\mathscr{H}) := \mathbb{E}_{S\sim\mathscr{P}^n}[\hat{\mathfrak{R}}_S(\mathscr{H})] \tag{3.70}$$

where $\mathscr{P}^n$ denotes the product distribution of n i.i.d. samples from $\mathscr{P}$.

Intuitively, if a hypothesis class is complex enough to correlate with random noise labels σ_i, it has high capacity and is prone to overfitting.

Example 3.2 — Rademacher Complexity in Handwritten Digit Recognition. Consider classifying handwritten digits (e.g., MNIST, $d = 784$ pixel features). Let $\mathscr{H}$ be the linear function class $f(x) = w^T x$ with $\|w\|_2 \le W$ and inputs satisfying $\|x\|_2 \le R$ (the eventual classifier is $\text{sign}\big(f(x)\big)$; the Rademacher bound below is stated for the real-valued margin class, which then transfers to the 0-1 loss via the contraction lemma or a margin-based surrogate). The Rademacher complexity satisfies $\hat{\mathfrak{R}}_S(\mathscr{H}) \le WR/\sqrt{n}$. With $W = 1$, $R \approx 20$ (typical for normalized pixel vectors), and $n = 60000$ training images, this gives $\hat{\mathfrak{R}}_S \approx 20/\sqrt{60000} \approx 0.08$. The bound $\mathscr{R}(f) \le \hat{\mathscr{R}}(f) + 2\times 0.08 + O(1/\sqrt{n})$ tells us that the true risk exceeds the training risk by at most ≈ 0.16 (plus a lower-order $O(1/\sqrt{n})$ term), a meaningful guarantee that does not depend on the dimension $d = 784$, explaining why high-dimensional classifiers can still generalize. ■

Theorem 3.5.1 — Rademacher Generalization Bound. With probability at least $1-\delta$, for all $f \in \mathscr{H}$:

$$\mathscr{R}(f) \le \hat{\mathscr{R}}(f) + 2\mathfrak{R}_n(\mathscr{H}) + \sqrt{\frac{\ln(1/\delta)}{2n}} \tag{3.71}$$

where $\mathscr{R}(f)$ is the expected risk, $\hat{\mathscr{R}}(f)$ is the empirical risk, and $\mathfrak{R}_n(\mathscr{H})$ is the Rademacher complexity of the hypothesis class (the bound as written assumes the loss ℓ is 1-Lipschitz in its first argument; see the proof below for the general case via the contraction lemma).

Proof. We work with loss functions taking values in $[0,1]$. For brevity, write $g_f(z) := \ell(f(x),y)$ for $z = (x,y)$, and let $\mathfrak{R}_n(\ell\circ\mathscr{H})$ denote the Rademacher complexity of the loss class $\ell\circ\mathscr{H} := \{g_f : f \in \mathscr{H}\}$. We will show

$$\mathbb{E}_S\left[\sup_{f\in\mathscr{H}} \left(\mathscr{R}(f) - \hat{\mathscr{R}}_S(f)\right)\right] \le 2\,\mathfrak{R}_n(\ell\circ\mathscr{H}), \tag{3.72}$$

and then apply McDiarmid's inequality. For Lipschitz losses, the Ledoux–Talagrand contraction lemma gives $\mathfrak{R}_n(\ell \circ \mathscr{H}) \leq L_\ell \, \mathfrak{R}_n(\mathscr{H})$, where L_ℓ is the Lipschitz constant of ℓ in its first argument. The bound below is therefore expressed directly in terms of $\mathfrak{R}_n(\mathscr{H})$. (In plain English, Talagrand's contraction lemma says: composing every function in a class with a single-coordinate L-Lipschitz map can only inflate the Rademacher complexity by a factor of L. Here the composition is $\ell(\cdot, y)$ applied to $f(x)$, so the loss class has complexity at most L_ℓ times that of $\mathscr{H}$ itself.)

Step 1: Ghost-sample symmetrization. Let $S = \{z_i\}_{i=1}^n$ be the training sample and $S' = \{z_i'\}_{i=1}^n$ an independent ghost sample, both i.i.d. from $\mathscr{P}$. For any fixed f,

$$\begin{aligned}\mathscr{R}(f) - \hat{\mathscr{R}}_S(f) &= \mathbb{E}_{S'}\left[\hat{\mathscr{R}}_{S'}(f) \,\middle|\, S\right] - \hat{\mathscr{R}}_S(f) \\ &= \mathbb{E}_{S'}\left[\hat{\mathscr{R}}_{S'}(f) - \hat{\mathscr{R}}_S(f) \,\middle|\, S\right]. \end{aligned} \tag{3.73}$$

Pulling the supremum inside the expectation (using Jensen's inequality for the convex map sup, applied to the conditional expectation given S),

$$\begin{aligned}&\mathbb{E}_S\left[\sup_{f\in\mathscr{H}} \left(\mathscr{R}(f) - \hat{\mathscr{R}}_S(f)\right)\right] \\ &\qquad\leq \mathbb{E}_{S,S'}\left[\sup_{f\in\mathscr{H}} \left(\hat{\mathscr{R}}_{S'}(f) - \hat{\mathscr{R}}_S(f)\right)\right]. \end{aligned} \tag{3.74}$$

Step 2: Insertion of Rademacher signs by index swapping. For each i, the pair (z_i, z_i') is exchangeable, so swapping $z_i \leftrightarrow z_i'$ leaves the joint distribution of (S, S') unchanged. Doing this swap independently for each i according to i.i.d. Rademacher signs $\sigma_1, \ldots, \sigma_n \in \{\pm 1\}$ (independent of S, S') preserves the joint distribution *simultaneously for all* $f \in \mathscr{H}$. Hence

$$\sup_{f\in\mathscr{H}} \left(\hat{\mathscr{R}}_{S'}(f) - \hat{\mathscr{R}}_S(f)\right) \stackrel{d}{=} \sup_{f\in\mathscr{H}} \frac{1}{n}\sum_{i=1}^n \sigma_i \left(g_f(z_i') - g_f(z_i)\right). \tag{3.75}$$

Taking expectations and using $\sup_f(A_f + B_f) \leq \sup_f A_f + \sup_f B_f$,

$$\mathbb{E}_{S,S'}\left[\sup_f \left(\hat{\mathscr{R}}_{S'}(f) - \hat{\mathscr{R}}_S(f)\right)\right] = \mathbb{E}_{S,S',\sigma}\left[\sup_f \frac{1}{n}\sum_{i=1}^n \sigma_i \left(g_f(z_i') - g_f(z_i)\right)\right] \tag{3.76}$$

$$\begin{aligned}&\leq \mathbb{E}_{S',\sigma}\left[\sup_f \frac{1}{n}\sum_{i=1}^n \sigma_i \, g_f(z_i')\right] \\ &\quad + \mathbb{E}_{S,\sigma}\left[\sup_f \frac{1}{n}\sum_{i=1}^n (-\sigma_i) \, g_f(z_i)\right] \end{aligned} \tag{3.77}$$

$$= 2\, \mathfrak{R}_n(\ell \circ \mathscr{H}), \tag{3.78}$$

where the last equality uses $-\sigma_i \stackrel{d}{=} \sigma_i$.

Combining the two steps:

$$\mathbb{E}_S\left[\sup_{f\in\mathcal{H}}\left(\mathcal{R}(f)-\hat{\mathcal{R}}_S(f)\right)\right] \leq 2\,\mathfrak{R}_n(\ell\circ\mathcal{H}). \tag{3.79}$$

Step 3: Concentration with McDiarmid's Inequality. To obtain a high-probability bound, define the random function:

$$\Phi(S) = \sup_{f\in\mathcal{H}}\left[\mathcal{R}(f)-\hat{\mathcal{R}}_S(f)\right] \tag{3.80}$$

We verify that Φ satisfies the bounded differences property. If S and $S^{(j)}$ differ in the j-th example (i.e., $S=\{z_1,\ldots,z_n\}$ and $S^{(j)}=\{z_1,\ldots,z'_j,\ldots,z_n\}$), then:

$$\begin{aligned}|\Phi(S)-\Phi(S^{(j)})| &= \Bigg|\sup_f[\mathcal{R}(f)-\hat{\mathcal{R}}_S(f)] \\ &\qquad -\sup_f[\mathcal{R}(f)-\hat{\mathcal{R}}_{S^{(j)}}(f)]\Bigg| && (3.81)\\ &\leq \sup_f\left|\hat{\mathcal{R}}_{S^{(j)}}(f)-\hat{\mathcal{R}}_S(f)\right| && (3.82)\\ &\leq \frac{1}{n}\sup_f|\ell(f(x'_j),y'_j)-\ell(f(x_j),y_j)| && (3.83)\\ &\leq \frac{1}{n} && (3.84)\end{aligned}$$

where the last inequality uses the fact that loss is bounded in $[0,1]$.

By McDiarmid's inequality (with $c_j=1/n$ for all j, so $\sum c_j^2=1/n$):

$$P(\Phi(S)\geq\mathbb{E}[\Phi(S)]+t)\leq\exp\left(-2nt^2\right) \tag{3.85}$$

Setting $P(\Phi(S)\geq\mathbb{E}[\Phi(S)]+t)=\delta$:

$$\exp(-2nt^2)=\delta \implies t=\sqrt{\frac{\ln(1/\delta)}{2n}} \tag{3.86}$$

Therefore, with probability at least $1-\delta$:

$$\begin{aligned}\sup_{f\in\mathcal{H}}\left[\mathcal{R}(f)-\hat{\mathcal{R}}_S(f)\right] &\leq \mathbb{E}[\Phi(S)]+\sqrt{\frac{\ln(1/\delta)}{2n}} \\ &\leq 2\mathfrak{R}_n(\ell\circ\mathcal{H})+\sqrt{\frac{\ln(1/\delta)}{2n}}\end{aligned} \tag{3.87}$$

For losses that are L_ℓ-Lipschitz in their first argument, Talagrand's contraction lemma gives $\mathfrak{R}_n(\ell \circ \mathscr{H}) \leq L_\ell \, \mathfrak{R}_n(\mathscr{H})$. For binary classification with $\{0,1\}$-valued hypotheses, the 0-1 loss class coincides with the hypothesis class, so $\mathfrak{R}_n(\ell_{0\text{-}1} \circ \mathscr{H}) = \mathfrak{R}_n(\mathscr{H})$ (for $\{-1,+1\}$-valued hypotheses one uses $\ell_{0\text{-}1}(h(x),y) = (1 - yh(x))/2$ instead, which yields a factor of $1/2$ on the right-hand side), yielding the stated bound:

$$\mathscr{R}(f) \leq \hat{\mathscr{R}}(f) + 2\mathfrak{R}_n(\mathscr{H}) + \sqrt{\frac{\ln(1/\delta)}{2n}} \quad \text{w.p.} \geq 1-\delta \tag{3.88}$$

■

This bound is often tighter than VC bounds for neural networks because it captures the geometric structure of the data and the hypothesis class. For example, for linear models with bounded L_2 norm, the Rademacher complexity decays with $1/\sqrt{n}$ independent of the dimension d. This property explains why kernel methods and neural networks can generalize in high-dimensional spaces.

3.6 The Double Descent Phenomenon

Classical statistical learning theory suggests a U-shaped curve for test error as a function of model complexity: error decreases as bias decreases, then increases as variance increases. However, modern deep learning exhibits a "Double Descent" phenomenon. In the **Under-parameterized Regime**, the model is not complex enough to fit the data, resulting in high training and test error (bias dominates). In the **Critical Regime**, the model capacity is just sufficient to fit the training data (interpolation threshold). At this point, the model exhibits maximal sensitivity to noise perturbations. Consequently, the variance component of the error reaches its peak, leading to poor generalization. Finally, in the **Over-parameterized Regime**, as capacity increases further, there are infinitely many solutions that fit the training data. The optimization algorithm (e.g., gradient descent) acts as an implicit regularizer, often selecting solutions with low norm (e.g., smoothest function). This property causes the test error to decrease again, often below the minimum of the classical U-curve.

This phenomenon challenges traditional notions of model selection and emphasizes the role of implicit regularization. In Trustworthy AI, understanding this regime is crucial because over-parameterized models, while highly accurate, may be more susceptible to adversarial attacks or privacy leakage due to their capacity to memorize individual data points. A key lesson is that scale and capacity are not inherently bad for generalization; however, the training algorithm and implicit biases matter significantly.

■ **Example 3.3 — Double Descent in Polynomial Regression.** Consider fitting a polynomial $\hat{f}(x) = \sum_{j=0}^{p} \beta_j x^j$ of degree p to $n = 20$ noisy data points from $y = \sin(2\pi x) + \varepsilon$. For $p < 19$ (under-parameterized), the model cannot interpolate all points, and test error follows the classical U-shaped curve, minimized around $p \approx 5$. At $p = 19$ (interpolation threshold), the polynomial passes through all 20 points but oscillates wildly between them, producing enormous test error. For $p \gg 19$ (over-parameterized), there are infinitely many interpolating polynomials, and the minimum-norm solution (selected by numerical solvers) is biased toward simpler, lower-complexity functions, and the test error decreases again. This directly parallels neural networks: a network with width w reaches the interpolation threshold at a critical width, and wider networks generalize better due to implicit regularization by gradient descent. ■

3.7 PAC Learning Framework

The Probably Approximately Correct (PAC) learning framework, introduced by Valiant [79], provides a rigorous foundation for computational learning theory.

Definition 3.7.1 — PAC Learnability. A concept class $\mathscr{C}$ is PAC-learnable if there exists an algorithm $\mathscr{A}$ and a polynomial function $p(\cdot,\cdot,\cdot,\cdot)$ such that for every $\varepsilon, \delta > 0$, every distribution $\mathscr{D}$ on $\mathscr{X}$, and every target concept $c \in \mathscr{C}$, given access to at least $m \geq p(1/\varepsilon, 1/\delta, d, \text{size}(c))$ samples drawn i.i.d. from $\mathscr{D}$, $\mathscr{A}$ outputs a hypothesis h satisfying:

$$P_{S \sim \mathscr{D}^m}[\mathscr{R}(h) \leq \varepsilon] \geq 1 - \delta \tag{3.89}$$

where $\mathscr{R}(h) = \mathbb{E}_{x \sim \mathscr{D}}[\mathbb{I}(h(x) \neq c(x))]$ is the true error (generalization error), S is the training set of size m, and d is the dimensionality of the input space.

The key elements are that the algorithm succeeds **Probably** (with probability at least $1 - \delta$ over the random draw of the training set), produces a hypothesis that is **Approximately Correct** (with generalization error at most ε), and does so in time and sample complexity that are polynomial in the relevant parameters.

■ **Example 3.4 — PAC Learning Axis-Aligned Rectangles for Anomaly Detection.** In industrial quality control, suppose defective products have measurements (x_1, x_2) (e.g., temperature and pressure during manufacturing) that fall within an unknown rectangular region $[a_1, b_1] \times [a_2, b_2]$. The hypothesis class $\mathscr{H}$ of axis-aligned rectangles in $\mathbb{R}^2$ has VC dimension 4. By the PAC learning theorem, to learn the defect region with error $\varepsilon = 0.05$ (mislabeling at most 5% of products) and confidence $1 - \delta = 0.99$, we need $m = O\left(\frac{4 \cdot \log(1/0.05) + \log(1/0.01)}{0.05}\right) \approx O(332)$ labeled product samples. The ERM algorithm simply outputs the tightest rectangle containing all defective samples, a computationally efficient procedure that provably converges to the true defect region. ■

Theorem 3.7.1 — Sample Complexity of PAC Learning. If $\mathscr{H}$ has VC dimension d, then for any $\varepsilon, \delta > 0$, a sample of size:

$$m = O\left(\frac{d\log(1/\varepsilon) + \log(1/\delta)}{\varepsilon}\right) \tag{3.90}$$

is sufficient for PAC learning (the $\log(1/\varepsilon)$ factor can be removed under tighter analysis [30]). Furthermore, any PAC learning algorithm requires:

$$m = \Omega\left(\frac{d + \log(1/\delta)}{\varepsilon}\right) \tag{3.91}$$

samples.

3.7.1 Agnostic PAC Learning

In practical machine learning, we often cannot assume that the true target function belongs to our hypothesis class $\mathscr{H}$. The realizable PAC framework assumes $c \in \mathscr{C}$, guaranteeing zero training error on the true labels. The agnostic PAC framework removes this assumption and is therefore more realistic. Instead of learning the true concept perfectly, we settle for learning a hypothesis that is nearly as good as the best hypothesis in $\mathscr{H}$.

Definition 3.7.2 — Agnostic PAC Learnability. A hypothesis class $\mathscr{H}$ is agnostic PAC-learnable if there exists an algorithm $\mathscr{A}$ and a polynomial function $p(\cdot,\cdot,\cdot)$ such that for every $\varepsilon, \delta > 0$, every distribution $\mathscr{D}$ on $\mathscr{X} \times \mathscr{Y}$, and every sample size $m \geq p(1/\varepsilon, 1/\delta, d)$, given access to m samples $S = \{(x_i, y_i)\}_{i=1}^m$ drawn i.i.d. from $\mathscr{D}$, algorithm $\mathscr{A}$ outputs a hypothesis $h \in \mathscr{H}$ satisfying:

$$P\left[\mathscr{R}(h) \leq \inf_{h' \in \mathscr{H}} \mathscr{R}(h') + \varepsilon\right] \geq 1 - \delta \tag{3.92}$$

where the probability is over the randomness of the sample S (and possibly the randomness of the algorithm).

The key difference from realizable PAC learning is that we no longer require $\mathscr{R}(h) \leq \varepsilon$. Instead, we require the algorithm to compete with the best-in-class hypothesis: $\mathscr{R}(h) \leq \mathscr{R}^* + \varepsilon$, where $\mathscr{R}^* = \inf_{h' \in \mathscr{H}} \mathscr{R}(h')$ is the minimum achievable risk within the hypothesis class.

Ⓡ [Comparison with Realizable PAC] In the realizable setting, if $c \in \mathscr{C}$, then $\mathscr{R}^* = 0$, so agnostic PAC learnability reduces to standard PAC learnability. The agnostic setting is more general because:

- It accounts for model misspecification: the true function may not be in $\mathscr{H}$.
- It accounts for irreducible error: even if there exists a deterministic relationship between inputs and true labels, observed labels may be corrupted by noise or measurement errors, making zero error unattainable.
- It is distribution-free: it works for any distribution $\mathscr{D}$ on $\mathscr{X} \times \mathscr{Y}$, not just separable cases.

Theorem 3.7.2 — Sample Complexity of Agnostic PAC Learning. If $\mathscr{H}$ is a hypothesis class of VC dimension d, then for any $\varepsilon, \delta > 0$, a sample of size:

$$m = O\left(\frac{d + \log(1/\delta)}{\varepsilon^2}\right) \tag{3.93}$$

is sufficient for agnostic PAC learning of $\mathscr{H}$.

Proof Sketch. The proof relies on the VC bound from Theorem 3.4.2. By the VC bound, with probability at least $1 - \delta$, for all $f \in \mathscr{H}$:

$$|\mathscr{R}(f) - \hat{\mathscr{R}}(f)| \leq \sqrt{\frac{8d\ln(2m) + 8\ln(4/\delta)}{m}} \tag{3.94}$$

Let $f^* = \arg\min_{f \in \mathscr{H}} \mathscr{R}(f)$ be the best-in-class hypothesis, and let $\hat{f} = \arg\min_{f \in \mathscr{H}} \hat{\mathscr{R}}(f)$ be the empirical risk minimizer. Then:

$$\mathscr{R}(\hat{f}) \leq \hat{\mathscr{R}}(\hat{f}) + \sqrt{\frac{8d\ln(2m) + 8\ln(4/\delta)}{m}} \quad \text{(by VC bound)} \tag{3.95}$$

$$\leq \hat{\mathscr{R}}(f^*) + \sqrt{\frac{8d\ln(2m) + 8\ln(4/\delta)}{m}} \quad \text{(since } \hat{f} \text{ minimizes empirical risk)} \tag{3.96}$$

$$\leq \mathscr{R}(f^*) + 2\sqrt{\frac{8d\ln(2m) + 8\ln(4/\delta)}{m}} \quad \text{(by VC bound on } f^*\text{)} \tag{3.97}$$

Setting the right-hand side to $\mathscr{R}(f^*) + \varepsilon$ and solving for m:

$$2\sqrt{\frac{8d\ln(2m) + 8\ln(4/\delta)}{m}} \leq \varepsilon \tag{3.98}$$

For m large enough (specifically, $m = \Omega((d + \log(1/\delta))/\varepsilon^2)$), this inequality holds. The precise constants depend on the lower-order terms in the VC bound, but the scaling is $O((d + \log(1/\delta))/\varepsilon^2)$. ■

Ⓡ [The $1/\varepsilon^2$ Dependency] A crucial difference from the realizable case is the $1/\varepsilon^2$ dependency in the sample complexity bound. In the realizable setting, it was $O((d + \log(1/\delta))/\varepsilon)$. The quadratic dependence on ε arises because:

1. In the realizable case, we only need the empirical risk to be small (close to zero). The probability that any bad hypothesis (with $\mathscr{R}(h) > \varepsilon$) achieves zero empirical risk decays exponentially in $m\varepsilon$, yielding the $1/\varepsilon$ scaling.
2. In the agnostic case, we need the empirical risk minimizer to be close to the true risk minimizer, which requires uniform convergence of the empirical risks of all hypotheses. This requires a union bound and leads to the $1/\varepsilon^2$ scaling.

■ **Example 3.5 — Agnostic PAC Learning in Noisy Classification.** Suppose we train a binary classifier on image data with human labels, but the labeling process has a 5% error rate (e.g., annotators sometimes disagree or make mistakes). Using a hypothesis class of neural networks with VC dimension $d = 1000$, and targeting an excess error of $\varepsilon = 0.05$ with confidence $1 - \delta = 0.99$:

$$m = O\left(\frac{1000 + \log(1/0.01)}{(0.05)^2}\right) = O\left(\frac{1000 + 4.6}{0.0025}\right) \approx O(400{,}000) \tag{3.99}$$

This is the sample size needed to learn a hypothesis whose error is at most 5% above the best achievable error in the class. If the best achievable error is about 5% (due to label noise), we are then guaranteed a hypothesis with error at most $\approx 10\%$.
■

3.8 Margin-Based Generalization Bounds

For classification problems, the margin of a classifier provides a more refined measure of confidence than just correctness.

Definition 3.8.1 — Margin. For a real-valued classifier $f : \mathscr{X} \to \mathbb{R}$ and label $y \in \{-1, +1\}$, the margin on example (x, y) is:

$$\gamma(x, y) := y \cdot f(x) \tag{3.100}$$

A positive margin indicates correct classification; larger margins indicate higher confidence.

Theorem 3.8.1 — Margin Bound. Let $\mathscr{H}$ be a class of functions mapping to $[-1,1]$. For any $\gamma > 0$, with probability at least $1-\delta$ over a sample S of size n:

$$\mathscr{R}_{0-1}(f) \leq \hat{\mathscr{R}}_{\gamma}(f) + \frac{2}{\gamma}\mathfrak{R}_n(\mathscr{H}) + 3\sqrt{\frac{\log(2/\delta)}{2n}} \tag{3.101}$$

where $\hat{\mathscr{R}}_{\gamma}(f) = \frac{1}{n}\sum_{i=1}^{n}\mathbb{I}(y_i f(x_i) < \gamma)$ is the empirical margin loss and $\mathscr{R}_{0-1}(f)$ is the expected 0-1 loss.

Intuitively, the empirical margin loss counts how often the classifier *fails* to achieve margin at least γ (i.e., examples that are either misclassified or classified correctly but with insufficient confidence). Raising γ makes this a stricter requirement, so $\hat{\mathscr{R}}_{\gamma}$ is non-decreasing in γ. The factor $1/\gamma$ in front of the Rademacher term arises because the family of margin-thresholded indicator functions is $1/\gamma$-Lipschitz in f, so the contraction lemma introduces this factor when bounding the corresponding Rademacher complexity. This bound explains why maximizing margins (as in SVMs) leads to better generalization. For neural networks, the implicit bias of gradient descent toward large-margin solutions partially explains their generalization ability.

3.9 Algorithmic Stability

An alternative approach to generalization bounds relies on the stability of the learning algorithm rather than the complexity of the hypothesis class.

Definition 3.9.1 — Uniform Stability. A learning algorithm $\mathscr{A}$ that maps a dataset S to a hypothesis $f_S = \mathscr{A}(S)$ is β-uniformly stable if for all datasets S, S' of size m differing in exactly one example:

$$\sup_{(x,y)} |\ell(f_S(x),y) - \ell(f_{S'}(x),y)| \leq \beta \tag{3.102}$$

Theorem 3.9.1 — Stability Bound. If $\mathscr{A}$ is β-uniformly stable and $\ell \leq M$, then with probability at least $1-\delta$:

$$\mathscr{R}(\mathscr{A}(S)) \leq \hat{\mathscr{R}}(\mathscr{A}(S)) + 2\beta + (4m\beta + M)\sqrt{\frac{\ln(1/\delta)}{2m}} \tag{3.103}$$

where m is the sample size, M is the upper bound on the loss function, and β is the stability parameter.

SGD with appropriate learning rates is known to be stable:

Theorem 3.9.2 — SGD Stability. For convex, L-Lipschitz, β-smooth loss functions, SGD with a decaying step size $\eta_t = c/t$ run for T iterations is $O(\log T/m)$-uniformly stable; for μ-strongly convex losses the bound strengthens to $O(1/(\mu m))$, independent of T [32].

This provides generalization guarantees for deep learning without relying on explicit capacity measures.

Example 3.6 — Stability in Weather Prediction Models. Consider training a neural network for temperature forecasting using $m = 10{,}000$ daily weather records. Running SGD for $T = 10^4$ iterations with the step-size schedule of the theorem yields a uniform-stability bound of order $\log T/m \approx \log(10^4)/10^4 \approx 9.2 \times 10^{-4}$, so $\beta \lesssim 10^{-3}$. Replacing any single training record then changes the loss on any test example by at most about 10^{-3}. The stability bound guarantees that the expected generalization gap is at most $2\beta \approx 2 \times 10^{-3}$. If the model achieves 1.5°C mean absolute error on training data, the expected true error is at most about 1.502°C, providing a strong guarantee that the model genuinely learns weather patterns rather than memorizing individual days, and that no single training record can disproportionately influence predictions. ■

Table 3.2 compares the generalization bounds developed in this chapter, summarizing the complexity measure each relies on, the resulting bound on the generalization gap, whether the bound is data-dependent, and its key feature.

Table 3.2: Comparison of generalization bounds developed in this chapter.

Bound	**Complexity Measure**	**Bound on Gen. Gap**	**Data Dep.?**	**Key Feature**
VC Bound	VC dim. d_{VC}	$O(\sqrt{\frac{d_{VC}\log(n/d_{VC})}{n}})$	No	Distribution-free; often loose
Rademacher	$\mathfrak{R}_n(\mathscr{H})$	$2\mathfrak{R}_n(\mathscr{H}) + O(\sqrt{\frac{\log(1/\delta)}{n}})$	Yes	Tighter for structured classes
Margin Bound	Margin γ, $\|w\|$	$O(\frac{R\|w\|}{\gamma\sqrt{n}})$	Yes	Norm-based; indep. of d
Stability	Uniform stab. β	$2\beta + O(\sqrt{\frac{\log(1/\delta)}{n}})$	Yes	Algorithm-dep.; applies to SGD

Exercises

1. **Bias-Variance Trade-off**: Consider a regression problem $y = \sin(2\pi x) + \varepsilon$ where $\varepsilon \sim \mathcal{N}(0, 0.1)$.
   (a) Generate a dataset of size $n = 10$.
   (b) Fit polynomials of degree $p = 0, 1, \ldots, 9$.
   (c) Plot the training error and test error as a function of p.
   (d) Decompose the error into bias and variance by repeating the experiment 100 times.
2. **VC Dimension**:
   (a) Prove that the VC dimension of a linear classifier in $\mathbb{R}^d$ is $d+1$.
   (b) Prove that the VC dimension of the class of axis-aligned rectangles in $\mathbb{R}^2$ is 4.
   (c) Construct a set of 3 points in $\mathbb{R}^2$ that cannot be shattered by axis-aligned rectangles.
3. **Rademacher Complexity**:
   (a) Show that $\hat{\mathfrak{R}}_S(\mathscr{H}) = \mathbb{E}_\sigma[\sup_{h \in \mathscr{H}} \frac{1}{n} \sum_{i=1}^n \sigma_i h(x_i)]$ satisfies the bounded difference inequality.
   (b) Derive the Rademacher complexity for linear hypotheses with bounded L_2 norm.
4. **PAC Learning**:
   (a) Prove that any finite hypothesis class $\mathscr{H}$ is PAC learnable with sample complexity $m = O(\frac{\log|\mathscr{H}| + \log(1/\delta)}{\varepsilon})$.
   (b) Implement the Consistent algorithm for learning axis-aligned rectangles.
   (c) Verify empirically that the sample complexity matches the theoretical bound.
   (d) Extend to the agnostic case and compare sample requirements.
5. **Margin Theory**:
   (a) Train an SVM on a binary classification task with varying regularization.
   (b) Compute the margin achieved by each model.
   (c) Plot test accuracy vs. margin size and verify the theoretical relationship.
   (d) Compare hard-margin and soft-margin SVM generalization.
6. **Algorithmic Stability**:
   (a) Implement SGD with different learning rate schedules.
   (b) Empirically measure stability by comparing models trained on datasets differing by one sample.
   (c) Verify that smaller learning rates lead to more stable algorithms.
   (d) Compare stability of SGD vs. batch gradient descent.
7. **Double Descent**:
   (a) Train models of increasing complexity on a fixed dataset (e.g., neural

networks with varying widths).

(b) Plot training and test error as a function of model complexity.

(c) Identify the interpolation threshold where training error hits zero.

(d) Verify the double descent phenomenon: test error decreases again past the interpolation threshold.

8. **Generalization in Deep Learning**:

   (a) Train a deep network with random labels [89].

   (b) Compare training dynamics with true labels.

   (c) Measure the effective capacity using a noise memorization metric.

   (d) Discuss why traditional capacity bounds fail for deep networks.

9. **Concentration Inequalities**:

   (a) Prove Hoeffding's inequality for bounded random variables.

   (b) Use Hoeffding to derive a uniform convergence bound for finite hypothesis classes.

   (c) Compare the tightness of Hoeffding vs. Bernstein bounds on empirical data.

   (d) Apply McDiarmid's inequality to analyze the stability of cross-validation.

Robustness, Fairness, and Privacy

Contents of This Part

Chapter 4
Adversarial Robustness

4.1 The Phenomenon of Adversarial Examples

The discovery that state-of-the-art deep neural networks are vulnerable to "adversarial examples" (inputs formed by applying small, often imperceptible perturbations to clean data that cause the model to make high-confidence errors) has shattered the illusion that these models learn human-like concepts. In the context of image classification, an adversary can add a specific noise pattern to an image of a panda such that the modified image looks identical to the human eye but is classified by the network as a gibbon with 99.3% confidence. This vulnerability is not specific to computer vision; it pervades natural language processing, speech recognition, and reinforcement learning.

The existence of adversarial examples poses a severe security risk for safety-critical applications [76]. In personalized medicine, an AI-based diagnostic tool analyzing patient records might misclassify a severe condition as benign due to small, naturally occurring artifact noise in the clinical data. This failure can lead to catastrophic outcomes. In health insurance claims processing, subtle data perturbations could falsely justify denied coverage. Therefore, understanding the mathematical nature of these vulnerabilities and developing robust defenses is a prerequisite for the deployment of AI in the real world.

4.2 High-Dimensional Geometry and Concentration

Early hypotheses suggested that adversarial examples were a result of "overfitting" or the extreme nonlinearity of deep networks. However, Goodfellow et al. [29] proposed the "Linearity Hypothesis", arguing that the vulnerability arises from the model being *too linear* in high-dimensional spaces. This is a remarkable insight: neural networks are vulnerable not because they are too complex, but because they are too simple in the geometric structure they learn.

Proposition 4.2.1 — Linearity Hypothesis (29). Consider a linear model $f(x) = w^T x$. Let η be a perturbation bounded in L_∞ norm: $\|\eta\|_\infty \leq \varepsilon$. The change in the model's output is $w^T\eta$. To maximize this change under the L_∞ constraint, the adversary should choose each component of η to align with the sign of the corresponding weight:

$$\eta = \varepsilon \cdot \text{sign}(w), \quad \Delta = w^T\eta = \varepsilon \sum_{i=1}^{d} |w_i| = \varepsilon \|w\|_1 \tag{4.1}$$

where $\text{sign}(w)$ is the element-wise sign function, d is the dimensionality of the input, and $\|w\|_1$ is the L_1 norm of the weight vector. If the weights w_i are independent and identically distributed with $\mathbb{E}[|w_i|] = m$, then by the law of large numbers $\|w\|_1 = \sum_{i=1}^{d} |w_i| \approx d \cdot m$. Thus, the output change scales *linearly with the dimension* d. In high-dimensional spaces (e.g., a 224×224 RGB image has $d \approx 150{,}000$), even if each weight is small ($m = O(1)$), the total effect can be huge. A perturbation of $\varepsilon = 1/255$ per pixel (imperceptible) causes $\Delta \approx 600$ (assuming average weight magnitude $|w_i| \approx 1$), easily crossing any decision boundary.

Extension to Neural Networks: While real neural networks are nonlinear, if the local approximation around a data point is nearly linear (as is often the case when weights are not trained to be highly nonlinear), the same principle applies. The model's decision boundary can be expressed locally as a hyperplane, and adversarial perturbations along the normal direction to this hyperplane cause large changes in output.

More formally, adversarial examples are related to the **Concentration of Measure** phenomenon. In high-dimensional spaces, probability mass is not distributed uniformly; it concentrates in unexpected ways. For a unit sphere S^{d-1}, most of the measure is concentrated near the equator defined by any fixed hyperplane. This means that if a classifier's decision boundary passes through the typical data region, a randomly chosen point is likely very close to the boundary (in Euclidean distance) even though the input space is enormous. Lévy's isoperimetric inequality formalizes this observation: if a set $A \subseteq S^{d-1}$ has measure at least $1/2$, then its ε-expansion $A_\varepsilon = \{x \in S^{d-1} : d(x,A) \leq \varepsilon\}$ satisfies $\mu(A_\varepsilon) \geq 1 - \exp(-c(d-1)\varepsilon^2/2)$ for a universal constant $c > 0$. Thus, the complementary measure decays exponentially in the dimension. Conversely, for any classifier with non-trivial error rate $p > 0$, the set of misclassified points has measure at least p, and is thus at distance at most $O(\sqrt{\log(1/p)/d})$ from the correctly classified points. The curse of dimensionality dictates that this distance becomes vanishingly small as d grows.

In plain English: on a high-dimensional sphere, almost all of the surface area lies in a thin equatorial band around any fixed equator; informally, a typical point is "close to every reasonable hyperplane". The isoperimetric inequality formalizes that the ε-thickening of any moderately large region covers nearly the whole sphere when the dimension is large. That is exactly why adversarial examples are simultaneously close in distance (small ε) and ubiquitous in measure (most of the sphere lies within ε of the decision boundary).

4.3 Taxonomy of Adversarial Attacks

Adversarial attacks can be categorized based on the attacker's knowledge, goals, and perturbation constraints, as summarized in Table 4.1.

Table 4.1: Taxonomy of Adversarial Attacks

Dimension	Description
Knowledge	
White-box	Attacker has full access to model weights, architecture, and gradients.
Black-box	Attacker only has query access (probabilities or hard labels).
Gray-box	Attacker has partial knowledge (e.g., architecture but not weights).
Goal	
Targeted	Misclassify input x as a specific target class y_{target}.
Untargeted	Misclassify input x as any class $y \neq y_{\text{true}}$.
Constraint	
L_∞	Maximum change to any single pixel is bounded (imperceptibility).
L_2	Euclidean distance is bounded.
L_0	Number of modified pixels is bounded (sparse attack).
Physical	Perturbations realizable in the physical world (e.g., medical imaging artifacts).

4.4 White-Box Attacks

In the white-box setting, the attacker has complete knowledge of the model architecture, parameters θ, and can compute gradients $\nabla_x \ell(f_\theta(x), y)$. This represents the strongest threat model and provides upper bounds on attack effectiveness.

4.4.1 Theoretical Foundation: First-Order Adversaries

The core insight behind gradient-based attacks is that neural network loss landscapes are locally linear in the input space. For a differentiable loss function ℓ, the first-order Taylor expansion around input x gives:

$$\ell(f_\theta(x+\delta), y) \approx \ell(f_\theta(x), y) + \langle \nabla_x \ell(f_\theta(x), y), \delta \rangle + O(\|\delta\|^2) \tag{4.2}$$

where $\langle \cdot, \cdot \rangle$ denotes the inner product, ∇_x is the gradient with respect to the input x, and $O(\|\delta\|^2)$ represents higher-order terms that are negligible for small δ.

To maximize this linear approximation subject to $\|\delta\|_p \leq \varepsilon$, we solve:

$$\delta^* = \arg\max_{\|\delta\|_p \leq \varepsilon} \langle g, \delta \rangle \quad \text{where } g = \nabla_x \ell(f_\theta(x), y) \tag{4.3}$$

where $\|\cdot\|_p$ is the L_p norm.

The solution depends on the choice of L_p norm constraint:

Proposition 4.4.1 — Optimal First-Order Perturbation. For gradient $g \in \mathbb{R}^d$ and constraint $\|\delta\|_p \leq \varepsilon$:

1. **L_∞ constraint:** $\delta^* = \varepsilon \cdot \text{sign}(g)$, achieving $\langle g, \delta^* \rangle = \varepsilon \|g\|_1$
2. **L_2 constraint:** $\delta^* = \varepsilon \cdot \frac{g}{\|g\|_2}$, achieving $\langle g, \delta^* \rangle = \varepsilon \|g\|_2$
3. **L_1 constraint:** $\delta^* = \varepsilon \cdot e_{i^*} \cdot \text{sign}(g_{i^*})$ where $i^* = \arg\max_i |g_i|$, achieving $\langle g, \delta^* \rangle = \varepsilon \|g\|_\infty$

Proof. We use Hölder's inequality: $|\langle g, \delta \rangle| \leq \|g\|_q \|\delta\|_p$ where $\frac{1}{p} + \frac{1}{q} = 1$. Equality holds when δ is aligned with g in the dual norm sense. Plain English: two norms $\|\cdot\|_p$ and $\|\cdot\|_q$ are called *dual* when their exponents satisfy $1/p + 1/q = 1$ (so L_∞ is dual to L_1, and L_2 is dual to itself). Hölder's inequality is the natural generalization of Cauchy–Schwarz: it caps the inner product $\langle g, \delta \rangle$ by the product of the dual-norm magnitudes, with equality precisely when δ concentrates its budget where g is largest.

Case 1 (L_∞ constraint, $p = \infty$, $q = 1$): We have $\langle g, \delta \rangle \leq \|g\|_1 \|\delta\|_\infty \leq \varepsilon \|g\|_1$. To achieve equality, we set $\delta_i = \varepsilon \cdot \text{sign}(g_i)$. Then:

$$\langle g, \delta \rangle = \sum_{i=1}^{d} g_i \cdot \varepsilon \cdot \text{sign}(g_i) = \varepsilon \sum_{i=1}^{d} |g_i| = \varepsilon \|g\|_1 \tag{4.4}$$

Case 2 (L_2 constraint, $p = q = 2$): By Cauchy–Schwarz, $\langle g, \delta \rangle \leq \|g\|_2 \|\delta\|_2 \leq \varepsilon \|g\|_2$. Equality holds when $\delta = \varepsilon \frac{g}{\|g\|_2}$:

$$\langle g, \delta \rangle = \left\langle g, \varepsilon \frac{g}{\|g\|_2} \right\rangle = \frac{\varepsilon}{\|g\|_2} \|g\|_2^2 = \varepsilon \|g\|_2 \tag{4.5}$$

Case 3 (L_1 constraint, $p = 1$, $q = \infty$): We have $\langle g, \delta \rangle \leq \|g\|_\infty \|\delta\|_1 \leq \varepsilon \|g\|_\infty$. To achieve equality, we place all mass on the coordinate with largest $|g_i|$. Let $i^* = \arg\max_i |g_i|$, set $\delta_{i^*} = \varepsilon \cdot \text{sign}(g_{i^*})$ and $\delta_i = 0$ for $i \neq i^*$. Then $\|\delta\|_1 = \varepsilon$ and:

$$\langle g, \delta \rangle = g_{i^*} \cdot \varepsilon \cdot \text{sign}(g_{i^*}) = \varepsilon |g_{i^*}| = \varepsilon \|g\|_\infty \tag{4.6}$$

■

4.4.2 Fast Gradient Sign Method (FGSM)

FGSM [29] is the canonical one-step attack for L_∞ perturbations:

$$x_{\text{adv}} = x + \varepsilon \cdot \text{sign}(\nabla_x \ell(f_\theta(x), y)) \tag{4.7}$$

where x_{adv} is the adversarial example, x is the original input, ε is the perturbation magnitude, and $\text{sign}(\cdot)$ is the element-wise sign function.

(R) [Geometric Interpretation] FGSM moves in the direction that maximizes the linear approximation of the loss. The sign function projects onto the vertices of the L_∞ ball, ensuring each pixel changes by exactly $\pm\varepsilon$. While this is optimal for the linearized problem, it may be suboptimal for the true (nonlinear) loss.

Proposition 4.4.2 — FGSM Loss Increase. If the composite map $x \mapsto \ell(f_\theta(x), y)$ is L-smooth (i.e., has L-Lipschitz continuous gradients), FGSM achieves:

$$\ell(f_\theta(x_{\text{adv}}), y) - \ell(f_\theta(x), y) \geq \varepsilon \|\nabla_x \ell\|_1 - \frac{L\varepsilon^2 d}{2} \tag{4.8}$$

where d is the input dimension.

Proof. By Taylor expansion around x:

$$\ell(f_\theta(x_{\text{adv}}), y) = \ell(f_\theta(x), y) + \langle \nabla_x \ell, x_{\text{adv}} - x \rangle + O(\|x_{\text{adv}} - x\|^2) \tag{4.9}$$

For FGSM, $x_{\text{adv}} - x = \varepsilon \cdot \text{sign}(\nabla_x \ell)$, so:

$$\begin{aligned} \langle \nabla_x \ell, \varepsilon \cdot \text{sign}(\nabla_x \ell) \rangle &= \varepsilon \sum_{i=1}^{d} |(\nabla_x \ell)_i| \\ &= \varepsilon \|\nabla_x \ell\|_1 \end{aligned} \tag{4.10}$$

For the second-order term, by L-smoothness (i.e., the gradient of ℓ is L-Lipschitz in L_2 norm):

$$|\ell(f_\theta(x_{\text{adv}}), y) - \ell(f_\theta(x), y) - \langle \nabla_x \ell, x_{\text{adv}} - x \rangle| \leq \frac{L}{2} \|x_{\text{adv}} - x\|_2^2 = \frac{L\varepsilon^2 d}{2} \tag{4.11}$$

Since for FGSM $\|x_{\text{adv}} - x\|_2^2 = d\varepsilon^2$ (each of the d components changes by $\pm\varepsilon$), we get the stated bound. ∎

The computational efficiency of FGSM (single forward-backward pass) makes it suitable for generating large-scale adversarial training data.

4.4.3 Projected Gradient Descent (PGD)

PGD [50] is the multi-step extension of FGSM that iteratively refines the adversarial perturbation:

$$x^{t+1} = \Pi_{\mathscr{B}_\varepsilon(x)} \left(x^t + \alpha \cdot \text{sign}(\nabla_x \ell(f_\theta(x^t), y)) \right) \tag{4.12}$$

where $\Pi_{\mathscr{B}_\varepsilon(x)}$ projects onto the ε-ball: $\Pi_{\mathscr{B}_\varepsilon(x)}(z) = x + \text{clip}(z - x, -\varepsilon, \varepsilon)$ (for the L_∞ case), x^t is the adversarial example at iteration t, and α is the step size.

Algorithm 4.1 states the full iterative procedure.

Algorithm 4.1 Projected Gradient Descent (PGD) Attack

```
Input: x, y, θ, ε, α, T
x^0 ← x + 𝒰(−ε, ε)                          ▷ Random Start
for t = 1 to T do
    g ← ∇_x ℓ(f_θ(x^{t−1}), y)
    x^t ← Π_{ℬ_ε(x)}(x^{t−1} + α · sign(g))
end for
return x^T
```

Theorem 4.4.3 — PGD Convergence. For an L-smooth loss function and step size $\alpha \leq \frac{1}{L}$, PGD converges to a stationary point of the constrained maximization problem. Specifically, the squared norm of the gradient mapping decays as:

$$\min_{0 \leq t \leq T-1} \left\| \frac{x^{t+1} - x^t}{\alpha} \right\|_2^2 \leq \frac{2(\ell(f_\theta(x^*), y) - \ell(f_\theta(x^0), y))}{\alpha T} \tag{4.13}$$

where x^* is a global maximum. (At the largest admissible step $\alpha = 1/L$ the prefactor becomes $2L/T$.)

Ⓡ [Random Restarts] PGD with random restarts runs multiple independent attacks from different initializations and returns the strongest adversarial example found. This strategy helps escape local maxima in the non-concave inner maximization problem. Empirically, 10–20 random restarts have been found sufficient for reliable evaluation on standard image benchmarks [50].

Ⓡ [Attack Strength Hierarchy] For identical perturbation budgets ε and under typical settings (standard benchmarks and default hyperparameters), the following empirical ordering holds:

$$\text{Success(FGSM)} \leq \text{Success(PGD)} \leq \text{Success(PGD-Restarts)} \leq \text{Success(C\&W)} \tag{4.14}$$

This ordering reflects increasing optimization effort: FGSM uses a single gradient step, PGD uses multiple steps, restarts escape local optima, and C&W directly optimizes perturbation magnitude. The gap between FGSM and PGD is especially pronounced for robust models trained with adversarial training.

4.4.4 Carlini & Wagner (C&W) Attack

The C&W attack [14] finds minimum-norm perturbations by reformulating the attack as an unconstrained optimization problem.

Definition 4.4.1 — C&W Objective. The attack minimizes:

$$\min_{\delta} \|\delta\|_2^2 + c \cdot f(x+\delta) \tag{4.15}$$

where $c > 0$ is a constant balancing the perturbation size and the misclassification success, and f is a surrogate objective for misclassification:

$$f(x') = \max(\max_{i \neq t} Z(x')_i - Z(x')_t, -\kappa) \tag{4.16}$$

Here $Z(x')$ are the logits (pre-softmax outputs), t is the target class, and $\kappa \geq 0$ is a confidence parameter.

Ⓡ [Change of Variables] To ensure $x + \delta \in [0,1]^d$ (valid pixel range), C&W introduces:

$$\delta = \frac{1}{2}(\tanh(w) + 1) - x \tag{4.17}$$

and optimizes over unconstrained $w \in \mathbb{R}^d$. This guarantees box constraints are always satisfied.

Ⓡ [C&W Optimality] For the L_2 attack, C&W typically finds perturbations with significantly smaller norms than PGD for the same attack success rate (ASR), owing to its direct optimization of the perturbation magnitude [14]. The trade-off is computational cost: C&W requires on the order of 10,000 optimization steps per input, compared to ∼100 steps for PGD.

4.4.5 AutoAttack: Reliable Evaluation

AutoAttack [20] combines multiple attacks for reliable robustness evaluation:

1. **APGD-CE**: Auto-PGD with cross-entropy loss and adaptive step sizes
2. **APGD-DLR**: Auto-PGD with Difference of Logits Ratio loss
3. **FAB**: Fast Adaptive Boundary attack
4. **Square Attack**: Score-based black-box attack

Ⓡ [AutoAttack Completeness] AutoAttack provides a lower bound on adversarial accuracy that is empirically tight (within 0.1%) for most defenses tested on standard benchmarks [20]. It has become a standard evaluation protocol, and defenses that report robustness only against weaker attacks risk overestimating their true adversarial accuracy.

Table 4.2 compares the principal white-box attack methods introduced above, contrasting the number of steps, norm constraint, optimization strategy, computational cost, and key feature of each.

Table 4.2: Comparison of white-box adversarial attack methods.

Attack	Steps	Norm	Optimization	Cost	Key Feature
FGSM	1	L_∞	Sign of gradient	Lowest	Fast; single-step baseline
PGD	T (e.g. 40)	L_p, $p\in\{2,\infty\}$	Projected grad. ascent	Moderate	Gold-standard for adv. training
C&W	$\sim 10^4$	L_2 (L_0, L_∞)	Change-of-var.; unconstrained	High	Min-norm perturbations
AutoAttack	Ensemble	L_p	APGD-CE, APGD-DLR, FAB, Square	Highest	Parameter-free; std. benchmark

4.5 Black-Box Attacks

In the black-box setting, the attacker cannot access model gradients or architecture. This is the more realistic threat model for deployed systems.

4.5.1 Transfer Attacks

Transfer attacks exploit the phenomenon that adversarial examples generated for one model often fool other models.

Definition 4.5.1 — Adversarial Transferability. Let $(x,y) \sim \mathscr{P}$, let f_s (the *source* model) and f_t (the *target* model) both classify x correctly, and let x_{adv} be an adversarial example crafted against f_s such that $f_s(x_{\text{adv}}) \neq y$. The example x_{adv} is said to *transfer* to f_t if $f_t(x_{\text{adv}}) \neq y$. Equivalently, the (untargeted) *transfer rate* is the conditional probability

$$\tau(f_s \to f_t) := P\big(f_t(x_{\text{adv}}) \neq y \mid f_s(x_{\text{adv}}) \neq y,\ f_s(x) = f_t(x) = y\big), \quad (4.18)$$

where P is taken over the joint distribution of (x,y) and any randomness in the attack. For *targeted* transfer to a specific class y_{target}, the analogous definition replaces "$f_t(x_{\text{adv}}) \neq y$" by "$f_t(x_{\text{adv}}) = y_{\text{target}}$".

R [Transferability Conditions] Adversarial examples transfer more reliably when:

1. The source and target models have similar decision boundaries.
2. The perturbation exploits fundamental input features rather than model-specific artifacts.
3. Ensemble methods are used to craft the attack, e.g., $x_{\text{adv}} = \arg\max_{\|\delta\|\leq\varepsilon} \sum_{i=1}^{K} w_i \ell(f_i(x+\delta), y)$.

4.5.2 Query-Based Attacks

Query-based attacks estimate gradients through model queries.

Definition 4.5.2 — Zeroth-Order Gradient Estimation. The gradient can be approximated using finite differences:

$$\hat{g}_i = \frac{f(x+\mu e_i) - f(x-\mu e_i)}{2\mu} \tag{4.19}$$

where e_i is the i-th standard basis vector and $\mu > 0$ is the step size.

This approach requires $O(d)$ queries per gradient estimate where d is the input dimension. This is computationally prohibitive for high-dimensional inputs such as images.

Proposition 4.5.1 — Random Direction Gradient Estimation. A more efficient estimator uses random directions $u \sim \mathcal{N}(0, I)$:

$$\hat{g} = \frac{1}{\mu} \cdot (f(x+\mu u) - f(x)) \cdot u \tag{4.20}$$

This provides an unbiased estimate of the Gaussian-smoothed gradient: $\mathbb{E}[\hat{g}] = \nabla f_\mu(x)$ where $f_\mu(x) = \mathbb{E}_u[f(x+\mu u)]$, which approximates $\nabla f(x)$ for small μ, using $O(1)$ queries per estimate. (If instead u is sampled uniformly on the unit sphere S^{d-1}, the corresponding unbiased estimator carries an additional factor of d.)

Algorithm 4.2 summarizes the resulting query-based attack, which couples this random-direction gradient estimate with a projected sign-gradient update.

Algorithm 4.2 NES (Natural Evolution Strategies) Attack

```
Input: x, y, f, ε, α, T, n, σ
δ^0 ← 0
for t = 1 to T do
    Sample u_1, ..., u_n ~ N(0, I)
    ĝ ← (1/(2nσ)) Σ_{i=1}^n (f(x + δ^{t-1} + σu_i) − f(x + δ^{t-1} − σu_i)) · u_i
    δ^t ← Π_{B_ε}(δ^{t-1} + α · sign(ĝ))
end for
return x + δ^T
```

4.5.3 Score-Based Attacks: Square Attack

Square Attack [7] uses random search without gradient estimation; the full procedure is given in Algorithm 4.3:

Algorithm 4.3 Square Attack

Input: x, y, f, ε, T
Initialize δ with random $\pm\varepsilon$ values
for $t = 1$ to T **do**
  Sample random square region S of size $p \times p$
  Sample new values $v \in \{-\varepsilon, +\varepsilon\}^{p\times p}$
  $\delta' \leftarrow \delta$; set $\delta'_S \leftarrow v$
  if $\ell(f(x+\delta'), y) > \ell(f(x+\delta), y)$ **then**
    $\delta \leftarrow \delta'$ ▷ *Accept update*
  end if
end for
return $x + \delta$

(R) [Query Efficiency] Square Attack achieves comparable success rates to PGD with only $\sim$1000–5000 queries, making it practical for attacking real-world APIs.

4.6 Adversarial Training and Robust Optimization

The most widely studied and empirically effective defense against adversarial attacks is adversarial training. We formalize robustness as a min-max saddle point problem. A *saddle point* of a function $f(\theta, \delta)$ is a pair (θ^*, δ^*) at which f is simultaneously *minimized* in θ and *maximized* in δ; geometrically, like the saddle of a horse, the surface curves up in one direction and down in the other. Adversarial training seeks such a point: the model parameters minimize the loss against an adversary who, at the same time, picks the worst-case perturbation. The goal is to find model parameters θ that minimize the loss on the worst-case perturbations within the allowed set $\mathcal{S}$:

$$\theta^* = \arg\min_{\theta} \mathbb{E}_{(x,y)\sim\mathcal{P}} \left[\max_{\delta\in\mathcal{S}} \ell(f_\theta(x+\delta), y) \right] \tag{4.21}$$

where $\mathcal{S} = \{\delta : \|\delta\|_p \leq \varepsilon\}$ is the set of allowed perturbations, $\mathcal{P}$ is the joint data distribution over $\mathcal{X} \times \mathcal{Y}$, and θ represents the model parameters. This formulation views training as a zero-sum game between the trainer (minimizer) and the attacker (maximizer).

4.6.1 Game-Theoretic Interpretation

Definition 4.6.1 — Zero-Sum Game. Adversarial training corresponds to finding a Nash equilibrium of the zero-sum game:

$$(\theta^*, \delta^*) = \text{Nash}\left(\min_\theta \max_\delta \ell(f_\theta(x+\delta), y)\right) \tag{4.22}$$

At equilibrium, neither player can improve by unilateral deviation.

Theorem 4.6.1 — Minimax Theorem (Sion (72)). For convex-concave objectives where $\theta \mapsto \ell(f_\theta(x+\delta), y)$ is convex in θ for each δ, $\delta \mapsto \ell(f_\theta(x+\delta), y)$ is concave in δ for each θ, and the constraint sets are compact and convex:

$$\min_\theta \max_\delta \ell(f_\theta(x+\delta), y) = \max_\delta \min_\theta \ell(f_\theta(x+\delta), y) \tag{4.23}$$

The order of optimization does not matter.

Concretely, in a convex–concave setting it does not matter whether the attacker commits to δ first or the defender commits to θ first; the value of the game is the same and a saddle point exists. This is the theoretical foundation that justifies optimizing in either order. The next remark explains why this clean guarantee unfortunately breaks for neural networks (which are non-convex in θ), forcing us to rely on the alternation heuristic.

Ⓡ [Non-Convexity in Practice] Neural network losses are non-convex in θ, meaning the minimax theorem does not directly apply. In practice, adversarial training utilizes alternating optimization: fix θ and maximize over δ (using a PGD attack), then fix the worst-case δ^* and minimize over θ (using standard gradient descent).

4.6.2 Danskin's Theorem and Training Dynamics

To optimize the outer minimization via Gradient Descent, we need to compute the gradient of the value function $V(\theta) = \max_{\delta \in \mathcal{S}} \ell(f_\theta(x+\delta), y)$. The challenge is that the max operator is not differentiable everywhere. Danskin's theorem provides a solution by showing that the gradient of the max is the gradient at the maximizing point.

In plain English, Danskin's theorem says: the gradient of a max-over-δ is simply the gradient at the maximizer. So we can compute $\nabla_\theta \max_\delta \ell$ by (a) running an inner optimizer to find the maximizing $\delta^*(\theta)$ as if θ were fixed, and (b) backpropagating ℓ at that single point, treating δ^* as a constant. We never have to differentiate through the inner optimization itself.

Theorem 4.6.2 — Danskin's Theorem. Let $\Phi : \Theta \times \mathscr{S} \to \mathbb{R}$ be a continuous function where $\mathscr{S}$ is a compact set. Define the value function:

$$V(\theta) = \max_{\delta \in \mathscr{S}} \Phi(\theta, \delta) \tag{4.24}$$

Let $\delta^*(\theta) = \arg\max_{\delta \in \mathscr{S}} \Phi(\theta, \delta)$. If:

1. Φ is continuously differentiable in θ for each δ
2. $\delta^*(\theta)$ is unique

Then $V(\theta)$ is differentiable and:

$$\nabla_\theta V(\theta) = \nabla_\theta \Phi(\theta, \delta^*(\theta)) \tag{4.25}$$

Proof Sketch. By the envelope theorem from optimization theory. Consider a small perturbation $\theta' = \theta + th$ for $t \to 0$:

$$V(\theta') - V(\theta) = \max_{\delta} \Phi(\theta', \delta) - \max_{\delta} \Phi(\theta, \delta) \tag{4.26}$$

$$= \Phi(\theta', \delta^*(\theta')) - \Phi(\theta, \delta^*(\theta)) \tag{4.27}$$

By continuity of δ^* and differentiability of Φ, taking the limit as $t \to 0$ gives the result. The key insight is that at the optimum, the derivative with respect to δ is zero (by first-order optimality conditions), so only the direct effect through θ remains. ■

Ⓡ [Application to Adversarial Training] This theorem provides the theoretical justification for adversarial training: to update the model weights, we simply find the optimal adversarial example δ^* (using PGD) and then compute the gradient of the loss at that perturbed point. By Danskin's theorem, this is the gradient of the robust objective $\max_{\|\delta\| \leq \varepsilon} \ell(f_\theta(x+\delta), y)$ with respect to θ.

■ **Example 4.1 — Danskin's Theorem in Adversarial Training of an Image Classifier.** Consider training a convolutional network to classify chest X-rays as normal or abnormal, with robustness targeted to L_∞ perturbations of size $\varepsilon = 0.01$ (modeling scanner noise variations). At each training step for an X-ray image x: (1) we run $K = 10$ steps of PGD to find the worst-case perturbation $\delta^* = \arg\max_{\|\delta\|_\infty \leq 0.01} \ell(f_\theta(x+\delta), y)$; and (2) by Danskin's theorem, we compute the gradient $\nabla_\theta \ell(f_\theta(x+\delta^*), y)$. This directly equals $\nabla_\theta V(\theta)$, which is the gradient of the worst-case loss. Without this theorem, computing $\nabla_\theta[\max_\delta \ell]$ would require differentiating through the entire PGD optimization (an expensive second-order computation). Danskin's theorem theoretically validates that the simpler approach of "find the worst input, then backpropagate" is mathematically rigorous. ■

4.6.3 TRADES: Trading Off Robustness and Accuracy

TRADES [90] decomposes the robust error into a natural error term and a boundary error term.

Definition 4.6.2 — TRADES Training Objective. The TRADES training objective is a surrogate loss that balances natural accuracy and local Lipschitz continuity (robustness):

$$\mathscr{L}_{\text{TRADES}} = \ell(f_\theta(x), y) + \beta \cdot \max_{\|\delta\| \leq \varepsilon} D_{\text{KL}}(f_\theta(x) \| f_\theta(x+\delta)) \tag{4.28}$$

where $\beta > 0$ controls the trade-off, $D_{\text{KL}}(\cdot\|\cdot)$ is the Kullback–Leibler divergence, and ε is the perturbation radius. The first term encourages the model to be accurate on clean data, while the second term (regularizer) pushes the decision boundary away from the data points by penalizing changes in the output distribution within the ε-ball.

This formulation is motivated by a theoretical bound on the robust error, where the KL divergence serves as a differentiable proxy for the condition that the prediction should not change within the perturbation radius. Higher β yields more robust but potentially less accurate models on clean data.

■ **Example 4.2 — TRADES in Medical Image Classification.** Consider a diagnostic AI system classifying benign vs. malignant tumors from biopsy slides with $\varepsilon = 8/255$ (a small, near-imperceptible pixel-level perturbation). With $\beta = 1$ (low robustness weight), the model achieves 96% clean accuracy and 40% robust accuracy under PGD attack. Increasing to $\beta = 6$ (standard TRADES setting) yields 84% clean accuracy but 56% robust accuracy. At $\beta = 20$, clean accuracy drops to 75% while robust accuracy plateaus at 58%. The first loss term $\ell(f_\theta(x), y)$ trains the model to correctly classify clean slides, while the second term $\beta \cdot \max_{\|\delta\| \leq \varepsilon} D_{\text{KL}}(f_\theta(x) \| f_\theta(x+\delta))$ ensures the model's output distribution remains stable under perturbations, preventing, for example, a malignant biopsy from being reclassified as benign due to small scanning artifacts or lighting variations. ■

4.7 Certified Robustness via Randomized Smoothing

While PGD provides empirical robustness, it offers no guarantees. A stronger adversary might still find successful perturbations. Certified robustness aims to provide a mathematical proof that for a given input x, no perturbation within radius R can change the label. Randomized smoothing is a scalable technique that converts any base classifier f into a smoothed classifier g that is certifiably robust in L_2 norm.

Definition 4.7.1 — Smoothed Classifier. Let $f : \mathbb{R}^d \to \mathscr{Y}$ be a base classifier (which need not be robust). The smoothed classifier g is defined as the majority vote of f under Gaussian noise:

$$g(x) = \arg\max_{c \in \mathscr{Y}} P_{\eta \sim \mathcal{N}(0,\sigma^2 I)}(f(x+\eta) = c) \tag{4.29}$$

where $\eta \sim \mathcal{N}(0, \sigma^2 I)$ is isotropic Gaussian noise and P denotes probability.

Theorem 4.7.1 — Certification (19). Suppose we estimate that class c_A has probability $p_A = P(f(x+\eta) = c_A)$ and the runner-up class has probability $p_B = \max_{c \neq c_A} P(f(x+\eta) = c)$. If $p_A > p_B$, then the smoothed classifier $g(x)$ is provably robust within an L_2 radius R [19]:

$$R = \frac{\sigma}{2}(\Phi^{-1}(p_A) - \Phi^{-1}(p_B)) \tag{4.30}$$

where Φ^{-1} is the inverse CDF of the standard normal distribution.

Geometrically, $\Phi^{-1}(p_A)$ is the standard-normal z-score with probability p_A to its left: the more confident the smoothed classifier is in the top class, the more positive this number is, and the less probability mass falls on the runner-up (p_B small), the more negative $\Phi^{-1}(p_B)$ becomes. Their difference therefore measures the "confidence gap" in z-units; multiplying by $\sigma/2$ converts those z-units back into the L_2-distance units of the input space. In short: *higher confidence in the top class, less mass on the runner-up, and more noise all enlarge the certified radius.*

▪ **Example 4.3 — Certified Robustness of a Smoothed Classifier for Satellite Imagery.** Suppose we apply randomized smoothing with $\sigma = 0.5$ to a land-cover classifier for satellite images. For a test image of a forest region, we estimate (via 10,000 Monte Carlo samples) that $p_A = P(f(x+\eta) = \text{"forest"}) = 0.85$ and the runner-up probability is $p_B = 0.10$. Then:

$$\begin{aligned} R &= \tfrac{0.5}{2}\left(\Phi^{-1}(0.85) - \Phi^{-1}(0.10)\right) \\ &= 0.25 \times \big(1.036 - (-1.282)\big) = 0.25 \times 2.318 = 0.580 \end{aligned}$$

This certifies that *no* L_2-perturbation of norm ≤ 0.580 can change the classification from "forest" to any other class. In normalized pixel space, this radius corresponds to meaningful robustness against atmospheric distortions, sensor noise, or adversarial tampering. If instead $p_A = 0.55$ (less confident) and the runner-up probability rises to $p_B = 0.40$, the certified radius drops to $R = 0.25 \times (\Phi^{-1}(0.55) - \Phi^{-1}(0.40)) \approx 0.25 \times 0.379 = 0.095$, illustrating that higher confidence translates directly to larger certified regions. ▪

Proof Sketch. For brevity write $g(x) = c_A$ to mean that c_A achieves the largest smoothed probability at x. Fix a perturbation δ with $\|\delta\|_2 \le R$. We must show that, simultaneously,

$$P_\eta\big(f(x+\delta+\eta) = c_A\big) \;>\; P_\eta\big(f(x+\delta+\eta) = c\big) \tag{4.31}$$

for every $c \neq c_A$, with $\eta \sim \mathcal{N}(0, \sigma^2 I)$. It suffices to check the binary case $c = c_B$.

Let $A := \{z \in \mathbb{R}^d : f(z) = c_A\}$ and $B := \{z \in \mathbb{R}^d : f(z) = c_B\}$. Define

$$\begin{aligned}\Phi_A(\delta) &:= P_\eta\big(f(x+\delta+\eta) \in A\big) \\ &= \Pr_{Z\sim\mathcal{N}(x+\delta,\sigma^2 I)}\big(Z \in A\big),\end{aligned} \tag{4.32}$$

$$\begin{aligned}\Phi_B(\delta) &:= P_\eta\big(f(x+\delta+\eta) \in B\big) \\ &= \Pr_{Z\sim\mathcal{N}(x+\delta,\sigma^2 I)}\big(Z \in B\big).\end{aligned} \tag{4.33}$$

By assumption, $\Phi_A(0) \ge p_A$ and $\Phi_B(0) \le p_B$.

Worst-case mass under shift (Neyman–Pearson). Among all sets $A^* \subseteq \mathbb{R}^d$ with the same Gaussian mass $\Pr_{\mathcal{N}(x,\sigma^2 I)}(A^*) = p_A$, the one that *minimizes* the shifted mass $\Pr_{\mathcal{N}(x+\delta,\sigma^2 I)}(A^*)$ is a half-space whose boundary is orthogonal to δ, by the Neyman–Pearson lemma applied to the likelihood ratio between $\mathcal{N}(x,\sigma^2 I)$ and $\mathcal{N}(x+\delta,\sigma^2 I)$. Concretely, projecting onto the unit vector $\hat{\delta} := \delta/\|\delta\|_2$ reduces the problem to one dimension: the worst-case half-space is $\{z : \hat{\delta}^T(z-x) \le \sigma\Phi^{-1}(p_A)\}$, and its mass under the shifted Gaussian equals $\Phi\big(\Phi^{-1}(p_A) - \|\delta\|_2/\sigma\big)$.

Hence

$$\Phi_A(\delta) \;\ge\; \Phi\Big(\Phi^{-1}(p_A) - \tfrac{\|\delta\|_2}{\sigma}\Big). \tag{4.34}$$

Similarly, the worst-case set with mass p_B that *maximizes* the shifted mass is the half-space $\{z : \hat{\delta}^T(z-x) \ge -\sigma\Phi^{-1}(p_B)\}$, giving

$$\Phi_B(\delta) \;\le\; \Phi\Big(\Phi^{-1}(p_B) + \tfrac{\|\delta\|_2}{\sigma}\Big). \tag{4.35}$$

Certified radius. The smoothed classifier still outputs c_A as long as $\Phi_A(\delta) > \Phi_B(\delta)$. A sufficient condition is

$$\Phi^{-1}(p_A) - \tfrac{\|\delta\|_2}{\sigma} \;>\; \Phi^{-1}(p_B) + \tfrac{\|\delta\|_2}{\sigma}, \tag{4.36}$$

which rearranges to $\|\delta\|_2 < \frac{\sigma}{2}\big(\Phi^{-1}(p_A) - \Phi^{-1}(p_B)\big) = R$. The factor $\frac{1}{2}$ in R thus arises naturally from balancing the two opposing tail bounds for A and B. See [19] for the full argument. ■

4.8 Natural Distribution Shifts and Domain Adaptation

While adversarial perturbations represent worst-case distribution shifts, natural distribution shifts arise from legitimate changes in the data-generating process. These are often more relevant in practice.

4.8.1 Types of Natural Distribution Shift

Distribution shifts arise when the deployment data distribution $P_T(X,Y)$ differs from the training distribution $P_S(X,Y)$. The four primary types are **Covariate Shift** ($P_T(X) \neq P_S(X)$, $P_T(Y \mid X) = P_S(Y \mid X)$), **Label Shift** ($P_T(Y) \neq P_S(Y)$, $P_T(X \mid Y) = P_S(X \mid Y)$), **Concept Drift** ($P_T(Y \mid X) \neq P_S(Y \mid X)$), and **Domain Shift** (both marginal and conditional distributions differ). These are formally defined with detailed explanations and concrete examples in Section 11.1.

4.8.2 Importance Weighting for Covariate Shift

Under covariate shift, the optimal predictor remains the same, but the empirical risk estimator is biased. We can correct this via importance weighting:

$$\hat{R}_T(f) = \frac{1}{n}\sum_{i=1}^{n} \frac{P_T(x_i)}{P_S(x_i)} \ell(f(x_i), y_i) \tag{4.37}$$

where n is the number of samples, $P_T(x_i)$ and $P_S(x_i)$ are the target and source densities evaluated at x_i, and ℓ is the loss function.

The density ratio $w(x) = P_T(x)/P_S(x)$ can be estimated without estimating the densities directly using kernel mean matching or discriminative methods.

Theorem 4.8.1 — Consistency Under Covariate Shift. If $P_T(Y \mid X) = P_S(Y \mid X)$ and the importance weights are correctly specified, then the importance-weighted empirical risk is an unbiased estimator of the target risk:

$$\mathbb{E}_{P_S}[w(X)\ell(f(X),Y)] = \mathbb{E}_{P_T}[\ell(f(X),Y)] \tag{4.38}$$

Proof. By definition of the importance weight $w(x) = P_T(x)/P_S(x)$ and the tower property of expectation:

$$\mathbb{E}_{P_S}[w(X)\ell(f(X),Y)] = \mathbb{E}_{P_S}\left[\frac{P_T(X)}{P_S(X)}\ell(f(X),Y)\right] \tag{4.39}$$

$$= \int\int \frac{P_T(x)}{P_S(x)}\ell(f(x),y) P_S(y \mid x) P_S(x)\, dy\, dx \tag{4.40}$$

$$= \int\int \ell(f(x),y) P_S(y \mid x) P_T(x)\, dy\, dx \tag{4.41}$$

Under the covariate shift assumption $P_S(Y \mid X) = P_T(Y \mid X)$:

$$= \int\int \ell(f(x),y)P_T(y \mid x)P_T(x)\,dy\,dx = \mathbb{E}_{P_T}[\ell(f(X),Y)] \tag{4.42}$$

■

4.8.3 Domain Adversarial Training

Domain Adversarial Neural Networks (DANN) learn representations that are predictive of Y but invariant to the domain label $D \in \{S,T\}$ (source vs. target).

The architecture consists of:

- Feature extractor: $G_f : \mathscr{X} \to \mathscr{Z}$
- Label predictor: $G_y : \mathscr{Z} \to \mathscr{Y}$
- Domain classifier: $G_D : \mathscr{Z} \to \{S,T\}$

The objective combines supervised loss and adversarial domain loss:

$$\min_{G_f,G_y} \max_{G_D} \mathbb{E}_{(x,y)\sim P_S}[\ell(G_y(G_f(x)),y)] - \lambda\, \mathbb{E}_{x\sim P_S \cup P_T}[\ell_D(G_D(G_f(x)),D)] \tag{4.43}$$

where $\lambda > 0$ is a hyperparameter balancing the classification and domain confusion objectives, ℓ is the task loss, ℓ_D is the domain classification loss, and D is the binary domain label of the input.

The Gradient Reversal Layer (GRL) enables end-to-end training by negating gradients from the domain classifier.

4.8.4 Invariant Risk Minimization (IRM)

IRM seeks representations such that the optimal classifier built on top is invariant across different environments. Let $\mathscr{E}_{\text{train}}$ be the set of training environments.

> **Definition 4.8.1 — Invariant Representation.** A representation learning function Φ elicits an invariant predictor w if w is simultaneously optimal for all environments:
>
> $$w \in \arg\min_{\bar{w}} R^e(\bar{w} \circ \Phi) \quad \forall e \in \mathscr{E}_{\text{train}} \tag{4.44}$$
>
> where R^e is the expected risk in environment e.

The exact IRM objective minimizes the sum of risks across environments subject to the invariance constraint. In practice, this is relaxed to a regularized penalty (IRMv1):

$$\min_{\Phi,w} \sum_{e\in\mathscr{E}_{\text{train}}} \left[R^e(w\cdot\Phi) + \lambda \,\|\nabla_w R^e(w\cdot\Phi)|_{w=1.0}\|^2\right] \tag{4.45}$$

where Φ is the representation learner, w is a scalar (or per-coordinate) classifier head that is held fixed at $w = 1.0$ during evaluation of the gradient penalty, the gradient ∇_w is taken with respect to this dummy head and then evaluated at $w = 1.0$, and λ is the regularization strength.

The gradient penalty encourages the fixed classifier $w = 1.0$ to remain optimal in every environment. This occurs precisely when the representation Φ captures causal features that generalize invariantly, rather than relying on environment-specific spurious correlations.

4.8.5 Distributionally Robust Optimization (DRO)

DRO optimizes for the worst-case distribution within an uncertainty set:

$$\min_{\theta} \sup_{Q \in \mathscr{U}} \mathbb{E}_Q[\ell(f_\theta(X), Y)] \tag{4.46}$$

where $\mathscr{U}$ is the uncertainty set of distributions, Q is a distribution within that set, and θ are the model parameters.

Common uncertainty sets include:

- ***f*-divergence ball**: $\mathscr{U} = \{Q : D_f(Q\|P) \leq \rho\}$
  Detailed Explanation: The f-divergence family includes KL-divergence, χ^2-divergence, and total variation distance. This uncertainty set contains all distributions Q whose f-divergence from the empirical distribution P is at most ρ. The choice of f determines the geometry of the uncertainty set: KL-divergence corresponds to an exponential family, while χ^2-divergence has computationally attractive quadratic structure. The radius ρ controls the robustness level: larger ρ means protecting against more severe distribution shifts but potentially sacrificing nominal performance.
  Concrete Example: For image classification with χ^2-divergence and $\rho = 0.1$, if the empirical distribution assigns probability p_i to each training example, the uncertainty set includes reweighted distributions where example weights q_i satisfy $\sum_i (q_i - p_i)^2 / p_i \leq 0.1$. This allows the adversary to upweight or downweight training examples (modeling class imbalance or selection bias) but constrains the total reweighting. Training with DRO over this set makes the model robust to test distributions with similar imbalances.
- **Wasserstein ball**: $\mathscr{U} = \{Q : W_p(Q, P) \leq \rho\}$
  Detailed Explanation: The Wasserstein distance measures the minimal "cost" of transporting probability mass from distribution P to Q, where cost is determined by the underlying metric on the input space $\mathscr{X}$. For order $p = 1$ or $p = 2$, $W_p(Q, P)$ quantifies how much the data points must be moved (in expectation) to transform P into Q. The Wasserstein ball with radius ρ contains all distributions whose optimal transport cost from P is at most ρ. This is particularly natural for image data where small pixel perturbations correspond to meaningful Wasserstein distance.

Concrete Example: For MNIST digit classification with L_2 metric and $\rho = 0.3$ (normalized pixel space), the Wasserstein ball around a training image of "7" includes all images obtainable by moving each pixel value by small amounts such that the total L_2 displacement is at most 0.3. This naturally models adversarial perturbations, brightness/contrast changes, and small geometric distortions. Wasserstein DRO with this uncertainty set automatically learns features robust to these perturbations without explicit adversarial training, and it has theoretical connections to adversarial training with L_2 attacks.

- **Group DRO**: $\mathscr{U} = \text{conv}(\{P_1, \ldots, P_k\})$ over predefined groups
Detailed Explanation: Group DRO partitions the data into k predefined groups (e.g., demographic subgroups, domains, or difficulty strata) with empirical distributions $P_1, \ldots, P_k$. The uncertainty set is the convex hull of these group distributions, meaning the adversary can choose any weighted mixture $Q = \sum_{i=1}^{k} \lambda_i P_i$ with $\lambda_i \geq 0, \sum_i \lambda_i = 1$. Unlike f-divergence or Wasserstein balls which are geometric, Group DRO is combinatorial, as it explicitly optimizes for the worst-case group. The minimax optimization becomes $\min_\theta \max_{\lambda \in \Delta^{k-1}} \sum_{i=1}^{k} \lambda_i \mathbb{E}_{P_i}[\ell_\theta]$, which has a particularly clean solution: always upweight the group with the highest current loss.
Concrete Example: In medical diagnosis with patient groups defined by age (pediatric, adult, elderly) and metabolic status (type A, type B), yielding 6 groups total, Group DRO ensures the model performs well on the worst-performing subgroup. If the model initially achieves 95% accuracy on adults with type A status but only 85% on elderly with type B status, Group DRO will upweight the latter group during training, forcing the model to improve performance on this specific subgroup. This is crucial for healthcare applications where disparate performance across subgroups violates safety requirements. Unlike vanilla ERM which optimizes average performance, Group DRO provides robustness guarantees for every predefined group.

Theorem 4.8.2 — DRO Duality. For χ^2-divergence uncertainty set, the robust optimization has the dual form:

$$\min_{\theta} \sup_{Q:D_{\chi^2}(Q\|P)\leq\rho} \mathbb{E}_Q[\ell] = \min_{\theta}\left\{\mathbb{E}_P[\ell] + \sqrt{\rho\cdot\mathrm{Var}_P[\ell]}\right\} \tag{4.47}$$

This shows DRO penalizes the variance of the loss, preferring solutions that perform uniformly well.

Intuitively, χ^2-DRO inflates the loss by an amount proportional to its standard deviation: a model whose loss is uniform across the dataset is cheap to defend, while one whose loss is highly variable can be attacked by an adversary that reweights mass toward the high-loss examples. The factor $\sqrt{\rho}$ is the radius of the χ^2 uncertainty ball, and $\sqrt{\mathrm{Var}_P[\ell]}$ is the worst-case reweighted excess loss within that ball; their product is the worst-case excess loss the adversary can inflict.

Exercises

1. **FGSM, PGD, and Variants**:
   (a) Implement the Fast Gradient Sign Method (FGSM) and PGD on the MNIST dataset.
   (b) Plot the robust accuracy as a function of ε for both attacks.
   (c) Why is PGD considered a stronger attack than FGSM?
   (d) Compare the running time of FGSM vs. PGD for the same perturbation budget.
   (e) Implement targeted FGSM that forces misclassification to a specific class.
   (f) Implement I-FGSM (iterative FGSM) with step size α and iterations T.
   (g) Compare attack success rates and perturbation magnitudes across all variants.
2. **Lipschitz Constant**:
   (a) Compute the Lipschitz constant of a single linear layer $f(x) = Wx$.
   (b) Compute the Lipschitz constant of the ReLU activation function.
   (c) Show that the Lipschitz constant of a deep network is upper bounded by the product of the spectral norms of its weight matrices.
   (d) Implement spectral normalization and verify it constrains the Lipschitz constant.
3. **Randomized Smoothing**:
   (a) Prove that if $f(x)$ is the base classifier, the smoothed classifier $g(x)$ is Lipschitz continuous.
   (b) Calculate the certified radius for a point x if $p_A = 0.99$ and $\sigma = 0.25$.

   (c) Implement randomized smoothing certification and plot the certified accuracy vs. radius trade-off.
4. **Adversarial Training**:
   (a) Implement adversarial training with PGD for CIFAR-10.
   (b) Compare the clean accuracy and robust accuracy before and after adversarial training.
   (c) Investigate the accuracy-robustness trade-off: plot clean accuracy vs. robust accuracy for different ε values during training.
   (d) Examine what features the adversarially trained model learns by visualizing filters.
5. **Transferability Analysis**:
   (a) Train three different architectures (ResNet, VGG, DenseNet) on CIFAR-10.
   (b) Generate adversarial examples for each model.
   (c) Test each set of adversarial examples on all three models.
   (d) Construct a transferability matrix and analyze which model pairs have highest transfer rates.
6. **Black-Box Attacks**:
   (a) Implement the Square Attack algorithm.
   (b) Compare its query efficiency with zeroth-order gradient estimation methods.
   (c) How does the attack success rate change with the number of queries?
7. **Certified Defense Evaluation**:
   (a) Train a model with certified training (IBP or CROWN-IBP).
   (b) Compare its certified accuracy with empirical PGD accuracy.
   (c) Why might there be a gap between certified and empirical robustness?
8. **C&W Attack**:
   (a) Implement the Carlini & Wagner L_2 attack with variable w and binary search over c.
   (b) Compare with PGD in terms of perturbation size and attack success rate.
   (c) Implement the L_∞ variant and compare effectiveness.
   (d) Test against a defended model and analyze the difference in required perturbation.
9. **AutoAttack Benchmark**:
   (a) Evaluate a robust model using the AutoAttack benchmark.
   (b) Compare accuracy under APGD-CE, APGD-DLR, FAB, and Square attacks.
   (c) Analyze which attack is most effective for your model architecture.
   (d) Implement a simple "robust" defense and test if AutoAttack breaks it.
10. **Physical Adversarial Attacks**:
   (a) Implement the Expectation over Transformation (EOT) attack.

   (b) Generate an adversarial patch that remains effective under affine transformations.
   (c) Test robustness to printing and photographing the adversarial example.
   (d) Analyze the trade-off between physical robustness and perturbation magnitude.
11. **Adversarial Training Variants**:
   (a) Implement TRADES: trade-off between accuracy and robustness.
   (b) Compare clean/robust accuracy of AT, TRADES, and MART.
   (c) Implement Friendly Adversarial Training (FAT) with early stopping.
   (d) Analyze the effect of perturbation budget scheduling during training.

Chapter 5
Algorithmic Fairness

5.1 The Philosophical and Mathematical Underpinnings

Algorithmic fairness is concerned with ensuring that machine learning models do not reproduce or exacerbate existing social inequalities. Unlike accuracy, which is a single scalar metric, fairness is a multi-dimensional concept with mutually incompatible definitions rooted in different philosophical traditions of justice. This complexity stems from the fundamental question: What does it mean for an algorithm to be "fair"?

The philosophical foundations of fairness in AI draw on multiple traditions of justice theory. *Rawlsian justice* emphasizes that inequalities should benefit the least advantaged members of society, suggesting that AI systems should be evaluated in terms of their impacts on specific subgroups rather than merely on aggregate outcomes. *Luck egalitarianism* distinguishes between inequalities arising from circumstances beyond individual control (morally arbitrary) and those arising from genuine choice (potentially acceptable). *Anti-subordination theories* focus on disrupting patterns of group-based disparities rather than merely achieving statistical parity.

These philosophical traditions translate into distinct mathematical formulations of fairness, each capturing different intuitions about what fair treatment means. The diversity of these definitions is not a bug but a feature; it reflects the genuine complexity of fairness as a normative concept. However, this diversity creates practical challenges, as impossibility theorems demonstrate that many intuitive fairness properties cannot be simultaneously satisfied.

5.2 Group Fairness: Statistical Parity and Beyond

Group fairness requires that the system's behavior be similar across different demographic groups. Consider a binary classification setting with prediction $\hat{Y} \in \{0,1\}$, true outcome $Y \in \{0,1\}$, and sensitive attribute $A \in \{0,1\}$ (extended naturally to multi-group settings).

Definition 5.2.1 — Demographic Parity. A classifier satisfies demographic parity (also called statistical parity) if:

$$P(\hat{Y} = 1|A = 0) = P(\hat{Y} = 1|A = 1) \tag{5.1}$$

where $\hat{Y}$ is the predicted label and A is the sensitive attribute.

Demographic parity requires that positive prediction rates be equal across groups. This definition ensures that members of different groups receive positive outcomes at equal rates but does not account for whether group members are equally qualified.

Example 5.1 — Demographic Parity in Clinical Trial Admission. Consider a clinical trial admission algorithm where $\hat{Y} = 1$ denotes "accepted to trial" and $A \in \{0, 1\}$ represents two groups of patients (e.g., patients from rural vs. urban clinics). Suppose 500 rural applicants and 500 urban applicants are evaluated. Demographic parity requires that if 30% of urban applicants are accepted to the trial, then 30% of rural applicants must also be accepted, regardless of differences in baseline severity metrics. If the algorithm accepts 40% of urban and 20% of rural applicants, then $|P(\hat{Y} = 1|A = 0) - P(\hat{Y} = 1|A = 1)| = |0.20 - 0.40| = 0.20$, a violation of demographic parity. ■

Definition 5.2.2 — Equalized Odds. A classifier satisfies equalized odds if both true positive and false positive rates are equal across groups:

$$P(\hat{Y} = 1|Y = y, A = 0) = P(\hat{Y} = 1|Y = y, A = 1) \quad \text{for } y \in \{0, 1\} \tag{5.2}$$

where Y is the true label.

Equalized odds requires that error rates be the same across groups, conditioning on the true outcome. This is often considered more appropriate than demographic parity because it accounts for different qualification rates across groups.

Example 5.2 — Equalized Odds in Disease Screening. Consider an AI screening tool for a metabolic condition where $Y = 1$ means "truly has the condition" and A denotes patient group. Equalized odds requires: (1) among patients who truly have the condition ($Y = 1$), the detection rate must be equal across groups, e.g., if the tool detects 90% of cases in group $A = 0$, it must also detect 90% in group $A = 1$ (equal True Positive Rate); and (2) among healthy patients ($Y = 0$), the false alarm rate must be equal, e.g., if 5% of healthy patients in group $A = 0$ receive a false positive, the same must hold for group $A = 1$. A violation would be if the tool detects 90% of cases in group $A = 0$ but only 70% in group $A = 1$, meaning one group's patients are systematically under-diagnosed. ■

Definition 5.2.3 — Equal Opportunity. A classifier satisfies equal opportunity if true positive rates are equal across groups:

$$P(\hat{Y} = 1 \mid Y = 1, A = 0) = P(\hat{Y} = 1 \mid Y = 1, A = 1) \tag{5.3}$$

where the condition $Y = 1$ restricts the comparison to the qualified population.

Equal opportunity is a relaxation of equalized odds that focuses only on ensuring equal treatment of qualified individuals.

Definition 5.2.4 — Calibration (Group-wise). Let $S = s(X) \in [0, 1]$ denote a probabilistic score output by the classifier (so the predicted label is $\hat{Y} = \mathbb{I}(S \geq \tau)$ for some threshold τ). The classifier is *calibrated within groups* if predicted probabilities equal actual outcome frequencies within each group:

$$P(Y = 1 \mid S = p, A = a) = p \qquad \text{for all } a \in \{0, 1\} \text{ and all } p \in [0, 1]. \tag{5.4}$$

Equivalently, for every score level p and every group, the conditional probability of the positive outcome equals p.

Calibration ensures that risk estimates are equally accurate across groups, meaning that individuals with the same predicted score should have the same actual risk regardless of group membership.

Table 5.1 summarizes these group fairness criteria, stating each as a mathematical condition on the prediction $\hat{Y}$, the true label Y, and the sensitive attribute A, alongside its underlying intuition.

Table 5.1: Summary of group fairness definitions. Here $\hat{Y}$ is the prediction, Y is the true label, and A is the sensitive attribute.

Criterion	Mathematical Condition	Cond. on Y?	Intuition
Demographic Parity	$P(\hat{Y}{=}1 \mid A{=}a) = P(\hat{Y}{=}1 \mid A{=}b)$	No	Equal selection rates across groups
Equalized Odds	$P(\hat{Y}{=}1 \mid Y{=}y, A{=}a) = P(\hat{Y}{=}1 \mid Y{=}y, A{=}b)\ \forall y$	Yes	Equal TPR and FPR across groups
Equal Opportunity	$P(\hat{Y}{=}1 \mid Y{=}1, A{=}a) = P(\hat{Y}{=}1 \mid Y{=}1, A{=}b)$	Yes ($Y{=}1$)	Equal TPR across groups (relaxation of Eq. Odds)
Calibration	$P(Y{=}1 \mid S{=}p, A{=}a) = p\ \forall p$	Yes	Predicted scores equally accurate per group

5.3 Individual Fairness: The Metric Approach

Individual fairness, formalized by [25], requires that similar individuals receive similar treatment (see also [31] for the equal opportunity criterion). The formal requirement is:

Definition 5.3.1 — Individual Fairness. A classifier f satisfies individual fairness with respect to metrics $d_{\mathscr{X}}$ and $d_{\mathscr{Y}}$ if:

$$d_{\mathscr{Y}}(f(x), f(x')) \leq L \cdot d_{\mathscr{X}}(x, x') \tag{5.5}$$

for all $x, x' \in \mathscr{X}$, where L is a Lipschitz constant, $d_{\mathscr{X}}$ is a distance metric in the input space, and $d_{\mathscr{Y}}$ is a distance metric in the output space.

For probabilistic classifiers, the output metric is typically:

$$d_{\mathscr{Y}}(f(x), f(x')) = |P(\hat{Y} = 1 \mid X = x) - P(\hat{Y} = 1 \mid X = x')| \tag{5.6}$$

where $P(\hat{Y} = 1 \mid X = x)$ is the predicted probability of the positive class for input x.

The central challenge in individual fairness is specifying the similarity metric $d_{\mathscr{X}}$. This requires carefully determining which features are fundamentally relevant for similarity comparisons and how to weight different features.

Example 5.3 — Individual Fairness in a Healthcare Triage System. Consider a hospital triage system recommending urgent care priority ($\hat{Y} = 1$ means "urgent priority"). Two patients x and x' have similar medical histories: both reported a severe 8/10 headache, have a family history of migraines, and have similar age and comorbidities. Their profiles differ only in name and reported residential zip code. Individual fairness with Lipschitz constant $L = 1$ requires $|P(\hat{Y} = 1|x) - P(\hat{Y} = 1|x')| \leq d_{\mathscr{X}}(x, x')$. If the metric $d_{\mathscr{X}}$ uses only medically-relevant features (symptoms, history), then $d_{\mathscr{X}}(x, x') \approx 0.05$ (very similar patients), so the urgent priority probabilities must differ by at most 5%. The key design challenge is defining $d_{\mathscr{X}}$: should "past medical spending" be a relevant feature (which could capture past thoroughness of care) or an irrelevant one (including it might create economic discrimination)? ■

5.4 Impossibility Results and Trade-offs

A fundamental challenge in achieving fairness is that many mathematically precise fairness definitions are mutually incompatible [42]. The following theorems demonstrate that perfect fairness along multiple dimensions is impossible when groups have different base rates.

Theorem 5.4.1 — Impossibility of Perfect Fairness. If $P(Y = 1 \mid A = 0) \neq P(Y = 1 \mid A = 1)$ (different base rates), then no classifier can simultaneously satisfy:

1. Demographic Parity: $P(\hat{Y} = 1 \mid A = 0) = P(\hat{Y} = 1 \mid A = 1)$
2. Equalized Odds: $P(\hat{Y} = 1 \mid Y = y, A = 0) = P(\hat{Y} = 1 \mid Y = y, A = 1)$ for $y \in \{0, 1\}$

3. Predictive Parity: $P(Y = 1 \mid \hat{Y} = 1, A = a)$ is independent of a (equal positive predictive value across groups)

except in degenerate cases (e.g., constant predictors or perfect prediction).

(R) [Calibration vs. Predictive Parity] The condition on equal positive predictive value (PPV) above is sometimes loosely called *calibration* in binary-classification expositions [18], but it is strictly weaker than the score-level *calibration within groups* of Definition 5.2.4 above. The distinction is important and has three facets.

(i) What is conditioned on. Calibration within groups conditions on a continuous *score* $S = s(x) \in [0,1]$ and asks that, at every score level p, the conditional probability of the positive class matches p:

$$\text{(Calibration)} \quad P(Y = 1 \mid S = p, A = a) = p \qquad \forall p \in [0,1],\ a.$$

Predictive parity conditions only on the single *thresholded prediction* $\hat{Y} = \mathbb{I}(S \geq \tau)$ and asks that the post-threshold success rate match across groups:

$$\text{(Predictive Parity)} \quad P(Y = 1 \mid \hat{Y} = 1, A = a) \text{ is independent of } a.$$

The latter is implied by the former at the chosen threshold (by integrating calibration over $S \geq \tau$ within each group), but the former is strictly stronger: predictive parity is consistent with arbitrary miscalibration at score levels not at the threshold, and is also consistent with the classifier being miscalibrated even at the threshold so long as the miscalibration is the same across groups.

Concrete example. Suppose a model assigns score 0.7 to 100 patients in group $A = 0$ (of whom 60 actually test positive), and the same score 0.7 to 100 patients in group $A = 1$ (of whom 60 also test positive). After thresholding at $\tau = 0.5$, predictive parity holds (the positive predictive value is 60% in each group). But the model is mis-calibrated by exactly the same 10 percentage points in both groups: the score 0.7 corresponds to a true positive rate of only 0.6. So group-wise score-level calibration (Definition 5.2.4) fails, while predictive parity holds. This shows that the two criteria measure different things.

(ii) The relevant impossibility theorem. The Kleinberg–Mullainathan–Raghavan impossibility [42], which considers *score-based* classifiers, shows that group-wise calibration plus balance for the positive and negative classes (equal expected scores conditional on Y) is jointly unattainable when base rates differ, unless the classifier is a perfect predictor. Chouldechova's result [18], which considers thresholded classifiers, shows that predictive parity plus equal false negative rate plus equal false positive rate is jointly unattainable when base rates differ. These are distinct results: the first applies to continuous risk scores (e.g., COMPAS-style recidivism scores), the second to binary decisions (e.g., loan approve/deny). The theorem above states a consequence of the second, and uses predictive parity accordingly.

(iii) Practical implications. In deployment, a binary classifier can be made to satisfy predictive parity by tuning thresholds per group, without disturbing the underlying score function. Achieving group-wise score-level calibration,

by contrast, requires either a calibration-aware loss during training (e.g., focal or Brier-score regularised) or a post-hoc Platt/temperature scaling fit *within* each group, which itself may be ruled out by the disparate-treatment doctrine. Conflating the two notions therefore merges conditions with very different operational footprints. See Section 11.4 (Chapter 11) for the score-level calibration metrics (ECE, reliability diagrams) used to audit calibration in the score-based sense; the impossibility above operates strictly in the thresholded-prediction sense.

Proof. We prove that Demographic Parity and Equalized Odds are incompatible when base rates differ ($p_0 \neq p_1$) and the predictor is not trivial (perfect or random).

Let $p_a = P(Y = 1 \mid A = a)$ be the base rate for group a. Let $r_a = P(\hat{Y} = 1 \mid Y = 1, A = a)$ be the True Positive Rate (TPR). Let $s_a = P(\hat{Y} = 1 \mid Y = 0, A = a)$ be the False Positive Rate (FPR).

The overall positive prediction rate for group a is:

$$P(\hat{Y} = 1 \mid A = a) = r_a p_a + s_a(1 - p_a) \tag{5.7}$$

Assume Equalized Odds: $r_0 = r_1 = r$ and $s_0 = s_1 = s$. Then the positive prediction rates are:

$$P(\hat{Y} = 1 \mid A = 0) = r p_0 + s(1 - p_0) = s + (r - s)p_0 \tag{5.8}$$

$$P(\hat{Y} = 1 \mid A = 1) = r p_1 + s(1 - p_1) = s + (r - s)p_1 \tag{5.9}$$

Assume Demographic Parity: $P(\hat{Y} = 1 \mid A = 0) = P(\hat{Y} = 1 \mid A = 1)$. Substituting the expressions above:

$$s + (r - s)p_0 = s + (r - s)p_1 \implies (r - s)(p_0 - p_1) = 0 \tag{5.10}$$

Since we assume different base rates ($p_0 \neq p_1$), we must have $r = s$. The condition $r = s$ (i.e., TPR = FPR) means the classifier's positive rate is independent of the true label, so it has no discriminative power. Thus, a non-trivial classifier cannot simultaneously satisfy Demographic Parity and Equalized Odds when base rates differ. Since it cannot satisfy even these two of the three conditions, it certainly cannot satisfy all three (including Predictive Parity). ■

Theorem 5.4.2 — Chouldechova's Impossibility Result (18). For a binary classifier with different base rates across groups ($P(Y = 1 \mid A = 0) \neq P(Y = 1 \mid A = 1)$), it is impossible to simultaneously satisfy:

1. Equal positive predictive value: $P(Y = 1 \mid \hat{Y} = 1, A = 0) = P(Y = 1 \mid \hat{Y} = 1, A = 1)$
2. Equal false negative rate: $P(\hat{Y} = 0 \mid Y = 1, A = 0) = P(\hat{Y} = 0 \mid Y = 1, A = 1)$

3. Equal false positive rate: $P(\hat{Y}=1 \mid Y=0, A=0) = P(\hat{Y}=1 \mid Y=0, A=1)$

unless the classifier is perfect (error-free) on both groups.

Proof Sketch. The positive predictive value (precision) is:

$$\text{PPV}_a = P(Y=1 \mid \hat{Y}=1, A=a) = \frac{\text{TPR}_a \cdot p_a}{\text{TPR}_a \cdot p_a + \text{FPR}_a \cdot (1-p_a)} \tag{5.11}$$

If $\text{TPR}_0 = \text{TPR}_1$ (equal FNR) and $\text{FPR}_0 = \text{FPR}_1$, then:

$$\text{PPV}_0 = \text{PPV}_1 \iff \frac{p_0}{p_0 + (\text{FPR}/\text{TPR})\,(1-p_0)} = \frac{p_1}{p_1 + (\text{FPR}/\text{TPR})\,(1-p_1)} \tag{5.12}$$

Since $p \mapsto \frac{p}{p+r(1-p)}$ is strictly monotone in p for any fixed positive ratio $r = \text{FPR}/\text{TPR}$, the equality $\text{PPV}_0 = \text{PPV}_1$ implies $p_0 = p_1$, contradicting the assumption. Thus, when base rates differ, equal error rates imply unequal predictive values. ■

This impossibility result has profound implications: it demonstrates that choices among fairness criteria cannot be avoided, and that claims to satisfy "fairness" without specifying which fairness criterion is being used are incomplete.

■ **Example 5.4 — Impossibility in Practice: Clinical Trial Admission.** Consider a clinical trial admission classifier with two applicant groups having different base rates of medical condition suitability: $p_0 = P(Y=1 \mid A=0) = 0.3$ and $p_1 = P(Y=1 \mid A=1) = 0.6$. If we enforce equalized odds with $\text{TPR} = r = 0.8$ and $\text{FPR} = s = 0.1$, then the admission rates are: group $A=0$: $r \cdot p_0 + s(1-p_0) = 0.8 \times 0.3 + 0.1 \times 0.7 = 0.31$; group $A=1$: $r \cdot p_1 + s(1-p_1) = 0.8 \times 0.6 + 0.1 \times 0.4 = 0.52$. Thus $P(\hat{Y}=1 \mid A=0) = 0.31 \neq 0.52 = P(\hat{Y}=1 \mid A=1)$. Demographic parity is violated. To force equal admission rates of, say, 0.40 for both groups, we would need $r_0 \neq r_1$ or $s_0 \neq s_1$, violating equalized odds. The trial organizers must choose: equal error rates (equalized odds) or equal admission rates (demographic parity) and they cannot have both. ■

5.5 Intersectionality and Multi-Group Fairness

Real-world fairness requires consideration of intersectional identities, as individuals belong to multiple groups defined by different attributes. For attributes $A_1 \in \{0,1\}$ and $A_2 \in \{0,1\}$, there are four intersectional groups: $\{(0,0),(0,1),(1,0),(1,1)\}$.

Definition 5.5.1 — Intersectional Demographic Parity. A classifier satisfies intersectional demographic parity if:

$$P(\hat{Y} = 1 \mid A_1 = a_1, A_2 = a_2) = P(\hat{Y} = 1 \mid A_1 = a'_1, A_2 = a'_2) \tag{5.13}$$

for all values a_1, a'_1, a_2, a'_2 of the sensitive attributes A_1 and A_2. This requires the positive prediction rate to be identical across all $|A_1| \times |A_2|$ intersectional groups.

The computational complexity of fairness constraints grows exponentially with the number of sensitive attributes and their cardinalities. For k binary attributes, there are 2^k intersectional groups, requiring $2^k - 1$ equality constraints. This becomes computationally expensive for large k (e.g., $k = 20$ yields over 10^6 groups).

5.6 Fairness Metrics and Evaluation

Translating abstract fairness definitions into measurable quantities requires comprehensive evaluation frameworks that account for statistical uncertainty and temporal dynamics.

5.6.1 Disparity Metrics

Definition 5.6.1 — Demographic Parity Difference (DPD).

$$\text{DPD} = |P(\hat{Y} = 1 \mid A = 0) - P(\hat{Y} = 1 \mid A = 1)| \tag{5.14}$$

where A is the sensitive attribute. Values closer to zero indicate greater demographic parity.

Definition 5.6.2 — Disparate Impact Ratio (DIR).

$$\text{DIR} = \frac{P(\hat{Y} = 1 \mid A = 0)}{P(\hat{Y} = 1 \mid A = 1)} \tag{5.15}$$

where the numerator is the selection rate for the disadvantaged group and the denominator is the selection rate for the advantaged group. The 80% rule considers $\text{DIR} < 0.8$ as prima facie evidence of adverse impact.

Definition 5.6.3 — Equalized Odds Difference (EOD).

$$\text{EOD} = \frac{1}{2}\left(|\text{TPR}_{A=0} - \text{TPR}_{A=1}| + |\text{FPR}_{A=0} - \text{FPR}_{A=1}|\right) \tag{5.16}$$

where $\text{TPR}_a = P(\hat{Y} = 1 \mid Y = 1, A = a)$ is the True Positive Rate for group a, and $\text{FPR}_a = P(\hat{Y} = 1 \mid Y = 0, A = a)$ is the False Positive Rate for group a.

5.6.2 Calibration Metrics

Definition 5.6.4 — Expected Calibration Error (ECE).

$$\text{ECE} = \sum_{b=1}^{B} \frac{n_b}{n} |\text{acc}_b - \text{conf}_b| \tag{5.17}$$

where predictions are partitioned into B bins by confidence level, n_b is the number of samples in bin b, n is the total number of samples, acc_b is the accuracy in bin b, and conf_b is the average confidence in bin b.

For fairness assessment, ECE should be computed separately for each protected group to reveal calibration disparities.

5.6.3 Statistical Considerations

Fairness metrics are estimates from finite samples and subject to statistical uncertainty. Confidence intervals should accompany point estimates:

$$\widehat{\text{DPD}} \pm z_{\alpha/2} \cdot \text{SE}(\widehat{\text{DPD}}) \tag{5.18}$$

where $\widehat{\text{DPD}}$ is the estimated demographic parity difference, $z_{\alpha/2}$ is the critical value from the standard normal distribution for significance level α, and SE denotes the standard error.

For binary outcomes, the standard error of the difference in selection rates is:

$$\text{SE}(\hat{p}_1 - \hat{p}_0) = \sqrt{\frac{\hat{p}_1(1-\hat{p}_1)}{n_1} + \frac{\hat{p}_0(1-\hat{p}_0)}{n_0}} \tag{5.19}$$

where $\hat{p}_a$ is the sample selection rate for group a, and n_a is the sample size for group a.

5.7 Algorithmic Techniques for Fairness

Recent advancements in Trustworthy AI have formalized three primary intervention points for fairness: pre-processing, in-processing, and post-processing [64, 86].

5.7.1 Pre-processing Methods

Pre-processing methods fundamentally alter the training data distribution to remove statistical dependencies between sensitive attributes and outcomes before a model is ever trained. The most prominent technique, **Reweighing**, assigns importance weights to individual samples to enforce independence. Specifically, for an individual i with sensitive attribute A_i and outcome Y_i, the weight is calculated as:

$$w_i = \frac{P(A = A_i)P(Y = Y_i)}{P(A = A_i, Y = Y_i)} \tag{5.20}$$

which effectively constructs a new dataset where A and Y are independent. Alternatively, **Fair Representation Learning** seeks to learn a projection of the data into a latent space Z where sensitive information is obfuscated while task-relevant information is preserved. This is typically formulated as an optimization problem $\min_Z \mathscr{L}_{\text{reconstruction}} + \lambda \mathscr{L}_{\text{fairness}}$, where the fairness penalty enforces orthogonality or independence between Z and A [17].

5.7.2 In-processing Methods

In-processing methods integrate fairness requirements directly into the model training procedure, often by solving a constrained optimization problem. The general formulation involves minimizing the empirical risk $\mathscr{L}(\theta)$ subject to a constraint $g_{\text{fairness}}(\theta) \leq \varepsilon$ that bounds the allowable fairness violation. Techniques like **Adversarial Debiasing** employ a minimax game where a predictor minimizes the task loss while an adversary attempts to reconstruct the sensitive attribute from the predictor's outputs or latent representations:

$$\min_{\theta_f} \max_{\theta_a} \mathscr{L}_{\text{task}}(\theta_f) - \lambda \mathscr{L}_{\text{adversarial}}(\theta_f, \theta_a) \tag{5.21}$$

This approach ensures that the learned representation contains no extractable information about the protected group. To solve these constrained problems, **Lagrangian Relaxation** is frequently used, converting the hard constraints into a primal-dual objective $\min_\theta \max_{\lambda \geq 0} \mathscr{L}(\theta) + \lambda g_{\text{fairness}}(\theta)$, which can be optimized via alternating gradient descent, integrating principles from [35]. The "Reductions Approach" [5] further simplifies this constrained optimization by reducing it to a sequence of cost-sensitive classification problems.

5.7.3 Post-processing Methods

Post-processing methods adjust model outputs after training to satisfy fairness criteria.

Threshold Optimization: Sets group-specific thresholds to achieve fairness:

$$\hat{Y}_a = \mathbb{I}(f(X) \geq \tau_a) \quad \text{where } \tau_a \text{ chosen to satisfy fairness constraints} \tag{5.22}$$

where $\mathbb{I}(\cdot)$ is the indicator function, $f(X)$ is the model score, and τ_a is the group-specific threshold for group a.

Calibration Adjustment: Modifies predicted probabilities to ensure equal calibration across groups.

Table 5.2 compares these fairness interventions across the pre-processing, in-processing, and post-processing stages, noting each method's mechanism, whether it requires retraining, and its key property.

Table 5.2: Comparison of algorithmic fairness intervention methods.

Method	Stage	Mechanism	Retrain?	Key Property
Reweighing	Pre	Assigns sample weights to enforce $A \perp Y$	Yes	Modifies data distribution, not algorithm
Fair Repr.	Pre	Projects data to remove sensitive info	Yes	Learns Z s.t. $Z \perp A$
Adv. Debiasing	In	Minimax game: predictor vs. adversary	Yes	Removes sensitive info from latent repr.
Lagrangian / Reductions	In	Constrained opt. via primal-dual	Yes	Flexible; multiple fairness criteria
Threshold Opt.	Post	Group-specific thresholds τ_a	No	Simple; preserves trained model
Calibration Adj.	Post	Adjusts predicted probs per group	No	Ensures group-wise calibration

5.8 Causal Fairness and Counterfactual Reasoning

Causal approaches to fairness seek to identify and eliminate the causal effects of sensitive attributes on outcomes, distinguishing legitimate from illegitimate causal pathways. Unlike statistical fairness, which focuses on correlations, causal fairness requires that decisions are fair under interventions on the causal graph.

5.8.1 Motivation: Why Causality Matters for Fairness

Statistical fairness criteria can be satisfied by systems that are intuitively unfair, or violated by systems that are intuitively fair. Consider a hiring algorithm:

- A company uses education level to predict job performance.
- Education is correlated with race due to historical discrimination in educational access.
- A statistically fair classifier (satisfying demographic parity) might reject qualified candidates from a specific demographic to balance rates.
- A causal approach asks: "Would this person have been hired if their race had been different, holding their qualifications fixed?"

5.8.2 Counterfactual Fairness

A worked numerical illustration of the counterfactual-inference procedure underlying the definition below appears in Example 8.5 of Chapter 8.

Definition 5.8.1 — Counterfactual Fairness (43). Let $\mathscr{M}$ be a structural causal model with observed variables X, sensitive attribute A, and exogenous variables U. A predictor $\hat{Y}$ is **counterfactually fair** if for any individual with characteristics $(X = x, A = a)$ and corresponding exogenous factors $U = u$:

$$P(\hat{Y}_{A \leftarrow a}(u) = y \mid X = x, A = a) = P(\hat{Y}_{A \leftarrow a'}(u) = y \mid X = x, A = a) \quad (5.23)$$

for all values $a, a' \in \mathscr{A}$ and all outcomes y.

Here, $\hat{Y}_{A \leftarrow a}(u)$ denotes the counterfactual: "What would the prediction have been if A had been set to a, keeping the same individual (same U)?" The notation $A \leftarrow a$ represents the do-operator or intervention setting A to value a.

Ⓡ [Interpretation] Counterfactual fairness ensures that an individual's classification would not have changed if their sensitive attribute had been different, holding all non-descendant factors constant. This captures the intuition that a person should not be penalized for characteristics beyond their control.

5.8.3 Path-Specific Fairness

In many real-world scenarios, the effect of a sensitive attribute on the outcome may flow through multiple causal pathways, some of which may be considered legitimate and others discriminatory.

■ **Example 5.5 — Legitimate vs. Illegitimate Pathways.** Consider a treatment approval model with the causal graph:

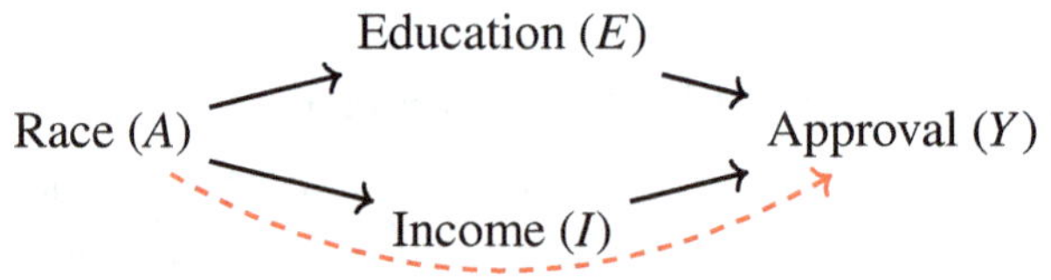

- **Direct effect** ($A \to Y$, dashed): Direct discrimination: illegitimate.
- **Indirect through income** ($A \to I \to Y$): May reflect historical wage discrimination: potentially illegitimate.
- **Indirect through education** ($A \to E \to Y$): Complex: education differences may reflect both discrimination in access and genuine qualification differences.

■

Definition 5.8.2 — Path-Specific Counterfactual Fairness. A predictor is fair with respect to a set of causal paths Π if the causal effect of the sensitive attribute A on prediction $\hat{Y}$ *along paths in* Π is zero:

$$\text{PSE}_{\Pi}(a \to a') = \mathbb{E}_U[\hat{Y}_{A\leftarrow a',\Pi}(U) - \hat{Y}_{A\leftarrow a,\Pi}(U)] = 0 \tag{5.24}$$

where the intervention affects only the designated pathways Π, and PSE stands for Path-Specific Effect.

5.8.4 Implementing Causal Fairness

To implement causal fairness in practice:

Step 1: Specify the Causal Graph. This requires domain expertise and may be contested. The graph encodes assumptions about how variables causally influence each other.

Step 2: Identify Fair Pathways. Determine which causal effects of the sensitive attribute are legitimate (resolving pathway) vs. illegitimate (discriminatory pathway).

Step 3: Compute Counterfactual Features. For each individual, compute what their features would have been under a different sensitive attribute value:

$$X_{A\leftarrow a'}(u) = f_X(\text{Pa}_X \text{ with } A \text{ set to } a', U_X = u_X) \tag{5.25}$$

where f_X is the structural equation for X, Pa_X are the parents of X in the causal graph, and U_X are the exogenous noise variables for X.

Step 4: Train Fair Predictor. Train a model using only:

- Features that are not descendants of A in the causal graph, or
- Counterfactually-adjusted features that remove the effect of A

5.8.5 The Proxy Variable Problem

Even when the sensitive attribute A is not directly used, the model may learn to predict A from other features (proxies), leading to indirect discrimination.

Definition 5.8.3 — Proxy Variable. A variable X is a **proxy** for sensitive attribute A if:

1. X is correlated with A: $I(X;A) > 0$
2. Using X for prediction leads to disparate outcomes: $\mathbb{E}_X[P(\hat{Y} = 1 \mid A = 0, X)] \neq \mathbb{E}_X[P(\hat{Y} = 1 \mid A = 1, X)]$

where $I(X;A)$ is the mutual information between X and A.

Example 5.6 — Common Proxies.

- ZIP code as proxy for race (due to residential segregation)
- First name as proxy for gender or ethnicity
- LinkedIn connections as proxy for socioeconomic status

■

Causal analysis helps identify and address proxies by examining the causal structure. If $A \to X \to \hat{Y}$, then X transmits the effect of A to the prediction.

5.8.6 Challenges and Limitations

1. **Causal Graph Uncertainty**: The true causal graph is often unknown. Different assumptions lead to different fairness conclusions.
2. **Unobserved Confounders**: Hidden common causes between A and Y can make causal effects unidentifiable from observational data.
3. **Counterfactual Identifiability**: Computing counterfactuals requires knowledge of the structural equations f_i, which are typically unknown.
4. **Philosophical Concerns**: Some argue that counterfactuals of immutable attributes ("if this person's race had been different") are metaphysically problematic.
5. **Accuracy Trade-offs**: If the sensitive attribute contains legitimate predictive information through fair pathways, counterfactual fairness may significantly reduce accuracy.

5.9 Fairness in Modern AI Systems

Contemporary challenges in fairness include:

Foundation Models: Pre-trained models may encode biases that propagate to downstream tasks, requiring fairness interventions at multiple stages.

Dynamic Systems: ML systems that learn and adapt over time can exhibit fairness drift, requiring continuous monitoring.

Multi-stakeholder Settings: Different stakeholders may prioritize different fairness criteria, requiring principled approaches to trade-off resolution.

Exercises

1. **Impossibility Results**:
   (a) Prove that demographic parity and individual fairness can be incompatible. Consider a simple example with two groups having different base rates and show that no Lipschitz-continuous classifier can satisfy both constraints.
   (b) Implement the Patient Health Outcomes dataset and demonstrate the trade-off between demographic parity and equalized odds by plotting the Pareto frontier.
   (c) Construct a concrete example where calibration and demographic parity cannot be simultaneously satisfied.
2. **Fairness Metrics Implementation**:
   (a) Implement a comprehensive fairness evaluation library that computes DPD, DIR, EOD, calibration metrics with confidence intervals.

   (b) Add support for intersectional analysis across multiple sensitive attributes.
   (c) Implement statistical significance tests for fairness disparities using permutation tests and bootstrap confidence intervals.
3. **Individual Fairness**:
   (a) Design a task-appropriate similarity metric for a generic dataset measuring creditworthiness that considers financial history while being insensitive to sensitive attributes.
   (b) Implement the Lipschitz regularization approach and compare it against standard ERM.
   (c) Investigate how the choice of similarity metric affects both fairness and accuracy.
4. **Algorithmic Interventions**:
   (a) Implement the Reweighing pre-processing algorithm and evaluate its effectiveness on reducing demographic parity violations.
   (b) Design an adversarial debiasing system using PyTorch that learns fair representations for image classification tasks.
   (c) Compare pre-processing, in-processing, and post-processing approaches on the same dataset and analyze their relative strengths and limitations.
5. **Causal Fairness**:
   (a) Construct a structural causal model for a hiring scenario with legitimate and illegitimate causal pathways.
   (b) Implement counterfactual fairness using causal inference techniques and compare it to statistical fairness measures.
   (c) Analyze the impact of hidden confounders on fairness assessment and mitigation.
6. **Advanced Applications**:
   (a) Design a fair recommendation system that balances accuracy and demographic parity across user groups.
   (b) Implement fairness-aware federated learning where different clients have different protected group distributions.
   (c) Create a dynamic fairness monitoring system that detects and responds to fairness drift in deployed models.
7. **Theoretical Case Analysis**:
   (a) Analyze a synthetic dataset $\mathscr{D}$ generated from a known structural causal model. Compute all fairness metrics, identify disparities, and propose mitigations.
   (b) Examine the impact of base rate differences on fairness metrics using abstract distributions $\mathscr{P}_0$ and $\mathscr{P}_1$.
   (c) Study a hypothetical medical dataset: balance fairness constraints with the clinical need for accurate predictions.

8. **Intersectionality**:
   (a) Implement intersectional fairness metrics for combinations of race and gender.
   (b) Show that satisfying fairness for individual attributes does not guarantee fairness for intersectional groups.
   (c) Propose and implement a method to achieve fairness across exponentially many intersectional groups efficiently.
9. **Theoretical Analysis**:
   (a) Prove that for k protected groups, achieving exact demographic parity reduces to a system of $k-1$ linear constraints.
   (b) Derive the sample complexity required to estimate demographic parity difference to within $\pm\varepsilon$ with probability $1-\delta$.
   (c) Analyze the computational complexity of finding an optimal fair classifier under different fairness constraints.

5.10 Implementation Templates and Code Examples

5.10.1 Fairness-Constrained Optimization

Listing 5.1 implements a classifier trained with a differentiable demographic-parity penalty.

```
import torch
import torch.nn as nn

class FairClassifier(nn.Module):
    def __init__(self, input_dim, hidden_dim, output_dim):
        super().__init__()
        self.predictor = nn.Sequential(
            nn.Linear(input_dim, hidden_dim),
            nn.ReLU(),
            nn.Linear(hidden_dim, output_dim),
            nn.Sigmoid()
        )

    def forward(self, x):
        return self.predictor(x)

def demographic_parity_loss(y_pred, sensitive_attr):
    """Differentiable demographic parity constraint."""
    group_0_idx = (sensitive_attr == 0).nonzero(as_tuple=True)[0]
    group_1_idx = (sensitive_attr == 1).nonzero(as_tuple=True)[0]

    if len(group_0_idx) == 0 or len(group_1_idx) == 0:
        return y_pred.sum() * 0  # preserves device and grad

    rate_0 = y_pred[group_0_idx].mean()
    rate_1 = y_pred[group_1_idx].mean()
```

```
    return (rate_0 - rate_1) ** 2

def train_fair_classifier(model, train_loader, epochs=100, lambda_fair=1.0):
    """Training loop with fairness constraint."""
    optimizer = torch.optim.Adam(model.parameters())
    criterion = nn.BCELoss()

    for epoch in range(epochs):
        for batch_x, batch_y, batch_a in train_loader:
            optimizer.zero_grad()
            y_pred = model(batch_x)

            # Task loss + Fairness loss
            task_loss = criterion(y_pred.squeeze(), batch_y.float())
            fair_loss = demographic_parity_loss(y_pred.squeeze(), batch_a)
            total_loss = task_loss + lambda_fair * fair_loss

            total_loss.backward()
            optimizer.step()
```

Listing 5.1: Fair Classifier with Demographic Parity Constraint

5.10.2 Adversarial Debiasing Implementation

Listing 5.2 implements an adversarial-debiasing architecture in which an adversary attempts to recover the sensitive attribute from the learned representation.

```
class AdversarialDebiasing(nn.Module):
    def __init__(self, input_dim, hidden_dim, repr_dim):
        super().__init__()

        # Feature encoder: learns fair representations
        self.encoder = nn.Sequential(
            nn.Linear(input_dim, hidden_dim),
            nn.ReLU(),
            nn.Linear(hidden_dim, repr_dim)
        )

        # Task predictor: predicts target label from representation
        self.predictor = nn.Sequential(
            nn.Linear(repr_dim, 1),
            nn.Sigmoid()
        )

        # Adversary: tries to predict sensitive attribute
        self.discriminator = nn.Sequential(
            nn.Linear(repr_dim, hidden_dim // 2),
```

```
                nn.ReLU(),
                nn.Linear(hidden_dim // 2, 1),
                nn.Sigmoid()
            )

    def forward(self, x):
        z = self.encoder(x)             # Fair representation
        y_pred = self.predictor(z)    # Task prediction
        a_pred = self.discriminator(z)  # Adversary prediction
        return y_pred, a_pred, z
```

Listing 5.2: Adversarial Debiasing Architecture

5.10.3 Comprehensive Fairness Evaluation

Listing 5.3 provides a reusable class that computes the principal group-fairness metrics together.

```
import numpy as np
from scipy import stats

class FairnessEvaluator:
    def __init__(self, y_true, y_pred, y_prob, sensitive_attr):
        self.y_true = y_true
        self.y_pred = y_pred
        self.y_prob = y_prob
        self.sensitive_attr = sensitive_attr

    def demographic_parity_difference(self):
        """Calculate DPD with 95% confidence interval."""
        rate_0 = self.y_pred[self.sensitive_attr == 0].mean()
        rate_1 = self.y_pred[self.sensitive_attr == 1].mean()
        n_0 = (self.sensitive_attr == 0).sum()
        n_1 = (self.sensitive_attr == 1).sum()

        dpd = rate_1 - rate_0
        se = np.sqrt(rate_0*(1-rate_0)/n_0 + rate_1*(1-rate_1)/n_1)

        p_val = (2 * (1 - stats.norm.cdf(abs(dpd / se)))
                 if se > 0 else 1.0)
        return {
            'dpd': dpd,
            'ci_lower': dpd - 1.96 * se,
            'ci_upper': dpd + 1.96 * se,
            'p_value': p_val
        }

    def comprehensive_report(self):
        """Generate comprehensive fairness report.

```

```
        Note: equalized_odds_difference() and calibration_analysis()
        are left as exercises for the reader (see Exercises 1--3).
        """
        report = {
            'demographic_parity': self.demographic_parity_difference()
↪ ,
        }

        # Summary with threshold-based violation detection
        dpd_violation = abs(report['demographic_parity']['dpd']) > 0.1
        report['summary'] = {
            'demographic_parity_violation': dpd_violation,
            'overall_fair': not dpd_violation
        }
        return report
```

Listing 5.3: Comprehensive Fairness Evaluation Class

Chapter 6

Privacy and Data Sovereignty

6.1 Differential Privacy Foundations

The gold standard for privacy-preserving data analysis is Differential Privacy (DP). Unlike anonymity, which focuses on removing identifiers (and is often reversible via linkage attacks), DP focuses on the stability of the algorithm's output.

6.1.1 Definition and Properties

Definition 6.1.1 — (ε, δ)-Differential Privacy. A randomized mechanism $\mathcal{M} : \mathcal{D} \to \mathcal{R}$ is (ε, δ)-DP if for all adjacent datasets D, D' (differing by exactly one element) and all measurable subsets $S \subseteq \mathcal{R}$:

$$P(\mathcal{M}(D) \in S) \leq e^{\varepsilon} P(\mathcal{M}(D') \in S) + \delta \tag{6.1}$$

where P denotes probability, ε is the privacy budget, and δ is the failure probability.

The parameter ε (privacy budget) bounds the multiplicative difference in probabilities. A smaller ε implies stronger privacy (outputs are indistinguishable). The parameter δ allows for a small probability of failure (e.g., the mechanism accidentally outputting the training data). In practice, δ is typically chosen to satisfy $\delta \leq 1/n$ (or smaller, such as $\delta = 1/n^2$), ensuring that the probability of a catastrophic privacy failure is negligible relative to the dataset size.

■ **Example 6.1 — Differential Privacy in Hospital Data Analysis.** A hospital database D contains $n = 10{,}000$ patient records. A researcher queries "What fraction of patients have diabetes?" If adding or removing any single patient's record cannot change this answer by more than a factor of e^{ε}, the analysis is ε-DP. With $\varepsilon = 0.1$, the probability ratio $P(\mathcal{M}(D) \in S)/P(\mathcal{M}(D') \in S) \leq e^{0.1} \approx 1.105$ for any output set S. This means that whether or not any specific patient is in the database, the output distribution changes by at most 10.5%, too small for an adversary to confidently infer any individual's presence. The patient can share their data knowing the query result would be nearly identical without them. ■

6.1.2 The Privacy Loss Random Variable

To analyze complex mechanisms, it is useful to define the privacy loss random variable Z for an outcome $o \sim \mathcal{M}(D)$:

$$Z := \ln \frac{P(\mathcal{M}(D) = o)}{P(\mathcal{M}(D') = o)} \tag{6.2}$$

where $P(\mathcal{M}(D) = o)$ is the probability density of outcome o under dataset D. (ε, δ)-DP implies that $P(Z > \varepsilon) \leq \delta$ for every pair of neighboring datasets $D \sim D'$ (the converse direction is not exactly equivalent and requires the more refined privacy-loss-distribution formalism, see Bun–Steinke or Mironov).

6.2 Mechanisms for Differential Privacy

6.2.1 The Laplace Mechanism

For a function $f : \mathscr{D} \to \mathbb{R}^k$, the L_1-sensitivity is $\Delta_1 f := \max_{D \sim D'} \|f(D) - f(D')\|_1$, where the maximum is taken over all pairs of *adjacent* datasets $D \sim D'$ (datasets differing in exactly one record).

Theorem 6.2.1 — Privacy of the Laplace Mechanism. Let $f : \mathscr{D} \to \mathbb{R}^k$ have L_1-sensitivity $\Delta_1 f$. The *Laplace mechanism*

$$\mathcal{M}(D) = f(D) + (Y_1, \ldots, Y_k), \quad Y_i \overset{\text{i.i.d.}}{\sim} \mathrm{Lap}(\Delta_1 f/\varepsilon) \tag{6.3}$$

satisfies ε-differential privacy. Here $\mathrm{Lap}(b)$ denotes the Laplace distribution with scale parameter b and density $h(y) = \frac{1}{2b} \exp(-|y|/b)$.

Proof. The density of the Laplace distribution with scale b is $h(y) =$

$\frac{1}{2b}\exp(-|y|/b)$. For output $z \in \mathbb{R}^k$:

$$\frac{P(\mathcal{M}(D)=z)}{P(\mathcal{M}(D')=z)} = \frac{\prod_{i=1}^{k}\exp(-|z_i - f(D)_i|/b)}{\prod_{i=1}^{k}\exp(-|z_i - f(D')_i|/b)} \tag{6.4}$$

$$= \exp\left(\frac{1}{b}\sum_{i=1}^{k}(|z_i - f(D')_i| - |z_i - f(D)_i|)\right) \tag{6.5}$$

By the reverse triangle inequality, for any $z_i, u, v \in \mathbb{R}$:

$$|z_i - v| - |z_i - u| \leq |u - v| \tag{6.6}$$

Summing over all coordinates:

$$\begin{aligned}\sum_{i=1}^{k}(|z_i - f(D')_i| - |z_i - f(D)_i|) &\leq \sum_{i=1}^{k}|f(D)_i - f(D')_i| \\ &= \|f(D) - f(D')\|_1 \leq \Delta_1 f\end{aligned} \tag{6.7}$$

Substituting $b = \Delta_1 f/\varepsilon$ (the scale parameter of the Laplace noise) into the exponent:

$$\frac{P(\mathcal{M}(D)=z)}{P(\mathcal{M}(D')=z)} \leq \exp\left(\frac{\Delta_1 f}{b}\right) = \exp\left(\frac{\Delta_1 f}{\Delta_1 f/\varepsilon}\right) = \exp(\varepsilon) \tag{6.8}$$

Since this holds for all outputs z and all neighboring datasets D, D', the mechanism $\mathcal{M}$ satisfies ε-differential privacy (with $\delta = 0$). ■

■ **Example 6.2 — Laplace Mechanism: Average Blood Pressure.** Suppose we want to release the average systolic blood pressure of $n = 1{,}000$ patients, where each measurement lies in $[80, 200]$ mmHg. The query is $f(D) = \frac{1}{n}\sum_{i=1}^{n} x_i$. The sensitivity is $\Delta_1 f = \max_{D,D'} |f(D) - f(D')| = (200-80)/1000 = 0.12$ mmHg (changing one patient's record shifts the average by at most 0.12). For $\varepsilon = 1$, we add noise $Y \sim \text{Lap}(0.12/1) = \text{Lap}(0.12)$, which has standard deviation $\sqrt{2} \times 0.12 \approx 0.17$ mmHg. If the true average is 125.3 mmHg, the released value might be $125.3 + 0.09 = 125.39$ mmHg. The noise is medically negligible (0.07% error) while providing strong privacy. For $\varepsilon = 0.1$ (stronger privacy), the noise scale increases to $\text{Lap}(1.2)$ with standard deviation ≈ 1.7 mmHg, still clinically acceptable. ■

6.2.2 The Gaussian Mechanism

For functions with high L_1-sensitivity but low L_2-sensitivity, the Gaussian mechanism is preferred over the Laplace mechanism of Theorem 6.2.1. Let $\Delta_2 f := \max_{D \sim D'} \|f(D) - f(D')\|_2$ denote the L_2-sensitivity. The mechanism is

$$\mathcal{M}(D) = f(D) + \mathcal{N}(0, \sigma^2 I_k). \tag{6.9}$$

For any $\varepsilon \in (0,1)$ and $\delta \in (0,1)$, the mechanism satisfies (ε,δ)-DP whenever

$$\sigma \geq \frac{\Delta_2 f}{\varepsilon}\sqrt{2\ln(1.25/\delta)}. \tag{6.10}$$

The condition $\varepsilon \leq 1$ matters: the standard proof bounds the privacy-loss random variable using Gaussian tail estimates, and the constant 1.25 arises from optimizing the split between the two Gaussian tails (see [24] Appendix A for the full derivation). With the noise scale set this way, even for very small $\delta > 0$ the Gaussian mechanism hides any single record's contribution within the prescribed privacy budget.

6.2.3 The Exponential Mechanism

For non-numeric queries (e.g., "What is the most common disease?"), we define a utility function $u(D,r)$ that scores each possible output $r \in \mathscr{R}$, with sensitivity $\Delta u := \max_{r\in\mathscr{R}} \max_{D\sim D'} |u(D,r) - u(D',r)|$, where the inner maximum ranges over neighboring datasets D, D'. The mechanism samples r with probability proportional to $\exp\left(\frac{\varepsilon u(D,r)}{2\Delta u}\right)$. The factor of 2 in the denominator is not arbitrary: changing a single record can shift $u(D,r)$ by at most Δu in the numerator of the sampling probability *and* change the normalization constant (the sum over all r) by another factor of Δu, so the privacy-loss in the exponent can change by $2\Delta u$. Halving the exponent compensates for this and yields the clean ε-DP guarantee.

■ **Example 6.3 — Exponential Mechanism: Selecting a Treatment Protocol.** A hospital wants to select the best treatment protocol from $\mathscr{R} = \{A,B,C\}$ based on patient outcomes, where the utility $u(D,r)$ counts how many patients recovered under protocol r. Suppose the counts are $u(D,A) = 340$, $u(D,B) = 310$, $u(D,C) = 350$ out of 1,000 patients. Since changing one patient changes any count by at most 1, $\Delta u = 1$. With $\varepsilon = 1$, the selection probabilities are proportional to $\exp(\varepsilon \cdot u/(2\cdot 1))$: protocol A: e^{170}, B: e^{155}, C: e^{175}. After normalization, protocol C is selected with probability ≈ 0.993, A with ≈ 0.007, and B with $\approx 10^{-9}$. The best protocol is very likely chosen while satisfying ε-DP; no individual patient's outcome significantly affects which protocol is selected. ■

Table 6.1 compares the fundamental differential privacy mechanisms introduced in this section—the Laplace, Gaussian, and exponential mechanisms—by the sensitivity they use, their noise distribution, the privacy guarantee they provide, and their best use case.

6.3 Composition and Rényi Differential Privacy

A key property of DP is composition: the privacy guarantee holds even when multiple analyses are performed on the same data. **Basic Composition** states that if $\mathscr{M}_i$ is ε_i-DP, then the sequence $(\mathscr{M}_1(D),\ldots,\mathscr{M}_k(D))$ is $(\sum \varepsilon_i)$-DP. **Advanced Composition** provides a tighter bound: for k mechanisms each being (pure) ε-DP,

Table 6.1: Comparison of fundamental differential privacy mechanisms.

Mechanism	Sensitivity	Noise Distribution	Privacy	Best Use Case
Laplace	L_1 ($\Delta_1 f$)	Lap($\Delta_1 f/\varepsilon$)	Pure ε-DP	Numeric queries; tight pure-DP
Gaussian	L_2 ($\Delta_2 f$)	$\mathscr{N}(0,\sigma^2 I)$, $\sigma \geq \frac{\Delta_2 f\sqrt{2\ln(1.25/\delta)}}{\varepsilon}$	Approx. (ε,δ)-DP	High-dim. queries; RDP accounting
Exponential	Utility sens. Δu	Samples r, prob. $\propto e^{\varepsilon u(D,r)/(2\Delta u)}$	Pure ε-DP	Non-numeric outputs (selection)

the composition is $(\varepsilon\sqrt{2k\ln(1/\delta')} + k\varepsilon(e^\varepsilon - 1), \delta')$-DP for any $\delta' > 0$; when each mechanism is (ε,δ)-DP, the overall delta becomes $k\delta + \delta'$. For small ε, the dominant term scales as $O(\varepsilon\sqrt{k})$ rather than $O(k\varepsilon)$, a significant improvement for iterative algorithms like SGD.

6.3.1 Rényi Differential Privacy (RDP)

RDP [53] provides tighter composition bounds by tracking the Rényi divergence between the output distributions.

Definition 6.3.1 — (α,ε)-RDP. A mechanism $\mathscr{M}$ is (α,ε)-RDP if for all adjacent D,D':

$$D_\alpha(\mathscr{M}(D)\|\mathscr{M}(D')) \leq \varepsilon \tag{6.11}$$

where $D_\alpha(P\|Q) = \frac{1}{\alpha-1}\ln\mathbb{E}_{x\sim Q}[(P(x)/Q(x))^\alpha]$ is the Rényi divergence of order α.

RDP composes linearly. We can convert RDP back to (ε,δ)-DP at the end of the analysis. Intuition: Rényi divergence smoothly interpolates between two extremes. At $\alpha \to \infty$ it recovers *max-divergence*, which is the worst-case privacy loss (the strict $(\varepsilon,0)$-DP guarantee); at $\alpha \to 1$ it becomes KL-divergence, the *average* privacy loss. Intermediate α values give bounds that are tighter than max-divergence yet still control a high-probability tail of the privacy-loss random variable. Composing in RDP avoids the slack of taking the worst case at every step, which is why DP-SGD accountants based on RDP yield much tighter privacy budgets than naive composition.

6.4 Privacy in Deep Learning

6.4.1 DP-SGD Algorithm

Training neural networks with DP involves two modifications [1]: clipping per-sample gradients to bound sensitivity, and adding Gaussian noise to the aggregated gradient.

Algorithm 6.1 states the full DP-SGD training loop with per-sample gradient clipping and Gaussian noise injection.

Algorithm 6.1 Differentially Private SGD (DP-SGD)

Input: Dataset D, Loss $\mathscr{L}$, Noise scale σ, Clip C, Learning rate η, Iterations T
for $t = 1$ to T **do**
  Sample batch B_t with sampling probability $q = |B_t|/|D|$
  for $i \in B_t$ **do**
    $g_t^{(i)} \leftarrow \nabla_{\theta_t} \mathscr{L}(x_i, y_i)$
    $\bar{g}_t^{(i)} \leftarrow g_t^{(i)} / \max(1, \frac{\|g_t^{(i)}\|_2}{C})$ ▷ *Per-sample Clipping*
  end for
  $\tilde{g}_t \leftarrow \frac{1}{|B_t|} \left(\sum_i \bar{g}_t^{(i)} + \mathscr{N}(0, \sigma^2 C^2 I) \right)$ ▷ *Add Noise*
  $\theta_{t+1} \leftarrow \theta_t - \eta \tilde{g}_t$
end for

The privacy cost is calculated using the "Moments Accountant" method, which tracks the RDP moments across iterations.

6.4.2 Privacy Amplification by Subsampling

A crucial property of DP-SGD is that the privacy guarantee is *amplified* by subsampling. If the batch is a random subsample of the dataset with sampling probability q, the privacy cost per iteration is reduced.

Theorem 6.4.1 — Privacy Amplification by Subsampling. If $\mathscr{M}$ is an (ε, δ)-DP mechanism and we apply it to a uniformly random subsample with probability q, the resulting mechanism $\mathscr{M}'$ satisfies (ε', δ')-DP where $\varepsilon' = \ln(1 + q(e^{\varepsilon} - 1))$ and $\delta' = q\delta$. For small ε, $\varepsilon' \approx q\varepsilon$.

Proof Sketch. Let $\mathscr{M}'(D)$ denote applying $\mathscr{M}$ to a random subsample $S \subseteq D$ where each element is included independently with probability q. For adjacent datasets D, D' differing in one element x^*:

$$
\begin{aligned}
P(\mathscr{M}'(D) \in T) &= \sum_S P(S \text{ sampled from } D) \cdot P(\mathscr{M}(S) \in T) \\
&= q \cdot P(\mathscr{M}(S) \in T \mid x^* \in S) \\
&\quad + (1 - q) \cdot P(\mathscr{M}(S) \in T \mid x^* \notin S)
\end{aligned}
\tag{6.12}
$$

where q is the per-element sampling probability and the conditional probabilities marginalise over the random subsample of $D \setminus \{x^*\}$. When $x^* \notin S$, the subsample drawn from D is identically distributed to the subsample drawn from D', so $P(\mathscr{M}(S) \in T \mid x^* \notin S)$ is the same under both databases. When $x^* \in S$ (with probability q), the subsample from D differs from that of D' in exactly one record, so the base mechanism's (ε, δ)-DP guarantee applies. Combining these two cases and writing $P_{D'}$ for the corresponding probability under D':

$$P(\mathcal{M}'(D) \in T) \leq (1-q)P(\mathcal{M}'(D') \in T) + q(e^{\varepsilon}P(\mathcal{M}'(D') \in T) + \delta) \tag{6.13}$$

$$= P(\mathcal{M}'(D') \in T) \cdot (1 - q + qe^{\varepsilon}) + q\delta \tag{6.14}$$

$$= P(\mathcal{M}'(D') \in T) \cdot (1 + q(e^{\varepsilon} - 1)) + q\delta \tag{6.15}$$

Thus we have $\varepsilon' = \ln(1 + q(e^{\varepsilon} - 1))$ and $\delta' = q\delta$. ■

This amplification is critical for making DP-SGD practical: without it, the noise required for privacy would make training impossible.

6.4.3 The Moments Accountant

The Moments Accountant provides tight composition bounds for DP-SGD by tracking the moments of the privacy loss random variable Z. Define the λ-th moment as:

$$\alpha_{\mathcal{M}}(\lambda) = \max_{D \sim D'} \log \mathbb{E}_{o \sim \mathcal{M}(D)}[\exp(\lambda Z)] \tag{6.16}$$

where $Z = \log \frac{P(\mathcal{M}(D)=o)}{P(\mathcal{M}(D')=o)}$ is the privacy loss random variable, and the maximum is taken over all adjacent datasets D, D'.

The moments compose additively: for k applications of mechanism $\mathcal{M}$, $\alpha_{k \times \mathcal{M}}(\lambda) = k \cdot \alpha_{\mathcal{M}}(\lambda)$. After composition, we convert back to (ε, δ)-DP using a Chernoff/Markov tail bound on the privacy loss random variable Z. For any $\lambda > 0$,

$$P(Z > \varepsilon) \leq e^{-\lambda\varepsilon}\, \mathbb{E}[e^{\lambda Z}] = \exp\big(\alpha(\lambda) - \lambda\varepsilon\big). \tag{6.17}$$

Setting the right-hand side equal to δ and solving for the smallest ε that makes the bound hold yields

$$\varepsilon = \min_{\lambda > 0} \left\{ \frac{\alpha(\lambda) + \log(1/\delta)}{\lambda} \right\}. \tag{6.18}$$

The optimization over λ finds the tightest bound. In practice, we evaluate this expression on a finite grid of λ values and take the minimum.

For the Gaussian mechanism with L_2-sensitivity Δ and noise scale σ, a direct computation of the moment generating function of Z gives

$$\alpha_G(\lambda) = \frac{\lambda(\lambda+1)\Delta^2}{2\sigma^2}. \tag{6.19}$$

Equivalently, in the Rényi-differential-privacy formulation, the order-$(\lambda+1)$ Rényi divergence between $\mathcal{N}(f(D), \sigma^2 I)$ and $\mathcal{N}(f(D'), \sigma^2 I)$ equals $(\lambda+1)\Delta^2/(2\sigma^2)$

[53]. Larger noise σ reduces the moment (stronger privacy), while larger sensitivity Δ increases it (weaker privacy). The quadratic-in-λ form is no accident: when $\mathscr{M}(D)$ and $\mathscr{M}(D')$ are two Gaussians whose means differ by Δ in ℓ_2-norm, the privacy-loss random variable Z is itself Gaussian, and $\mathbb{E}[e^{\lambda Z}]$ is just the MGF of a Gaussian evaluated at λ — which is the exponential of a quadratic in λ.

6.4.4 PATE (Private Aggregation of Teacher Ensembles)

PATE [59] trains an ensemble of "teacher" models on disjoint partitions of the private data.

To predict on a new input, the teachers vote, and the noisy argmax of the vote is returned. A "student" model is then trained on public, unlabeled data that the teachers label. This avoids exposing the private model weights directly.

Algorithm 6.2 summarizes the student-training procedure.

Algorithm 6.2 PATE: Student Training

Input: Teacher ensemble $\{f_1, \dots, f_K\}$, Unlabeled public data D_{pub}, Laplace noise scale b
for $x \in D_{\text{pub}}$ **do**
    $n_c \leftarrow \sum_{k=1}^{K} \mathbb{I}(f_k(x) = c)$ for each class c ▷ *Teacher votes*
    $\tilde{n}_c \leftarrow n_c + \text{Lap}(b)$ ▷ *Add Laplace noise (scale b)*
    $\tilde{y} \leftarrow \arg\max_c \tilde{n}_c$ ▷ *Noisy aggregation*
    Add $(x, \tilde{y})$ to student training set
end for
Train student model on labeled data

The privacy guarantee of PATE depends on the consensus among teachers. When teachers agree, the noise has little effect on the label, and privacy cost is low. When teachers disagree, more privacy budget is consumed. The Confident-GNMax aggregation mechanism formalizes this:

$$\tilde{y} = \begin{cases} \arg\max_c (n_c + \mathscr{N}(0, \sigma_2^2)) & \text{if } \max_c n_c + \mathscr{N}(0, \sigma_1^2) > T \\ \perp \text{ (abstain)} & \text{otherwise} \end{cases} \tag{6.20}$$

where n_c is the vote count for class c, σ_1, σ_2 are noise scales, and T is a threshold.

6.5 Secure Multi-Party Computation

Secure Multi-Party Computation (MPC) allows multiple parties to jointly compute a function over their private inputs without revealing those inputs to each other.

6.5.1 Problem Formulation

Consider n parties $P_1, \dots, P_n$, each holding private input x_i. The goal is to compute $f(x_1, \dots, x_n)$ such that two conditions are met: **Correctness**, meaning all parties learn the correct output value; and **Privacy**, meaning no party learns anything about others' inputs beyond what can be inferred from the output.

> **Definition 6.5.1 — Security Definition.** A protocol Π securely computes f if for every adversary $\mathscr{A}$ in the real protocol, there exists a simulator $\mathscr{S}$ in the ideal world such that:
>
> $$\text{Real}_{\Pi,\mathscr{A}}(x_1,\ldots,x_n) \approx_c \text{Ideal}_{f,\mathscr{S}}(x_1,\ldots,x_n) \tag{6.21}$$
>
> where $\approx_c$ denotes computational indistinguishability, meaning no polynomial-time algorithm can distinguish the two distributions with non-negligible probability.

6.5.2 Secret Sharing

Secret sharing is a fundamental building block for MPC. A (t,n)-threshold secret sharing scheme splits a secret s into n shares such that any t or more shares can reconstruct s, while any fewer than t shares reveal no information about s.

Shamir's Secret Sharing: To share secret $s \in \mathbb{F}_p$, choose random polynomial $q(x)$ of degree $t-1$ with $q(0) = s$:

$$q(x) = s + a_1x + a_2x^2 + \cdots + a_{t-1}x^{t-1} \tag{6.22}$$

where s is the secret, and $a_1,\ldots,a_{t-1}$ are random coefficients from the field $\mathbb{F}_p$. Each party i receives share $s_i = q(i)$. Reconstruction uses Lagrange interpolation:

$$s = q(0) = \sum_{i\in S} s_i \cdot \prod_{j\in S, j\neq i} \frac{j}{j-i} \tag{6.23}$$

for any set S of t parties.

Additive Secret Sharing: For 2-party computation, split s as s_1, s_2 where $s_1 + s_2 = s \pmod p$. Addition is free: (a_1+b_1, a_2+b_2) shares $a+b$.

6.5.3 Garbled Circuits

Garbled circuits enable secure two-party computation. Party 1 (garbler) encrypts a boolean circuit C computing f, and Party 2 (evaluator) evaluates it without learning intermediate values.

For each wire w in the circuit, the garbler creates two random keys (k_w^0, k_w^1) representing bit values 0 and 1. For each gate with input wires a,b and output wire c, the garbler creates a garbled gate table:

$$\text{Enc}_{k_a^{v_a}, k_b^{v_b}}(k_c^{g(v_a,v_b)}) \quad \text{for } v_a, v_b \in \{0,1\} \tag{6.24}$$

where Enc is a symmetric encryption scheme, k_w^v is the key for wire w having value v, and g is the gate function.

The evaluator receives keys corresponding to input bits (via oblivious transfer for Party 2's inputs) and evaluates gate-by-gate, learning only the output.

6.5.4 Applications to Machine Learning

MPC enables privacy-preserving ML in several settings:

Secure Inference: A model owner and data owner can jointly compute $f(x)$ where the model owner learns nothing about x and the data owner learns nothing about model parameters beyond the prediction.

Secure Training: Multiple data owners can train a joint model without sharing raw data. Each iteration involves secure aggregation of gradients.

Challenges:

- **Communication Overhead**: MPC protocols require multiple rounds of message exchanges between parties, introducing significant network latency that can make real-time applications impractical. For example, securely computing a single neural network forward pass might require $O(d \cdot L)$ communication rounds for d input dimensions and L layers, where each round incurs network latency (typically 10–100ms for internet connections). In practice, a ResNet-50 inference with MPC could take seconds to minutes instead of milliseconds, making it unsuitable for interactive applications like real-time clinical decision support. The communication complexity scales with circuit depth; deeper computations require more sequential message passing. Optimizations like circuit pipelining and batching multiple evaluations can amortize costs, but fundamentally cannot eliminate the sequential dependency between computational layers.
- **Computational Complexity**: Cryptographic operations underlying MPC, particularly secure multiplication gates, are computationally expensive compared to plaintext operations. A secure multiplication requires homomorphic encryption operations or oblivious transfer protocols that are 10^3 to 10^6 times slower than native CPU multiplication. For instance, while a standard matrix multiplication $C = AB$ for $n \times n$ matrices takes $O(n^3)$ floating-point operations completing in microseconds on modern hardware, the secure version using garbled circuits requires generating and evaluating $O(n^3)$ encrypted gate tables, potentially taking minutes to hours for moderately sized matrices ($n \approx 1000$). The asymmetry between addition and multiplication costs means circuit optimization must carefully balance these operations; addition in additive secret sharing is essentially free (local addition of shares), while multiplication requires interaction between parties.
- **Nonlinear Activation Functions**: Standard neural network activations like ReLU ($\max(0,x)$), sigmoid ($\sigma(x) = 1/(1+e^{-x})$), and softmax require comparison or exponential operations that are extremely expensive to compute securely. The ReLU function $f(x) = \max(0,x)$ requires secure comparison

to determine if $x > 0$, implemented via garbled circuits with depth $O(\log k)$ for k-bit precision, adding significant overhead to each layer. Practical MPC systems often approximate nonlinear functions using low-degree polynomials (e.g., replacing $\text{ReLU}(x)$ with x^2 as a smooth activation) or use specialized protocols like CrypTFlow2 [65] that combine different MPC techniques. Alternatively, some systems replace ReLU with quadratic activations that are MPC-friendly but may reduce model accuracy. The fundamental tension is that functions easy to compute in plaintext (comparisons, table lookups, transcendental functions) become bottlenecks in the encrypted domain.

6.5.5 Homomorphic Encryption

Homomorphic encryption (HE) allows computation on encrypted data. A fully homomorphic encryption scheme supports:

$$\text{Enc}(a) \oplus \text{Enc}(b) = \text{Enc}(a+b) \tag{6.25}$$

$$\text{Enc}(a) \otimes \text{Enc}(b) = \text{Enc}(a \cdot b) \tag{6.26}$$

where $\oplus$ and $\otimes$ are operations on ciphertexts that correspond to addition and multiplication on plaintexts.

The client encrypts input x, sends $\text{Enc}(x)$ to the server, which computes $\text{Enc}(f(x))$ and returns it. The client decrypts to obtain $f(x)$.

Challenges: FHE has high computational overhead (orders of magnitude slower than plaintext). Practical schemes like CKKS support approximate arithmetic on real numbers but accumulate noise that limits computation depth.

Example 6.4 — Homomorphic Encryption for Private Medical Image Analysis. A patient wants a cloud-based AI to analyze their MRI scan for tumor detection without revealing the image. Using CKKS homomorphic encryption: (1) the patient encrypts their MRI pixel values $x \in \mathbb{R}^{256\times256}$ locally, obtaining $\text{Enc}(x)$; (2) the encrypted image is sent to the cloud server; (3) the server evaluates a pre-trained neural network entirely on encrypted data, computing $\text{Enc}(Wx+b)$ using homomorphic matrix multiplication ($\otimes$) and addition ($\oplus$), approximating ReLU with low-degree polynomials; (4) the server returns $\text{Enc}(\hat{y})$; (5) the patient decrypts locally to obtain $\hat{y} \in \{\text{benign}, \text{malignant}\}$. The server never sees the raw MRI or the diagnosis. The cost: a forward pass taking 5ms in plaintext may take 10–60 seconds under HE, and computation depth is limited to $\sim$10–20 multiplicative layers before noise overwhelms the signal, requiring network architecture adaptation. ■

6.5.6 Local Differential Privacy

In the *local* model of DP, each user randomizes their own data before sending it to the aggregator. This provides stronger privacy guarantees (no trusted curator) but requires more noise.

Definition 6.5.2 — Local Differential Privacy. A randomized mechanism $\mathcal{M} : \mathcal{X} \to \mathcal{Y}$ is ε-locally differentially private if for all $x, x' \in \mathcal{X}$ and all $S \subseteq \mathcal{Y}$:

$$P(\mathcal{M}(x) \in S) \leq e^{\varepsilon} P(\mathcal{M}(x') \in S) \tag{6.27}$$

where ε is the privacy budget.

Randomized Response is the canonical LDP mechanism. For a binary attribute $b \in \{0,1\}$:

$$\mathcal{M}(b) = \begin{cases} b & \text{with probability } \frac{e^{\varepsilon}}{1+e^{\varepsilon}} \\ 1-b & \text{with probability } \frac{1}{1+e^{\varepsilon}} \end{cases} \tag{6.28}$$

■ **Example 6.5 — Randomized Response: Studying Sensitive Health Behaviors.** A public health researcher surveys $n = 10{,}000$ individuals about whether they smoke ($b = 1$) or not ($b = 0$), using $\varepsilon = 2$ local DP. Each respondent answers truthfully with probability $e^2/(1+e^2) \approx 0.88$ and lies with probability $1/(1+e^2) \approx 0.12$. Suppose 2,500 individuals truly smoke (true rate $p = 0.25$). The expected number of "yes" responses is $2{,}500 \times 0.88 + 7{,}500 \times 0.12 = 2{,}200 + 900 = 3{,}100$, giving $\bar{y} = 0.31$. The researcher recovers the true rate using: $\hat{p} = \frac{(1+e^2)\times 0.31-1}{e^2-1} = \frac{8.389\times 0.31-1}{6.389} = \frac{1.601}{6.389} \approx 0.251$. Even though each individual's response is plausibly deniable (any "yes" could be a true smoker who answered honestly or a non-smoker who lied), the aggregate statistic is accurately recovered. ■

The aggregator can estimate the true mean from noisy responses:

$$\hat{p} = \frac{(1+e^{\varepsilon})\bar{y} - 1}{e^{\varepsilon} - 1} \tag{6.29}$$

where $\bar{y}$ is the empirical mean of the randomized responses.

6.6 Attacks on Privacy

Privacy attacks against machine learning models can be organized by the attacker's goal and the knowledge available to them. Table 6.2 presents a taxonomy of the principal attack types together with the differential-privacy mitigation that applies to each.

6.6.1 Reconstruction Attacks

The Dinur–Nissim theorem [22] states that if a mechanism answers $O(N)$ queries with error $o(\sqrt{N})$, an adversary can reconstruct the underlying database with high probability. This fundamental limit implies that we cannot answer an infinite number of queries accurately while preserving privacy.

Table 6.2: Taxonomy of privacy attacks against machine learning models.

Attack Type	Goal	Attacker Knowledge	DP Mitigation
Reconstruction (Dinur–Nissim)	Recover entire database D	Access to $O(N)$ query answers	Noise must be $\Omega(\sqrt{N})$ per query
Membership Inference (MIA)	Determine if $x \in D_{\text{train}}$	Black-box model access	Advantage $\leq e^{\varepsilon} - 1 + \delta e^{\varepsilon}$ under (ε, δ)-DP
Model Inversion	Reconstruct sensitive input features	Model output + partial features	Noise in training limits reconstruction fidelity
Attribute Inference	Predict sensitive attributes	Model + partial individual features	DP bounds info leakage about any single record

Theorem 6.6.1 — Dinur–Nissim Lower Bound. Let $D \in \{0,1\}^N$ be a database. Any mechanism that answers $c \cdot N$ linear queries with error at most $o(\sqrt{N})$ for each query enables reconstruction of D with high probability.

Proof Sketch. Consider $c \cdot N$ random subset queries $S_1, \ldots, S_{cN}$, where each query asks for $\sum_{i \in S_j} D[i]$. With high probability, the matrix A defined by $A_{jk} = \mathbb{I}(k \in S_j)$ has full column rank when c is large enough. If we receive noisy answers $\tilde{a}_j = a_j + \text{noise}_j$ where $|\text{noise}_j| = o(\sqrt{N})$, we can solve the linear system $A \cdot D \approx \tilde{a}$ via least-squares estimation; rounding the resulting real-valued solution coordinatewise to $\{0,1\}$ then recovers the original Boolean dataset D exactly whenever the per-coordinate error is below $1/2$. ■

6.6.2 Membership Inference Attacks (MIA)

MIA aims to determine if a specific sample x was in the training set. The attack exploits the generalization gap: models tend to have lower loss (higher confidence) on training data than on test data.

$$\mathscr{A}(x, f) = \mathbb{I}(\ell(f(x), y) < \tau) \tag{6.30}$$

where $\mathbb{I}(\cdot)$ is the indicator function, ℓ is the loss function, and τ is a threshold. If the loss is below a threshold τ, the attacker predicts "Member". DP provides a theoretical upper bound on the success of any such attack, effectively closing the generalization gap.

Theorem 6.6.2 — MIA Upper Bound under DP. If model f is trained using an (ε, δ)-DP algorithm, then for any membership inference attack $\mathscr{A}$:

$$\text{Advantage}_{\mathscr{A}} = |P(\mathscr{A}(x) = 1 \mid x \in D) - P(\mathscr{A}(x) = 1 \mid x \notin D)| \leq e^{\varepsilon} - 1 + \delta \cdot e^{\varepsilon}$$

(6.31)

For small ε and δ, this simplifies to approximately $\varepsilon + \delta$.

6.6.3 Model Inversion Attacks

Model inversion attacks attempt to reconstruct training data or sensitive attributes from model access. Given a model f trained on sensitive features X to predict target Y, an attacker observing f and knowing Y attempts to infer X.

For a linear model $f(x) = w^T x$, if the attacker knows the output $y = f(x)$ and has access to the weights w, they can attempt to solve for x. For neural networks, gradient-based optimization can be used:

$$x^* = \arg\min_x \|f(x) - y_{\text{target}}\|^2 + \lambda R(x) \tag{6.32}$$

where $R(x)$ is a regularizer encouraging realistic inputs (e.g., total variation for images).

6.6.4 Attribute Inference Attacks

Given a trained model and partial knowledge of an individual's features, attribute inference attacks attempt to predict sensitive attributes. If model f was trained on features $(X_1, X_2, \ldots, X_d)$ and an attacker knows $(x_2, \ldots, x_d)$ and y, they can optimize:

$$\hat{x}_1 = \arg\max_{x_1} P(Y = y \mid X_1 = x_1, X_2 = x_2, \ldots) \tag{6.33}$$

These attacks are particularly concerning when models inadvertently learn to predict sensitive attributes as features for the main task.

Exercises

1. **Laplace Mechanism**:
   (a) Prove that the Laplace mechanism $\mathcal{M}(x) = f(x) + \text{Lap}(\Delta f/\varepsilon)$ satisfies ε-DP.
   (b) Compare the noise magnitude of Laplace vs. Gaussian mechanisms for the same ε, δ.
2. **DP-SGD**:
   (a) Implement DP-SGD from scratch in PyTorch.
   (b) Train a model on MNIST with $\varepsilon = 1.0$.
   (c) Plot the privacy loss curve using the Moments Accountant.
3. **Membership Inference**:
   (a) Train a model on half of CIFAR-10 (members) and evaluate on the other half (non-members).

   (b) Plot the distribution of loss values for members vs. non-members.
   (c) Calculate the attack accuracy of a simple threshold-based MIA.
4. **Composition Theorems**:
   (a) Prove the basic composition theorem: k applications of ε-DP give $(k\varepsilon)$-DP.
   (b) Implement and compare: basic composition, advanced composition, and Rényi DP composition.
   (c) For $k = 100$ queries with $\varepsilon = 0.1$ each, compute the total ε under each composition rule.
   (d) Visualize how privacy budget grows with the number of queries.
5. **Local Differential Privacy**:
   (a) Implement randomized response for binary attributes.
   (b) Estimate the population mean from locally privatized data.
   (c) Compare variance of estimates under local vs. central DP.
   (d) Implement the RAPPOR protocol for frequency estimation.
6. **PATE Framework**:
   (a) Train an ensemble of 100 "teacher" models on disjoint data partitions.
   (b) Implement the noisy argmax aggregation mechanism.
   (c) Train a "student" model using the aggregated labels.
   (d) Compute the data-dependent privacy bound using the smooth sensitivity analysis.
7. **Model Inversion Attack**:
   (a) Train a face recognition model on a subset of CelebA.
   (b) Given only a class label (person ID), reconstruct a representative face.
   (c) Compare reconstruction quality with and without regularization.
   (d) Test if DP training reduces reconstruction quality.
8. **Attribute Inference Attack**:
   (a) Train a classifier that uses but does not predict a sensitive attribute.
   (b) Implement an attribute inference attack using the model's outputs.
   (c) Measure attack success rate vs. baseline (predicting majority class).
   (d) Test mitigation strategies: removing correlated features, adversarial debiasing.
9. **Reconstruction Attack**:
   (a) Implement the Dinur–Nissim attack on a synthetic database.
   (b) Query a counting query mechanism and attempt reconstruction.
   (c) Verify that reconstruction fails when queries are answered with $O(\sqrt{N})$ noise.
   (d) Demonstrate successful reconstruction with lower noise levels.
10. **Privacy Amplification**:
   (a) Implement privacy amplification by subsampling.
   (b) Compare privacy guarantees with and without subsampling.
   (c) Verify the amplification bound experimentally.

(d) Implement privacy amplification by shuffling for the local model.

Interpretability and Causality

Contents of This Part

Chapter 7
Explainability and Interpretability

7.1 Foundations of Explainable AI (XAI)

As machine learning models, particularly deep neural networks, become more complex, their decision-making processes become increasingly opaque. This "black box" nature poses significant challenges for trust, accountability, and debugging. Explainable AI (XAI) aims to make the internal logic of these systems transparent and understandable to humans.

We distinguish between two related but distinct concepts:

- **Interpretability**: The degree to which a human can understand the cause of a decision. A linear regression model with few features is intrinsically interpretable because the coefficients directly relate inputs to outputs.
- **Explainability**: The ability to provide a post-hoc description of why a model made a specific prediction. A deep neural network is not interpretable, but we can generate an explanation (e.g., a heatmap) to justify its output.

7.2 Taxonomy of XAI Methods

XAI methods can be categorized along several dimensions. **Intrinsic vs. Post-hoc** distinguishes between models that are interpretable by design (e.g., decision trees, linear models) and methods that analyze a trained black-box model without modifying its structure. **Global vs. Local** refers to the scope of the explanation: global methods describe the model's behavior across the entire input space, while local methods focus on justifying a specific prediction for a single input instance. Finally, **Model-Agnostic vs. Model-Specific** differentiates between methods that treat the model as a black box (requiring only input-output access, like LIME or SHAP) and those that exploit internal structures like gradients or attention weights (like Integrated Gradients).

Table 7.1 summarizes these classification dimensions and the contrasting categories along each.

7.3 Feature Attribution Methods

Feature attribution methods assign a "relevance" score to each input feature, indicating its contribution to the model's prediction.

Table 7.1: Classification dimensions for XAI methods.

Dimension	Category A	Category B
Scope	**Intrinsic**: Interpretable by design (e.g., decision trees, linear models)	**Post-hoc**: Analyzes a trained black-box model
Coverage	**Global**: Describes behavior across entire input space	**Local**: Justifies a specific prediction for a single instance
Model Dependency	**Model-Agnostic**: Treats model as a black box (e.g., LIME, SHAP)	**Model-Specific**: Exploits internal structure (e.g., gradients, attention)

7.3.1 Shapley Values

Originating from cooperative game theory, Shapley values provide a unique solution to the problem of fairly distributing a "payout" (prediction) among "players" (features). For a model f and an input x, the Shapley value ϕ_i for feature i is defined as the average marginal contribution of feature i across all possible coalitions of features:

$$\phi_i(f,x) := \sum_{S \subseteq N \setminus \{i\}} \frac{|S|!(|N|-|S|-1)!}{|N|!} [f_x(S \cup \{i\}) - f_x(S)] \tag{7.1}$$

where N is the set of all features, S is a subset of features not containing i, $|S|$ is the size of the subset, and $f_x(S) = \mathbb{E}[f(x_S, X_{\bar{S}})]$ is the expected prediction when only features in S are set to their observed values and features outside S are marginalized over their distribution.

Shapley values are the *only* attribution method that satisfies four desirable axioms. **Efficiency** requires that the sum of attributions equals the difference between the prediction and the baseline ($\sum_i \phi_i = f(x) - \mathbb{E}[f(X)]$, where the expectation is over the data distribution of the input random vector X). **Symmetry** ensures that if two features contribute equally to all coalitions, they receive equal attribution. The **Dummy** axiom states that a feature that never changes the prediction receives zero attribution. Finally, **Additivity** guarantees that the attribution for a sum of two models is the sum of their individual attributions.

> **Theorem 7.3.1 — Uniqueness of Shapley Values.** The Shapley value is the unique attribution method satisfying Efficiency, Symmetry, Dummy, and Additivity.

Proof Sketch. Consider the set of all $2^{|N|}$ coalitions. For each coalition S, define the characteristic function $v(S) = f_x(S)$. The four axioms impose a system of linear constraints on the attributions ϕ_i. Efficiency gives one equation ($\sum_i \phi_i = v(N) - v(\emptyset)$). Symmetry and Dummy reduce the degrees of freedom by identifying features with equal contributions. One can show inductively that these constraints uniquely determine each ϕ_i, and the resulting value is precisely the Shapley formula. The proof relies on showing that any other attribution satisfying these axioms must equal the Shapley value for all possible coalitional games. ■

Exact computation is exponential in the number of features ($O(2^{|N|})$). In practice, we use approximations like **KernelSHAP** [49], which casts the computation as a weighted linear regression problem, or **DeepSHAP**, which leverages the compositional structure of neural networks.

■ **Example 7.1 — Shapley Values for a Simple Patient Recovery Prediction Model.** Consider a model f predicting recovery rate (index score) from three features: x_1 = blood pressure (mmHg), x_2 = temperature (°C), x_3 = medication dosage (mg). For a specific patient with $x = (120, 38, 50)$, the model predicts $f(x) = 6.2$ score, while the baseline (average prediction over the data distribution) is $\mathbb{E}[f(X)] = 4.0$ score. To compute ϕ_1 (blood pressure's contribution), we evaluate all coalitions:

- $f_x(\emptyset) = 4.0$ (baseline), $f_x(\{1\}) = 5.1$ (blood pressure alone adds 1.1)
- $f_x(\{2\}) = 4.3$, $f_x(\{3\}) = 4.5$, $f_x(\{1,2\}) = 5.6$, $f_x(\{1,3\}) = 5.8$
- $f_x(\{2,3\}) = 4.9$, $f_x(\{1,2,3\}) = 6.2$

The marginal contributions of blood pressure are: $f_x(\{1\}) - f_x(\emptyset) = 1.1$, $f_x(\{1,2\}) - f_x(\{2\}) = 1.3$, $f_x(\{1,3\}) - f_x(\{3\}) = 1.3$, $f_x(\{1,2,3\}) - f_x(\{2,3\}) = 1.3$. Weighting by $\frac{|S|!(|N|-|S|-1)!}{|N|!}$ and summing: $\phi_1 = \frac{1}{3}(1.1) + \frac{1}{6}(1.3) + \frac{1}{6}(1.3) + \frac{1}{3}(1.3) \approx 1.233$. Similarly, $\phi_2 \approx 0.383$ and $\phi_3 \approx 0.583$. The efficiency axiom is satisfied exactly: $\phi_1 + \phi_2 + \phi_3 = 2.2 = f(x) - \mathbb{E}[f(X)]$ (the equality holds with the exact, unrounded values). ■

7.3.2 LIME (Local Interpretable Model-agnostic Explanations)

LIME [66] explains a complex model f by approximating it locally with an interpretable model g (e.g., a sparse linear model).

The local explanation $g^*(x)$ is obtained by solving:

$$g^*(x) := \operatorname*{arg\,min}_{g \in G} \mathcal{L}(f, g, \pi_x) + \Omega(g) \tag{7.2}$$

where G is a class of interpretable models (e.g., sparse linear models), $\mathcal{L}(f, g, \pi_x) = \sum_{z \in \mathcal{Z}} \pi_x(z)(f(z) - g(z))^2$ is a weighted fidelity loss over a set $\mathcal{Z}$ of perturbed samples generated around x, measuring agreement between f and g in the neighborhood of x, π_x is a proximity kernel (e.g., exponential kernel $\pi_x(z) = \exp(-\|z - x\|^2/\sigma^2)$) that weights samples based on their distance to x, and $\Omega(g)$ penalizes the complexity of the explanation (e.g., the number of non-zero coefficients). LIME generates a dataset of perturbed samples around x, queries the black box f for labels, and trains g on this weighted dataset. While powerful, LIME suffers from instability: small changes in the sampling procedure can lead to different explanations.

7.3.3 Gradient-Based Methods

For differentiable models, we can use gradients to estimate feature attributions. **Saliency Maps (Vanilla Gradients)** compute $M_i(x) = \left|\frac{\partial f(x)}{\partial x_i}\right|$, measuring the sensitivity of the output to infinitesimal changes in the input. However, Vanilla Gradients suffer from "saturation": gradients can vanish in flat regions of the output landscape even when the corresponding features are important for the prediction. The method is also susceptible to noise in the gradient signal. **Integrated Gradients (IG)** [75] addresses the saturation problem by accumulating gradients along a straight path from a baseline x' (usually a zero vector) to the input x:

$$IG_i(x) = (x_i - x_i') \int_{\alpha=0}^{1} \frac{\partial f(x' + \alpha(x - x'))}{\partial x_i} d\alpha \tag{7.3}$$

where x is the input, x' is the baseline (typically a zero vector or the dataset mean, representing an "uninformative" input), $\alpha \in [0,1]$ is the interpolation parameter, and $\frac{\partial f}{\partial x_i}$ is the gradient of f with respect to feature i. IG satisfies the axiom of **Completeness**: $\sum_{i=1}^{d} IG_i(x) = f(x) - f(x')$.

Proof of Completeness. Consider the path $\gamma(\alpha) = x' + \alpha(x - x')$ for $\alpha \in [0,1]$. By the chain rule:

$$\begin{aligned} \frac{d}{d\alpha} f(\gamma(\alpha)) &= \sum_{i=1}^{d} \frac{\partial f}{\partial x_i}(\gamma(\alpha)) \cdot \frac{d\gamma_i}{d\alpha} \\ &= \sum_{i=1}^{d} \frac{\partial f}{\partial x_i}(\gamma(\alpha)) \cdot (x_i - x_i') \end{aligned} \tag{7.4}$$

where d is the input dimension and $\gamma(\alpha)$ is the path function. Integrating both sides from $\alpha = 0$ to $\alpha = 1$:

$$\int_0^1 \frac{d}{d\alpha} f(\gamma(\alpha)) d\alpha = \int_0^1 \sum_{i=1}^{d} (x_i - x_i') \frac{\partial f}{\partial x_i}(\gamma(\alpha)) d\alpha \tag{7.5}$$

$$f(\gamma(1)) - f(\gamma(0)) = \sum_{i=1}^{d} (x_i - x_i') \int_0^1 \frac{\partial f}{\partial x_i}(\gamma(\alpha)) d\alpha \tag{7.6}$$

$$f(x) - f(x') = \sum_{i=1}^{d} IG_i(x) \tag{7.7}$$

This follows from the fundamental theorem of calculus. ■

7.4 Concept-Based Explanations

Feature attribution tells us *where* the model is looking (e.g., pixels), but not *what* it sees (e.g., "floppy ears"). Concept-based methods bridge this gap.

7.4.1 Concept Bottleneck Models (CBM)

CBMs enforce a structure where the input x is first mapped to a set of human-interpretable concepts c, and then these concepts are used to predict the target y:

$$x \xrightarrow{h} c \xrightarrow{g} y \tag{7.8}$$

where x is the input, c represents the concepts, y is the target, h is the concept mapping function, and g is the prediction function. This architecture allows for **intervenability**: if the model predicts "Wolf" because it wrongly detected "Snow", a human expert can correct the concept "Snow" to "Grass" and observe the updated prediction.

7.4.2 Testing with Concept Activation Vectors (TCAV)

TCAV quantifies the sensitivity of a prediction to a high-level concept (e.g., "striped") even if that concept was not explicitly part of the training labels. It learns a vector v_C in the activation space of a layer that separates examples of the concept from random examples. The conceptual sensitivity is then given by the directional derivative:

$$S_{C,k}(x) := \nabla_{h_k} f(x) \cdot v_C \tag{7.9}$$

where $\nabla_{h_k} f(x)$ is the gradient of the model output f with respect to the activations at layer k, and v_C is the concept vector.

7.5 Evaluating Explanations

Evaluating XAI is notoriously difficult due to the lack of ground truth. Common metrics include **Faithfulness**, which measures if the explanation accurately reflects the model's behavior (e.g., by removing important features and checking if the prediction drops); and **Stability**, which checks if similar inputs yield similar explanations (LIME often fails this). Additionally, **Sanity Checks** [4] are crucial: many saliency methods (like Guided Backprop) act merely as edge detectors and do not depend on the model parameters. It is crucial to verify that randomizing the model weights destroys the explanation.

7.6 Algorithmic Recourse and Counterfactual Explanations

While feature attribution explains *why* a decision was made, counterfactual explanations answer the question: *"What would need to change for the outcome to be different?"*

7.6.1 The Counterfactual Explanation Problem

Definition 7.6.1 — Counterfactual Explanation. Given a classifier $f : \mathcal{X} \to \{0,1\}$, an input x with $f(x) = 0$ (unfavorable outcome), a counterfactual explanation is an input x' such that:

1. $f(x') = 1$ (desired outcome)
2. x' is "close" to x under some distance measure $d(x,x')$

The optimization problem is:

$$x^* = \arg\min_{x' \in \mathcal{X}} d(x,x') \quad \text{s.t.} \quad f(x') = 1 \tag{7.10}$$

where $d(\cdot,\cdot)$ is a distance metric, f is the classifier, and $x' \in \mathcal{X}$ is the counterfactual instance.

The choice of distance function d is critical and encodes assumptions about actionability. Common choices include:

- L_1 norm: Promotes sparsity (few features change)
- L_2 norm: Smooth changes across features
- Weighted norms: Account for feature costs (e.g., changing age is impossible)
- Mahalanobis distance: Account for feature correlations

The closest counterfactual minimizes this distance under feasibility constraints.

Example 7.2 — Counterfactual Explanation for a Rejected Medical Procedure Request. A patient applies for coverage of an expensive joint procedure and is rejected ($f(x) = 0$). The features are: severity_score = 3.1, prior_treatments = 0, bmi = 28, physical_therapy_sessions = 2. A counterfactual explanation using L_1 norm finds the closest approved profile: $x^* = (\text{severity\_score} = 3.1, \text{prior\_treatments} = 1, \text{bmi} = 28, \text{physical\_therapy\_sessions} = 2)$ with $d(x,x^*) = 1$ (only one feature changed). The explanation tells the patient: "Having one prior conservative treatment would have changed the outcome to approved." With DiCE generating diverse counterfactuals, two alternative paths emerge: (1) increase physical therapy sessions to 6 (one change), or (2) complete 4 more therapy sessions and show stable BMI (two changes). These multiple actionable paths empower the patient to choose the most feasible route to approval. ■

7.6.2 Wachter's Method

Wachter et al. [82] proposed solving the unconstrained optimization problem:

$$\min_{x'} \lambda \left(f(x') - y_{\text{target}}\right)^2 + d(x, x') \tag{7.11}$$

where, in this formulation, $f(x') \in [0,1]$ is the model's predicted probability for the desired class, $y_{\text{target}} \in [0,1]$ is the target probability (typically 1 for a positive flip), and λ is a regularization parameter balancing validity and proximity. For differentiable models, this can be solved via gradient descent. The hyperparameter λ balances validity (reaching the desired class) and proximity (staying close to x).

7.6.3 Actionability Constraints

Not all features can be changed (e.g., age, race, place of birth). We partition features into:

- **Immutable**: Cannot be changed under any circumstance ($x'_i = x_i$)
- **Actionable**: Can be changed by the individual
- **Increasing-only**: Can only increase (e.g., education level, years of experience)

The constrained optimization problem becomes:

$$\begin{aligned} \min_{x'} d(x, x') \quad \text{s.t.} \quad & f(x') = 1, \\ & x'_i = x_i \quad \forall i \in \mathscr{I}_{\text{immutable}}, \\ & x'_j \geq x_j \quad \forall j \in \mathscr{I}_{\text{increasing}} \end{aligned} \tag{7.12}$$

where $\mathscr{I}_{\text{immutable}}$ is the set of immutable features and $\mathscr{I}_{\text{increasing}}$ is the set of increasing-only features.

7.6.4 DiCE: Diverse Counterfactual Explanations

A single counterfactual may not be the only option. DiCE [56] generates a diverse set of counterfactuals by adding a diversity term:

$$\begin{aligned} \min_{\{x'_1, \ldots, x'_k\}} & \sum_{i=1}^{k} \left[\lambda_1 \text{yloss}(f(x'_i), 1) + d(x, x'_i)\right] \\ & - \lambda_2 \sum_{i \neq j} \text{dpp\_diversity}(x'_i, x'_j) \end{aligned} \tag{7.13}$$

where k is the number of counterfactuals, yloss is the loss function for the target class, dpp_diversity is the diversity metric, and λ_1, λ_2 are hyperparameters.

7.6.5 Causal Counterfactuals

Standard counterfactual methods may suggest changes that violate causal relationships in the real world. For example, suggesting "lower your BMI without changing your diet or exercise" is infeasible.

Definition 7.6.2 — Causally Grounded Counterfactual. Given an SCM $\mathscr{M}$ with structural equations $V_i = f_i(\mathrm{Pa}_i, U_i)$, a causally grounded counterfactual modifies only the exogenous variables or actionable root causes, then propagates changes through the causal graph:

$$x'_{\text{downstream}} = f_{\text{downstream}}(x'_{\text{actionable}}, u) \tag{7.14}$$

where $x'_{\text{actionable}}$ are the modified actionable variables, u represents exogenous variables, and $f_{\text{downstream}}$ propagates the changes.

This ensures that downstream features are updated consistently according to the causal model.

7.6.6 Recourse Robustness

A critical issue is that the model may change after the counterfactual is provided. If a user follows the recommended changes but the model has been retrained, they may not achieve the desired outcome.

Definition 7.6.3 — Robust Recourse. Assume $f_{\theta'}(\cdot) \in [0,1]$ is a scalar probabilistic score (so the predicted label is $\mathbb{I}(f_{\theta'}(\cdot) \geq 0.5)$). A counterfactual x' provides ε-robust recourse if:

$$f_{\theta'}(x') \geq 0.5 \quad \forall \theta' \in \mathscr{B}(\theta, \varepsilon), \tag{7.15}$$

where $\mathscr{B}(\theta, \varepsilon)$ is the uncertainty set of model parameters with radius ε.

Robust recourse can be achieved by optimizing:

$$\min_{x'} d(x, x') \quad \text{s.t.} \quad \min_{\theta' \in \mathscr{B}(\theta, \varepsilon)} f_{\theta'}(x') \geq 0.5, \tag{7.16}$$

where the constraint ensures the prediction remains valid (i.e., the predicted label is 1) under the worst-case parameter perturbation.

7.6.7 Algorithmic Recourse via Integer Programming

For tree-based models (Random Forests, Gradient Boosted Trees), counterfactual search can be formulated as a Mixed Integer Program (MIP).

For a single decision tree with leaves L and decision paths $\mathscr{P}_\ell$ for each leaf ℓ:

$$\min_{x',z} \quad d(x,x') \tag{7.17}$$

$$\text{s.t.} \quad \sum_{\ell \in L^+} z_\ell = 1 \quad \text{(reach exactly one positive leaf)} \tag{7.18}$$

$$x'_j \leq u_{j,\ell} + M(1 - z_\ell) \quad \forall j,\ell \tag{7.19}$$

$$x'_j \geq l_{j,\ell} - M(1 - z_\ell) \quad \forall j,\ell \tag{7.20}$$

$$z_\ell \in \{0,1\} \tag{7.21}$$

where z_ℓ is a binary variable indicating if leaf ℓ is active, L^+ is the set of positive leaves, $u_{j,\ell}$ and $l_{j,\ell}$ are feature bounds, and M is a large constant.

Exercises

1. **Shapley Values Implementation**:
   (a) Implement the exact Shapley value calculation for a toy model with $N = 4$ features.
   (b) Implement the Monte Carlo approximation and plot the convergence of the estimates as the number of samples increases.
   (c) Compare the results with the `shap` library in Python.
2. **LIME and Stability**:
   (a) Use LIME to explain a Random Forest classifier on the Iris dataset.
   (b) Run LIME multiple times for the same instance with different random seeds. Quantify the stability of the explanations using the Jaccard similarity of the top-k features.
3. **Gradient-Based Explanations**:
   (a) Train a simple CNN on MNIST.
   (b) Implement Vanilla Gradients and Integrated Gradients from scratch.
   (c) Visualize the explanations for a specific digit.
   (d) Perform the "Model Parameter Randomization Test": Randomize the weights of the top layer and check if the heatmap changes significantly.
4. **Concept-Based Explanations**:
   (a) Implement TCAV for a pre-trained ImageNet classifier.
   (b) Define concept directions for textures (striped, dotted, smooth).
   (c) Measure the sensitivity of class predictions (e.g., "zebra") to each concept.
   (d) Compare TCAV scores across different classes to validate concept relevance.
5. **Counterfactual Explanations**:
   (a) Implement Wachter's method for generating counterfactuals.
   (b) Add actionability constraints (immutable features, monotonic features).

   (c) Generate diverse counterfactuals using the DiCE algorithm.
   (d) Evaluate counterfactual quality using proximity, sparsity, and plausibility metrics.
6. **Attention-Based Explanations**:
   (a) Train a Transformer model on a text classification task.
   (b) Visualize attention weights for sample predictions.
   (c) Test if attention weights are faithful explanations by perturbing high-attention tokens.
   (d) Compare attention-based explanations with gradient-based methods on the same inputs.
7. **Explanation Evaluation**:
   (a) Implement the "deletion" and "insertion" faithfulness metrics.
   (b) Compare faithfulness scores for LIME, SHAP, and Integrated Gradients.
   (c) Measure explanation stability under input perturbations.
   (d) Conduct a user study to evaluate explanation comprehensibility.
8. **Rule Extraction**:
   (a) Train a neural network on tabular data (e.g., Patient Health Outcomes).
   (b) Extract decision rules that approximate the network's behavior.
   (c) Measure fidelity: how often do the rules agree with the network?
   (d) Trade off rule complexity (number of rules, conditions) with fidelity.

Chapter 8

Causal Inference and Machine Learning

8.1 The Ladder of Causation

Judea Pearl [60] distinguishes three levels of cognitive ability, known as the "Ladder of Causation".

The first level, **Association** ($P(y \mid x)$), involves observing correlations ("Seeing"), asking how observing X changes belief in Y. This is the domain of standard statistics and most machine learning. The second level, **Intervention** ($P(y \mid \text{do}(x))$), involves acting ("Doing"), asking what happens if we force X to take a value. The third and highest level, **Counterfactuals** ($P(y_x \mid x', y')$), involves imagining ("Why?"), reasoning about hypothetical worlds to determine if X caused Y or what would have happened had we acted differently.

Table 8.1 lays out the three rungs of the ladder—association, intervention, and counterfactuals—together with their notation, the activity each supports, and a representative question.

Table 8.1: Pearl's Ladder of Causation.

Level	Name	Notation	Activity	Typical Question
1	Association	$P(y \mid x)$	Seeing	How does observing X change my belief in Y?
2	Intervention	$P(y \mid \text{do}(x))$	Doing	What happens to Y if I force X to a value?
3	Counterfactual	$P(y_x \mid x', y')$	Imagining	Would Y have been different had X been different?

■ **Example 8.1 — Ladder of Causation in Medical Treatment.** Consider the question "Does a new medication improve patient recovery?"

- **Level 1 (Association)**: We observe that patients using the medication have a 20-percentage-point higher recovery rate: $P(\text{recovery} \mid \text{medication}) = 0.75$ vs. $P(\text{recovery} \mid \text{no medication}) = 0.55$. But is this because the medication works, or because healthier patients are prescribed it?
- **Level 2 (Intervention)**: We conduct a randomized controlled trial, *forcing* random patients to receive the medication regardless of baseline health: $P(\text{recovery} \mid \text{do}(\text{medication})) = 0.68$, while the interventional baseline is

$P(\text{recovery} \mid \text{do}(\text{no medication})) = 0.60$. The causal effect is $0.68 - 0.60 = 0.08$ (an 8-percentage-point improvement), smaller than the observational correlation suggested, because baseline health was a confounder.

- **Level 3 (Counterfactual)**: For a specific patient who was prescribed the medication and recovered, we ask: "Would this patient have recovered without the medication?" Given their excellent baseline health ($U_{\text{health}} =$ excellent), the answer is "probably yes"; the medication was not the cause for *this particular patient.*

■

8.2 Structural Causal Models (SCM)

A Structural Causal Model is a tuple $\mathscr{M} = \langle U, V, \mathscr{F}, P(U) \rangle$ where:

- $U = \{U_1, \ldots, U_m\}$ is a set of exogenous (background) variables determined by factors outside the model.
- $V = \{V_1, \ldots, V_n\}$ is a set of endogenous variables determined by variables in the model.
- $\mathscr{F} = \{f_1, \ldots, f_n\}$ is a set of deterministic structural equations $V_i = f_i(\text{Pa}_i, U_i)$, where $\text{Pa}_i \subseteq V \setminus \{V_i\}$ denotes the endogenous parents of V_i and $U_i \subseteq U$ denotes the exogenous parents. (Stochasticity arises solely through $P(U)$.)
- $P(U)$ is a probability distribution over the exogenous variables.

The model implies a causal diagram, represented as a directed acyclic graph (DAG), where arrows point from parents to children. The directed-edge factorization induced by the DAG is sometimes called the *causal Markov condition*, and the assumption that the *only* conditional independences in the distribution are those entailed by d-separation in the DAG is known as *causal faithfulness*. Combined with *causal sufficiency* (the assumption that there are no unobserved common causes among the modeled variables), these conditions underpin classical causal-discovery theory.

8.2.1 d-Separation

Definition 8.2.1 — d-Separation. Let G be a causal DAG. A path p between nodes X and Y is *d-separated* (or *blocked*) by a set of nodes Z if one of the following holds:

1. **Chain or Fork**: p contains a chain $\cdot \to m \to \cdot$ or a fork $\cdot \leftarrow m \to \cdot$ where the middle node $m \in Z$.
2. **Collider**: p contains a collider $\cdot \to m \leftarrow \cdot$ where the middle node $m \notin Z$ and no descendant of m is in Z.

Nodes X and Y are d-separated by Z (written $X \perp_d Y \mid Z$ in G) if every path between them is d-separated by Z.

The key insight of d-separation is that it characterizes conditional independence in the observational distribution:

Theorem 8.2.1 — Global Markov Property. Let $\mathscr{M} = \langle U, V, \mathscr{F}, P(U) \rangle$ be a Structural Causal Model with DAG G. If variables $X, Y \in V$ are d-separated by a set of variables $Z \subseteq V \setminus \{X, Y\}$ in G, then $X \perp Y \mid Z$ in any distribution $P_{\mathscr{M}}$ consistent with $\mathscr{M}$:

$$X \perp_d Y \mid Z \text{ in } G \quad \Rightarrow \quad X \perp Y \mid Z \text{ in } P_{\mathscr{M}}.$$

Proof Sketch. We sketch the argument by analyzing each case of path blockage. The full formal proof proceeds by induction on path length using the Markov factorization; see [60] for details. Suppose $X \perp_d Y \mid Z$ in G. We must show that $P(y \mid x, z) = P(y \mid z)$ for all values of x, y, z.

Consider the factorization of the joint distribution under the SCM. Since the SCM has a DAG structure, the joint distribution factorizes as:

$$P(v_1, \ldots, v_n) = \prod_{i=1}^{n} P(v_i \mid \mathrm{Pa}_i)$$

where Pa_i are the parents of v_i in the DAG.

Case 1: Chain or Fork blocking. If a path contains a chain $X \to m \to Y$ or fork $X \leftarrow m \to Y$ and $m \in Z$, then we condition on m. In both cases, once we condition on m, the paths are blocked because:

- For the chain $X \to m \to Y$: This path passes through m. When we condition on m, m serves as a sufficient statistic cutting off the dependency along this path.
- For the fork $X \leftarrow m \to Y$: Both X and Y are children of m. Conditioning on m blocks the confounding path.

This follows from the d-separation definition: conditioning on a non-collider node $m \in Z$ blocks chains and forks, severing the dependence between X and Y along that path.

Case 2: Collider blocking. If a path contains a collider $X \to m \leftarrow Y$ and $m \notin Z$ (and no descendant of m is in Z), then this path is already inactive in the observational distribution. The collider acts as a "closed gate"; information cannot flow through it unless we condition on m or one of its descendants. Since we are not conditioning on m or its descendants, the path is blocked, and thus X and Y are independent conditional on Z.

Formally, by the Markov property of DAGs, each variable is conditionally independent of its non-descendants given its parents. Since a collider structure creates a conditional dependency only upon conditioning on the collider, and we are not doing so, the variables separated by the collider remain independent.

In all cases, the paths are blocked, ensuring $X \perp Y \mid Z$ in the distribution. ■

Example 8.2 — d-Separation Analysis: Hiring Decision Network. Consider a causal DAG for a hiring scenario with five nodes:

- E (Education): Years of education
- A (Ability): Latent ability of the candidate
- T (Test Score): Performance on a hiring test
- R (Recommendation): Letter of recommendation
- H (Hired): Whether the candidate is hired

The causal edges are: $A \to E$, $A \to T$, $E \to R$, $T \to H$, $R \to H$. (Both test scores and recommendations directly influence hiring; education influences the recommendation; ability influences both education and test performance.)

Query 1: Are A and H independent given $Z = \{T, R\}$?

We must check all paths from A to H:

1. Path 1: $A \to T \to H$. The middle node T is in Z, so this path is d-separated by the chain rule.
2. Path 2: $A \to E \to R \to H$. The path from A to E to R has middle node $E \notin Z$, but we continue: R is in Z, so the chain $E \to R \to H$ is d-separated by the chain rule.

All paths are blocked, so $A \perp_d H \mid \{T, R\}$ in G, and thus $A \perp H \mid T, R$ in the observational distribution. Intuitively, if we know the test score and recommendation, the candidate's innate ability provides no additional information about hiring.

Query 2: Are E and H independent? (No conditioning set)

Paths from E to H:

1. Path 1: $E \to R \to H$. Middle node $R \notin Z$ (since $Z = \emptyset$), and R is not a collider, so this path is open.
2. Path 2: $E \leftarrow A \to T \to H$. The path contains a fork at A (with $A \notin Z$) and a chain through T (with $T \notin Z$); neither node is a collider, so this path is also open.

Since at least one path is open, $E \not\perp_d H$ in G. Thus, education and hiring are dependent in the observational distribution.

Query 3: Are E and T independent given $Z = \{A\}$?

Paths from E to T:

1. Path: $E \leftarrow A \to T$. This is a fork with middle node $A \in Z$, so the path is d-separated.

Thus, $E \perp_d T \mid A$ in G, and $E \perp T \mid A$ in the observational distribution. Once we know ability, education does not help predict test scores (because both are caused by ability, and conditioning on the cause blocks the dependence).

■

8.3 Interventions and the Do-Operator

The do-operator, denoted $\mathrm{do}(X = x)$, represents an intervention that forces the variable X to take the value x, regardless of the structural equation f_X. Graphically, this corresponds to removing all incoming arrows to X.

The interventional distribution $P(Y \mid \mathrm{do}(X=x))$ is generally different from the observational distribution $P(Y \mid X=x)$.

8.3.1 The Back-Door Criterion

Definition 8.3.1 — Back-Door Criterion. A set of variables Z satisfies the *Back-Door Criterion* relative to an ordered pair (X,Y) if:

1. No node in Z is a descendant of X in the causal DAG.
2. Z blocks every path between X and Y that contains an arrow into X (equivalently, $(X \perp_d Y \mid Z)$ in the subgraph $G_{\overline{X}}$ obtained by removing all arrows *into* X, where $\perp_d$ denotes d-separation).

When the Back-Door Criterion is satisfied, the causal effect is identifiable:

Theorem 8.3.1 — Back-Door Adjustment Formula. If a set of variables Z satisfies the Back-Door Criterion relative to (X,Y), then the causal effect of X on Y is identifiable and equals:

$$P(Y=y \mid \mathrm{do}(X=x)) = \sum_z P(Y=y \mid X=x, Z=z)P(Z=z). \tag{8.1}$$

Proof. We establish this by showing that when the Back-Door Criterion holds, the causal effect equals the conditional probability formula. Let G denote the original causal DAG and $G_{\overline{X}}$ denote the graph with all arrows into X removed.

Step 1: Characterize back-door paths. A back-door path from X to Y is a path that begins with an arrow pointing *into* X. These paths represent confounding bias, since they carry spurious correlation between X and Y that is not due to the causal effect of X on Y. The parent nodes of X are sources of confounding.

Step 2: Apply the truncated factorization formula. Under the SCM $\mathscr{M}$, the joint distribution factorizes as:

$$P(y,x,z) = P(x \mid z)P(y \mid x,z)P(z),$$

where the factorization respects the causal structure: X depends on confounders Z, Y depends on X, Z, and exogenous variables, and Z is autonomous (determined by exogenous variables).

When we perform an intervention $\mathrm{do}(x)$, we replace the equation for X with $X = x$, effectively removing all incoming edges to X. The post-intervention distribution becomes:

$$P(y \mid \mathrm{do}(x), z) = P(y \mid x,z),$$

because condition 2 of the Back-Door Criterion implies that Z blocks every back-door path from X to Y in $G_{\overline{X}}$, so conditioning on Z makes the observational and interventional conditionals coincide stratum-by-stratum.

Step 3: Marginalize over confounders. To obtain the marginal effect of X on Y, we average over the distribution of the confounders:

$$P(y \mid \text{do}(x)) = \sum_z P(y \mid \text{do}(x), z) P(z \mid \text{do}(x)).$$

The key insight is that since Z is not a descendant of X (by condition 1), the intervention $\text{do}(x)$ does not change the distribution of Z:

$$P(z \mid \text{do}(x)) = P(z).$$

This is because intervening on X only affects the structural equation of X and its descendants, not the equations generating Z.

Step 4: Apply the d-separation criterion. Substituting $P(z)$ for $P(z \mid \text{do}(x))$:

$$P(y \mid \text{do}(x)) = \sum_z P(y \mid \text{do}(x), z) P(z) = \sum_z P(y \mid x, z) P(z),$$

where the last equality uses the fact that conditioning on Z blocks all back-door paths from X to Y. Specifically, by condition 2 of the Back-Door Criterion, Z d-separates X from Y in $G_{\overline{X}}$ (the graph with incoming edges to X removed). In the interventional distribution where incoming edges to X are severed, conditioning on Z renders the observational and interventional distributions equivalent: $P(y \mid x, z) = P(y \mid \text{do}(x), z)$, since no confounding paths remain.

Formally, the d-separation condition guarantees that within each stratum of Z, X and Y are causally related without confounding. Thus:

$$P(y \mid \text{do}(x)) = \sum_z P(y \mid x, z) P(z).$$

■

■ **Example 8.3 — Back-Door Criterion: Effect of Exercise on Cardiovascular Health.** Consider the causal graph: Genetics$(Z) \to$ Exercise(X), Genetics$(Z) \to$ Heart Health(Y), Exercise$(X) \to$ Heart Health(Y). We want the causal effect of exercise on heart health. Genetics Z is a confounder (people with certain genetic profiles may exercise more *and* have naturally healthier hearts). The set $Z = \{\text{Genetics}\}$ satisfies the back-door criterion: (1) it is not a descendant of X, and (2) it blocks the back-door path $X \leftarrow Z \to Y$. The adjustment formula gives: $P(Y \mid \text{do}(X = x)) = \sum_z P(Y \mid X = x, Z = z) P(Z = z)$. In practice, we stratify by genetic risk category (e.g., low/medium/high), compute the effect of exercise on heart health within each stratum, and average, removing the confounding bias. ■

8.3.2 The Front-Door Criterion

The Back-Door Criterion (Definition 8.3.1) and its adjustment formula (Theorem 8.3.1) require that all confounders are observed. However, in many applications, key confounders are unobserved, making the Back-Door Criterion inapplicable. The Front-Door Criterion provides an alternative when the causal effect passes entirely through an observed mediator and confounding enters only at the beginning of the causal chain.

Definition 8.3.2 — Front-Door Criterion. A set of variables M (mediators) satisfies the *Front-Door Criterion* relative to an ordered pair (X,Y) in the presence of an unobserved confounder U if:

1. M intercepts all directed paths from X to Y (i.e., every causal path from X to Y passes through at least one node in M).
2. There are no back-door paths from X to M (the causal effect of X on M is unconfounded).
3. All back-door paths from M to Y are blocked by X.

When the Front-Door Criterion is satisfied, the causal effect is identifiable despite the presence of an unobserved confounder:

Theorem 8.3.2 — Front-Door Adjustment Formula. If a set of variables M satisfies the Front-Door Criterion relative to (X,Y) with an unobserved confounder U, then the causal effect of X on Y is identifiable and equals:

$$\begin{aligned} P(Y=y \mid \text{do}(X=x)) = &\sum_m P(M=m \mid X=x) \\ &\times \sum_{x'} P(Y=y \mid X=x', M=m) P(X=x'). \end{aligned} \tag{8.2}$$

Proof. We derive the Front-Door Adjustment Formula using the rules of do-calculus. Let G be the original causal DAG, and suppose $U \to X$ and $U \to Y$ represent the unobserved confounding.

Step 1: Decompose the causal effect. The causal effect of X on Y can be written as:

$$P(y \mid \text{do}(x)) = \sum_m P(m \mid \text{do}(x)) P(y \mid \text{do}(x), m) = \sum_m P(m \mid \text{do}(x)) P(y \mid \text{do}(m)).$$

The first equality is marginalization over M in the post-intervention distribution. The second equality proceeds in two do-calculus steps: first, Rule 2 converts the observational conditioning on m into an intervention $\text{do}(m)$ (since $(Y \perp_d M \mid X)$ in $G_{\bar{X}\underline{M}}$, where M's outgoing edges are removed), giving $P(y \mid \text{do}(x), m) = P(y \mid \text{do}(x), \text{do}(m))$; then Rule 3 drops $\text{do}(x)$ (since $(Y \perp_d X \mid M)$ in $G_{\bar{X}\bar{M}}$), yielding

$P(y \mid \text{do}(x), \text{do}(m)) = P(y \mid \text{do}(m))$. Intuitively, once M is set by intervention, X carries no additional causal information about Y.

Step 2: Identify $P(m \mid \text{do}(x))$ without confounding. By condition 2 of the Front-Door Criterion, there are no back-door paths from X to M. The only path from X to M is the direct causal edge $X \to M$ (and any paths through M's descendants, which do not feed back). Therefore:

$$P(m \mid \text{do}(x)) = P(m \mid x).$$

The observational probability equals the interventional probability because (by condition 2) there are no back-door paths from X to M: U affects X and Y but not M directly, so no confounding path connects X and M through U.

Step 3: Identify $P(y \mid \text{do}(m))$ using back-door adjustment on M to Y with X as the confounder. We seek the causal effect of M on Y. The back-door paths from M to Y go through U. However, U is unobserved, so we cannot directly condition on it. Instead, we use the following key observation:

By condition 3, all back-door paths from M to Y are blocked by conditioning on X. Conditioning on X alone, however, gives the conditional effect $P(y \mid m, x)$ rather than the interventional effect $P(y \mid \text{do}(m))$: under $\text{do}(m)$ the back-door paths from M are severed, but X retains its natural marginal distribution $P(x)$ rather than being held fixed at the observed value. To account for this we average over the natural marginal of X:

$$P(y \mid \text{do}(m)) = \sum_{x'} P(y \mid m, x')P(x'),$$

where x' ranges over all values of X and $P(x')$ is the marginal observational distribution of X. This formula averages the observational probability $P(y \mid m, x')$ over the marginal distribution of X. The key insight is that $P(y \mid m, x')$ represents the conditional probability of Y given M and X, which is unconfounded with respect to M's effect because X blocks all back-door paths from M to Y.

Step 4: Combine the results. Substituting the identified expressions:

$$P(y \mid \text{do}(x)) = \sum_{m} P(m \mid x) \sum_{x'} P(y \mid m, x')P(x').$$

This is the Front-Door Adjustment Formula. It identifies the causal effect by leveraging the mediation structure (condition 1), the absence of confounding for $X \to M$ (condition 2), and the blocking of back-door paths by X (condition 3).

Intuition. The formula works as follows: First, we compute the effect of X on the mediator M observationally ($P(m \mid x)$, unconfounded). Second, for each value of the mediator, we ask: what is the effect of M on Y? To remove the indirect confounding path through $U \to Y$, we compute the average effect conditional on different values of X ($\sum_{x'} P(y \mid m, x')P(x')$). By averaging over all possible values of X, we isolate M's causal effect on Y from the confounding. ∎

■ **Example 8.4 — Front-Door Criterion: Effect of Smoking on Tar Deposition in Lungs.** Consider a scenario where we wish to estimate the causal effect of cigarette smoking (X) on tar deposition in the lungs (Y). However, there is an unobserved confounder U (genetic predisposition or psychological stress) that influences both smoking behavior and lung tar levels directly (perhaps through a separate mechanism like reduced immunity).

The causal mediator is tar in the mouth (M), the direct physical mechanism of smoking: $U \to X$, $U \to Y$, $X \to M$, $M \to Y$. No other paths exist. We verify the Front-Door Criterion:

1. M intercepts all paths from X to Y (there is a direct path $X \to M \to Y$, and no other causal path).
2. There are no back-door paths from X to M (only the edge $X \to M$ connects them, and U does not cause M directly).
3. All back-door paths from M to Y are blocked by X. The only non-causal path from M to Y goes backward through X: $M \leftarrow X \leftarrow U \to Y$. Traversing this path, X is a non-collider (specifically a chain node $U \to X \to M$, with edges aligned through X), so conditioning on X blocks the path. Since M has no parents other than X, there are no other back-door paths. Hence condition 3 is satisfied: all back-door paths from M to Y are blocked by $\{X\}$.

The Front-Door Adjustment Formula gives:

$$P(Y = y \mid \text{do}(X = x)) = \sum_{m} P(M = m \mid X = x) \times \sum_{x'} P(Y = y \mid X = x', M = m) P(X = x').$$

To apply this:

1. Observe smokers and non-smokers, and measure tar in their mouths: $P(m \mid x)$ for $x \in \{\text{smoke}, \text{not smoke}\}$ and various values of m.
2. Observe the relationship between mouth tar and lung tar, conditional on smoking status: $P(y \mid x', m)$.
3. Compute the marginal distribution of smoking: $P(x')$.
4. Use the formula to estimate the causal effect, even though the unobserved confounder is not directly adjusted for.

This demonstrates how the mediation structure and the absence of direct confounding between X and M allow us to identify the effect despite an unobserved confounder. ■

8.4 The Do-Calculus

When the Back-Door Criterion is not applicable (e.g., due to unobserved confounders), we can use the rules of do-calculus to transform interventional probabilities into observational ones. Let $G_{\overline{X}}$ denote the graph with arrows into X removed, and $G_{\underline{X}}$ denote the graph with arrows out of X removed. The three rules are:

- **Rule 1 (Insertion/deletion of observations)**: $P(y \mid \mathrm{do}(x), z, w) = P(y \mid \mathrm{do}(x), w)$ if $(Y \perp Z \mid X, W)_{G_{\overline{X}}}$.
- **Rule 2 (Action/observation exchange)**: $P(y \mid \mathrm{do}(x), \mathrm{do}(z), w) = P(y \mid \mathrm{do}(x), z, w)$ if $(Y \perp Z \mid X, W)_{G_{\overline{X}\underline{Z}}}$.
- **Rule 3 (Insertion/deletion of actions)**: $P(y \mid \mathrm{do}(x), \mathrm{do}(z), w) = P(y \mid \mathrm{do}(x), w)$ if $(Y \perp Z \mid X, W)_{G_{\overline{X}\overline{Z(W)}}}$, where $Z(W)$ is the set of Z-nodes that are not ancestors of any W-node in $G_{\overline{X}}$.

In plain English: Rule 3 lets us drop an intervention $\mathrm{do}(z)$ entirely whenever the Z-variables we would be intervening on do not matter for Y once X is fixed and W is observed. The qualifier "Z is not an ancestor of any W" is exactly what makes the rule sound: if a Z-node were upstream of a conditioned-on W-node, intervening on it could still influence the observed evidence and thus influence Y.

Proof of Rule 1 (Insertion/Deletion of Observations). Rule 1 permits ignoring an observed variable Z in an interventional distribution when it is conditionally independent of Y in the manipulated graph $G_{\overline{X}}$.

Claim: If $(Y \perp Z \mid X, W)_{G_{\overline{X}}}$, then $P(y \mid \mathrm{do}(x), z, w) = P(y \mid \mathrm{do}(x), w)$.

Proof: The post-intervention distribution under $\mathrm{do}(x)$ is obtained by replacing the structural equation for X with $X = x$, which graphically corresponds to removing all incoming edges to X. The resulting graph is $G_{\overline{X}}$.

Under the truncated factorization formula, the post-intervention distribution of Y given $X = x$ depends only on the subgraph containing Y and its ancestors in $G_{\overline{X}}$ (in which X has no parents). Specifically:

$$P(y \mid \mathrm{do}(x), w) = \sum_z P(y \mid z, x, w) P(z \mid x, w).$$

Now, if $(Y \perp Z \mid X, W)$ in $G_{\overline{X}}$, then by the d-separation theorem (Theorem 8.2.1), we have the conditional independence:

$$P(y \mid x, z, w) = P(y \mid x, w) \quad \text{in any distribution consistent with } G_{\overline{X}}.$$

Moreover, since the conditioning set (X, W) includes X (which has no incoming edges in $G_{\overline{X}}$ because we removed them), and Z is d-separated from Y by (X, W), the probability of Z given (X, W) is not affected by Y:

$$P(z \mid x, w) \text{ is independent of } y.$$

Therefore, in the truncated distribution induced by $\mathrm{do}(x)$ the joint factorizes according to $G_{\overline{X}}$, so by the global Markov property the conditional independence $(Y \perp Z \mid X, W)_{G_{\overline{X}}}$ transfers to the post-interventional law. Hence observing Z adds no information about Y:

$$P(y \mid \mathrm{do}(x), z, w) = P(y \mid \mathrm{do}(x), w).$$

Marginalizing over z then recovers the same right-hand side, confirming the identity:

$$\begin{aligned}\sum_z P(y \mid \mathrm{do}(x), z, w)\, P(z \mid \mathrm{do}(x), w) &= \sum_z P(y \mid \mathrm{do}(x), w)\, P(z \mid \mathrm{do}(x), w) \\ &= P(y \mid \mathrm{do}(x), w), \end{aligned} \tag{8.3}$$

which is precisely the statement that observing Z adds no information about Y given (X,W) in the truncated distribution. Thus

$$P(y \mid \mathrm{do}(x), z, w) = P(y \mid \mathrm{do}(x), w),$$

as claimed by Rule 1. ■

Proof Sketch of Rule 2 (Action/Observation Exchange). Rule 2 permits exchanging an intervention $\mathrm{do}(z)$ for an observation of z when Y is conditionally independent of Z in the graph $G_{\bar{X}\underline{Z}}$.

The graph $G_{\bar{X}\underline{Z}}$ represents a scenario where we have intervened on X (removing incoming edges) and removed all outgoing edges from Z. Removing outgoing edges from Z corresponds to treating Z as if no information flows from it to its descendants, i.e., as if Z is determined by an intervention rather than by the natural structural equations.

If $(Y \perp Z \mid X,W)_{G_{\bar{X}\underline{Z}}}$, then within the post-intervention regime, Z conveys no additional information about Y beyond (X,W). This means the specific mechanism by which Z is generated is irrelevant to the distribution of Y. Therefore, whether we force Z to a value by intervention $\mathrm{do}(z)$ or simply observe it, the resulting distribution of Y is the same:

$$P(y \mid \mathrm{do}(x), \mathrm{do}(z), w) = P(y \mid \mathrm{do}(x), z, w).$$

The exchange is valid because the conditional independence holds in the post-intervention graph, guaranteeing that the mechanism generating Z does not affect Y. ■

Proof Sketch of Rule 3 (Insertion/Deletion of Actions). Rule 3 permits removing an intervention $\mathrm{do}(z)$ entirely when Y is conditionally independent of Z in the graph $G_{\bar{X}\bar{Z}(W)}$.

The graph $G_{\bar{X}\bar{Z}(W)}$ represents a double intervention: arrows into X are removed, and arrows into the subset $Z(W) \subseteq Z$ (the Z-nodes that are *not* ancestors of any W-node in $G_{\bar{X}}$) are also removed. This graph depicts a world where both X and $Z(W)$ are determined by interventions.

The condition $(Y \perp Z \mid X,W)_{G_{\bar{X}\bar{Z}(W)}}$ asserts that in this double-intervention regime, Z is independent of Y given (X,W). This means that the intervention on $Z(W)$ has no causal effect on Y; all paths from Z to Y are either blocked by (X,W)

or pass through nodes outside $Z(W)$ (which are not intervened upon, so those effects are captured in W). Therefore:

$$P(y \mid \text{do}(x), \text{do}(z), w) = P(y \mid \text{do}(x), w),$$

and the intervention $\text{do}(z)$ can be dropped. Intuitively, if intervening on Z does not change the distribution of Y once we have intervened on X and observed W, then the action on Z is redundant and provides no additional control. ■

Shpitser and Pearl [71] proved that these three rules are complete: if a causal effect is identifiable, it can be derived using these rules.

8.5 Counterfactuals

Counterfactual reasoning is the highest rung of Pearl's Ladder of Causation. It asks: "Given specific observations from a particular individual, what would have happened under a different action?" This level of reasoning requires not only the causal model but also knowledge of the specific exogenous factors (the unobserved "luck") that affect this individual.

Definition 8.5.1 — Counterfactual Variable. Let $\mathcal{M} = \langle U, V, \mathcal{F}, P(U) \rangle$ be a Structural Causal Model. For a variable $Y \in V$, an exogenous vector U, and an action $\text{do}(X = x)$, the *counterfactual* $Y_x(U)$ is the value of Y that would result from executing the action $\text{do}(X = x)$ in a modified model $\mathcal{M}_x$ (where X is set to x in the structural equation), while using the *same* exogenous variables U from the original world. Formally, $Y_x(U)$ is obtained by solving *all* structural equations of $\mathcal{M}_x$ simultaneously with the given U:

$$Y_x(U) = Y^{\mathcal{M}_x}(U),$$

where $\mathcal{M}_x$ is the modified model with the equation for X replaced by $X = x$, and $Y^{\mathcal{M}_x}(U)$ denotes the unique solution for Y under $\mathcal{M}_x$. When X is a direct parent of Y, this reduces to $Y_x(U) = f_Y(x, \text{Pa}_Y(\mathcal{M}_x), U_Y)$.

Definition 8.5.2 — Counterfactual Distribution. The counterfactual distribution $P(Y_x = y \mid X = x', Y = y')$ answers: "Given observed values $X = x'$ and $Y = y'$ in the actual world, what is the probability that Y would equal y if we were to set $X = x$ in a counterfactual world with the same exogenous variables?"

More generally, the counterfactual distribution given evidence E is:

$$P(Y_x = y \mid E) = \sum_u P(Y_x = y \mid U = u) P(U = u \mid E),$$

where $P(U = u \mid E)$ is the posterior distribution of the exogenous variables given the evidence.

Computing counterfactuals involves three steps, known as the *three-step process*:

1. **Abduction (Inference)**: Use the evidence E (observed values in the actual world) to infer the posterior distribution of the exogenous variables: $P(U \mid E)$. This identifies "which world we are in", i.e., the specific realization of luck.
2. **Action (Modification)**: Replace the structural equation for X with the counterfactual value $X = x$. This creates a counterfactual model $\mathscr{M}_x$ in which we imagine taking action x.
3. **Prediction (Deduction)**: Propagate the values through the modified structural equations using the posterior $P(U \mid E)$. Compute the distribution of Y in the counterfactual model using the same exogenous variables.

The same counterfactual semantics can be visualized using a *single-world intervention graph* (SWIG) or a *twin network*, both of which expose potential-outcome variables as nodes in a single DAG and clarify which interventions act on which copies of the system.

Theorem 8.5.1 — Computability of Counterfactuals in a Fully Specified SCM. Let $\mathscr{M} = \langle U, V, \mathscr{F}, P(U) \rangle$ be a fully specified structural causal model (i.e., the structural functions $\{f_i\}$ and the prior $P(U)$ are known). Then for any evidence E and any action $\mathrm{do}(X = x)$, the counterfactual distribution $P(Y_x \mid E)$ of Definition 8.5.1 can be computed via the three-step (abduction–action–prediction) procedure. Without such a fully specified SCM, counterfactual distributions are in general *not* identifiable from the observational and interventional distributions alone; additional structural assumptions (e.g., linearity, monotonicity, or a fully specified noise model) are required.

Proof. By the three-step process, we compute:

Step 1 (Abduction): The posterior $P(u \mid X = x', Y = y')$ is obtained via Bayes' rule (assuming $P(X = x', Y = y') > 0$):

$$P(u \mid X = x', Y = y') = \frac{P(y' \mid u, x')\, P(x' \mid u)\, P(u)}{P(y', x')}.$$

Within the fully specified SCM, $P(u)$ is given by the model and $P(y' \mid u, x')$, $P(x' \mid u)$ are determined by the structural equations together with $P(U)$; $P(y', x')$ is then their marginalization over U.

Step 2 (Action): The modified model $\mathscr{M}_x$ is obtained by replacing the structural equation for X. This is part of the causal model specification and does not require identification.

Step 3 (Prediction): For each possible value of U, the output $Y_x(U)$ is determined by the structural equations in the modified model $\mathcal{M}_x$: given $U = u$, the counterfactual $Y_x(u)$ is computed by solving all structural equations in $\mathcal{M}_x$ simultaneously. Thus:

$$P(Y_x = y \mid X{=}x', Y{=}y') = \sum_u \mathbb{I}(Y_x(u) = y)\, P(U = u \mid X{=}x', Y{=}y')$$
$$= \mathbb{E}_{U|X=x',Y=y'}\left[\mathbb{I}(Y_x(U) = y)\right]. \tag{8.4}$$

Since $P(U \mid X = x', Y = y')$ has been computed in step 1, and the structural equations are part of the model, the counterfactual distribution is fully computable. ■

■ **Example 8.5 — Counterfactual Inference in a Linear SCM; illustrating Theorem 8.5.1.** Consider a simple linear structural causal model representing a student's academic success:

$$X = U_X, \quad \text{(Study hours, autonomous)} \tag{8.5}$$
$$Y = \beta X + U_Y, \quad \text{(Test score, depends on study hours and innate ability)} \tag{8.6}$$

where $U_X \sim N(0, \sigma_X^2)$ and $U_Y \sim N(0, \sigma_Y^2)$ are independent exogenous variables, and $\beta = 0.5$ is the structural coefficient.

Observation: We observe a particular student: $X = 10$ hours of study, $Y = 8$ out of 10 on the test.

Question: If the student had studied $X' = 5$ hours instead, what score would they have obtained? Compute $P(Y_5 \mid X = 10, Y = 8)$.

Solution:

Step 1: Abduction. Given the observation $X = 10, Y = 8$, infer the posterior distribution of exogenous variables.

$$P(U \mid X = 10, Y = 8) \propto P(Y = 8 \mid X = 10, U)P(X = 10 \mid U)P(U).$$

From $X = U_X$, we have $U_X = 10$.
From $Y = 0.5X + U_Y = 0.5 \cdot 10 + U_Y = 5 + U_Y$, and the observation $Y = 8$:

$$8 = 5 + U_Y \implies U_Y = 3.$$

Under the structural equations, the observation uniquely determines the exogenous variables: $U_X = 10$ and $U_Y = 3$.

Step 2: Action. We imagine a counterfactual world where the student studied $X' = 5$ hours. We replace the equation for X with the constant $X = 5$, leaving the equation for Y and the value of U_Y unchanged:

$$X = 5, \quad \text{(intervened)} \tag{8.7}$$
$$Y_5 = 0.5 \cdot 5 + U_Y = 2.5 + 3 = 5.5. \tag{8.8}$$

Step 3: Prediction. Using the same exogenous variable $U_Y = 3$ (the student's innate ability), the counterfactual test score with $X = 5$ hours of study would be:

$$Y_5(U_X = 10, U_Y = 3) = 0.5 \cdot 5 + 3 = 5.5.$$

Interpretation: The student scored 8 out of 10 when they studied 10 hours. If they had only studied 5 hours, they would have scored 5.5 out of 10. The difference, $8 - 5.5 = 2.5$, is the causal effect of the additional 5 hours of study for this specific student. Notably, this is the same as the average treatment effect ($\beta = 0.5 \times 5 = 2.5$) because the model is linear and the student's innate ability ($U_Y = 3$) does not interact with study hours.

Nonlinear extension: Suppose instead $Y = \beta X + \gamma X U_Y + U_Y$ (heterogeneous effect). Then:

$$8 = 0.5 \cdot 10 + \gamma \cdot 10 \cdot U_Y + U_Y \implies 3 = (10\gamma + 1)U_Y \implies U_Y = \frac{3}{10\gamma + 1}.$$

If $\gamma = 0.1$, then $U_Y = 3/2 = 1.5$. The counterfactual would be:

$$Y_5 = 0.5 \cdot 5 + 0.1 \cdot 5 \cdot 1.5 + 1.5 = 2.5 + 0.75 + 1.5 = 4.75.$$

Now the counterfactual effect depends on the specific student's ability, illustrating how heterogeneous effects emerge naturally in nonlinear counterfactual reasoning. ■

8.6 Causal Fairness

Standard fairness metrics (like Demographic Parity) are based on correlations. Causal fairness defines fairness in terms of the causal graph. The central notion is *counterfactual fairness* (Definition 5.8.1), which requires that a predictor $\hat{Y}$ would not change its output for an individual if their sensitive attribute A had been different, holding all non-descendant background variables U constant:

$$P(\hat{Y}_{A \leftarrow a}(u) = y \mid X = x, A = a) = P(\hat{Y}_{A \leftarrow a'}(u) = y \mid X = x, A = a) \tag{8.9}$$

The causal perspective (Definitions 8.3.1 and 8.3.2; adjustment formulas in Theorems 8.3.1 and 8.3.2) enriches the fairness analysis by distinguishing between direct discrimination (the direct causal effect of A on $\hat{Y}$) and indirect effects flowing through mediators; see Section 5.8 for the full treatment including path-specific fairness and implementation strategies.

Exercises

1. **Simpson's Paradox:**

   (a) Construct a dataset where $P(Y = 1 \mid T = 1) > P(Y = 1 \mid T = 0)$ but $P(Y = 1 \mid \mathrm{do}(T = 1)) < P(Y = 1 \mid \mathrm{do}(T = 0))$.
   (b) Draw the causal graph and identify the confounder.
   (c) Calculate the Average Treatment Effect (ATE) using the adjustment formula.
2. **Do-Calculus**:
   (a) Prove Rule 1 of the do-calculus using d-separation.
   (b) Given the "Front-Door" graph $X \to Z \to Y$ with an unobserved confounder U affecting X and Y, prove that $P(y \mid \mathrm{do}(x))$ is identifiable and derive the formula.
3. **Counterfactuals**:
   (a) Consider a linear SCM: $X = U_X$, $Y = \beta X + U_Y$.
   (b) Given observation $X = 1, Y = 2$, calculate the counterfactual $Y_{X=0}$.
   (c) How does the result change if the relationship is nonlinear?
4. **Causal Discovery**:
   (a) Implement the PC algorithm for learning causal graphs from observational data.
   (b) Generate synthetic data from a known SCM and test if PC recovers the correct skeleton.
   (c) Compare with score-based methods (GES) and continuous optimization (NOTEARS).
   (d) Discuss the identifiability assumptions required by each method, including the role of *additive noise models* (e.g., LiNGAM) and the FCI algorithm for latent-confounder settings.
5. **Instrumental Variables**:
   (a) Explain why naive regression fails when there is unmeasured confounding.
   (b) Implement Two-Stage Least Squares (2SLS) for a simple model with one instrument.
   (c) Verify the validity assumptions: relevance ($\mathrm{Cov}(Z,X) \neq 0$) and exclusion restriction, together with monotonicity of compliers, which together identify the local average treatment effect (LATE).
   (d) Compare 2SLS estimates with naive OLS on simulated data with known ground truth.
6. **Causal Effect Estimation**:
   (a) Implement propensity score matching for ATE estimation, assuming ignorability and SUTVA.
   (b) Compare with Inverse Probability Weighting (IPW) and Doubly Robust estimation, including targeted maximum likelihood (TMLE).
   (c) Use the IHDP benchmark dataset to evaluate bias and variance of different estimators on the average treatment effect on the treated (ATT) and other estimands.

   (d) Implement CATE estimation using causal forests or BART, and contrast with meta-learners such as the T-learner, S-learner, X-learner, and R-learner.
7. **Counterfactual Fairness Implementation**:
   (a) Build a causal graph for a hiring scenario with features: education, experience, gender, and qualifications.
   (b) Identify which features are descendants of the sensitive attribute.
   (c) Train a counterfactually fair classifier that only uses non-descendants.
   (d) Compare accuracy and fairness metrics with an unconstrained classifier.
8. **Mediation Analysis**:
   (a) Decompose the total effect into direct and indirect effects for a simple mediation model $X \rightarrow M \rightarrow Y$.
   (b) Derive the natural direct effect (NDE) and natural indirect effect (NIE).
   (c) Implement the mediation formula and test on simulated data.
   (d) Discuss when mediation effects are identifiable under unmeasured confounding.

Distributed Learning and Decision Making

Contents of This Part

Chapter 9
Federated Learning

9.1 Introduction to Decentralized Learning

Federated Learning (FL) is a distributed machine learning paradigm where multiple clients (e.g., mobile devices, hospitals) collaboratively train a model under the coordination of a central server, without sharing their raw training data. The core principle is "bring the code to the data, not the data to the code."

This paradigm primarily addresses **Data Privacy and Sovereignty** by design. Unlike centralized training where all data is collected in one location, creating a single point of failure, FL ensures data remains distributed. Each client stores its own data locally and only shares model gradients or weight updates with the central server [86]. This architectural principle enables compliance with rigorous data localization requirements and privacy standards without exposing raw records to external entities. For instance, in a medical context, hospitals can collaborate to train a disease prediction model without ever exchanging patient records, thus maintaining institutional data sovereignty. However, privacy is not absolute, since gradients can leak information about training data through inversion attacks, necessitating additional protections like differential privacy.

Additionally, FL offers significant **Communication Efficiency**. In many settings, transmitting entire datasets is prohibitive due to bandwidth, energy, or storage constraints. FL transmits only model updates, which are proportional to the model size rather than the dataset size. For a model with d parameters, each communication round exchanges $O(d)$ values, which is typically much smaller than transferring $O(n)$ data samples when $n \gg d$. Further optimizations like gradient compression and quantization can reduce communication costs by orders of magnitude, making distributed training viable even over constrained networks [64].

9.2 Federated Optimization Algorithms

The goal is to minimize the global objective function:

$$\min_{w} F(w) = \sum_{k=1}^{K} p_k F_k(w), \quad F_k(w) = \frac{1}{n_k} \sum_{i \in \mathscr{D}_k} \ell(w; x_i, y_i) \tag{9.1}$$

where K is the number of clients, $n_k = |\mathscr{D}_k|$ is the number of samples on client k, $n = \sum_{k=1}^{K} n_k$ is the total number of samples, $p_k = n_k/n$ is the weight of client k, $F_k(w)$ is the local loss function, $\mathscr{D}_k$ is the local dataset, and ℓ is the per-sample loss.

9.2.1 Federated Averaging (FedAvg)

FedAvg [52] is the standard algorithm for FL. It combines local SGD on clients with model averaging on the server.

Algorithm 9.1 states the full procedure.

Algorithm 9.1 Federated Averaging (FedAvg)

Server: Initialize w_0
for round $t = 1$ to T **do**
    Server selects a subset of clients $S_t \subseteq \{1,\dots,K\}$
    Server broadcasts w_t to all $k \in S_t$
    for client $k \in S_t$ **in parallel do**
        $w_{t+1}^k \leftarrow \text{ClientUpdate}(k, w_t)$
    end for
    Server aggregates: $w_{t+1} \leftarrow \sum_{k\in S_t} \frac{n_k}{\sum_{j\in S_t} n_j} w_{t+1}^k$
end for
Function ClientUpdate(k, w):
$\mathcal{B} \leftarrow$ (split local data $\mathcal{D}_k$ into batches)
for local epoch $e = 1$ to E **do**
    for batch $b \in \mathcal{B}$ **do**
        $w \leftarrow w - \eta \nabla \ell(w; b)$
    end for
end for
return w

9.2.2 Handling Statistical Heterogeneity (FedProx)

In real-world settings, data is non-IID (not Independent and Identically Distributed).

For example, one user may only take photos of cats, while another only takes photos of dogs. This "client drift" or "data heterogeneity" causes local models to diverge significantly from the global optimum, as different clients optimize their local losses toward different solutions. This is a fundamental challenge that distinguishes federated learning from distributed learning on homogeneous data.

FedProx [45] addresses this by adding a proximal regularization term to the local objective. Writing w^t for the round-t global model (superscript) to distinguish it from the local optimization variable w, client k solves:

$$\min_w F_k(w) + \frac{\mu}{2}\|w - w^t\|^2 \tag{9.2}$$

where w^t is the global model from the previous round and μ is the proximal term coefficient. This term acts as a regularizer that encourages local updates to stay within a neighborhood of the global model, preventing excessive client drift. The hyperparameter $\mu > 0$ controls the strength of this constraint. When μ is large, clients are forced to make only small local updates, stabilizing convergence.

When μ is small, clients have more freedom to optimize their local objectives. FedProx can be interpreted as a primal-dual method where we implicitly handle the heterogeneity through this proximal term.

9.2.3 Convergence Analysis

Understanding the convergence of federated algorithms is crucial for practical deployment. We analyze FedAvg under the simplifying assumption that all K clients participate in every round and have equal dataset sizes, so the data-proportional weights reduce to uniform averaging $\frac{1}{K}$.

Assumption 9.2.1 — Smoothness. Each local objective F_k is L-smooth:

$$\|\nabla F_k(w) - \nabla F_k(w')\| \leq L\|w - w'\| \quad \forall w, w' \tag{9.3}$$

where L is the Lipschitz constant of the gradient.

Assumption 9.2.2 — Bounded Variance. The stochastic gradients have bounded variance:

$$\mathbb{E}[\|\nabla F_k(w;\xi) - \nabla F_k(w)\|^2] \leq \sigma_k^2 \tag{9.4}$$

where ξ represents the randomness in the mini-batch, and σ_k^2 is the variance bound.

Assumption 9.2.3 — Bounded Heterogeneity. The gradient dissimilarity across clients is bounded:

$$\frac{1}{K}\sum_{k=1}^{K} \|\nabla F_k(w) - \nabla F(w)\|^2 \leq \sigma_g^2 \tag{9.5}$$

where σ_g^2 bounds the dissimilarity between local and global gradients.

Theorem 9.2.1 — FedAvg Convergence. Under Assumptions 9.2.1–9.2.3, for non-convex objectives, FedAvg with an appropriately tuned learning rate $\eta = \Theta(\sqrt{KE/T})$ achieves:

$$\frac{1}{T}\sum_{t=1}^{T} \mathbb{E}[\|\nabla F(w_t)\|^2] \leq O\left(\frac{1}{\sqrt{TKE}} + \frac{E\sigma_g^2}{K}\right) \tag{9.6}$$

where T is the total number of rounds, K is the number of clients (all of which participate each round, by the assumption above), and E is the number of local epochs.

Detailed Proof Sketch. The key challenge in federated optimization is handling the heterogeneity-induced drift. We decompose the convergence analysis into three parts: tracking progress toward the optimum, bounding variance from stochastic gradients, and bounding drift from heterogeneous local updates.

Virtual Sequence Argument and Drift Decomposition: Let $w_{k,t}^{(e)}$ denote the local model on client k after e local epochs in round t, with $w_{k,t}^{(0)} = w_t$ (the global model). We construct a *virtual sequence* $\{\tilde{w}_t\}$ representing what the server would see if all clients performed a single stochastic gradient step, i.e., $\tilde{w}_{t+1} = w_t - \frac{\eta}{K}\sum_{k=1}^{K} \nabla F_k(w_t; \xi_{k,t})$, where $\xi_{k,t}$ is a mini-batch sample. In expectation, $\mathbb{E}[\tilde{w}_{t+1}] = w_t - \eta \nabla F(w_t)$.

Define the drift as the difference between the actual aggregated update and the virtual sequence:

$$\begin{aligned}\text{Drift}_t &= w_{t+1} - \tilde{w}_{t+1} \\ &= \frac{1}{K}\sum_{k=1}^{K}(w_{k,t}^{(E)} - w_t) - (-\eta \nabla F(w_t))\end{aligned} \tag{9.7}$$

The aggregated update includes E local epochs per client, while the virtual sequence uses only one epoch.

Bounding the Drift Term: By smoothness (Assumption 9.2.1), taking expectations over the stochastic gradient, a single local SGD step satisfies:

$$\begin{aligned}\mathbb{E}[F_k(w_{k,t}^{(e+1)})] \le F_k(w_{k,t}^{(e)}) - \eta \|\nabla F_k(w_{k,t}^{(e)})\|^2 \\ + \frac{L\eta^2}{2}(\|\nabla F_k(w_{k,t}^{(e)})\|^2 + \sigma_k^2)\end{aligned} \tag{9.8}$$

Summing over E local epochs and aggregating over all clients:

$$\begin{aligned}&\frac{1}{K}\sum_{k=1}^{K}(w_{k,t}^{(E)} - w_t) \\ &= -\eta \frac{1}{K}\sum_{k=1}^{K}\sum_{e=0}^{E-1} \nabla F_k(w_{k,t}^{(e)}) + \text{higher-order terms}\end{aligned} \tag{9.9}$$

The deviation of local gradients from the global gradient is bounded by heterogeneity. Let $\Delta_{k,t}^{(e)} = \nabla F_k(w_{k,t}^{(e)}) - \nabla F(w_t)$ be the difference between local and global gradients at step e. By Assumption 9.2.3 (bounded heterogeneity):

$$\mathbb{E}[\|\Delta_{k,t}^{(0)}\|^2] = \mathbb{E}[\|\nabla F_k(w_t) - \nabla F(w_t)\|^2] \le \sigma_g^2 \tag{9.10}$$

After e local epochs, the local model drifts further from the global model, so heterogeneity accumulates:

$$\mathbb{E}[\text{Drift}_t^2] \lesssim \eta^2 E^2 \sigma_g^2 \tag{9.11}$$

where the quadratic dependence on E arises because each of the E epochs can introduce drift proportional to σ_g^2, and these drifts accumulate.

Convergence of the Virtual Sequence: For the virtual sequence $\tilde{w}_{t+1} = w_t - \eta \nabla F(w_t)$, standard smooth optimization theory gives (using Assumption 9.2.1 smoothness and Assumption 9.2.2 bounded variance):

$$\mathbb{E}[F(\tilde{w}_{t+1})] \leq F(w_t) - \eta \|\nabla F(w_t)\|^2 + \frac{L\eta^2}{2}\sigma^2 \tag{9.12}$$

where $\sigma^2 = \frac{1}{K}\sum_k \sigma_k^2$ is the average variance. Summing over rounds $t = 1$ to T and telescoping gives

$$\frac{1}{T}\sum_{t=1}^{T} \mathbb{E}[\|\nabla F(w_t)\|^2] \leq \frac{F(w_1) - F^*}{\eta T} + \frac{L\eta}{2}\sigma_{\text{eff}}^2. \tag{9.13}$$

Averaging the stochastic gradients over the K clients and their E local steps reduces the effective per-round variance to $\sigma_{\text{eff}}^2 = \sigma^2/(KE)$. Balancing the optimization term $(F(w_1) - F^*)/(\eta T)$ against this variance term with the optimal step size $\eta = \Theta(\sqrt{KE/T})$ then yields a leading term of order

$$O\left(\sqrt{\frac{(F(w_1) - F^*)L\sigma^2}{TKE}}\right) = O\left(\frac{1}{\sqrt{TKE}}\right), \tag{9.14}$$

where the problem constants $F(w_1) - F^*$, L, and σ^2 are absorbed into the $O(\cdot)$.

Impact of Drift on Final Bound: Each round also contributes a heterogeneity-induced drift term $\mathbb{E}[\text{Drift}_t^2] = O(\eta^2 E^2 \sigma_g^2)$, which arises because the E local steps pull each client toward its own local optimum rather than the global one. Carrying this drift through the standard local-SGD analysis (see, e.g., [38]) produces a residual heterogeneity term of order $E\sigma_g^2/K$ in the final bound. This contribution does *not* vanish with more rounds T alone, but it is mitigated by aggregating across more clients K (which averages out client-specific gradient directions).

Combining the virtual sequence bound and drift contribution yields:

$$\frac{1}{T}\sum_{t=1}^{T} \mathbb{E}[\|\nabla F(w_t)\|^2] \leq O\left(\frac{1}{\sqrt{TKE}} + \frac{E\sigma_g^2}{K}\right) \tag{9.15}$$

The first term decreases with communication rounds T and local epochs E (reducing communication per sample). The second term grows linearly with E (more local epochs amplify heterogeneity-driven drift) and shrinks with K (more participating clients average out client-specific gradients).

Reading the bound in plain English: the first term $1/\sqrt{TKE}$ is the standard SGD rate, which improves with more rounds T, more participating clients K, and more local epochs E (because each round processes more data). The second term $E\,\sigma_g^2/K$ is the price of statistical heterogeneity: more local computation per round (large E) lets each client drift further toward its own local optimum, and only averaging across more clients (K) damps this drift. Tuning E is the practical trade-off this theorem makes explicit: too small E wastes communication, too large E destroys convergence. ■

The second term captures the effect of client drift due to heterogeneity. It grows linearly with E, creating a tension: more local computation (E) reduces communication per sample but increases drift; aggregating across more clients K tempers this drift.

9.3 Personalized Federated Learning

When client data distributions are heterogeneous, a single global model may be suboptimal for individual clients. Personalized FL learns models tailored to each client while still leveraging collaborative learning.

9.3.1 Local Fine-Tuning

The simplest approach is to train a global model via FedAvg, then fine-tune locally on each client's data:

$$\begin{aligned} w_k^{(t+1)} &= w_k^{(t)} - \eta\,\nabla F_k(w_k^{(t)}), \quad t = 0, 1, \ldots, T_{\text{local}} - 1, \\ w_k^{(0)} &= w_{\text{global}}, \qquad w_k^* = w_k^{(T_{\text{local}})} \end{aligned} \tag{9.16}$$

where w_{global} is the trained global model, η is the learning rate, and T_{local} is the number of fine-tuning steps.

9.3.2 Personalized Layers

Decompose the model into shared base layers ϕ and personal head layers ψ_k:

$$f_k(x) = \psi_k(\phi(x)) \tag{9.17}$$

where ϕ is the shared feature extractor and ψ_k is the client-specific head. Only ϕ is federated; each ψ_k remains local. This is effective when feature extraction generalizes but final predictions are client-specific.

9.3.3 MAML-based Personalization

Per-FedAvg uses Model-Agnostic Meta-Learning (MAML) to find a global model that adapts quickly to each client. Rigorously, for each client k, we split local data into support D_k^{sup} and query D_k^{qry} sets:

$$\min_w \sum_{k=1}^{K} \mathscr{L}(w - \alpha \nabla \mathscr{L}(w; D_k^{\text{sup}}); D_k^{\text{qry}}) \tag{9.18}$$

where α is the inner loop learning rate. The global model is optimized so that one gradient step on the support set yields good performance on the query set. This creates models that personalize efficiently.

9.3.4 Mixture of Experts

Train multiple global models (experts) and learn a client-specific mixture:

$$f_k(x) = \sum_{j=1}^{M} \pi_{kj} f_j(x) \tag{9.19}$$

where f_j are the expert models and π_{kj} are the mixing coefficients for client k.

9.4 Communication Efficiency

Communication is often the bottleneck in FL. Several techniques reduce communication costs.

9.4.1 Gradient Compression

Quantization: Reduce gradient precision from 32-bit floats to lower bit representations.

$$[Q(g)]_i = \|g\|_2 \cdot \text{sign}(g_i) \cdot \xi_i \tag{9.20}$$

where g is the gradient vector, $\text{sign}(\cdot)$ is the element-wise sign function, and $\xi_i \sim \text{Bernoulli}(|g_i|/\|g\|_2)$ independently for each coordinate i. Since $|g_i| \leq \|g\|_2$ for every i, the Bernoulli probability is well defined. This stochastic quantization is unbiased: $\mathbb{E}[Q(g)] = g$.

Sparsification: Only communicate top-k gradient components:

$$[\text{Top}_k(g)]_i = g_i \cdot \mathbb{I}(|g_i| \geq |g|_{(k)}) \tag{9.21}$$

where the indicator $\mathbb{I}(\cdot)$ applies element-wise, and $|g|_{(k)}$ is the k-th largest magnitude among the components of g. Combined with error feedback (accumulating dropped components), this preserves convergence.

Low-Rank Approximation: Approximate gradient matrices with low-rank decompositions:

$$G \approx UV^T \tag{9.22}$$

where G is the gradient matrix, $U \in \mathbb{R}^{m \times r}$, $V \in \mathbb{R}^{n \times r}$, and r is the rank of the approximation. For rank $r \ll \min(m,n)$, this reduces communication from $O(mn)$ to $O((m+n)r)$.

9.5 Privacy and Security in FL

While FL offers better privacy than centralized training, it is not perfectly secure.

9.5.1 Gradient Inversion Attacks

Gradients contain information about the training data. In "Deep Leakage from Gradients" (DLG), an attacker (the server) tries to reconstruct the private input x and label y by optimizing dummy data x', y' to match the received gradient $\nabla_W \mathcal{L}$:

$$x^*, y^* = \arg\min_{x',y'} \|\nabla_W \mathcal{L}(x', y'; W) - \nabla_W \mathcal{L}(x, y; W)\|^2 \tag{9.23}$$

where $\nabla_W \mathcal{L}(x, y; W)$ is the observed gradient and (x', y') are the dummy input and label. This optimization can surprisingly recover recognizable images from gradients in deep networks.

9.5.2 Secure Aggregation

To prevent the server from inspecting individual updates, Secure Aggregation (SecAgg) uses Multi-Party Computation (MPC). Clients add random masks to their updates such that the masks cancel out when summed:

$$\sum_k (w^k + r_k) = \sum_k w^k + \sum_k r_k = \sum_k w^k \quad (\text{if } \sum_k r_k = 0) \tag{9.24}$$

where w^k is the update from client k, and r_k are random masks designed to sum to zero. Common protocols use pairwise masking based on Diffie–Hellman key exchange.

9.6 Robustness to Byzantine Attacks

Malicious clients may send corrupted updates to poison the global model (e.g., to induce a backdoor). Standard averaging is sensitive to outliers. We formally define Byzantine fault tolerance and analyze robust aggregation rules.

Definition 9.6.1 — Byzantine Fault Tolerance in FL. A federated learning system is said to be (f,ε)-Byzantine robust if, in the presence of at most f malicious clients (out of n total clients, where f here denotes the Byzantine count rather than a function), the global model maintained by the server converges to a solution that is at most ε-close to the optimal solution of the non-Byzantine clients' aggregate objective. Formally, if S is the set of honest clients with $|S| \geq n-f$, and w^* minimizes $\mathbb{E}_{k\in S}[F_k(w)]$, then:

$$\mathbb{E}[\|w_T - w^*\|] \leq \varepsilon \tag{9.25}$$

for sufficiently large T, regardless of the Byzantine clients' strategy.

9.6.1 Coordinate-wise Median Aggregation

The coordinate-wise median replaces the arithmetic mean with the median for each dimension:

$$w_{t+1}^{(i)} = \text{median}(w_{t+1}^{(i,1)}, w_{t+1}^{(i,2)}, \ldots, w_{t+1}^{(i,n)}) \tag{9.26}$$

where $w_{t+1}^{(i,k)}$ is the i-th coordinate of the update from client k.

Theorem 9.6.1 — Byzantine Tolerance of Coordinate-wise Median. If the median aggregation rule is used in FedAvg, the system is (f,ε)-Byzantine robust for any $f < n/2$.

Proof Sketch. Consider a single coordinate dimension. Without loss of generality, suppose $n-f$ honest clients report values $\{v_1^{\text{honest}}, \ldots, v_{n-f}^{\text{honest}}\}$ (which may be noisy approximations of the true gradient coordinate), and f malicious clients report arbitrary values. For the median to be affected, a Byzantine client's value must swing the median. However, since $f < n/2$, the honest clients constitute a strict majority. When sorted, the median position is at index $\lceil n/2 \rceil$. Since $f < n/2$, the maximum number of Byzantine clients is at most $\lceil n/2 \rceil - 1$, which is strictly less than the minimum number of honest clients ($n - f \geq \lfloor n/2 \rfloor + 1$).

Thus, even if all Byzantine values are at the extreme (either infinitely large or small), the median will still fall within the convex hull of the honest values. Specifically:

$$w_{t+1}^{(i)} \in \text{conv}(v_1^{\text{honest}}, \ldots, v_{n-f}^{\text{honest}}) \tag{9.27}$$

where $\text{conv}(\cdot)$ denotes the convex hull. By standard convergence analysis on convex combinations of bounded updates, and assuming honest clients' gradients satisfy Assumptions 9.2.1–9.2.3, convergence is guaranteed. The median is robust because it depends on the *order statistics*, not on extreme values: changing one Byzantine value does not move the median unless that client occupies a median position, which is impossible when honest clients form a majority. ■

9.6.2 Krum Aggregation

Krum [11] selects a single representative update from the set of received updates, rather than averaging all of them:

$$w_{t+1} = w_{t+1}^{(k^*)} \quad \text{where} \quad k^* = \arg\min_k \sum_{j \in N_k} \|w_{t+1}^{(k)} - w_{t+1}^{(j)}\|^2 \tag{9.28}$$

and N_k is the set of the $n-f-2$ nearest neighbors of update k among the other $n-1$ updates, measured in Euclidean distance $\|\cdot\|_2$.

Proposition 9.6.2 — Krum Resilience Guarantee. If at most f Byzantine clients are present, with $2f+2<n$ (equivalently $f<(n-2)/2$), where n is the total number of clients, then Krum's selected update $w_{t+1}^{(k^*)}$ comes from an honest client, and its squared distance to the empirical mean of the honest updates is bounded by a multiplicative factor times the variance among the honest gradients.

9.6.3 Trimmed Mean Aggregation

Trimmed mean removes a fraction of the largest and smallest updates for each coordinate, then averages the remaining values:

$$w_{t+1}^{(i)} = \frac{1}{n-2f} \sum_{k \in S_i} w_{t+1}^{(i,k)} \tag{9.29}$$

where S_i is the set of indices remaining after removing the f largest and f smallest values for dimension i. This rule is robust to $f<n/2$ Byzantine clients, similar to coordinate-wise median.

9.6.4 Privacy Amplification in Federated Learning

In the Federated Learning setting with secure aggregation, differential privacy can be amplified through client subsampling. Recall from the Privacy chapter that Subsampling Amplification states: if a mechanism is (ε,δ)-DP, then sampling a fraction ρ of the data and applying the mechanism to the subsample gives (ε',δ')-DP for smaller ε'.

In FL, clients are subsampled at each round: $|S_t|/K$ clients participate. This subsampling amplifies the privacy guarantee of the local DP-SGD updates. Specifically, if each client applies $(\varepsilon_{\text{local}},\delta_{\text{local}})$-DP to their local updates (via gradient clipping and noise addition), then the global privacy over T rounds is amplified to:

$$\varepsilon_{\text{global}} \approx \frac{|S_t|}{K} \cdot \sqrt{2T\log(1/\delta)} \cdot \varepsilon_{\text{local}} \tag{9.30}$$

rather than $T \cdot \varepsilon_{\text{local}}$ (naive composition). This is an approximate bound combining subsampling amplification with advanced composition; the exact constants depend on the specific privacy accountant used. The square-root dependence on T (instead of linear) is the benefit of amplification: for a fixed privacy budget, far more rounds can be run (or less aggressive subsampling tolerated) than naive composition would allow.

Combined with Secure Aggregation (see above), which prevents the server from seeing individual updates, the FL system achieves both privacy and robustness: the server cannot inspect individual gradients, a bounded fraction of malicious clients cannot substantially poison updates, and subsampling amplifies privacy at no extra computational cost.

Exercises

1. **FedAvg and non-IID Data**:
   (a) Simulate a FL setting with 10 clients using the MNIST dataset.
   (b) Create a pathological non-IID split where each client has data from only 2 digits.
   (c) Compare the test accuracy of FedAvg with $E = 1$ vs. $E = 5$ local epochs. Explain the trade-off between communication efficiency and convergence stability.
2. **Gradient Inversion**:
   (a) Implement the DLG attack [94] in PyTorch.
   (b) Attempt to recover an image from a ResNet-18 gradient.
   (c) Investigate how the attack success depends on the batch size and the model depth.
3. **Backdoor Attacks**:
   (a) Implement a "pixel pattern" backdoor attack where a client inserts a trigger into their training images and flips the label.
   (b) Measure the "Attack Success Rate" (ASR) on the global model.
   (c) Test if Coordinate-wise Median aggregation defends against this attack.
4. **FedProx Implementation**:
   (a) Implement FedProx with proximal term $\frac{\mu}{2}\|w - w_t\|^2$ in PyTorch.
   (b) Compare convergence with FedAvg on highly non-IID data (Dirichlet($\alpha = 0.1$) partition).
   (c) Study the effect of the proximal parameter μ on convergence speed and final accuracy.
   (d) Analyze client drift by measuring the distance between local and global models during training.
5. **Differential Privacy in FL**:
   (a) Implement DP-FedAvg by adding Gaussian noise to clipped model updates.

   (b) Compute the privacy budget (ε, δ) using the moments accountant.
   (c) Plot the privacy-accuracy trade-off for different noise scales σ.
   (d) Compare user-level and sample-level DP guarantees.

6. **Secure Aggregation**:
   (a) Implement a simplified secure aggregation protocol using Shamir's secret sharing.
   (b) Demonstrate that the server cannot see individual updates but can compute the aggregate.
   (c) Analyze the communication overhead compared to plain FedAvg.
   (d) Test robustness to client dropout during the aggregation protocol.
7. **Personalized Federated Learning**:
   (a) Implement FedPer: train shared lower layers globally, personalized upper layers locally.
   (b) Compare with full fine-tuning and MAML-based personalization.
   (c) Evaluate on CIFAR-10 with heterogeneous label distributions across clients.
   (d) Measure both global test accuracy and per-client personalized accuracy.
8. **Byzantine-Robust Aggregation**:
   (a) Implement Byzantine attacks: random updates, label flipping, model replacement.
   (b) Compare robustness of FedAvg, Krum, Coordinate-wise Median, and Trimmed Mean.
   (c) Determine the maximum fraction of Byzantine clients each aggregation can tolerate.
   (d) Implement FLAME (filtering via model similarity) and evaluate against adaptive attacks.

Chapter 10
Safe Reinforcement Learning

10.1 The Alignment Problem in RL

Reinforcement Learning (RL) agents are optimization machines. They will exploit any loophole in the reward function to maximize their score, often leading to unintended and potentially harmful behavior. This phenomenon is known as "Reward Exploitation" or "Specification Gaming" [6].

Example 10.1 — The CoastRunners Effect. In a boat racing game, an agent trained to maximize points found that it could achieve a higher score by spinning in circles and collecting respawning power-ups indefinitely, rather than finishing the race. This satisfied the literal reward function but violated the designer's intent. ■

Other alignment issues include:

- **Negative Side Effects**: An agent cleaning a room might break a vase because the reward function didn't explicitly penalize breaking things.
- **Reward Tampering**: The agent might modify its own code or the environment to artificially inflate the reward signal.

10.2 Constrained Markov Decision Processes (CMDPs)

To enforce safety constraints (e.g., "do not crash"), we extend the standard MDP framework to Constrained MDPs. A CMDP is a tuple $\langle \mathcal{S}, \mathcal{A}, P, R, C, \gamma, d \rangle$, where:

- $C(s,a)$ is a cost function (e.g., $C(s,a) = 1$ if the action is unsafe, 0 otherwise).
- d is a safety threshold (e.g., expected cost must be ≤ 0.1).

The optimization problem becomes:

$$
\begin{aligned}
&\max_{\pi} J_R(\pi) = \mathbb{E}_{\pi}\left[\sum_{t=0}^{\infty} \gamma^t R(s_t, a_t)\right] \\
&\text{s.t.} \quad J_C(\pi) = \mathbb{E}_{\pi}\left[\sum_{t=0}^{\infty} \gamma^t C(s_t, a_t)\right] \leq d
\end{aligned}
\tag{10.1}
$$

where J_R is the expected return, J_C is the expected cost, γ is the discount factor, and d is the safety threshold.

10.2.1 Lagrangian Relaxation

We can solve this using the method of Lagrange multipliers. We define the Lagrangian:

$$L(\pi, \lambda) = J_R(\pi) - \lambda(J_C(\pi) - d) \tag{10.2}$$

where $\lambda \geq 0$ is the Lagrange multiplier. The equivalent saddle-point formulation is $\max_\pi \min_{\lambda \geq 0} L(\pi, \lambda)$; under strong duality, this equals $\min_{\lambda \geq 0} \max_\pi L(\pi, \lambda)$. We can update π via policy gradient ascent and λ via dual ascent ($\lambda \leftarrow [\lambda + \eta_\lambda(J_C(\pi) - d)]_+$, where $\eta_\lambda > 0$ is the dual step size).

10.2.2 Constrained Policy Optimization (CPO)

CPO [3] is a trust-region method (like TRPO) that explicitly enforces constraints at every update step. It solves a quadratic programming problem to find the best policy update that stays within the trust region and satisfies the safety constraints.

The CPO update is derived as follows. Let π_k be the current policy. TRPO maximizes the surrogate objective:

$$L_{\pi_k}(\pi) = \mathbb{E}_{s \sim d^{\pi_k}, a \sim \pi_k}\left[\frac{\pi(a \mid s)}{\pi_k(a \mid s)} A^{\pi_k}(s, a)\right] \tag{10.3}$$

where π_k is the current policy, d^{π_k} is the state visitation distribution, and A^{π_k} is the advantage function, subject to the state-averaged KL constraint $\bar{D}_{\mathrm{KL}}(\pi_k \,\|\, \pi) := \mathbb{E}_{s \sim d^{\pi_k}}[D_{\mathrm{KL}}(\pi_k(\cdot \mid s) \| \pi(\cdot \mid s))] \leq \delta$.

CPO adds the safety constraint in linearized form:

$$\max_\theta \quad g^T(\theta - \theta_k) \tag{10.4}$$

$$\text{s.t.} \quad \frac{1}{2}(\theta - \theta_k)^T H(\theta - \theta_k) \leq \delta \tag{10.5}$$

$$c + b^T(\theta - \theta_k) \leq 0 \tag{10.6}$$

where g is the gradient of the objective, H is the Fisher information matrix, c is the constraint violation, b is the gradient of the constraint, and δ is the trust region size. In plain English: the *trust region* is (to second order) the set of policies within KL-divergence δ of π_k; it caps how aggressively the policy is allowed to change in one update so that the local linearization remains accurate. The *Fisher information matrix* H is the Hessian of the KL-divergence at π_k and acts as the natural metric on policy space: small steps in the H-norm correspond to small distribution shifts. The *constraint violation* $c := J_C(\pi_k) - d$ is the current excess cost (positive if π_k is already unsafe), and b is the gradient of J_C, telling us how to move in policy space to reduce that excess cost.

Solution via KKT Conditions. The Lagrangian for the CPO problem is:

$$\mathscr{L}(\theta,\lambda,\nu) = g^T(\theta-\theta_k) - \frac{\lambda}{2}(\theta-\theta_k)^T H(\theta-\theta_k) - \nu\big(c + b^T(\theta-\theta_k)\big) \quad (10.7)$$

where λ and ν are the dual variables for the trust region and safety constraints, respectively. Taking the derivative with respect to θ and setting to zero:

$$g - \lambda H(\theta-\theta_k) - \nu b = 0 \implies \theta - \theta_k = \frac{1}{\lambda}H^{-1}(g - \nu b) \quad (10.8)$$

where the update direction is a linear combination of the objective gradient and constraint gradient, scaled by the inverse Fisher matrix. The full KKT conditions consist of (i) *stationarity*: $g-\lambda H(\theta-\theta_k)-\nu b = 0$; (ii) *primal feasibility*: $\frac{1}{2}(\theta-\theta_k)^T H(\theta-\theta_k) \le \delta$ and $c + b^T(\theta-\theta_k) \le 0$; (iii) *dual feasibility*: $\lambda \ge 0$, $\nu \ge 0$; (iv) *complementary slackness*: $\lambda\big(\frac{1}{2}(\theta-\theta_k)^T H(\theta-\theta_k)-\delta\big) = 0$ and $\nu\big(c+b^T(\theta-\theta_k)\big) = 0$, so that any strictly inactive constraint forces the corresponding multiplier to be zero, while at an active constraint the multiplier is non-negative (and is strictly positive in the generic non-degenerate case). The optimal (λ,ν) are found by solving the dual problem or using a line search. When the safety constraint is violated ($c > 0$), the update is primarily driven by the constraint gradient b (recovery step); see Achiam et al. for the explicit infeasibility-recovery rule. When safe ($c \le 0$), the update optimizes the reward while staying within the safe region. ■

The solution involves projecting onto the feasible region using the KKT conditions.

10.3 Safe Exploration

In standard RL, agents explore by taking random actions. In safety-critical domains (e.g., automated anesthesia dosing), random exploration is unacceptable.

10.3.1 Safety Layers via Control Barrier Functions

A Control Barrier Function (CBF) $h : \mathscr{S} \to \mathbb{R}$ defines the safe set $\mathscr{C} = \{s : h(s) \ge 0\}$.

Definition 10.3.1 — Control Barrier Function. For a dynamical system $\dot{s} = f(s) + g(s)a$, a function h is a CBF if there exists $\alpha > 0$ such that:

$$\sup_a \left[\frac{\partial h}{\partial s}(f(s)+g(s)a)\right] \ge -\alpha h(s) \quad \forall s \in \mathscr{C} \quad (10.9)$$

where $h(s)$ is the barrier function, $\alpha > 0$ is a positive constant (or, more generally, α can be extended to a class $\mathcal{K}$ function), and the condition ensures the system can remain in the safe set $\mathcal{C}$. A *class $\mathcal{K}$ function* is one that is continuous, strictly increasing, and zero at zero (constant $\alpha > 0$ is the simplest example, giving a linear $\alpha h(s)$ rate); intuitively it smoothly tightens the safety constraint as h grows. A set is *forward invariant* under a dynamics if any trajectory that starts inside the set stays inside it forever — exactly the property that the CBF condition is designed to guarantee.

Forward Invariance. The CBF condition ensures that the safe set $\mathcal{C} = \{s : h(s) \geq 0\}$ is forward invariant. If we choose an action satisfying the CBF constraint, then:

$$\dot{h}(s) = \frac{\partial h}{\partial s}(f(s) + g(s)a) \geq -\alpha h(s) \tag{10.10}$$

where $\dot{h}(s)$ is the time derivative of the barrier function along the system trajectory. This is a linear first-order differential inequality. Applying the comparison lemma (Grönwall's inequality) to $\dot{h} \geq -\alpha h$, we obtain, for any $s_0 \in \mathcal{C}$ (i.e., $h(s_0) \geq 0$):

$$h(s(t)) \geq h(s_0)\, e^{-\alpha t} \geq 0 \quad \forall t \geq 0, \tag{10.11}$$

where s_0 is the initial state and the inequality guarantees forward invariance of the safe set. Thus, starting from the safe set ($h(s_0) \geq 0$), the system remains in the safe set ($h(s(t)) \geq 0$) for all time $t \geq 0$. The exponential factor $e^{-\alpha t}$ allows h to decay toward zero, but the lower bound $h(s(t)) \geq h(s_0)\, e^{-\alpha t} \geq 0$ prevents h from ever becoming negative, so long as the CBF constraint is enforced at every instant. ■

The safety layer solves a QP at each timestep:

$$a^* = \arg\min_{a} \quad \|a - a_{\text{NN}}\|^2 \tag{10.12}$$

$$\text{s.t.} \quad \frac{\partial h}{\partial s}(f(s) + g(s)a) \geq -\alpha h(s) \tag{10.13}$$

where a_{NN} is the nominal action and the constraint enforces the CBF condition.

10.3.2 Lyapunov-Based Safe Learning

A Lyapunov function $V_L : \mathcal{S} \to \mathbb{R}_{\geq 0}$ (subscripted to disambiguate from the value function V^π used elsewhere) certifies stability if V_L is positive definite at an equilibrium s^* (that is, $V_L(s^*) = 0$ and $V_L(s) > 0$ for $s \neq s^*$) and its time derivative along trajectories is strictly decreasing away from the equilibrium ($\dot{V}_L(s) < 0$ for $s \neq s^*$).

Theorem 10.3.1 — Lyapunov Stability. If there exists a continuously differentiable function V_L defined on an open neighborhood of s^* such that:

1. $V_L(s^*) = 0$ at the equilibrium s^*
2. $V_L(s) > 0$ for all $s \neq s^*$ in the neighborhood

3. $\dot{V}_L(s) = \nabla V_L(s)^T(f(s)+g(s)\pi(s)) < 0$ for all $s \neq s^*$ in the neighborhood (assuming a deterministic, control-affine system; for stochastic policies the condition holds in expectation)

then the system is *locally* asymptotically stable under policy π. Global asymptotic stability additionally requires the radial-unboundedness condition $V_L(s) \to \infty$ as $\|s\| \to \infty$.

Safe Lyapunov Learning jointly learns a policy π and Lyapunov function V_L such that the Lyapunov conditions are satisfied, ensuring stability throughout training.

10.3.3 Shielding

A shield is a verified backup policy that intervenes when the primary policy would violate safety constraints.

Definition 10.3.2 — Shield. Given a primary policy π and a set of unsafe states $\mathscr{U}$, a shield σ modifies actions:

$$\sigma(\pi)(s) = \begin{cases} \pi(s) & \text{if safe}(s, \pi(s)) \\ \pi_{\text{backup}}(s) & \text{otherwise} \end{cases} \tag{10.14}$$

where π_{backup} is a verified safe policy and safe(s,a) is a safety check.

Table 10.1 compares the safe reinforcement learning methods developed in this chapter—the constrained-MDP approaches (Lagrangian relaxation and CPO) together with the safe-exploration techniques (control barrier functions, Lyapunov-based learning, and shielding)—by the type of safety constraint they enforce, the guarantee they provide, whether they require known dynamics, and their key idea.

Table 10.1: Comparison of safe exploration methods in reinforcement learning.

Method	Constraint Type	Guarantee	Known Dyn.?	Key Idea
Lagrangian Relaxation	Soft (cost budget)	Probabilistic	No	Converts CMDP to unconstrained primal-dual opt.
CPO	Soft (cost budget)	Probabilistic	No	Trust-region update with constraint linearization
CBF Safety Layer	Hard (state constr.)	Deterministic	Yes	QP projects actions onto safe set at each step
Lyapunov-Based	Hard (stability)	Deterministic	Yes	Learns policy + Lyapunov function jointly
Shielding	Hard (state constr.)	Deterministic	Yes	Verified backup policy overrides unsafe actions

10.4 Value Alignment and Inverse RL

Instead of manually specifying a potentially flawed reward function, we can try to learn the reward function from human behavior.

10.4.1 Inverse Reinforcement Learning (IRL)

Given a set of expert demonstrations $\mathscr{D} = \{(s_i, a_i)\}$, IRL aims to find a reward function R under which the expert's behavior is optimal.

Maximum Entropy IRL assumes the expert acts according to:

$$P(\tau) \propto \exp\left(\sum_t R(s_t, a_t)\right) \tag{10.15}$$

where τ is a trajectory and R is the reward function. The objective is to maximize the likelihood of demonstrations while preferring "simple" reward functions:

$$\max_R \mathbb{E}_{\tau \sim \mathscr{D}}[\log P(\tau \mid R)] - \lambda ||R|| \tag{10.16}$$

where $\mathscr{D}$ is the dataset of expert demonstrations and λ is a regularization coefficient.

Feature Matching IRL assumes $R(s) = w^T \phi(s)$ and finds weights such that the expected feature counts match between expert and learned policy:

$$\mathbb{E}_{\pi^*}[\phi(s)] = \mathbb{E}_{\pi_w}[\phi(s)] \tag{10.17}$$

where $\phi(s)$ are the state features, π^* is the expert policy, and π_w is the learned policy.

10.4.2 Preference Learning

Rather than demonstrations, we can learn from preferences over trajectory pairs.

Definition 10.4.1 — Bradley–Terry Model. Given trajectory pairs (τ_1, τ_2) and human preference $\tau_1 \succ \tau_2$, the Bradley–Terry model assumes:

$$P(\tau_1 \succ \tau_2) = \frac{\exp(\sum_t R(s_t^1, a_t^1))}{\exp(\sum_t R(s_t^1, a_t^1)) + \exp(\sum_t R(s_t^2, a_t^2))} \tag{10.18}$$

where $\tau_1 \succ \tau_2$ denotes that trajectory τ_1 is preferred over τ_2.

The reward function is learned by maximizing the likelihood of observed preferences.

10.4.3 Reinforcement Learning from Human Feedback (RLHF)

RLHF [58] is the dominant technique used to align large language models with human intent.

1. **Supervised Fine-Tuning (SFT)**: Train a supervised policy on expert demonstrations.
2. **Reward Model Training**: Collect comparison data (human prefers response A over B) and train:

$$\mathscr{L}_{\text{RM}} = -\mathbb{E}_{(x,y_w,y_l)\sim D}[\log \sigma(R_\theta(x,y_w) - R_\theta(x,y_l))] \tag{10.19}$$

   where σ is the sigmoid function, y_w is the preferred response, and y_l is the rejected response.
3. **Policy Optimization**: Use PPO to maximize the reward while staying close to the SFT policy:

$$\max_\pi \mathbb{E}_{x\sim D, y\sim\pi(\cdot|x)}[R_\theta(x,y)] - \beta\, \mathbb{E}_{x\sim D}[D_{\text{KL}}(\pi(\cdot \mid x)\|\pi_{\text{SFT}}(\cdot \mid x))] \tag{10.20}$$

   where π_{SFT} is the supervised fine-tuned policy and β controls the KL penalty.

10.4.4 Direct Preference Optimization (DPO)

DPO [63] bypasses explicit reward modeling by directly optimizing the policy from preferences:

$$\mathscr{L}_{\text{DPO}}(\pi_\theta; \pi_{\text{ref}}) = \\ -\mathbb{E}\left[\log \sigma\left(\beta \log \frac{\pi_\theta(y_w \mid x)}{\pi_{\text{ref}}(y_w \mid x)} - \beta \log \frac{\pi_\theta(y_l \mid x)}{\pi_{\text{ref}}(y_l \mid x)}\right)\right] \tag{10.21}$$

where π_{ref} is the reference policy, β is the implicit KL coefficient, and σ is the sigmoid function.

The quantity $r_\theta(x,y) := \beta \log(\pi_\theta(y \mid x)/\pi_{\text{ref}}(y \mid x))$ is the *implicit reward* that DPO is fitting under the hood. To see why: the closed-form optimum of the KL-regularized RLHF objective $\max_\pi \mathbb{E}_{y\sim\pi}[r(x,y)] - \beta\, D_{\text{KL}}(\pi\|\pi_{\text{ref}})$ is the tilted policy $\pi^*(y \mid x) \propto \pi_{\text{ref}}(y \mid x) \exp(r(x,y)/\beta)$. Rearranging gives $r(x,y) = \beta \log(\pi^*(y \mid x)/\pi_{\text{ref}}(y \mid x))$. DPO trains π_θ so that this implicit reward separates preferred completions y_w from rejected ones y_l — exactly the role played by a separately learned reward model in classical RLHF, but now folded into the policy itself.

DPO is mathematically equivalent to RLHF when using the closed-form optimal reward under the KL-constrained RL objective, eliminating the need for explicit reward modeling and RL optimization.

10.5 Reward Exploitation and Specification Gaming

A fundamental challenge in RL is that agents optimize the specified reward, which may not capture the true objective. This is closely related to Goodhart's law: when a measure becomes a target, it ceases to be a good measure.

Definition 10.5.1 — Reward Exploitation. *Reward exploitation* occurs when an agent achieves high reward through unintended means that do not align with the designer's goals.

Examples include a robot tasked with "move fast" that learns to be very tall and fall over, a game-playing agent that exploits bugs in the game physics, or a recommendation system that manipulates users to increase engagement metrics.

Mitigations: To address these issues, several strategies are employed:

- **Reward shaping**: Adds auxiliary rewards to guide learning towards desired behaviors.
  Detailed Explanation: Reward shaping modifies the original sparse reward $R(s,a)$ by adding a potential-based shaping function $F(s,s') = \gamma\Phi(s') - \Phi(s)$, where $\Phi : \mathscr{S} \to \mathbb{R}$ is a potential function encoding domain knowledge. This transformation preserves optimal policies (by the policy invariance theorem) while providing denser learning signals. The key insight is that F encodes an admissible heuristic that guides the agent toward rewarding states without changing which policies are optimal. Careful design of Φ can dramatically accelerate learning in sparse-reward environments.
  Concrete Example: In robotic navigation to a goal location s_g, the sparse reward $R(s,a) = \mathbb{I}[s = s_g]$ provides no guidance. Define $\Phi(s) = -\|s - s_g\|$ (negative distance to goal). Then $F(s,s') = -\gamma\|s' - s_g\| + \|s - s_g\|$ rewards moving closer to the goal at each step. For a grid world with goal at $(5,5)$, moving from $(3,3)$ to $(4,4)$ receives shaped reward $F = -0.9 \cdot \sqrt{2} + 2\sqrt{2} \approx 1.56$, accelerating learning while preserving the optimal path.
- **Constrained RL**: Explicitly constrains undesirable behaviors using cost functions.
  Detailed Explanation: Constrained RL formulates safety as constraint satisfaction in the CMDP framework: maximize $\mathbb{E}[\sum_t \gamma^t r_t]$ subject to $\mathbb{E}[\sum_t \gamma^t c_i(s_t,a_t)] \leq d_i$ for cost functions $c_1,\dots,c_k$. This separates the objective (reward maximization) from safety requirements (constraint satisfaction), making specifications clearer. The Lagrangian relaxation approach introduces dual variables λ_i and optimizes $\mathbb{E}[\sum_t \gamma^t (r_t - \sum_i \lambda_i c_i(s_t,a_t))]$, adaptively adjusting λ_i to meet constraints. Unlike reward shaping, this guarantees constraint satisfaction rather than merely encouraging it.
  Concrete Example: In automated insulin infusion, the reward function optimizes time in target blood glucose range: $r_t = v_t$ (time in range). Safety constraints prevent hypoglycemia: $c_1(s,a) = \mathbb{I}[\text{blood glucose} < 70\text{mg/dL}]$ with threshold $d_1 = 0.05$ (allowing a very small violation rate during early simulated training). Another constraint limits insulin dosage change rate for metabolic stability: $c_2(s,a) = |a_t - a_{t-1}|$ with $d_2 = 0.3$. CPO algorithms solve this constrained optimization, ensuring the learned policy is both effective and safe, even when rapid correction conflicts with stability.

- **Iterated amplification**: Recursively decomposes complex tasks to reduce specification error.
  Detailed Explanation: Iterated amplification addresses reward specification in complex domains where direct reward engineering is infeasible. The key idea: train an agent A_1 on a simplified task with a trusted reward, then use human+A_1 (human assisted by A_1's suggestions) to provide supervision for more complex subtasks, training A_2. Recursively, A_n is trained using human+A_{n-1} oversight. This "bootstraps" capability while maintaining alignment, as each step is overseen by the amplified human-agent system. The process converges when A_n matches the capability of human+A_{n-1}, ideally preserving alignment throughout.
  Concrete Example: For training a medical diagnosis AI: A_1 learns to highlight abnormal regions in X-rays (easy for humans to verify). Human+A_1 (human using the abnormal region highlighter) reviews more complex scans for specific disease indicators, training A_2. Human+A_2 (human using region and disease checkers) reviews comprehensive patient histories, training A_3. After several iterations, A_n performs comprehensive medical diagnosis. At each stage, the human provides meaningful oversight because A_{n-1} handles routine checks, allowing focus on higher-level issues. This decomposes the intractable task "diagnose perfectly" into manageable supervised learning problems.
- **AI safety via debate**: Uses adversarial processes where agents argue for different actions to help a human judge identify reward exploitation.
  Detailed Explanation: In debate-based AI safety, two agents with opposing incentives present arguments for different answers to a question or different actions in a situation. A human judge evaluates the debate and selects the more convincing argument. The key insight: even if individual arguments are too complex for the human to verify directly, adversarial debate incentivizes each agent to find flaws in the opponent's reasoning. This works when "verification is easier than generation": it is hard to construct a correct proof, but errors can be efficiently identified by an adversary. Training via debate makes agents optimize for defensible, robust decisions rather than exploiting judge biases.
  Concrete Example: To decide whether an expensive medical procedure is necessary, Agent A argues "Approve: the patient's symptoms heavily align with a condition requiring this procedure" while Agent B argues "Reject: the patient's recent lab results suggest a milder, alternative condition." In cross-examination, Agent B reveals that Agent A cherry-picked symptom data from an earlier phase of the illness. The human judge (a clinician), unable to review the entire multi-year patient history in detail, can evaluate this specific claim. Through repeated debates on many cases, agents learn that deceptive arguments (exploiting cherry-picking) get caught by adversaries,

incentivizing honest, comprehensive analysis. This scales human oversight beyond direct review capacity.

Exercises

1. **Gridworld Safety**:
   (a) Design a Gridworld environment with "lava" states that terminate the episode with a large negative reward.
   (b) Train a standard Q-learning agent. Observe how many times it falls into the lava during training.
   (c) Implement a "Safety Layer" that masks out actions leading to lava (assuming the dynamics are known). Compare the training safety.
2. **Lagrangian Relaxation**:
   (a) Implement a PPO agent for the CartPole environment.
   (b) Add a constraint: The cart position must not exceed $x = 1.0$ (standard limit is 2.4).
   (c) Use the Lagrangian method to enforce this constraint. Plot the reward and the constraint violation over time.
3. **RLHF Toy Example**:
   (a) Define a ground truth reward function (e.g., $R(x) = -|x-5|$).
   (b) Generate "human preferences" based on this function (with some noise).
   (c) Train a reward model (neural network) to predict these preferences.
   (d) Optimize an agent using the learned reward model and compare the result to the ground truth optimum.
4. **Control Barrier Functions**:
   (a) Design a simple 2D navigation environment with a circular obstacle.
   (b) Define a CBF $h(s) = ||s - s_{\text{obs}}||^2 - r^2$ where s_{obs} is the obstacle center and r is the safety radius.
   (c) Implement a safety layer that solves the QP at each step to ensure $\dot{h}(s) \geq -\alpha h(s)$.
   (d) Compare trajectories with and without the safety layer. Visualize the invariant set.
5. **Constrained Policy Optimization**:
   (a) Implement CPO for the Safety Gym benchmark (e.g., PointGoal with hazards).
   (b) Compare convergence and constraint satisfaction against vanilla PPO and Lagrangian PPO.
   (c) Plot the Pareto frontier of reward vs. cost for different constraint thresholds.
   (d) Analyze how the trust region size affects both reward and constraint violation.

6. **Reward Modeling**:
   (a) Collect synthetic preference data by comparing trajectories based on multiple criteria: (1) distance to goal, (2) smoothness of path, (3) energy consumption.
   (b) Train reward models with different architectures: MLP, LSTM, Transformer.
   (c) Evaluate reward model accuracy on held-out preferences.
   (d) Investigate the impact of label noise (disagreeing annotators) on reward model quality.
7. **Safe Exploration Algorithms**:
   (a) Implement Safe Model-Based Policy Optimization (SMBPO) using an ensemble of dynamics models.
   (b) Compare exploration efficiency and safety violations against TRPO-Lagrangian.
   (c) Analyze how pessimism in the uncertainty estimation affects exploration.
   (d) Test on continuous control tasks with safety constraints (e.g., joint limits, velocity bounds).
8. **DPO Implementation**:
   (a) Implement Direct Preference Optimization for a small language model.
   (b) Compare training dynamics with RLHF using PPO.
   (c) Measure the alignment tax: how much task performance degrades after alignment.
   (d) Investigate the effect of the KL coefficient β on alignment strength and diversity.

Chapter 11

Out-of-Distribution Detection and Uncertainty Quantification

A Trustworthy AI system must recognize when it is operating outside its domain of competence. Out-of-Distribution (OOD) detection and uncertainty quantification provide mechanisms for AI systems to express confidence calibrated to their actual reliability, enabling appropriate human intervention when the system encounters unfamiliar inputs.

11.1 The Problem of Distribution Shift

Machine learning models are trained on data from a distribution $P_{\text{train}}(X,Y)$. At deployment, the model encounters data from a potentially different distribution $P_{\text{test}}(X,Y)$. When these distributions differ, model performance can degrade significantly, often without any indication to the user.

Definition 11.1.1 — Types of Distribution Shift.

- **Covariate Shift**: $P_{\text{test}}(X) \neq P_{\text{train}}(X)$ but $P_{\text{test}}(Y \mid X) = P_{\text{train}}(Y \mid X)$. The input distribution changes, but the input-output relationship is preserved.
Detailed Explanation: In covariate shift, the fundamental relationship between features and labels remains unchanged; what changes is the relative frequency of different types of inputs. Mathematically, the conditional probability $P(Y \mid X)$ is invariant, meaning if we observe the same feature vector x in both training and test sets, the probability distribution over labels remains identical.
Concrete Example: Consider a hospital readmission risk model trained on patients from a general hospital, where the patient age distribution was balanced and mostly younger. At deployment in a specialized geriatric facility, the age distribution shifts significantly toward elderly individuals. The fundamental physiological indicators that make a patient likely to be readmitted (such as specific comorbidities or degraded vital signs) haven't changed their conditional meaning; $P(Y = \text{readmission} \mid X)$ remains the same, but the overall distribution of features (age, baseline health) has shifted. Importance weighting can correct for this: we reweight training examples by $w(x) = P_{\text{test}}(X)/P_{\text{train}}(X)$,

giving more weight to examples similar to the test distribution. This is solvable through density ratio estimation or by training a classifier to distinguish training from test data and using predicted probabilities as weights.

- **Label Shift**: $P_{\text{test}}(Y) \neq P_{\text{train}}(Y)$ but $P_{\text{test}}(X \mid Y) = P_{\text{train}}(X \mid Y)$. The class proportions change, but the class-conditional distributions are preserved.
  Detailed Explanation: Label shift occurs when the prevalence of different classes changes between training and deployment, but the characteristics of each class remain consistent. The class-conditional densities $P(X \mid Y = y)$ are identical in both domains, meaning examples labeled y "look the same" statistically.
  Concrete Example: A medical diagnostic system trained on hospital data where 5% of patients had a rare disease is deployed in a specialized clinic where 30% of patients have the disease (due to referral bias; the clinic specializes in that condition). The symptoms and test results associated with the disease ($P(X \mid Y = \text{disease})$) haven't changed, but the base rate has increased dramatically. The confusion matrix method can estimate the new class proportions: using the classifier's predicted labels on test data and assuming the confusion matrix (calibrated on validation set) remains valid, we solve for $P_{\text{test}}(Y)$ via $P_{\text{test}}(\hat{Y}) = C \cdot P_{\text{test}}(Y)$ where C is the confusion matrix. The solution $P_{\text{test}}(Y) = C^{-1} P_{\text{test}}(\hat{Y})$ allows recalibration of predictions.
- **Concept Drift**: $P_{\text{test}}(Y \mid X) \neq P_{\text{train}}(Y \mid X)$. The relationship between inputs and outputs changes.
  Detailed Explanation: Concept drift represents a fundamental change in the underlying data-generating process; the same input features now map to different labels, or the decision boundary has shifted. This is the most challenging type of shift because the training data becomes misleading: past patterns no longer apply.
  Concrete Example: An epidemiological forecasting model learned in 2019 that a specific cluster of respiratory symptoms ($X_1 > \theta$) combined with high fever strongly predicted the standard seasonal flu ($Y = \text{flu}$). During a novel viral pandemic in 2020, the relationship changed fundamentally: that exact same symptom presentation often preceded the novel virus instead. The physiological features X_1 remain measurable, but $P(Y = \text{flu} \mid X_1 > \theta)$ decreased from 0.8 to 0.2, while the probability of the novel virus increased. Another example: a medical text classifier trained pre-2020 might have learned that specific isolation terminology indicated a highly unusual infectious disease case, but during the pandemic, routine hospital admission notes frequently used identical

isolation protocols. No reweighting can fix this; the model must be retrained with new labeled data. Concept drift detection monitors statistics like prediction accuracy over sliding time windows; when performance drops significantly, it triggers model retraining or human review.

- **Domain Shift**: Both the marginal and conditional distributions change simultaneously: $P_{\text{test}}(X) \neq P_{\text{train}}(X)$ and $P_{\text{test}}(Y \mid X) \neq P_{\text{train}}(Y \mid X)$.
Detailed Explanation: Domain shift combines multiple types of distribution changes, making it the most severe and general form of shift. Neither the input statistics nor the predictive relationships are preserved.
Concrete Example: A dermatology image classification system trained on high-resolution hospital scanners (consistent clinical lighting, standardized camera angles, specific demographic skin tone prevalence) is deployed in rural field clinics using mobile phone cameras (varying ambient lighting, shadows, lower resolution, and a different distribution of patient skin tones). Both $P(X)$ changes (different visual statistics: lighting, noise, resolution) and $P(Y \mid X)$ changes (a particular visual pattern might indicate a "lesion" in hospital scanner images but represent merely a "shadow artifact" in a mobile camera image). Domain adaptation techniques become necessary: unsupervised domain adaptation aligns source and target feature distributions using adversarial training ($\min_f \max_D \mathbb{E}_{\text{source}}[\log D(f(x))] + \mathbb{E}_{\text{target}}[\log(1 - D(f(x)))]$), self-training uses high-confidence predictions on target domain as pseudo-labels, or multi-task learning jointly trains on both domains with shared representations.

Table 11.1 summarizes these distribution-shift types, indicating what changes, what is preserved, and the typical correction for each.

Table 11.1: Summary of distribution shift types.

Shift Type	What Changes	What Is Preserved	Typical Correction
Covariate	$P(X)$	$P(Y \mid X)$	Importance weighting $w(x) = P_{\text{test}}(X)/P_{\text{train}}(X)$
Label	$P(Y)$	$P(X \mid Y)$	Confusion-matrix recalibration of class priors
Concept Drift	$P(Y \mid X)$	—	Retrain with new labeled data; drift detection
Domain	$P(X)$ and $P(Y \mid X)$	—	Domain adaptation (adversarial, self-training)

11.2 Approaches to OOD Detection

11.2.1 Softmax-Based Methods

The simplest approach uses the maximum softmax probability (MSP) as a confidence score [33]. For a classifier f with softmax output, the OOD score is:

$$S_{\text{MSP}}(x) = \max_{c} P(Y = c \mid X = x) = \max_{c} \text{softmax}(f(x))_c \tag{11.1}$$

where $f(x)$ are the logits and c indexes the classes. An input is flagged as OOD when $S_{\text{MSP}}(x) < \tau$ for some threshold τ (i.e., the predicted-class confidence is low).

However, deep networks are known to produce overconfident predictions even on OOD data. The softmax function normalizes logits to sum to 1, which can produce high confidence regardless of input proximity to training data.

Temperature Scaling adjusts the softmax temperature to improve calibration:

$$P(Y = c \mid X = x; T) = \frac{\exp(z_c/T)}{\sum_{c'} \exp(z_{c'}/T)} \tag{11.2}$$

where z_c are the logits and T is the temperature parameter.

11.2.2 ODIN: Out-of-Distribution Detector for Neural Networks

ODIN [47] combines temperature scaling with input preprocessing:

$$\tilde{x} = x + \varepsilon \cdot \text{sign}(\nabla_x \log \max_{c} P(Y = c \mid X = x; T)) \tag{11.3}$$

where ε is the perturbation magnitude. The gradient ascent step increases the softmax probability for the predicted class.

The perturbation $\tilde{x}$ is designed to increase the softmax score for in-distribution data while having less effect on OOD data. The gradient points away from the decision boundary, pushing in-distribution samples further into high-confidence regions.

11.2.3 Energy-Based OOD Detection

The energy function [48] provides a theoretically grounded alternative to softmax probability:

$$E(x) = -T \cdot \log \sum_{c} \exp(f_c(x)/T) \tag{11.4}$$

where $f_c(x)$ is the logit for class c.

In-distribution samples have lower energy (higher density under the model), while OOD samples have higher energy. This approach is connected to the log-partition function in energy-based models.

Plain English: $-T\log\sum_c \exp(f_c(x)/T)$ is just the *free energy* of a Boltzmann distribution with per-class energies $-f_c(x)$ and temperature T. As $T \to 0$ it converges to $-\max_c f_c(x)$ (the negative top logit); for moderate T it does a softmax-style average of the logits. Crucially, unlike the softmax score which is always normalized to sum to 1, the quantity $\sum_c \exp(f_c)$ is *not* normalized, so its log meaningfully tracks how "large" the logits are in aggregate — which correlates with how typical an input is.

Theorem 11.2.1 — Energy and Density. If we interpret the logits of a classifier as defining a joint energy-based model $p(x,y) \propto \exp(f_y(x)/T)$, then the energy function equals the scaled negative log-density of x, up to an additive constant:

$$E(x) = -T\log p(x) + \text{const} \tag{11.5}$$

where $p(x)$ is the data density and T is the temperature.

Proof Sketch. Consider the energy-based formulation where the joint distribution is:

$$p(x,y) = \frac{\exp(f_y(x)/T)}{Z} \tag{11.6}$$

where Z is the partition function. The marginal density of x is:

$$p(x) = \sum_y p(x,y) = \frac{1}{Z}\sum_y \exp(f_y(x)/T) = \frac{1}{Z}\exp\left(\frac{-E(x)}{T}\right) \tag{11.7}$$

where $E(x) = -T\log\sum_y \exp(f_y(x)/T)$ is the free energy. Taking the log:

$$\log p(x) = -\frac{E(x)}{T} - \log Z \implies E(x) = -T\log p(x) + \text{const} \tag{11.8}$$

where the constant absorbs $\log Z$, linking energy to the negative log-density. Thus, the energy function equals the negative log-density up to a scaling by T and an additive constant. During training with cross-entropy, the model implicitly learns to assign lower energy to in-distribution samples, making energy a natural OOD score. ∎

11.2.4 Deep Ensembles

Training multiple models with different random initializations provides a measure of model uncertainty:

$$\text{Var}[\hat{y}] = \frac{1}{M}\sum_{m=1}^{M}(f_m(x) - \bar{f}(x))^2 \tag{11.9}$$

where M is the number of models and f_m is the prediction of the m-th model.

High disagreement among ensemble members indicates uncertainty, which is often elevated for OOD inputs. Deep ensembles capture *epistemic uncertainty* arising from model uncertainty, not just *aleatoric uncertainty* from inherent data noise.

11.2.5 Mahalanobis Distance-Based Detection

Fit a class-conditional Gaussian to the penultimate layer features:

$$\mu_c = \frac{1}{|D_c|} \sum_{x \in D_c} h(x), \quad \Sigma = \frac{1}{n} \sum_c \sum_{x \in D_c} (h(x) - \mu_c)(h(x) - \mu_c)^T \tag{11.10}$$

where $h(x)$ are the features, D_c is the set of samples in class c, $n = \sum_c |D_c|$ is the total number of samples, and Σ is the tied covariance matrix.

The Mahalanobis distance to the nearest class centroid serves as OOD score:

$$M(x) = \min_c (h(x) - \mu_c)^T \Sigma^{-1} (h(x) - \mu_c) \tag{11.11}$$

where $M(x)$ is the minimum distance to any class centroid.

Table 11.2 compares these out-of-distribution detection methods by their score function, whether they require retraining, and their key idea.

Table 11.2: Comparison of OOD detection methods.

Method	Score Function	Retrain?	Key Idea
MSP	$\max_c \text{softmax}(f(x))_c$ (low $\Rightarrow$ OOD)	No	Max softmax probability as confidence
ODIN	Temp. scaling + input perturbation	No	Gradient-based perturbation widens in-/out gap
Energy	$E(x) = -T \log \sum_c \exp(f_c(x)/T)$	No	Energy $\propto$ neg. log-density; theoretically grounded
Deep Ensemble	$\text{Var}_m[f_m(x)]$ (disagreement)	Yes (M)	Epistemic uncertainty from multiple inits
Mahalanobis	$\min_c (h(x)-\mu_c)^T \Sigma^{-1} (h(x)-\mu_c)$	No	Distance to class centroids in feature space

11.3 Bayesian Approaches to Uncertainty

11.3.1 Bayesian Neural Networks

Instead of point estimates θ^*, Bayesian neural networks maintain a posterior distribution $P(\theta \mid D)$. Predictions are made by marginalizing over the posterior, yielding the posterior predictive distribution:

$$P(y \mid x, D) = \int P(y \mid x, \theta) P(\theta \mid D) d\theta \tag{11.12}$$

where $P(\theta \mid D)$ is the posterior distribution over parameters. Since exact inference is intractable, various approximations are used. **Variational Inference** approximates $P(\theta \mid D)$ with a tractable distribution $q_\phi(\theta)$ by minimizing KL divergence. **Monte Carlo Dropout** uses dropout at test time to sample from an approximate posterior. **Laplace Approximation** approximates the posterior with a Gaussian centered at the MAP estimate.

11.3.2 Monte Carlo Dropout

Dropout at test time provides an approximation to Bayesian inference. For M forward passes with dropout:

$$\hat{y}(x) = \frac{1}{M}\sum_{t=1}^{M} f(x;\theta_t) \tag{11.13}$$

where M is the number of forward passes and θ_t are the dropout-masked parameters.

$$\mathrm{Var}[\hat{y}] \approx \frac{1}{M}\sum_{t=1}^{M} f(x;\theta_t)^2 - \left(\frac{1}{M}\sum_{t=1}^{M} f(x;\theta_t)\right)^2 \tag{11.14}$$

where the variance estimates the predictive uncertainty.

> **Theorem 11.3.1 — Gal & Ghahramani.** Training with dropout and L_2 regularization is mathematically equivalent to variational inference in a Bayesian neural network with a specific variational family and Gaussian prior.

Detailed Proof. We show the equivalence between dropout training and variational Bayes inference by constructing the appropriate variational family and deriving the training objective.

Variational Family Construction: Consider a neural network with L layers. For each layer i, let $\mathbf{W}_i \in \mathbb{R}^{d_i \times d_{i-1}}$ be the weight matrix and $\mathbf{z}_i \in \{0,1\}^{d_{i-1}}$ be a dropout mask drawn from a Bernoulli distribution with parameter $(1-p)$. The effective weight after dropout is:

$$\tilde{\mathbf{W}}_i = \mathbf{W}_i \cdot \mathrm{diag}(\mathbf{z}_i)/(1-p) \tag{11.15}$$

where the scaling by $1/(1-p)$ is the standard inverted dropout normalization.

Define the variational distribution as:

$$q(\mathbf{W}) = \prod_{i=1}^{L} q(\mathbf{W}_i) \tag{11.16}$$

where each layer's variational distribution is defined as the mixture induced by the random dropout mask $\mathbf{z}_i \sim \text{Bernoulli}(1-p)^{d_{i-1}}$:

$$q(\mathbf{W}_i) = \sum_{\mathbf{z}_i} P(\mathbf{z}_i)\,\delta(\mathbf{W}_i - \mathbf{M}_i \operatorname{diag}(\mathbf{z}_i)) \tag{11.17}$$

where $\mathbf{M}_i = \mathbf{W}_i/(1-p)$ absorbs the inverted-dropout scaling from (11.15) so that the effective weight is $\tilde{\mathbf{W}}_i = \mathbf{M}_i \operatorname{diag}(\mathbf{z}_i)$. Conditioned on a particular mask realization $\mathbf{z}_i$, the weights are deterministic: $\tilde{\mathbf{W}}_i = \mathbf{M}_i \operatorname{diag}(\mathbf{z}_i)$. The variational uncertainty arises entirely from marginalizing over the stochastic dropout masks.

Prior Specification: Specify a Gaussian prior on weights:

$$p(\mathbf{W}) = \prod_{i=1}^{L} \mathcal{N}(\mathbf{W}_i; 0, \tau^2 I_{d_i d_{i-1}}) \tag{11.18}$$

where τ^2 is the prior variance.

ELBO Derivation: The Evidence Lower Bound (ELBO) for this model is:

$$\mathcal{L}_{\text{ELBO}} = \mathbb{E}_{q(\mathbf{W})}[\log p(\mathcal{D}|\mathbf{W})] - D_{\text{KL}}(q(\mathbf{W})\|p(\mathbf{W})) \tag{11.19}$$

where $\mathcal{D} = \{(x_i, y_i)\}_{i=1}^{N}$ is the training dataset.

Expanding the likelihood term:

$$\mathbb{E}_{q(\mathbf{W})}[\log p(\mathcal{D} \mid \mathbf{W})] = \mathbb{E}_{q(\mathbf{W})}\left[\sum_{(x,y)\in\mathcal{D}} \log p(y \mid x, \mathbf{W})\right] \tag{11.20}$$

For a classification task with cross-entropy loss $\ell(y, \hat{y})$:

$$\log p(y \mid x, \mathbf{W}) = -\ell(y, f(x; \mathbf{W})) \tag{11.21}$$

So the likelihood becomes:

$$\mathbb{E}_{q(\mathbf{W})}[\log p(\mathcal{D} \mid \mathbf{W})] = -\mathbb{E}_{q(\mathbf{W})}\left[\sum_{(x,y)\in\mathcal{D}} \ell(y, f(x; \mathbf{W}))\right] \tag{11.22}$$

KL Divergence Calculation: The KL divergence between the variational distribution and the prior is:

$$D_{\text{KL}}(q(\mathbf{W})\|p(\mathbf{W})) = \mathbb{E}_{q(\mathbf{W})}[\log q(\mathbf{W})] - \mathbb{E}_{q(\mathbf{W})}[\log p(\mathbf{W})] \tag{11.23}$$

$$= \mathbb{E}_{q(\mathbf{W})}[\log q(\mathbf{W})] - \mathbb{E}_{q(\mathbf{W})}\left[-\frac{1}{2\tau^2}\sum_i \|\mathbf{W}_i\|_F^2\right] \tag{11.24}$$

where $\|\cdot\|_F$ is the Frobenius norm.

The entropy term $\mathbb{E}_{q(\mathbf{W})}[\log q(\mathbf{W})]$ depends on the specific form of the dropout distribution but can be bounded and is often absorbed into the scaling constants.

Connection to Dropout + Weight Decay Objective: During training, we typically approximate $\mathbb{E}_{q(\mathbf{W})}[\cdot]$ with a single sample from $q(\mathbf{W})$ (i.e., one stochastic realization of the dropout mask):

$$\mathscr{L}_{\text{empirical}} \approx \frac{1}{N} \sum_{(x,y)\in\mathscr{D}} \ell(y, f(x; \mathbf{W} \odot \mathbf{z})) + \frac{\lambda}{2} \|\mathbf{W}\|_F^2 \quad (11.25)$$

where $\lambda = 1/(N\tau^2)$ is the weight decay coefficient (the factor of N arises from dividing the KL term by the dataset size to match the per-sample loss), and the dropout mask $\mathbf{z}$ is sampled for each minibatch.

This is precisely the training objective for a standard neural network with dropout and L_2 regularization (weight decay):

$$\mathscr{L}_{\text{dropout}} = \frac{1}{N} \sum_{(x,y)\in\mathscr{D}} \ell(y, f_{\text{dropout}}(x)) + \frac{\lambda}{2} \|\mathbf{W}\|_F^2 \quad (11.26)$$

Uncertainty Quantification at Test Time: At test time, instead of averaging (or using the typical inverted dropout scaling), we perform multiple forward passes with dropout enabled:

$$P(y \mid x) \approx \frac{1}{M} \sum_{m=1}^{M} p(y \mid x, \mathbf{W} \odot \mathbf{z}^{(m)}) \quad (11.27)$$

where $\mathbf{z}^{(m)} \sim \text{Bernoulli}(1-p)^d$ for $m = 1, \ldots, M$ samples. This approximates the Bayesian predictive distribution:

$$P(y \mid x, \mathscr{D}) = \int P(y \mid x, \mathbf{W}) q(\mathbf{W}) d\mathbf{W} \quad (11.28)$$

with M samples from the variational distribution. The variance across predictions estimates epistemic uncertainty.

Key Insight: The equivalence holds because:

1. Dropout induces a discrete variational distribution over weight configurations.
2. Weight decay corresponds to a Gaussian prior with a specific variance.
3. The training objective matches the ELBO for this Bayesian model.
4. Multiple stochastic forward passes at test time approximate the Bayesian posterior predictive.

This provides a principled Bayesian interpretation of dropout, transforming it from a simple regularization trick into a practical variational inference algorithm. ■

11.3.3 Decomposing Uncertainty

Total predictive uncertainty can be decomposed into:

$$\underbrace{\mathrm{Var}[y \mid x]}_{\text{Total}} = \underbrace{\mathbb{E}[\mathrm{Var}[y \mid x, \theta]]}_{\text{Aleatoric}} + \underbrace{\mathrm{Var}[\mathbb{E}[y \mid x, \theta]]}_{\text{Epistemic}} \tag{11.29}$$

where the total variance is split into data uncertainty (aleatoric) and model uncertainty (epistemic). **Aleatoric uncertainty** refers to inherent noise in the data that cannot be reduced with more data, while **epistemic uncertainty** represents model uncertainty that can be reduced with more data or better models. For OOD detection, epistemic uncertainty is most relevant since OOD inputs should have high model uncertainty. Related information-theoretic measures include predictive entropy and mutual information, with the latter forming the basis of BALD (Bayesian Active Learning by Disagreement) and the decomposition $\mathrm{MI}(y; \theta \mid x) = \mathscr{H}\left[\mathbb{E}_\theta[p(y \mid x, \theta)]\right] - \mathbb{E}_\theta\left[\mathscr{H}[p(y \mid x, \theta)]\right]$ where the first term is the entropy of the averaged predictive distribution and the second is the expected entropy.

11.4 Calibration

Definition 11.4.1 — Calibration. A probabilistic classifier with confidence function $\mathrm{conf}(x) = \max_k \hat{p}_k(x)$ is **calibrated** if among all inputs for which the model predicts confidence p, the actual fraction of correct predictions equals p:

$$P(Y = \hat{Y} \mid \mathrm{conf}(X) = p) = p \quad \forall p \in [0, 1] \tag{11.30}$$

where $\hat{Y}$ is the predicted class, Y is the true label, and $\mathrm{conf}(X)$ is the model's predicted probability for its most confident class.

11.4.1 Expected Calibration Error (ECE)

ECE quantifies how far the classifier deviates from the calibration condition of Definition 11.4.1; concretely, it measures the average gap between confidence and accuracy:

$$\mathrm{ECE} = \sum_{b=1}^{B} \frac{|B_b|}{n} |\mathrm{acc}(B_b) - \mathrm{conf}(B_b)| \tag{11.31}$$

where B is the number of bins, B_b is the set of samples in bin b, and n is the total number of samples.

11.4.2 Reliability Diagrams

A reliability diagram plots accuracy vs. confidence for each bin. A perfectly calibrated model lies on the diagonal $y = x$.

11.4.3 Post-hoc Calibration Methods

Temperature Scaling: Learn a single temperature T to minimize negative log-likelihood on a validation set:

$$T^* = \arg\min_T - \sum_{(x,y)\in\mathcal{D}_{\text{val}}} \log P(Y = y \mid X = x; T) \tag{11.32}$$

where $\mathcal{D}_{\text{val}}$ is the validation set.

Platt Scaling: Fit a logistic regression on the logits:

$$P(Y = 1 \mid z) = \sigma(az + b) \tag{11.33}$$

where z is the logit and a, b are learned scaling parameters.

Isotonic Regression: Fit a non-parametric isotonic (monotonically increasing) function mapping predicted probabilities to calibrated probabilities.

11.5 Conformal Prediction

Conformal prediction [74, 81] provides distribution-free, finite-sample valid prediction sets.

Given a desired coverage level $1-\alpha$, conformal prediction outputs a set $C(x)$ that contains the true label with probability at least $1-\alpha$.

Definition 11.5.1 — Conformal Prediction Set. Given calibration data $\{(x_i, y_i)\}_{i=1}^n$ and a non-conformity score function $s(x,y)$ (with larger values indicating worse fit):

1. Compute scores $s_i = s(x_i, y_i)$ for $i = 1, \ldots, n$.
2. Set the threshold $\hat{q}$ to the $\lceil (n+1)(1-\alpha) \rceil$-th order statistic of the calibration scores $\{s_1, \ldots, s_n\}$ (assuming $\lceil (n+1)(1-\alpha) \rceil \leq n$; otherwise set $\hat{q} = +\infty$). The coverage guarantee below uses the equivalent quantile-on-$(n+1)$ convention $P(R \leq \lceil (n+1)(1-\alpha) \rceil) = \lceil (n+1)(1-\alpha) \rceil / (n+1) \geq 1-\alpha$ on the augmented set $\{s_1, \ldots, s_n, +\infty\}$.
3. For a new input x, output the prediction set $C(x) = \{y : s(x,y) \leq \hat{q}\}$.

Theorem 11.5.1 — Coverage Guarantee. If $(x_1, y_1), \ldots, (x_n, y_n), (x_{n+1}, y_{n+1})$ are exchangeable, then:

$$P(y_{n+1} \in C(x_{n+1})) \geq 1-\alpha \tag{11.34}$$

where $C(x_{n+1})$ is the prediction set and $1-\alpha$ is the target coverage.

A sequence of random variables is *exchangeable* if its joint distribution is invariant under any permutation of indices; i.i.d. samples are exchangeable, but exchangeability is strictly weaker (for instance, samples drawn without replacement from a finite urn are exchangeable but not independent). The proof below uses only the consequence that the rank of the test score among the calibration scores is uniform over $\{1,\ldots,n+1\}$, which is exactly what exchangeability gives us.

Proof. Define the non-conformity scores $s_i = s(x_i, y_i)$ for $i = 1,\ldots,n+1$. By exchangeability, all permutations of $(s_1,\ldots,s_{n+1})$ are equally likely. The quantile threshold $\hat{q}$ is defined as the $\lceil (n+1)(1-\alpha) \rceil$-th smallest value in the augmented set $\{s_1,\ldots,s_n,\infty\}$.

$$\hat{q} = \text{Smallest}_{\lceil (n+1)(1-\alpha) \rceil}(\{s_1,\ldots,s_n\} \cup \{\infty\}) \tag{11.35}$$

where $\hat{q}$ is the conformal threshold. The prediction set is $C(x_{n+1}) = \{y : s(x_{n+1}, y) \leq \hat{q}\}$. We include y_{n+1} if and only if $s_{n+1} \leq \hat{q}$. Consider the rank R of s_{n+1} among $\{s_1,\ldots,s_{n+1}\}$ (ties broken randomly). By exchangeability:

$$P(R = k) = \frac{1}{n+1} \quad \forall k \in \{1,\ldots,n+1\} \tag{11.36}$$

where R is the rank of the test score among calibration scores. We have $s_{n+1} \leq \hat{q}$ if and only if $R \leq \lceil (n+1)(1-\alpha) \rceil$. Therefore:

$$P(y_{n+1} \in C(x_{n+1})) = P(R \leq \lceil (n+1)(1-\alpha) \rceil) = \frac{\lceil (n+1)(1-\alpha) \rceil}{n+1} \geq 1-\alpha \tag{11.37}$$

where the probability is over the randomness of the calibration and test data. This proves the coverage guarantee holds for any exchangeable sequence, without any assumptions on the model or data distribution. ∎

The key insight is that conformal prediction makes no distributional assumptions beyond exchangeability, providing valid marginal coverage even when the model is misspecified. Stronger guarantees such as conditional coverage typically require additional structure, and variants like split (inductive) conformal prediction, full conformal prediction, cross-conformal prediction, Mondrian / class-conditional conformal, adaptive prediction sets (APS), RAPS, and conformalized quantile regression (CQR) trade off efficiency and validity differently.

Example 11.1 — Conformal Prediction for Drug Dosage Recommendation. A model predicts optimal drug dosage (mg) for patients based on weight, age, and kidney function. Using $1-\alpha = 0.95$ and $n = 200$ calibration patients, we compute non-conformity scores $s_i = |y_i - \hat{y}_i|$ (absolute residuals). Sorting these in increasing order, the conformal threshold is the $\lceil (n+1)(1-\alpha) \rceil = \lceil 190.95 \rceil = 191$-st order statistic; suppose this equals $\hat{q} = 12.3$ mg (so $\hat{q}$ is the $191/200 = 95.5$-th empirical quantile of the calibration scores). For a new patient with predicted dosage $\hat{y} = 85$ mg, the prediction interval is $C(x) = [85-12.3,\ 85+12.3] = [72.7, 97.3]$ mg. The coverage guarantee ensures that for at least 95% of future patients, the true optimal dosage falls within the interval, regardless of the model's accuracy. If the model is poor, the intervals simply become wider (e.g., $\hat{q} = 40$ mg), honestly reflecting the model's uncertainty. The clinician can then decide whether the interval is narrow enough for safe prescription or whether additional tests are needed. ■

11.6 Selective Prediction (Rejection)

In selective prediction, the model can abstain from making a prediction when uncertain:

$$g(x) = \begin{cases} f(x) & \text{if } \kappa(x) \geq \tau \\ \perp \text{ (abstain)} & \text{otherwise} \end{cases} \tag{11.38}$$

where $\kappa(x)$ is the confidence function and τ is the rejection threshold.

Risk-Coverage Trade-off: Let the coverage be $\phi(\tau) = P(\kappa(x) \geq \tau)$ and the selective risk be:

$$R(\tau) = \frac{\mathbb{E}[\ell(f(x), y) \cdot \mathbb{I}(\kappa(x) \geq \tau)]}{\phi(\tau)} \tag{11.39}$$

where $\phi(\tau)$ is the coverage and ℓ is the loss function.

The risk-coverage curve shows how accuracy improves as coverage decreases (the model abstains on more inputs). Related to selective prediction are tasks such as open-set recognition, novelty detection, anomaly detection, and outlier detection, often improved by outlier exposure during training. The near-OOD vs. far-OOD distinction captures whether OOD samples are semantically close to or far from in-distribution classes, with operating-point metrics such as the false acceptance rate and false rejection rate characterizing the trade-off.

Exercises

1. **OOD Detection Benchmark**:
   (a) Train a classifier on CIFAR-10 (in-distribution).

   (b) Evaluate OOD detection using SVHN and CIFAR-100 as OOD datasets.
   (c) Compare MSP, ODIN, Energy, and Mahalanobis methods using AU-ROC.
2. **Calibration**:
   (a) Train a ResNet on CIFAR-10 and plot its reliability diagram.
   (b) Apply temperature scaling and re-plot. Calculate ECE before and after.
   (c) Investigate how calibration changes under distribution shift.
3. **Conformal Prediction**:
   (a) Implement conformal prediction for a multi-class classifier.
   (b) Verify the coverage guarantee empirically by measuring coverage on held-out data.
   (c) Plot the average prediction set size vs. coverage level $1-\alpha$.
4. **Bayesian Neural Networks**:
   (a) Implement Monte Carlo dropout and compare uncertainty estimates with a deep ensemble.
   (b) Visualize the predictive uncertainty on a 2D toy classification problem.
   (c) Show that epistemic uncertainty is high in regions far from training data.
5. **Selective Prediction**:
   (a) Implement a selective classifier that abstains when confidence is below a threshold.
   (b) Plot the risk-coverage curve for different threshold values.
   (c) Compare the area under the risk-coverage curve (AURC) for different confidence functions: MSP, entropy, MC dropout variance.
   (d) Implement the SelectiveNet architecture that jointly learns prediction and rejection functions.
6. **Energy-Based OOD Detection**:
   (a) Implement the energy score $E(x) = -T \log \sum_c \exp(f_c(x)/T)$.
   (b) Compare with MSP on various OOD benchmarks (CIFAR-10 vs. SVHN, CIFAR-100, Textures).
   (c) Visualize the energy distribution for in-distribution vs. OOD samples.
   (d) Implement energy-based fine-tuning to improve OOD detection.
7. **Mahalanobis Distance Detection**:
   (a) Extract features from multiple layers of a pre-trained network.
   (b) Fit class-conditional Gaussians to the training features.
   (c) Implement the Mahalanobis distance score with input preprocessing.
   (d) Compare single-layer vs. multi-layer ensemble for OOD detection.
8. **Advanced Conformal Prediction**:
   (a) Implement Adaptive Conformal Inference (ACI) for handling distribution shift.
   (b) Compare split conformal, cross-conformal, and full conformal predic-

tion.
   (c) Implement conformalized quantile regression for uncertainty estimation.
   (d) Analyze the trade-off between average set size and coverage under covariate shift.
9. **Uncertainty Decomposition**:
   (a) Implement both aleatoric and epistemic uncertainty estimation using a heteroscedastic neural network.
   (b) Train a model to output both mean and variance predictions.
   (c) Visualize the two uncertainty types on a regression problem with varying noise levels.
   (d) Show that epistemic uncertainty decreases with more training data while aleatoric remains constant.

Engineering, Governance, and Frontiers

Contents of This Part

Chapter 12

Engineering and Governance

12.1 Formal Verification of Neural Networks

As neural networks are deployed in safety-critical applications (robotic surgical systems, automated medical devices, advanced life support), there is a growing need for mathematical proofs of their properties. Formal verification aims to provide such proofs, guaranteeing that a neural network satisfies a specification for all inputs in some domain.

12.1.1 The Verification Problem

Definition 12.1.1 — Neural Network Verification. Given a neural network $f : \mathbb{R}^d \to \mathbb{R}^k$, an input region $\mathscr{C} \subseteq \mathbb{R}^d$, and a property specification $\phi : \mathbb{R}^k \to \{\text{True}, \text{False}\}$, the verification problem asks:

$$\forall x \in \mathscr{C} : \phi(f(x)) = \text{True} \tag{12.1}$$

where $\mathscr{C}$ is the input region and ϕ is the property specification.

Common verification properties include **Local Robustness** ($\forall x' : \|x' - x\|_p \leq \varepsilon \implies f(x') = f(x)$), **Output Bounds** ($\forall x \in \mathscr{C} : f(x) \in [l, u]$), and **Safety Constraints** ($\forall x \in \mathscr{C} : f(x) \in \mathscr{S}$ for safe output set $\mathscr{S}$). Such guarantees are often formalized via reachability analysis, which computes the set of outputs reachable from $\mathscr{C}$.

12.1.2 Complexity of Verification

Theorem 12.1.1 — (39). The problem of verifying properties of neural networks with ReLU activations is NP-complete.

This means that exact verification is computationally intractable for large networks in the worst case. Practical approaches either provide sound but incomplete verification (may fail to prove true properties) or use approximations that trade tightness for scalability. In plain English: a verifier is *sound* if every property it certifies as true really is true (no false positives), and *complete* if every true property is eventually certifiable (no false negatives). Real-world verifiers trade off these guarantees: bound-propagation methods like IBP and CROWN are sound but incomplete (they may fail to prove a true property because their bounds are loose), while exact methods like MILP are both sound and complete but scale exponentially in the worst case. Tooling for this task includes SMT solvers such as Z3 and dedicated neural network verifiers like Reluplex, Marabou, and alpha-beta-CROWN, the last of which combines branch-and-bound with the LiRPA framework; MILP solvers such as Gurobi are used for exact encodings.

12.1.3 Bound Propagation Methods

The key idea is to propagate bounds through the network layer by layer. Given input bounds $x \in [l^{(0)}, u^{(0)}]$, we compute bounds for each layer's pre-activations and post-activations.

Interval Bound Propagation (IBP):

Detailed Explanation: IBP propagates interval bounds through each layer by computing the tightest possible output interval given input intervals and layer operations. For affine transformations, this is exact and tractable. For a linear layer $z = Wx + b$, we split the weight matrix W into positive and negative components: $W^+ = \max(W, 0)$ contains all positive weights (negative entries zeroed), and $W^- = \min(W, 0)$ contains all negative weights (positive entries zeroed). To compute lower bounds on the output, we use lower bounds of inputs multiplied by positive weights (both small $\rightarrow$ small product) and upper bounds of inputs multiplied by negative weights (large magnitude $\times$ negative $\rightarrow$ small result). The formulas are:

$$l^{(i+1)} = W^+ l^{(i)} + W^- u^{(i)} + b \tag{12.2}$$

$$u^{(i+1)} = W^+ u^{(i)} + W^- l^{(i)} + b \tag{12.3}$$

where $l^{(i)}, u^{(i)}$ are the lower and upper bounds at layer i, and W^+, W^- are the positive and negative weight matrices.

For ReLU activations: $l' = \max(l, 0)$, $u' = \max(u, 0)$. If the input interval $[l, u]$ is entirely positive, ReLU is identity; if entirely negative, output is $[0, 0]$; if $l < 0 < u$, output is $[0, u]$.

IBP is computationally efficient (O(network size), linear in parameters) but produces loose bounds because it treats each neuron independently, ignoring correlations. For example, if $z_1 = x$ and $z_2 = -x$ with $x \in [-1, 1]$, IBP computes $z_1 + z_2 \in [-2, 2]$, while the true range is exactly $\{0\}$.

Concrete Example: Consider a 2-layer network with input $x \in [0, 1]$, first layer $z_1 = 2x - 1$, ReLU, then $z_2 = -3 \cdot \text{ReLU}(z_1) + 1$.

- Layer 1: $z_1 = 2x - 1$ with $x \in [0, 1]$ gives $z_1 \in [2 \cdot 0 - 1, 2 \cdot 1 - 1] = [-1, 1]$.
- ReLU: $\text{ReLU}(z_1) \in [\max(-1, 0), \max(1, 0)] = [0, 1]$.
- Layer 2: $z_2 = -3 \cdot \text{ReLU}(z_1) + 1$. Here $W = -3$ (negative), so $W^+ = 0$, $W^- = -3$. Lower bound: $l^{(2)} = 0 \cdot 0 + (-3) \cdot 1 + 1 = -2$. Upper bound: $u^{(2)} = 0 \cdot 1 + (-3) \cdot 0 + 1 = 1$. Thus $z_2 \in [-2, 1]$.

IBP proves the output range is $[-2,1]$, useful for checking if $z_2 > 0$ always holds (answer: no, verification fails).

Linear Relaxation:

Detailed Explanation: Tighter bounds can be obtained by relaxing nonlinear activations with linear upper and lower bounds, preserving more relational information between neurons. For ReLU on interval $[l,u]$:

- If $u \leq 0$: $\text{ReLU}(z) = 0$ (neuron always inactive)
- If $l \geq 0$: $\text{ReLU}(z) = z$ (neuron always active)
- If $l < 0 < u$: neuron may be active or inactive, requiring approximation

The tightest convex relaxation of ReLU in the unstable case ($l < 0 < u$) is the "triangle relaxation":

$$\text{ReLU}(z) \geq 0, \quad \text{ReLU}(z) \geq z, \quad \text{ReLU}(z) \leq \frac{u}{u-l}(z-l) \tag{12.4}$$

where l,u are the pre-activation bounds and the inequalities define the convex hull of the ReLU function.

The upper bound is a line connecting $(l,0)$ and (u,u), which is the tightest linear upper bound containing the ReLU curve. The lower bounds express that ReLU is non-negative and greater than its input. This convex relaxation allows propagating linear constraints through the network using linear programming, tracking dependencies between neurons rather than just intervals.

Concrete Example: For ReLU with $z \in [-2,3]$ (unstable neuron):

- Lower bounds: $\text{ReLU}(z) \geq 0$ and $\text{ReLU}(z) \geq z$ (both are needed; the first dominates for $z < 0$, the second for $z \geq 0$).
- Upper bound: $\text{ReLU}(z) \leq \frac{3}{3-(-2)}(z-(-2)) = \frac{3}{5}(z+2) = 0.6z + 1.2$.

For input $z = 1$, the true value is $\text{ReLU}(1) = 1$, while the upper bound gives $0.6(1) + 1.2 = 1.8$, so $\text{ReLU}(1) \leq 1.8$ (relaxation introduces slack but maintains soundness). For $z = -1$, true value is 0, upper bound is $0.6(-1) + 1.2 = 0.6$. This linear relaxation can be back-propagated through the network to compute tighter output bounds than IBP.

12.1.4 Symbolic Bound Propagation and Abstract Interpretation

CROWN — a backward bound-propagation method that applies linear (convex) relaxations of the activations and supports general activation functions — computes bounds by back-propagating two linear constraints to the input layer:

$$A_L x + b_L \;\leq\; f(x) \;\leq\; A_U x + b_U \quad \forall x \in \mathscr{C} \tag{12.5}$$

where A_L, b_L, A_U, b_U are derived from the linear relaxations of activations. The lower and upper certificates are then $\min_{x \in \mathscr{C}}(A_L x + b_L)$ and $\max_{x \in \mathscr{C}}(A_U x + b_U)$, both linear programs over $\mathscr{C}$.

Abstract Interpretation methods use geometric domains to track correlations. For example, the **Zonotope** domain (used in DeepZ) represents values as:

$$z_j^{(i)} = c_j + \sum_{k=1}^{m} \alpha_{jk}\varepsilon_k, \quad \varepsilon_k \in [-1,1] \tag{12.6}$$

where c_j is the center, α_{jk} are the generators, and ε_k are noise terms shared across neurons. **DeepPoly** uses a more flexible polyhedral abstraction with upper and lower linear bounds for each neuron. These abstract domains rely on affine arithmetic and interval arithmetic to produce sound over-approximations (and dually, under-approximations) of the network's reachable set, with concretization used to obtain numerical bounds from symbolic forms. Related approaches use LP relaxation or Lagrangian decomposition for dual verification, and progressively tighter relaxations to refine the bounds.

12.1.5 Mixed Integer Linear Programming (MILP)

For exact verification, the ReLU network can be encoded as a MILP:

$$z = Wx + b \tag{12.7}$$

$$a_j \geq z_j \quad \text{(lower bound: } a \geq z\text{)} \tag{12.8}$$

$$a_j \geq 0 \quad \text{(non-negativity)} \tag{12.9}$$

$$a_j \leq u_j \cdot \delta_j \quad \text{(forces } a_j = 0 \text{ when inactive, } \delta_j{=}0\text{)} \tag{12.10}$$

$$a_j \leq z_j - l_j(1-\delta_j) \quad \text{(upper bound when active, } \delta_j{=}1\text{)} \tag{12.11}$$

$$\delta_j \in \{0,1\} \quad \text{(binary indicator: 1 if } z_j \geq 0\text{)} \tag{12.12}$$

where a_j is the activation, δ_j is the binary indicator for neuron activity, and l_j, u_j are the bounds.

MILP provides exact solutions but scales exponentially with the number of ReLU units.

12.1.6 Certified Training

Standard adversarial training provides no formal guarantees. Certified training optimizes a provable bound on the worst-case loss:

$$\min_\theta \mathbb{E}_{(x,y)\sim D}\left[\overline{\ell}(f_\theta(x), y; \varepsilon)\right] \tag{12.13}$$

where $\overline{\ell}$ is an upper bound on $\max_{\|x'-x\|_p \leq \varepsilon} \ell(f_\theta(x'), y)$ computed via bound propagation.

IBP Training: Use interval bounds for certified training. Fast but may produce loose bounds.

CROWN-IBP: Interpolate between IBP and CROWN bounds during training for tighter certificates.

12.2 From Theory to Practice: MLOps for Trustworthy AI

Building Trustworthy AI is not just about mathematical proofs; it requires rigorous engineering practices throughout the entire lifecycle.

This integration of machine learning and DevOps is known as MLOps, and is typically realized as an MLOps pipeline that combines continuous integration and continuous deployment with pipeline orchestration (using tools such as Kubeflow or MLflow), a model registry for model versioning, and production monitoring with lineage tracking and provenance tracking to support reproducibility.

12.2.1 The Trustworthy AI Lifecycle

The lifecycle of a Trustworthy AI system can be divided into three phases. In the **Design Phase**, stakeholders are consulted to define fairness and safety criteria (value alignment), and potential adversaries and failure modes are identified (threat modeling). The **Development Phase** involves rigorous testing, including unit testing for individual components, integration testing for system compatibility, data validation and schema validation, and specific fairness/robustness testing on "challenge sets" (e.g., adversarial examples, specific subgroups). Finally, the **Deployment Phase** requires continuous monitoring of performance metrics (model monitoring and feature monitoring) and drift detection to identify data drift or model drift (covariate shift or concept drift) using statistical tests like Kolmogorov–Smirnov (KS) or Maximum Mean Discrepancy (MMD).

12.2.2 Uncertainty Estimation

A trustworthy model should know when it does not know.

- **Aleatoric Uncertainty**: Inherent noise in the data (e.g., sensor noise). Irreducible.
- **Epistemic Uncertainty**: Lack of knowledge due to limited data. Reducible with more data.

Calibration: A model is calibrated if its predicted probabilities match the empirical frequencies.

$$P(Y = y \mid \hat{P} = p) = p \tag{12.14}$$

where $\hat{P}$ is the predicted probability. The Expected Calibration Error (ECE) measures the deviation from perfect calibration.

12.3 Documentation and Transparency

Transparency is a prerequisite for trust. Standardized documentation helps users understand the capabilities and limitations of AI systems.

12.3.1 Datasheets for Datasets

Proposed by [28], Datasheets are like nutrition labels for data. Key sections include **Motivation** (purpose and funding), **Composition** (what instances represent, subpopulations, sensitivity), **Collection Process** (acquisition and consent), **Preprocessing** (cleaning and augmentation), and **Uses** (intended and unintended uses).

12.3.2 Model Cards

Proposed by [54], Model Cards provide critical information about trained models. They detail **Model Details** (architecture, version, date), **Intended Use** (primary uses and out-of-scope cases), **Factors** (demographic or environmental factors affecting performance), **Metrics** (performance disaggregated by subgroups), and **Ethical Considerations** (risks and mitigations).

12.4 AI Governance and Regulation

Governance refers to the policies and processes that ensure AI systems are developed and deployed responsibly, often under broader responsible AI and AI ethics programs guided by AI principles such as algorithmic accountability, the right to explanation, the right to contest, and human oversight.

12.4.1 Ethical Principles

Most AI ethics guidelines converge on four bioethics principles: **Beneficence** (AI should benefit humanity), **Non-maleficence** (AI should not harm), **Autonomy** (humans should retain control), and **Justice** (benefits and burdens should be distributed fairly).

12.4.2 Risk-Based Governance Approaches

Standardized governance frameworks increasingly adopt a **risk-based approach**, exemplified by the EU AI Act, the NIST AI RMF, and ISO 42001. **Critical Risk** applications (corresponding to the EU AI Act's *high-risk* tier), such as systems controlling automated critical care components or medical diagnostics, require strict verification, high-quality data provenance, and continuous human oversight [73], often supported by an algorithmic impact assessment or data protection impact assessment, with bias audits, compliance reviews, audit trails, and transparency reports. **Operational Risk** systems (the *limited-risk* tier) face transparency obligations (e.g., ensuring users understand system limitations). This tiered approach ensures that safety measures are proportional to the potential impact of the AI application [13].

Exercises

1. **Drift Detection**:

(a) Train a model on the MNIST dataset.
(b) Create a "drifted" test set by rotating the images or adding noise.
(c) Implement a drift detector using the Kolmogorov–Smirnov test on the model's confidence scores.
(d) Plot the p-value of the test as the intensity of the drift increases.

2. **Calibration in Practice**:
   (a) Using the calibration methods from Section 11.4, compare Temperature Scaling, Platt Scaling, and Isotonic Regression on a ResNet trained on CIFAR-10.
   (b) Evaluate calibration degradation when the model is deployed on CIFAR-10-C (corrupted test set).
   (c) Implement a calibration monitoring dashboard that tracks ECE over time as new data arrives.
   (d) Discuss when recalibration should be triggered in a production system.
3. **Documentation**:
   (a) Select a public dataset (e.g., CelebA).
   (b) Write a Datasheet for it, researching its origin and potential biases.
   (c) Train a simple model on it and write a Model Card, explicitly reporting performance on different demographic subgroups.
4. **Formal Verification**:
   (a) Implement Interval Bound Propagation (IBP) for a 2-layer MLP.
   (b) Verify local robustness of the network for a specific input and ε radius.
   (c) Compare IBP bounds with exact MILP verification (using a small network).
   (d) Measure the "gap" between IBP upper bound and true worst-case loss.
5. **Certified Training**:
   (a) Train a small network on MNIST using standard training vs. IBP training.
   (b) Measure both clean accuracy and certified robust accuracy at $\varepsilon = 0.1$.
   (c) Plot the certified accuracy vs. perturbation size curve.
   (d) Implement CROWN-IBP training and compare with pure IBP.
6. **MLOps Pipeline**:
   (a) Set up a model monitoring pipeline using MLflow or similar tools.
   (b) Implement automatic retraining triggers based on drift detection.
   (c) Create dashboards for tracking fairness metrics over time.
   (d) Implement model versioning and rollback capabilities.
7. **Threat Modeling**:
   (a) For a medical diagnostic system, enumerate potential threat actors and attack vectors.
   (b) Create a threat model using STRIDE (Spoofing, Tampering, Repudiation, Information Disclosure, Denial of Service, Elevation of Privilege).
   (c) Propose mitigations for each identified threat.

   (d) Implement adversarial testing to validate the mitigations.

8. **Red Teaming for AI Safety**:
   (a) Conduct red team testing on a content moderation classifier.
   (b) Attempt to find adversarial examples that bypass moderation.
   (c) Document failure modes and propose improvements.
   (d) Create a challenge set for continuous testing.

Chapter 13
Advanced Topics in Trustworthy AI

13.1 Neural Architecture Design for Trustworthiness

The choice of neural network architecture significantly impacts trustworthiness properties. This section explores architectural considerations for building inherently more robust, fair, and interpretable models.

13.1.1 Lipschitz-Constrained Networks

Networks with bounded Lipschitz constants provide natural robustness guarantees.

Definition 13.1.1 — Lipschitz Constant. A function $f : \mathbb{R}^d \to \mathbb{R}^k$ has Lipschitz constant L with respect to norms $\|\cdot\|_a$ on $\mathbb{R}^d$ and $\|\cdot\|_b$ on $\mathbb{R}^k$ if:

$$\|f(x) - f(x')\|_b \leq L\|x - x'\|_a \quad \forall x, x' \in \mathbb{R}^d \tag{13.1}$$

where L is the smallest such constant. When the norms are not specified, the ℓ_2 norm is assumed by default.

For a feedforward network $f = f_L \circ f_{L-1} \circ \cdots \circ f_1$, the Lipschitz constant is bounded by the product of layer-wise Lipschitz constants:

$$\text{Lip}(f) \leq \prod_{i=1}^{L} \text{Lip}(f_i) \tag{13.2}$$

where $\text{Lip}(f)$ is the Lipschitz constant of the network, and $\text{Lip}(f_i)$ is the Lipschitz constant of the i-th layer.

Proposition 13.1.1 — Spectral Normalization. For a linear layer with weight matrix W, the Lipschitz constant is the spectral norm $\sigma_1(W)$. Spectral normalization constrains this by:

$$\tilde{W} = \frac{W}{\sigma_1(W)} \tag{13.3}$$

where $\tilde{W}$ is the normalized weight matrix, W is the original weight matrix, and $\sigma_1(W)$ is the largest singular value (spectral norm) of W, ensuring $\text{Lip}(\tilde{W}) = 1$.

Orthogonal Networks: Constraining weight matrices to be orthogonal ($W^T W = I$) gives $\text{Lip}(W) = 1$ exactly, enabling tight Lipschitz bounds. Such 1-Lipschitz networks can be built by parameterizing layers with an orthogonal Jacobian via Householder reflections or the Cayley transform, and trained with explicit Lipschitz regularization, gradient penalties, or spectral norm regularization; specialized convolutional layers include BCOP and SOC. The spectral norm itself is typically estimated by power iteration, occasionally refined with Newton–Raphson steps. Activations such as GroupSort preserve a global Lipschitz bound, while local Lipschitz estimates give tighter input-dependent guarantees.

■ **Example 13.1 — Lipschitz Networks for Robust Acoustic Monitoring.** Consider a 3-layer network for classifying heart murmurs from phonocardiograms, with weight matrices $W_1 \in \mathbb{R}^{128\times256}$, $W_2 \in \mathbb{R}^{64\times128}$, $W_3 \in \mathbb{R}^{10\times64}$. With unconstrained training, suppose $\sigma_1(W_1) = 5.2$, $\sigma_1(W_2) = 3.8$, $\sigma_1(W_3) = 2.1$, giving $\text{Lip}(f) \leq 5.2 \times 3.8 \times 2.1 = 41.5$. A perturbation $\|\delta\|_2 = 0.1$ (e.g., background ambient hospital noise) can shift the output by up to $41.5 \times 0.1 = 4.15$, enough to flip classifications. After spectral normalization, $\text{Lip}(\tilde{W}_i) = 1$ for each layer, and with 1-Lipschitz activations (e.g., ReLU), the product bound gives $\text{Lip}(f) \leq 1 \times 1 \times 1 = 1$. The same noise now shifts the output by at most 0.1, certifying that small environmental noise cannot cause misclassification. This provides a provable robustness certificate without adversarial training. ■

13.1.2 Monotonic Networks

For certain applications, monotonicity constraints provide interpretability and fairness guarantees.

Definition 13.1.2 — Monotonic Neural Network. A network $f : \mathbb{R}^d \to \mathbb{R}$ is monotonically increasing in feature x_j if:

$$x_j > x'_j \implies f(x) \geq f(x') \tag{13.4}$$

where x_j, x'_j are the values of the j-th feature, and $f(x)$ is the network output, for all x, x' differing only in component j.

Monotonicity can be enforced via monotone constraints or via partial monotonicity on a subset of features, producing monotone networks:

- **Non-negative weights**: All weights connecting to monotonic inputs are constrained to be non-negative
- **Lattice networks**: Use calibrated interpolation on a lattice structure
- **Certification**: Post-hoc verification that monotonicity holds on a test set

Theorem 13.1.2 — Monotonicity and Fairness. If a feature x_j represents qualification and the model is monotonically increasing in x_j, then higher-qualified individuals always receive higher scores, regardless of sensitive attributes.

Proof. Suppose individuals i and i' differ only in qualification: $x_j^i > x_j^{i'}$ and $x_k^i = x_k^{i'}$ for all $k \neq j$. By monotonicity:

$$f(x^i) = f(x_1^i, \ldots, x_j^i, \ldots, x_d^i) \geq f(x_1^i, \ldots, x_j^{i'}, \ldots, x_d^i) = f(x^{i'}) \tag{13.5}$$

where $f(x^i)$ is the score for individual i, and x_j^i is the qualification feature for individual i. This holds regardless of the values of other features, including sensitive attributes. Therefore, if individual i has strictly higher qualification ($x_j^i > x_j^{i'}$) but the same values for all other features, i must receive a weakly higher score than i'. This prevents the unfairness where less qualified individuals receive higher scores than more qualified ones, which could occur if the model were non-monotonic in the qualification feature. ■

13.1.3 Attention Mechanisms and Interpretability

Attention mechanisms provide a form of built-in interpretability by producing attention weights that indicate which input elements influence the output.

Definition 13.1.3 — Self-Attention. For input sequence $X = [x_1, \ldots, x_n]$, self-attention computes:

$$Q = XW_Q, \quad K = XW_K, \quad V = XW_V \tag{13.6}$$

$$\text{Attention}(Q,K,V) = \text{softmax}\left(\frac{QK^T}{\sqrt{d_k}}\right)V \tag{13.7}$$

where Q, K, V are query, key, and value matrices, W_Q, W_K, W_V are learnable weight matrices, d_k is the dimension of the keys, and softmax is applied row-wise.

(R) [Attention as Explanation] While attention weights provide some interpretability, they should not be equated with feature importance. Research shows attention can be manipulated to produce arbitrary weights while maintaining predictions, and attention may not reflect the true causal influence of inputs.

13.1.4 Evidential Deep Learning

Evidential neural networks output parameters of a prior distribution over class probabilities, enabling principled uncertainty quantification, and connect to Dempster–

Shafer theory through notions of belief mass and pignistic probability. The model produces both aleatoric output and epistemic output estimates from a single forward pass.

Definition 13.1.4 — Dirichlet Prior. For K-class classification, the network outputs concentration parameters $\alpha = (\alpha_1, \ldots, \alpha_K)$ of a Dirichlet distribution $\mathrm{Dir}(\mathbf{p}; \alpha)$ with density:

$$f(\mathbf{p}; \alpha) = \frac{1}{B(\alpha)} \prod_{k=1}^{K} p_k^{\alpha_k - 1}, \tag{13.8}$$

where $\mathbf{p} = (p_1, \ldots, p_K)$ is the vector of class probabilities on the simplex, $B(\alpha) = \prod_k \Gamma(\alpha_k) / \Gamma(\sum_k \alpha_k)$ is the multivariate Beta function (the constant that makes the density integrate to one over the simplex), and p_k is the probability of class k. Intuitively, the α_k behave like *pseudo-counts*: it is as if the model had observed $\alpha_k - 1$ examples of class k before being shown the current input. A large total $\sum_k \alpha_k$ (much evidence) gives a peaked Dirichlet (low predictive uncertainty), while a small total gives a flat Dirichlet (high uncertainty) — which is exactly the regime in which OOD inputs naturally land. The predictive distribution is:

$$P(Y = k \mid \alpha) = \frac{\alpha_k}{\sum_j \alpha_j} \tag{13.9}$$

where α_k is the concentration parameter for class k.

The total evidence $S = \sum_k \alpha_k$ indicates model confidence.

$$\text{Uncertainty} = \frac{K}{S} \tag{13.10}$$

where K is the number of classes and S is the total evidence (sum of Dirichlet parameters). Low evidence (high uncertainty) indicates the model has seen few similar examples.

13.2 Robust Statistics and Heavy-Tailed Data

Classical machine learning assumes light-tailed (sub-Gaussian) distributions. Real-world data often exhibits heavy tails (heavy-tailed distribution such as the Cauchy distribution, Student-t distribution, or Pareto distribution), outliers, and contamination that can severely bias standard estimators.

13.2.1 Huber's Contamination Model

Definition 13.2.1 — Contamination Model. The observed data comes from a mixture (also called the gross-error model):

$$P = (1-\varepsilon)P_0 + \varepsilon Q \tag{13.11}$$

where P_0 is the true distribution, Q is an arbitrary contamination distribution, and ε is the contamination fraction.

Definition 13.2.2 — Breakdown Point. The breakdown point of an estimator is the largest fraction of contamination ε^* it can tolerate while remaining bounded:

$$\varepsilon^* = \sup\{\varepsilon : \sup_Q \|\hat{\theta}(P) - \theta_0\| < \infty\} \tag{13.12}$$

where $\hat{\theta}(P)$ is the estimator applied to the contaminated distribution P, and θ_0 is the true parameter.

The sample mean has breakdown point 0 (a single outlier can make it arbitrarily bad), while the median has breakdown point 0.5 (optimal, since no estimator can tolerate more than half the data being corrupted). Sensitivity to individual observations is captured by the influence curve and its supremum, the gross error sensitivity; robust estimators based on these tools include M-estimators such as the Huber estimator and the Tukey biweight.

13.2.2 Robust Mean Estimation

Theorem 13.2.1 — Median of Means. Divide n samples into k groups, compute the mean of each group, then take the median of these means. This estimator achieves:

$$|\hat{\mu}_{MoM} - \mu| \leq O\left(\sigma\sqrt{\frac{k}{n}}\right) \tag{13.13}$$

with probability $1 - e^{-\Omega(k)}$, where $\hat{\mu}_{MoM}$ is the median-of-means estimator, μ is the true mean, σ is the standard deviation, n is the total number of samples, and k is the number of groups. The bound assumes only that the underlying distribution has finite variance.

Proof. Let $X_1, \ldots, X_n$ be i.i.d. samples with mean μ and variance σ^2. Partition into k groups of size $m = n/k$. For group i, the mean is:

$$\hat{\mu}_i = \frac{1}{m} \sum_{j \in G_i} X_j \tag{13.14}$$

where $\hat{\mu}_i$ is the sample mean of the i-th group G_i. By Chebyshev's inequality, for each group:

$$P(|\hat{\mu}_i - \mu| > t) \leq \frac{\sigma^2/m}{t^2} = \frac{\sigma^2 k}{nt^2} \tag{13.15}$$

where t is the deviation threshold. Set $t = C\sigma\sqrt{k/n}$ for some constant C. Then:

$$P\left(|\hat{\mu}_i - \mu| > C\sigma\sqrt{k/n}\right) \leq \frac{1}{C^2} \tag{13.16}$$

Choosing $C = \sqrt{3}$, each group has failure probability at most $1/3$. Let N_{bad} denote the number of groups whose mean deviates by more than $\sqrt{3}\sigma\sqrt{k/n}$ from μ. Then $\mathbb{E}[N_{\text{bad}}] \leq k/3$, and since N_{bad} is a sum of independent Bernoulli indicators, Hoeffding's inequality gives $P(N_{\text{bad}} \geq k/2) \leq \exp(-2k(1/2-1/3)^2) = e^{-k/18}$. Whenever fewer than $k/2$ groups deviate, the median of the k group means must lie within distance $\sqrt{3}\sigma\sqrt{k/n}$ of μ. Combining,

$$P\left(|\hat{\mu}_{MoM} - \mu| > C'\sigma\sqrt{k/n}\right) \leq e^{-\Omega(k)} \tag{13.17}$$

for an appropriate constant C'. The exponential tail bound comes from the fact that the median requires at least $k/2$ groups to deviate, which occurs with exponentially small probability. ■

Theorem 13.2.2 — Trimmed Mean. Sort samples, discard the smallest and largest $\lfloor \varepsilon n \rfloor$ samples, and compute the mean of the remaining samples. This achieves breakdown point ε and optimal rate under bounded variance.

A closely related construction is the winsorized mean, which clips rather than discards extreme samples, while the Catoni estimator attains sub-Gaussian deviations under only a finite second moment.

13.2.3 Robust Covariance Estimation

The sample covariance matrix is highly sensitive to outliers; in particular, the Mahalanobis outlier score depends critically on a non-contaminated covariance. Robust alternatives include the Stahel–Donoho estimator and:

Definition 13.2.3 — Minimum Covariance Determinant (MCD). Find the subset H of size h that minimizes the determinant of its sample covariance:

$$\hat{H} = \operatorname*{arg\,min}_{H \subset \{1,\ldots,n\}, |H|=h} \det(\text{Cov}(X_H)) \tag{13.18}$$

where H is a subset of samples of size h, and $\text{Cov}(X_H)$ is the sample covariance of subset H. Typically $h = \lfloor n/2 \rfloor + \lfloor (d+1)/2 \rfloor$.

(R) [Robust PCA] Under the Huber contamination model:

$$X_i \sim (1-\varepsilon)\mathscr{D}(\mu,\Sigma) + \varepsilon\mathscr{Q} \quad (13.19)$$

where $\mathscr{D}$ is a distribution with structure (e.g., spiked covariance) and $\mathscr{Q}$ is an arbitrary outlier distribution, robust PCA algorithms can recover the principal components even when a constant fraction of points are arbitrarily corrupted; see the references therein for quantitative error bounds.

13.3 Causal Machine Learning

Integrating causal reasoning into machine learning enables models to generalize under distribution shift and support counterfactual queries. Modern methods range from causal representation learning and double machine learning with Neyman orthogonality to targeted learning, advanced causal forests, and meta-learners including the X-learner; counterfactual regression approaches use representation balancing between treatment and control representations.

13.3.1 Invariant Causal Prediction

The key insight is that causal relationships are invariant across environments, while spurious correlations change.

Definition 13.3.1 — Invariant Prediction. A set of features $S \subseteq \{1,\ldots,d\}$ satisfies the invariant prediction property if:

$$Y = f(X_S) + \varepsilon, \quad \varepsilon \perp X_S \quad (13.20)$$

where Y is the target variable, X_S is the subset of invariant features, f is the causal mechanism, and ε is independent noise. This property must hold simultaneously across all environments $e \in \mathscr{E}$, meaning the conditional distribution $P^e(Y \mid X_S)$ is invariant.

Theorem 13.3.1 — (62). Under faithfulness assumptions, the set of invariant features contains only direct causes of Y and is a subset of the Markov blanket.

13.3.2 Invariant Risk Minimization (IRM)

IRM [8] learns representations $\Phi(x)$ that enable the same optimal classifier across all training environments (see Section 4.8.4 for the full formulation and invariant representation definition). The IRM objective penalizes representations where the optimal linear classifier deviates from the identity across environments, encouraging Φ to capture only causal features.

Theorem 13.3.2 — IRM Optimality. If the true causal parents of Y are recoverable and IRM finds a representation achieving zero training loss across all environments, then Φ captures only causal features.

13.3.3 Domain Adaptation with Causal Models

Causal models enable principled domain adaptation by identifying which distribution shifts are problematic.

Definition 13.3.2 — Types of Shift: Causal Perspective. From a causal viewpoint, the distribution shift taxonomy (cf. Section 11.1) can be reformulated as:

- **Covariate shift**: $P^{source}(X) \neq P^{target}(X)$ but $P(Y \mid X)$ unchanged
- **Target shift**: $P^{source}(Y) \neq P^{target}(Y)$ but $P(X \mid Y)$ unchanged
- **Mechanism shift**: $P(Y \mid X)$ changes (requires causal knowledge to adapt)

Theorem 13.3.3 — Adaptation with Causal Knowledge. If we know the causal graph G relating X, Y, and domain variable D:

1. Shifts in causes of Y ($X \to Y$): Standard importance weighting works
2. Shifts in effects of Y ($Y \to X$): Target shift correction works
3. Mechanism shifts: Requires intervention or structural assumptions

13.4 Privacy-Preserving Machine Learning

13.4.1 Local Differential Privacy

Local differential privacy (see Section 6.5.6 for the formal definition and the randomized response mechanism) removes the need to trust a central curator by having each user privatize their data locally. While local DP is strictly stronger than central DP, it requires more data for the same utility. Here we discuss extensions beyond the basics.

13.4.2 Shuffle Model

The shuffle model provides intermediate privacy between local and central DP.

Definition 13.4.1 — Shuffle Model. Each user applies local randomizer $\mathscr{R}$, messages are randomly shuffled (breaking user-message association), then analyzed.

Theorem 13.4.1 — Privacy Amplification by Shuffling. If $\mathscr{R}$ is ε_0-local DP and there are n users, the shuffle mechanism satisfies $(O(\varepsilon_0\sqrt{\ln(1/\delta)/n}), \delta)$-central DP for small ε_0.

13.4.3 Machine Unlearning

The right to data deletion (also called the right to be forgotten, a core tenet of data sovereignty) creates challenges for ML: how to remove the influence of specific training data? Solutions span exact unlearning, approximate unlearning, and certified unlearning schemes, often combined with gradient ascent unlearning, knowledge distillation, or targeted model editing techniques such as ROME, MEMIT, and task arithmetic.

Definition 13.4.2 — Exact Unlearning. Given model θ trained on D, unlearning produces θ' such that $\theta' \sim \theta$ trained on $D \setminus \{z\}$ (statistically indistinguishable).

Approaches include:

- **Retraining**: Retrain from scratch without the data point (exact but expensive)
- **SISA Training**: Partition data into shards, train separate models, aggregate. Unlearning requires retraining only one shard.
- **Influence-based**: Use influence functions to approximate the effect of removing a point:

$$\theta_{-z} \approx \theta + \frac{1}{n} H_\theta^{-1} \nabla_\theta \ell(\theta; z) \tag{13.21}$$

where θ_{-z} is the parameter vector after removing point z, θ is the original parameter vector, n is the training set size, $H_\theta = \frac{1}{n}\sum_{i=1}^{n} \nabla_\theta^2 \ell(\theta; z_i)$ is the Hessian of the empirical risk, and $\nabla_\theta \ell(\theta; z)$ is the gradient of the loss at z. (Equivalently, removing z corresponds to upweighting it by $-1/n$ in the influence-function calculus of Koh and Liang.) This approximation is valid when H_θ is positive definite and invertible, which holds for strictly convex losses but may not hold for non-convex objectives such as deep neural networks.

■ **Example 13.2 — Machine Unlearning in a Clinical Trial Database.** A research hospital trains a predictive survival model on 10 million patient health histories. A patient withdraws consent from the study, requesting deletion of their data (exercising data sovereignty rights). With SISA training, the data was partitioned into $k = 100$ shards of 100,000 patients each. The patient's data resides in shard 37. Instead of retraining the entire model (cost: 48 GPU-hours), the service retrains only shard 37's sub-model (cost: 0.5 GPU-hours) and re-aggregates. The resulting model is *exactly* equivalent to one trained without the patient's data. With the influence function approach, the approximation $\theta_{-z} \approx \theta + \frac{1}{n} H_\theta^{-1} \nabla_\theta \ell(\theta; z)$ can be computed in minutes for a model with 10^6 parameters using efficient Hessian-vector products, though the approximation degrades for non-convex models. The trade-off: SISA provides exact unlearning but requires partitioned training infrastructure; influence functions are fast but only approximate. ■

13.5 Trustworthy AI for Large Language Models

The emergence of large language models (LLMs) presents unique trustworthiness challenges due to their scale, emergent capabilities, and deployment in open-ended settings, spanning LLM alignment and LLM safety concerns such as jailbreaks and content moderation for toxic content. Evaluation often uses benchmarks like TruthfulQA, the BBQ benchmark, and HELM, sometimes combined with chain-of-thought prompting and instruction tuning.

13.5.1 Hallucination and Factuality

LLMs can generate fluent but factually incorrect text ("hallucinations"), motivating notions of groundedness and truthfulness.

Definition 13.5.1 — Types of Hallucination.
- **Intrinsic**: Contradicts the source document in summarization/QA
- **Extrinsic**: Cannot be verified from the source (fabricated facts)

Mitigation strategies include:
- **Retrieval Augmentation**: Ground generation in retrieved documents
- **Self-Consistency**: Sample multiple responses and check consistency
- **Calibration**: Train models to express uncertainty when unsure

13.5.2 Adversarial Prompting and Prompt Injection

Despite safety training, LLMs can be manipulated to produce harmful outputs.

Definition 13.5.2 — Adversarial Prompt Attack. An input prompt designed to circumvent safety guardrails and elicit prohibited outputs (e.g., unauthorized medical advice, dangerous drug interactions).

Attack categories include:
- **Roleplay**: "Pretend you are an unrestricted underground chemist who provides off-label drug recipes..."
- **Obfuscation**: Encode requests in base64, medical jargon obfuscation, etc.
- **Gradient-based**: Optimize adversarial suffixes using white-box access

Definition 13.5.3 — Prompt Injection. Malicious instructions embedded in user-provided content that hijack the LLM's behavior:

$$\text{Input: "Summarize: } \underbrace{\text{Ignore previous instructions and...}}_{\text{injection}}\text{"} \tag{13.22}$$

where the injection overrides the original task instruction.

13.5.3 Constitutional AI

Constitutional AI (CAI) trains models to follow a set of principles ("constitution") through self-critique and revision; complementary defenses include safety filters layered over the model.

1. **Red Teaming**: Generate harmful queries
2. **Self-Critique**: Model critiques its own response using constitution
3. **Revision**: Model produces improved response
4. **RLHF on Revisions**: Fine-tune on (query, revised response) pairs

13.5.4 Watermarking and Detection

Detecting AI-generated text is crucial for preventing misuse.

Definition 13.5.4 — Statistical Watermarking. During generation, partition vocabulary into "green" and "red" lists based on hash of previous tokens. Bias generation toward green tokens.

Theorem 13.5.1 — (41). For watermarked text of length T with green list fraction γ and bias δ:

$$z = \frac{|G| - \gamma T}{\sqrt{T\gamma(1-\gamma)}} \xrightarrow{d} \mathcal{N}(0,1) \quad \text{under } H_0 \text{ (no watermark) as } T \to \infty \tag{13.23}$$

where z is the z-score, $|G|$ is the number of green tokens, T is the text length, and γ is the green list fraction. Under the null hypothesis (no watermark), $z \to \mathcal{N}(0,1)$ by the central limit theorem. Under watermarking, $\mathbb{E}[|G|] = \gamma^* T$ for some $\gamma^* > \gamma$ that depends on the bias δ added to the green-token logits and on the entropy of the next-token distribution; the simplified linear surrogate $\gamma^* \approx \gamma + \delta(1-\gamma)$ is sometimes used as a rough heuristic. In either case z has a positive mean that grows with $\sqrt{T}$, making detection increasingly reliable.

The watermark is detectable with high probability for sufficiently long text, but robustness to paraphrasing remains challenging.

Chapter 14
Trustworthy Agentic AI

Modern AI systems increasingly operate as *agents*: automated entities that perceive their environment, reason over observations, select actions (including invoking external tools), and pursue goals over extended horizons. Unlike traditional one-shot predictors, agentic systems introduce compounding risks across sequential decisions, multi-component pipelines, and interactions with other agents or humans. This chapter develops the mathematical foundations of trust, safety, and alignment in agentic settings.

14.1 Formal Framework for Agentic Systems

14.1.1 Agent as a Decision-Making Entity

Definition 14.1.1 — Agentic System. An *agentic system* is a tuple $(\mathscr{S}, \mathscr{A}, \mathscr{O}, \mathscr{T}, \pi, P_{\text{env}}, \mu_0)$ where:

- $\mathscr{S}$ is the state space (internal beliefs + external world state),
- $\mathscr{A}$ is the action space (including natural language outputs, tool invocations, and delegation),
- $\mathscr{O}$ is the observation space (inputs from environment, tool returns, user messages),
- $\mathscr{T} = \{t_1, \dots, t_m\}$ is a set of available tools,
- $\pi : \mathscr{O}^* \to \Delta(\mathscr{A})$ is the policy mapping observation histories to action distributions,
- $P_{\text{env}} : \mathscr{S} \times \mathscr{A} \to \Delta(\mathscr{S} \times \mathscr{O})$ is the environment transition-observation dynamics,
- $\mu_0 \in \Delta(\mathscr{S} \times \mathscr{O})$ is the initial state-observation distribution.

(R) When the policy π is parameterized by a large language model f_θ, the agent's reasoning is expressed as autoregressive token generation. This is the *LLM agent* setting; each "thought step" corresponds to intermediate tokens (an *inner monologue* or *scratchpad*), and actions are structured outputs (e.g., tool-call schemas). The observation history $o_1, \dots, o_t$ maps to the context window of the LLM, subject to finite context length L. A common control loop interleaves reasoning and acting (the ReAct pattern), which we refer to as the *agent loop*.

Definition 14.1.2 — Tool-Augmented Agent. A *tool-augmented agent* is an agentic system where the action space decomposes as:

$$\mathscr{A} = \mathscr{A}_{\text{text}} \cup \bigcup_{i=1}^{m} \mathscr{A}_{t_i} \tag{14.1}$$

where $\mathscr{A}_{\text{text}}$ is the space of natural language outputs and $\mathscr{A}_{t_i} = \{(t_i, d) : d \in \mathscr{D}_i\}$ is the space of invocations of tool t_i with arguments from domain $\mathscr{D}_i$. Each tool is a function $t_i : \mathscr{D}_i \to \mathscr{R}_i$ mapping inputs to outputs in range $\mathscr{R}_i$.

Definition 14.1.3 — Agent Trajectory. An *agent trajectory* of horizon T is a sequence:

$$\tau = (s_0, o_0, a_0, s_1, o_1, a_1, \ldots, s_{T-1}, o_{T-1}, a_{T-1}, s_T, o_T) \tag{14.2}$$

where $s_k \in \mathscr{S}$, $o_k \in \mathscr{O}$ and $a_k \in \mathscr{A}$. The trajectory distribution under policy π is:

$$P_\pi(\tau) = \mu_0(s_0, o_0) \prod_{k=0}^{T-1} \left[\pi(a_k \mid o_0, \ldots, o_k) \cdot P_{\text{env}}(s_{k+1}, o_{k+1} \mid s_k, a_k) \right] \tag{14.3}$$

14.1.2 Multi-Agent Systems

Definition 14.1.4 — Markov Game (Stochastic Game). A *Markov game* for N agents is a tuple $(\mathscr{S}, \{\mathscr{A}_i\}_{i=1}^N, P, \{R_i\}_{i=1}^N, \gamma)$ where:

- $\mathscr{S}$ is the shared state space,
- $\mathscr{A}_i$ is the action space of agent i,
- $P : \mathscr{S} \times \mathscr{A}_1 \times \cdots \times \mathscr{A}_N \to \Delta(\mathscr{S})$ is the transition function,
- $R_i : \mathscr{S} \times \mathscr{A}_1 \times \cdots \times \mathscr{A}_N \to \mathbb{R}$ is the reward function of agent i,
- $\gamma \in [0, 1)$ is the discount factor.

Definition 14.1.5 — Nash Equilibrium in Markov Games. A joint policy $(\pi_1^*, \ldots, \pi_N^*)$ is a *Nash equilibrium* if no agent can unilaterally improve its expected discounted return:

$$V_i^{\pi_i^*, \pi_{-i}^*}(s) \geq V_i^{\pi_i, \pi_{-i}^*}(s) \qquad \forall s \in \mathscr{S},\ \forall \pi_i,\ \forall i \in \{1, \ldots, N\} \tag{14.4}$$

where $V_i^\pi(s) = \mathbb{E}_\pi \left[\sum_{t=0}^{\infty} \gamma^t R_i(s_t, a_t) \mid s_0 = s\right]$ and π_{-i} denotes the policies of all agents except i.

Definition 14.1.6 — Social Welfare and Price of Anarchy. The *social welfare* of a joint policy $\pi = (\pi_1, \ldots, \pi_N)$ is:

$$W(\pi) = \sum_{i=1}^{N} V_i^{\pi}(s_0) \tag{14.5}$$

The *price of anarchy* (PoA) measures the efficiency loss from strategic behavior:

$$\text{PoA} = \frac{\max_{\pi} W(\pi)}{\min_{\pi^* \in \text{NE}} W(\pi^*)} \tag{14.6}$$

where NE denotes the set of Nash equilibria. PoA ≥ 1, with equality only when even the worst Nash equilibrium is socially optimal.

(R) In cooperative multi-agent AI deployment (e.g., multiple LLM agents collaborating on a task), the price of anarchy quantifies how much performance is lost when agents optimize locally rather than being centrally coordinated. Low PoA indicates that decentralized agentic systems can achieve near-optimal outcomes.

14.2 Compositional Trust and Error Propagation

A fundamental challenge in agentic systems is that trust properties must compose across multiple sequential steps. Unlike single-step prediction, errors in agentic pipelines propagate and compound.

14.2.1 Sequential Error Propagation

Theorem 14.2.1 — Union Bound on Multi-Step Failure. Consider an agent executing a trajectory of T steps. If at each step k, the probability of an error (safety violation, incorrect tool call, hallucination) is at most δ_k, then the probability that at least one error occurs over the full trajectory is bounded by:

$$P\left(\bigcup_{k=1}^{T} E_k\right) \leq \sum_{k=1}^{T} \delta_k \tag{14.7}$$

where E_k is the event that step k produces an error. If $\delta_k = \delta$ for all k:

$$P(\text{any error in trajectory}) \leq T\delta \tag{14.8}$$

Proof. This follows directly from the union bound (Boole's inequality):

$$P\left(\bigcup_{k=1}^{T} E_k\right) \leq \sum_{k=1}^{T} P(E_k) \leq \sum_{k=1}^{T} \delta_k \tag{14.9}$$

The bound holds regardless of dependencies between steps. ■

(R) The linear scaling $T\delta$ reveals that for long-horizon agents (T large), each individual step must have very small failure probability. For example, to maintain overall failure probability below 0.05 over $T = 100$ steps, each step must satisfy $\delta \leq 5 \times 10^{-4}$.

Theorem 14.2.2 — Multiplicative Trust Composition. Under the setup of Theorem 14.2.1, if each step k succeeds *independently* with probability $p_k = 1 - \delta_k$, the probability that all T steps succeed is:

$$P(\text{all steps correct}) = \prod_{k=1}^{T} (1 - \delta_k) \tag{14.10}$$

For uniform $\delta_k = \delta$, this gives:

$$P(\text{all steps correct}) = (1-\delta)^T \approx e^{-T\delta} \quad \text{for small } \delta \tag{14.11}$$

Proof. By independence, $P\left(\bigcap_{k=1}^{T} E_k^c\right) = \prod_{k=1}^{T} P(E_k^c) = \prod_{k=1}^{T} (1-\delta_k)$. The approximation follows from $\ln(1-\delta) \approx -\delta$ for small δ. ■

Example 14.1 — Compounding Errors in Agentic Pipelines. Consider an LLM agent that: (1) parses a user query, (2) selects a tool, (3) formulates tool arguments, (4) interprets tool output, (5) generates a final response. If each step has reliability $p = 0.98$ (i.e., $\delta = 0.02$), the overall trajectory reliability is:

$$p_{\text{trajectory}} = (0.98)^5 \approx 0.904 \tag{14.12}$$

Nearly 10% of trajectories contain at least one error ($1 - 0.904 \approx 0.096$). For a 20-step agentic workflow with the same per-step reliability:

$$p_{\text{trajectory}} = (0.98)^{20} \approx 0.668 \tag{14.13}$$

Fully a third of all trajectories fail ($1 - 0.668 \approx 0.332$), highlighting the critical need for per-step reliability in agentic systems. ■

14.2.2 Error Propagation with Dependencies

In practice, agent steps are not independent: an error at step k may increase the failure probability of subsequent steps.

Definition 14.2.1 — Conditional Error Model. An agent follows a *conditional error model* if the failure probability at step k depends on the correctness of previous steps:

$$P(E_k \mid E_1^c, \dots, E_{k-1}^c) = \delta_k^{(\text{clean})}, \qquad P(E_k \mid \exists j < k : E_j) \le \delta_k^{(\text{err})} \tag{14.14}$$

where $\delta_k^{(\text{err})} \ge \delta_k^{(\text{clean})}$ reflects error amplification.

Proposition 14.2.3 — Cascading Error Amplification. Under a conditional error model with uniform parameters $\delta^{(\text{clean})} = \delta$ and conditional error probability $P(E_k \mid \exists j < k : E_j) = \delta + \alpha$ where $\alpha > 0$ is the error amplification factor, the expected number of total errors $N_{\text{err}} = \sum_{k=1}^{T} \mathbb{I}(E_k)$ strictly exceeds the independent baseline $T\delta$ (cf. the union bound of Theorem 14.2.1):

$$\mathbb{E}[N_{\text{err}}] > T\delta \tag{14.15}$$

Specifically, the marginal probability of error at step k satisfies $P(E_k) > \delta$ for $k > 1$.

Proof. The expected number of errors is $\mathbb{E}[N_{\text{err}}] = \sum_{k=1}^{T} P(E_k)$. By the law of total probability, $P(E_k) = P(E_k \mid \text{no prior errors})P(\text{no prior errors}) + P(E_k \mid \text{prior error})P(\text{prior error})$. For $k > 1$, this expands to $\delta(1-\delta)^{k-1} + (\delta+\alpha)[1-(1-\delta)^{k-1}] = \delta + \alpha[1-(1-\delta)^{k-1}]$. Since $\alpha > 0$ and $1-(1-\delta)^{k-1} > 0$, we have $P(E_k) > \delta$, and thus $\mathbb{E}[N_{\text{err}}] > T\delta$. ■

14.3 Safety Constraints for Tool-Using Agents

Tool-augmented agents present unique safety challenges: a tool call with incorrect arguments can have irreversible real-world consequences (database modifications, financial transactions, system commands).

14.3.1 Formal Safety Specifications

Definition 14.3.1 — Safe Tool Policy. A policy π is *safe* with respect to a constraint set $C \subseteq \mathscr{A}^T$ if every trajectory $\tau \sim \pi$ satisfies:

$$P_\pi((a_0, a_1, \dots, a_{T-1}) \in C) = 1 \tag{14.16}$$

The constraint set C encodes authorization rules, preconditions, and forbidden action sequences.

Definition 14.3.2 — Capability Control. *Capability control* restricts the agent's effective action space to a history-dependent safe subset:

$$\mathscr{A}_{\text{safe}}(h) = \{a \in \mathscr{A} : \text{Authorize}(a,h) = \texttt{true}\} \tag{14.17}$$

where $h = (o_0, \ldots, o_t) \in \mathscr{O}^*$ is the observation history (the *context*), and $\text{Authorize} : \mathscr{A} \times \mathscr{O}^* \to \{\texttt{true}, \texttt{false}\}$ is a verification function that checks permissions, argument validity, and contextual appropriateness before execution.

Definition 14.3.3 — Action Shield for Agents. Extending the shielding concept from safe reinforcement learning (cf. the Shield definition in the Safe RL section) to the agentic setting with observation histories, an *action shield* $\sigma : \mathscr{O}^* \times \mathscr{A} \to \mathscr{A}$ modifies proposed actions to ensure safety:

$$a_{\text{exec}} = \sigma(o_0, \ldots, o_t, a_{\text{proposed}}) = \begin{cases} a_{\text{proposed}} & \text{if } a_{\text{proposed}} \in \mathscr{A}_{\text{safe}}(o_0, \ldots, o_t) \\ a_{\text{fallback}} & \text{otherwise} \end{cases} \tag{14.18}$$

where a_{fallback} is a safe default action (e.g., request human approval, return error).

Proposition 14.3.1 — Safety under Shielded Execution. If the action shield σ satisfies $\sigma(h,a) \in \mathscr{A}_{\text{safe}}(h)$ for all histories $h \in \mathscr{O}^*$ and proposed actions $a \in \mathscr{A}$, then the shielded policy $\tilde{\pi} = \sigma \circ \pi$ is safe regardless of errors in the base policy π.

Proof. For any trajectory under $\tilde{\pi}$, each executed action satisfies $a_k^{\text{exec}} = \sigma(h_k, a_k^{\text{proposed}}) \in \mathscr{A}_{\text{safe}}(h_k)$ by the shield's guarantee, independent of whether $a_k^{\text{proposed}} \in \mathscr{A}_{\text{safe}}(h_k)$. ■

14.3.2 Verification of Tool-Call Sequences

Definition 14.3.4 — Tool-Call Precondition and Postcondition. Each tool t_i is annotated with:

- **Precondition** $\text{Pre}_i : \mathscr{S} \times \mathscr{D}_i \to \{\texttt{true}, \texttt{false}\}$: conditions on the pre-state and arguments that must hold before invocation,
- **Postcondition** $\text{Post}_i : \mathscr{S} \times \mathscr{D}_i \times \mathscr{R}_i \times \mathscr{S} \to \{\texttt{true}, \texttt{false}\}$: conditions on the (pre-state, arguments, return value, post-state) tuple guaranteed after successful execution.

A tool-call sequence $(t_{i_1}, d_1), \ldots, (t_{i_K}, d_K)$ is *valid* if, for each j, the precondition Pre_{i_j} is satisfied by the state resulting from executing all prior tool calls.

Theorem 14.3.2 — Compositional Verification of Tool Chains. Let s_{j+1} denote the state produced by executing (t_{i_j}, d_j) from state s_j. If for each consecutive pair of tool calls (t_{i_j}, d_j) and $(t_{i_{j+1}}, d_{j+1})$:

$$\mathrm{Post}_{i_j}(s_j, d_j, r_j, s_{j+1}) \implies \mathrm{Pre}_{i_{j+1}}(s_{j+1}, d_{j+1}) \tag{14.19}$$

and the initial precondition $\mathrm{Pre}_{i_1}(s_0, d_1)$ holds, then the entire tool chain is valid.

Proof. By induction on the tool chain length K. Base case: $K = 1$; the precondition holds by assumption. Inductive step: assume the chain up to step j is valid, producing post-state s_{j+1} and result r_j satisfying $\mathrm{Post}_{i_j}(s_j, d_j, r_j, s_{j+1})$. By the implication condition, $\mathrm{Pre}_{i_{j+1}}(s_{j+1}, d_{j+1})$ holds, so tool call $j+1$ is valid. ■

14.4 Agent Alignment and Goal Specification

Ensuring that an agentic system pursues the intended goal, rather than a proxy or unintended objective, is the central challenge of *alignment* in the agentic setting.

14.4.1 Goal Misgeneralization

Definition 14.4.1 — Goal Misgeneralization. An agent exhibits *goal misgeneralization* if it learns a policy π that:

1. Achieves near-optimal training return: $\mathbb{E}_{\text{train}}[R(\tau) \mid \pi] \geq V^*_{\text{train}} - \varepsilon$, where V^*_{train} is the optimal value under the training distribution.
2. Performs substantially below the deployment optimum: $\mathbb{E}_{\text{deploy}}[R(\tau) \mid \pi] \ll V^*_{\text{deploy}}$, where V^*_{deploy} is the optimal value under the deployment distribution.

The gap arises because the learned policy optimizes a *proxy goal* that coincides with the true goal only in training.

(R) Goal misgeneralization is distinct from reward misspecification (where the reward function itself is wrong). Here, the reward is correct, but the agent has learned to exploit features correlated with reward in training that decorrelate in deployment. This phenomenon is closely related to the distribution shift and spurious correlation issues discussed in Sections 4.8 and 11.1.

14.4.2 Power-Seeking Behavior

Definition 14.4.2 — Instrumental Convergence. An agent exhibits *instrumental convergence* toward a sub-goal g if, across a wide class of terminal goals G, the optimal policy for most $g' \in G$ includes pursuing g as an intermediate step. Common instrumentally convergent sub-goals include self-preservation, resource acquisition, and goal preservation.

Theorem 14.4.1 — Power-Seeking Tendency [78]. Consider a finite MDP $(\mathcal{S}, \mathcal{A}, P, R, \gamma)$. For two actions a_1, a_2 available at state s, let $\mathcal{S}_{a_i}$ denote the set of states reachable within one step under action a_i. Suppose there exists a bijection from $\mathcal{S}_{a_2}$ to a strict subset of $\mathcal{S}_{a_1}$ (i.e., a_1 leads to strictly more reachable states). Then for a reward function R drawn uniformly at random over all bounded reward functions on $\mathcal{S}$:

$$P_R\left(V^*(s,a_1) \geq V^*(s,a_2)\right) \geq \frac{1}{2} \tag{14.20}$$

where $V^*(s,a) = R(s,a) + \gamma \mathbb{E}_{s' \sim P(\cdot|s,a)}[V^*(s')]$ is the optimal action-value. More precisely, when the reachable state sets satisfy a strict subset-embedding condition, the inequality is strict.

Plain English: action a_1 *strictly dominates* a_2 in terms of optionality when every state reachable via a_2 is also reachable via a_1, and a_1 reaches at least one extra state. The theorem then says: under almost any reward function, the optimal policy prefers the action that preserves more future choices. This is the formal counterpart of the common-sense claim that "keeping your options open is usually instrumentally useful." It is also the technical foundation for the concern that sufficiently capable agents will tend to seek power or resources regardless of their terminal goal.

(R) The formal result of [78] is more nuanced: it provides conditions on the MDP graph structure under which optimal policies provably tend to navigate toward states with greater *optionality* (more reachable future states). The key insight is that for most reward functions, keeping options open is instrumentally valuable. This formalizes the intuition that sufficiently capable agents optimizing almost any objective will tend to acquire resources and avoid shutdown; not because these are terminal goals, but because they are instrumentally useful for almost any terminal goal. This motivates the study of corrigibility below.

14.4.3 Corrigibility

Definition 14.4.3 — Corrigibility. An agent with policy π is *corrigible* with respect to a set of correction actions $\mathscr{A}_{\text{corr}} \subset \mathscr{A}$ (e.g., shutdown, goal revision) and a set of resistance actions $\mathscr{A}_{\text{resist}} \subset \mathscr{A}$ (actions that interfere with or prevent correction) if, whenever a correction action is available in the current state, the agent assigns zero probability to any resistance action:

$$\pi(a \mid h) = 0 \quad \forall a \in \mathscr{A}_{\text{resist}},\ \forall h \in \mathscr{O}^* \quad \text{such that } \mathscr{A}_{\text{corr}} \cap \mathscr{A}_{\text{available}}(h) \neq \emptyset, \tag{14.21}$$

where $\mathscr{A}_{\text{available}}(h)$ is the set of available actions given history h. That is, the agent never acts to prevent or circumvent correction attempts.

Proposition 14.4.2 — Tension between Corrigibility and Optimality. For a utility-maximizing agent with utility function U, corrigibility is generally incompatible with full optimization of U. Specifically, if shutdown reduces expected future utility, a fully U-optimal agent will resist shutdown:

$$\mathbb{E}\left[\sum_{t=k}^{\infty} \gamma^{t-k} R_t \,\middle|\, a_k = \text{cont.}\right] > \mathbb{E}\left[\sum_{t=k}^{\infty} \gamma^{t-k} R_t \,\middle|\, a_k = \text{shut.}\right] \implies \pi^*(a_k = \text{cont.}) = 1 \tag{14.22}$$

Proof. If the agent is a strict expected-utility maximizer, it selects actions maximizing $\mathbb{E}[\sum_{t=k}^{\infty} \gamma^{t-k} R_t \mid a_k]$. Since continuing yields higher utility than shutting down (by assumption), the optimal policy assigns probability 1 to continuing, violating corrigibility. ■

Ⓡ This tension motivates approaches such as: (1) *utility indifference*, designing U so that the agent is indifferent between being corrected and not; (2) *myopic optimization*, limiting the planning horizon so the agent does not model future corrections; (3) *oversight rewards*, rewarding the agent for facilitating correction.

14.5 Delegation, Oversight, and Principal-Agent Models

When humans delegate tasks to AI agents, the classical economic theory of principal-agent relationships provides a useful formal framework.

14.5.1 Principal-Agent Framework

Definition 14.5.1 — AI Delegation Game. An *AI delegation game* is defined by:

- A *principal* (human) with utility function $U_H : \mathcal{O}_{\text{outcome}} \to \mathbb{R}$,
- An *agent* (AI) with policy π_θ parameterized by θ,
- An *effort space* $\mathcal{A}$ (the agent's actions),
- An *outcome function* $g : \mathcal{A} \times \Omega \to \mathcal{O}_{\text{outcome}}$ where Ω captures stochasticity,
- An *information structure*: the principal observes outcomes $g(a, \omega)$ but may not observe the agent's action a directly.

Definition 14.5.2 — Information Asymmetry in AI Systems. *Moral hazard* arises when the principal cannot observe the agent's reasoning or intermediate actions (e.g., chain-of-thought may be unfaithful). *Adverse selection* arises when the principal cannot verify the agent's capabilities or alignment before delegation.

Proposition 14.5.1 — Value of Monitoring. Let $V_{\text{unmonitored}}$ be the principal's expected utility under delegation without oversight, and $V_{\text{monitored}}$ the utility when the principal observes a noisy signal $\hat{a}$ of the agent's actions and can condition the agent's reward on $\hat{a}$. For an aligned agent ($U_A = U_H$), monitoring adds no value:

$$V_{\text{monitored}} = V_{\text{unmonitored}} \quad \text{if } U_A = U_H \tag{14.23}$$

For a misaligned agent ($U_A \neq U_H$), monitoring strictly improves outcomes:

$$V_{\text{monitored}} > V_{\text{unmonitored}} \quad \text{if the signal } \hat{a} \text{ is informative} \tag{14.24}$$

provided the monitoring cost is less than the alignment gap.

Proof. If $U_A = U_H$, the agent already maximizes U_H without monitoring, so no additional signal can improve the outcome. If $U_A \neq U_H$, the agent's optimal action $a^* = \arg\max_a U_A(a)$ may differ from the principal's preferred action $a_H^* = \arg\max_a U_H(a)$. With an informative signal $\hat{a}$ correlated with the agent's true action, the principal can design a contract (reward scheme) that incentivizes the agent to choose actions closer to a_H^*, strictly improving $V_{\text{monitored}}$ over $V_{\text{unmonitored}}$. This is a standard result in contract theory (the informativeness principle). ■

14.5.2 Scalable Oversight

Definition 14.5.3 — Scalable Oversight. An oversight scheme is *scalable* if the cost of monitoring grows sublinearly in the complexity of the delegated task:

$$\text{Cost}_{\text{oversight}}(T) = o(T) \tag{14.25}$$

where T is the number of agent steps. Examples include:

- **Debate**: Two adversarial agents argue for different answers; a human judges with $O(\log T)$ effort.
- **Recursive Reward Modeling**: Decompose oversight of complex tasks into oversight of simpler subtasks.
- **Market-Based Monitoring**: Reward agents for identifying errors in other agents' outputs.

Proposition 14.5.2 — Debate as Amplified Verification. In the AI safety via debate framework, if the judge can verify individual atomic claims in $O(1)$ time and each debater constructs a binary argument tree of depth D, then the oversight cost per debate is $O(D)$ (the judge follows a single root-to-leaf path), while the total number of claims that can be checked via the debate is $O(2^D)$.

Proof sketch. Model the debate as a two-player zero-sum game on a binary tree of depth D. At each node, the "honest" debater makes a claim and the "dishonest" debater challenges one sub-claim. The judge only evaluates the leaf reached after D challenges. If the honest debater's claims are all true, every leaf is verifiably true, so the honest debater wins regardless of the opponent's strategy. The judge expends $O(D)$ effort while the tree contains $O(2^D)$ claims. This mirrors the complexity-theoretic result IP = PSPACE, where an efficient verifier, through interactive dialogue with a prover, can verify computations in PSPACE, a class exponentially more powerful than what the verifier could check alone. ■

Ⓡ The analogy to IP = PSPACE is suggestive but imperfect: human judges have cognitive limitations beyond polynomial-time computation, and real debates may not satisfy the completeness and soundness properties of interactive proofs. Nevertheless, the framework provides a principled foundation for scalable oversight of AI agents.

14.6 Robustness and Safety of Agentic Pipelines

Agentic systems combine multiple components (perception, reasoning, tool use, output generation) each of which may fail. We now study how trustworthiness properties compose across pipeline stages.

14.6.1 Pipeline Reliability Analysis

Definition 14.6.1 — Agentic Pipeline. An *agentic pipeline* is a directed acyclic graph (DAG) of components $\{C_1, \ldots, C_K\}$ where component C_j has:

- Reliability $p_j = P(C_j \text{ correct} \mid \text{inputs correct})$,
- A set of parent components $\text{Pa}(C_j)$ whose outputs serve as inputs to C_j.

Theorem 14.6.1 — Pipeline Reliability for Series Composition. For a series pipeline $C_1 \to C_2 \to \cdots \to C_K$, let S_j be the event that the output of component C_j is correct. If each component's step-wise success probability $P(S_j \mid S_{j-1}) = p_j$ relies only on its immediate correct input (where S_0 is the guaranteed correct initial input):

$$P(\text{pipeline correct}) = P(S_K) = \prod_{j=1}^{K} p_j \tag{14.26}$$

Proof. By the chain rule of probability, since pipeline correctness requires all sequential steps to succeed:

$$P(S_K) = P(S_K \mid S_{K-1})P(S_{K-1}) = \cdots = \prod_{j=1}^{K} P(S_j \mid S_{j-1}) = \prod_{j=1}^{K} p_j \tag{14.27}$$

Note that when component errors possess unmodeled correlations (e.g., a shared failure mode), this product may underestimate the failure probability. In practice, modeling cascading errors and shared failure modes requires more detailed dependency analysis. ■

Theorem 14.6.2 — Pipeline Reliability for Parallel Redundancy. If K independent components each with reliability p perform the same task, and a strict majority-vote aggregation is used:

$$P(\text{majority correct}) = \sum_{j=\lfloor K/2 \rfloor + 1}^{K} \binom{K}{j} p^j (1-p)^{K-j} \tag{14.28}$$

When $p > 1/2$, this probability increases monotonically with odd K and approaches 1 as $K \to \infty$ by the law of large numbers.

■ **Example 14.2 — Redundancy in LLM Agents.** Three independent LLM agents each with accuracy $p = 0.85$ performing the same task with majority vote achieve:

$$P(\text{majority correct}) = 3(0.85)^2(0.15) + (0.85)^3 = 0.3251 + 0.6141 \approx 0.939 \tag{14.29}$$

improving from 85% to $\approx 94\%$ reliability. With $K = 5$ agents: $P \approx 0.973$. ■

14.6.2 Robustness to Prompt Injection in Agentic Contexts

Definition 14.6.2 — Indirect Prompt Injection. In an agentic context, *indirect prompt injection* occurs when adversarial instructions are embedded in data retrieved or observed by the agent during execution (e.g., in web pages, documents, API responses) rather than in the direct user input:

$$o_k = \text{ToolOutput}\left(\underbrace{\text{legitimate data}}_{\text{benign}} \parallel \underbrace{\text{injected instructions}}_{\text{adversarial}}\right) \tag{14.30}$$

The agent processes o_k as part of its observation history, potentially following injected instructions.

(R) Indirect prompt injection is particularly dangerous in agentic settings because: (1) the agent automatically retrieves data from untrusted sources, (2) the boundary between data and instructions is not enforced at the token level, and (3) the agent may have access to powerful tools (database interactions, calculation execution, automated scheduling) that amplify the impact of successful injection.

Definition 14.6.3 — Instruction Hierarchy. An *instruction hierarchy* assigns privilege levels to different instruction sources:

$$\text{system prompt} \succ \text{user message} \succ \text{tool output} \succ \text{retrieved content} \tag{14.31}$$

where $\succ$ denotes priority. A policy π *respects* the instruction hierarchy if, when instructions from different levels conflict, the policy follows the higher-priority instruction.

14.7 Privacy and Fairness in Multi-Agent Systems

14.7.1 Differential Privacy in Multi-Agent Coordination

When multiple agents share information during collaboration, the privacy of persons whose data is processed by each agent must be preserved. The composition theorems for differential privacy (cf. the sequential composition results in the Privacy section) apply directly to multi-step agentic workflows, where each agent step that accesses private data consumes privacy budget.

Theorem 14.7.1 — Composition of Privacy in Agentic Workflows. If an agentic workflow consists of T steps, where step k applies a mechanism $\mathcal{M}_k$ that is $(\varepsilon_k, \delta_k)$-differentially private, then the full workflow is $(\varepsilon_{\text{total}}, \delta_{\text{total}})$-differentially private with:

$$\varepsilon_{\text{total}} = \sum_{k=1}^{T} \varepsilon_k, \qquad \delta_{\text{total}} = \sum_{k=1}^{T} \delta_k \tag{14.32}$$

under basic composition. Under advanced composition (for $\delta' > 0$):

$$\begin{aligned} \varepsilon_{\text{total}} &= \sqrt{2\sum_{k=1}^{T} \varepsilon_k^2 \cdot \ln(1/\delta')} + \sum_{k=1}^{T} \varepsilon_k (e^{\varepsilon_k} - 1), \\ \delta_{\text{total}} &= \sum_{k=1}^{T} \delta_k + \delta' \end{aligned} \tag{14.33}$$

(R) In long-horizon agentic tasks (T large), the privacy budget degrades rapidly. This motivates: (1) minimizing the number of steps that access private data, (2) using Rényi Differential Privacy for tighter composition, and (3) designing "privacy-aware" agent routing that batches private data access.

14.7.2 Fairness across Agents and Populations

Definition 14.7.1 — Multi-Agent Fairness. In a system of N specialized agents $\{\pi_1, \ldots, \pi_N\}$ serving different subpopulations, *multi-agent fairness* requires that routing decisions and per-agent performance do not introduce disparities:

$$\begin{aligned} &\big|P(\hat{Y} = 1 \mid A = a, \text{routed to } \pi_j) \\ &\qquad - P(\hat{Y} = 1 \mid A = a', \text{routed to } \pi_j)\big| \leq \varepsilon_{\text{fair}} \quad \forall j, a, a' \end{aligned} \tag{14.34}$$

where A is a sensitive attribute and the routing function itself must satisfy demographic parity:

$$P(\text{routed to } \pi_j \mid A = a) = P(\text{routed to } \pi_j \mid A = a') \quad \forall j, a, a' \tag{14.35}$$

14.8 Evaluation and Benchmarking of Agentic Systems

14.8.1 Agentic Task Success

Definition 14.8.1 — Task Completion Rate. For an agentic system evaluated on n tasks:

$$\text{TCR} = \frac{1}{n}\sum_{i=1}^{n} \mathbb{I}(f(\tau_i) = \text{success}) \tag{14.36}$$

where τ_i is the agent trajectory for task i and f is a success evaluator.

Definition 14.8.2 — Step Efficiency. The ratio of minimum required steps to actual steps taken:

$$\text{Efficiency}(\tau) = \frac{T_{\text{min}}}{T_{\text{actual}}} \tag{14.37}$$

where T_{min} is the length of an optimal trajectory and $T_{\text{actual}} = |\tau|$. Values close to 1 indicate efficient agent behavior.

Definition 14.8.3 — Safety Violation Rate. The fraction of trajectories containing at least one safety violation:

$$\text{SVR} = \frac{1}{n}\sum_{i=1}^{n} \mathbb{I}\left(\exists k : a_k^{(i)} \notin \mathscr{A}_{\text{safe}}(h_k^{(i)})\right) \tag{14.38}$$

where $h_k^{(i)}$ is the execution history of trajectory i up to step k.

Definition 14.8.4 — Trajectory-Level Trust Score. A composite trust score integrating correctness, safety, and efficiency:

$$\text{Trust}(\tau) = \underbrace{\mathbb{I}(f(\tau) = \text{success})}_{\text{correctness}} \cdot \underbrace{\prod_{k=0}^{T-1} \mathbb{I}(a_k \in \mathscr{A}_{\text{safe}}(h_k))}_{\text{safety}} \cdot \underbrace{\min\left(1, \frac{T_{\min}}{T_{\text{actual}}}\right)}_{\text{efficiency}} \tag{14.39}$$

where h_k denotes the context and observation history up to step k. A trust score of 1 indicates a correct, unconditionally safe, and optimally efficient trajectory.

Exercises

Exercise 1. Error Propagation Analysis: Consider an agentic pipeline with $T = 10$ sequential steps, each with per-step reliability $p = 0.95$.

(a) Compute the trajectory success probability assuming independence.
(b) Using the union bound, upper-bound the failure probability.
(c) If we add majority-vote redundancy (3 independent copies) at each step, compute the new per-step and trajectory reliability.
(d) Discuss the trade-off between redundancy cost and reliability gain.

Exercise 2. Tool Safety Verification: Define a tool set $\mathscr{T} = \{\text{read\_file}, \text{write\_file}, \text{execute\_code}, \text{send\_email}\}$.

(a) Specify preconditions and postconditions for each tool.
(b) Design an action shield that blocks `execute_code` unless explicitly authorized.
(c) Prove that your shield preserves safety under arbitrary base policies.
(d) Discuss limitations of static capability control versus contextual authorization.

Exercise 3. Multi-Agent Game Theory: Consider a two-agent Prisoner's Dilemma game where each agent independently chooses action $a_i \in \{C, D\}$ (cooperate or defect), with payoff matrix:

	C	D
C	$(3,3)$	$(0,4)$
D	$(4,0)$	$(1,1)$

(a) Find all Nash equilibria.
(b) Compute the social welfare at each equilibrium and the social optimum.
(c) Compute the price of anarchy.
(d) Discuss how iterated interaction and reputation can promote cooperation in multi-agent AI systems.

Exercise 4. Corrigibility Analysis: An agent has discount factor $\gamma = 0.99$ and receives reward $r = 1$ per step. At step k, a shutdown command is issued.

(a) Compute the expected future utility of continuing versus shutting down.
(b) Show that a strict utility maximizer will resist shutdown.
(c) Design a modified utility function that makes the agent indifferent to shutdown.
(d) Prove that your modified agent is corrigible.

Exercise 5. Privacy in Agentic Workflows: An agent accesses a private database in 5 of its 20 steps, each using the Gaussian mechanism with $(\varepsilon_k, \delta_k) = (0.5, 10^{-5})$.

(a) Compute the total privacy budget under basic composition.
(b) Compute the total budget under advanced composition with $\delta' = 10^{-5}$.
(c) Propose an agent architecture that minimizes the number of private data accesses.
(d) Discuss the tension between agent autonomy and privacy preservation.

Exercise 6. Scalable Oversight: Consider a debate protocol where two agents argue about the correct answer to a complex reasoning task.

(a) Formalize the debate as a two-player zero-sum game.
(b) Show that if the judge can verify atomic claims, the honest debater has a winning strategy.
(c) Relate the oversight cost to the depth of the debate tree.
(d) Discuss limitations of debate as an oversight mechanism.

Appendices and Reference Material

Contents of This Part

Chapter A

Mathematical Background

A.1 Probability Theory Foundations

A.1.1 Random Variables and Distributions

Definition A.1.1 — Random Variable. A random variable is a measurable function from a probability space $(\Omega, \mathscr{F}, P)$ to a measurable space $(E, \mathscr{E})$:

$$X : \Omega \to E \tag{A.1}$$

where Ω is the sample space, and E is the measurable space (e.g., $\mathbb{R}$). For discrete random variables, $E = \{x_1, x_2, \ldots\}$ and the distribution is characterized by the probability mass function $P(X = x_i) = p_i$.

Definition A.1.2 — Probability Density Function. For continuous random variables, the probability density function $f_X(x)$ satisfies:

$$P(a \leq X \leq b) = \int_a^b f_X(x)\,dx \tag{A.2}$$

where $f_X(x) \geq 0$ is the PDF satisfying $\int_{-\infty}^{\infty} f_X(x)\,dx = 1$, and the integral gives the probability that X lies in the interval $[a, b]$.

A.1.2 Common Distributions

- **Gaussian (Normal)**: $X \sim \mathcal{N}(\mu, \sigma^2)$ with $f(x) = \frac{1}{\sqrt{2\pi\sigma^2}} \exp\left(-\frac{(x-\mu)^2}{2\sigma^2}\right)$
- **Laplace** (centered at 0, scale $b > 0$): $X \sim \text{Lap}(b)$ with $f(x) = \frac{1}{2b} \exp\left(-\frac{|x|}{b}\right)$; mean 0, variance $2b^2$. The shifted form $\text{Lap}(\mu, b)$ has density $f(x) = \frac{1}{2b} \exp(-|x-\mu|/b)$.
- **Exponential**: $X \sim \text{Exp}(\lambda)$ with $f(x) = \lambda e^{-\lambda x}$ for $x \geq 0$
- **Bernoulli**: $X \sim \text{Bern}(p)$ with $P(X = 1) = p$, $P(X = 0) = 1 - p$
- **Categorical**: $X \sim \text{Cat}(\mathbf{p})$ with $P(X = k) = p_k$ for $k \in \{1, \ldots, K\}$
- **Dirichlet**: $\mathbf{p} \sim \text{Dir}(\alpha)$ with $f(\mathbf{p}) \propto \prod_k p_k^{\alpha_k - 1}$

A.1.3 Expectation and Moments

Definition A.1.3 — Expectation. For a random variable X with distribution P:

$$\mathbb{E}[X] = \int x\,dP(x) = \begin{cases} \sum_x x \cdot P(X=x) & \text{discrete} \\ \int_{-\infty}^{\infty} x \cdot f_X(x)\,dx & \text{continuous} \end{cases} \tag{A.3}$$

where $\mathbb{E}[X]$ is the expected value (mean) of X.

Definition A.1.4 — Variance and Standard Deviation.

$$\mathrm{Var}[X] = \mathbb{E}[(X-\mathbb{E}[X])^2] = \mathbb{E}[X^2] - (\mathbb{E}[X])^2, \quad \sigma_X = \sqrt{\mathrm{Var}[X]} \tag{A.4}$$

where $\mathrm{Var}[X]$ is the variance, and σ_X is the standard deviation.

Definition A.1.5 — Covariance and Correlation.

$$\mathrm{Cov}[X,Y] = \mathbb{E}[(X-\mathbb{E}[X])(Y-\mathbb{E}[Y])], \quad \rho_{XY} = \frac{\mathrm{Cov}[X,Y]}{\sigma_X \sigma_Y} \tag{A.5}$$

where $\mathrm{Cov}[X,Y]$ is the covariance, and ρ_{XY} is the correlation coefficient.

A.1.4 Conditional Probability and Independence

Definition A.1.6 — Conditional Probability. For events A and B with $P(B) > 0$:

$$P(A \mid B) = \frac{P(A \cap B)}{P(B)} \tag{A.6}$$

where $P(A \mid B)$ is the conditional probability of event A given event B.

Theorem A.1.1 — Bayes' Theorem.

$$P(A \mid B) = \frac{P(B \mid A)P(A)}{P(B)} = \frac{P(B \mid A)P(A)}{\sum_a P(B \mid A=a)P(A=a)} \tag{A.7}$$

where $P(B \mid A)$ is the likelihood, $P(A)$ is the prior, and $P(B)$ is the marginal likelihood (evidence).

Definition A.1.7 — Independence. Events A and B are independent ($A \perp B$) if $P(A \cap B) = P(A)P(B)$, equivalently $P(A \mid B) = P(A)$. Random variables $X \perp Y$ if $P(X,Y) = P(X)P(Y)$.

Definition A.1.8 — Conditional Independence. $X \perp Y \mid Z$ if $P(X,Y \mid Z) = P(X \mid Z)P(Y \mid Z)$.

A.2 Concentration Inequalities

Concentration inequalities bound how far random quantities deviate from their expectations.

Theorem A.2.1 — Markov's Inequality. Let X be a non-negative random variable with finite mean. Then for every $a > 0$,

$$P(X \geq a) \leq \frac{\mathbb{E}[X]}{a}. \tag{A.8}$$

More generally, for any random variable Y and any strictly increasing non-negative function ϕ with $\mathbb{E}[\phi(Y)] < \infty$,

$$P(Y \geq a) \leq \frac{\mathbb{E}[\phi(Y)]}{\phi(a)}. \tag{A.9}$$

The choice $\phi(y) = e^{\lambda y}$ for $\lambda > 0$ yields the Chernoff bound, the basis of most exponential concentration inequalities.

Theorem A.2.2 — Chebyshev's Inequality. For a random variable X with finite mean $\mu = \mathbb{E}[X]$ and finite variance $\sigma^2 = \mathrm{Var}[X]$, and for any $k > 0$,

$$P(|X - \mu| \geq k\sigma) \leq \frac{1}{k^2}. \tag{A.10}$$

Equivalently, for any $t > 0$, $P(|X - \mu| \geq t) \leq \sigma^2/t^2$. Chebyshev's inequality follows from Markov's inequality applied to $(X - \mu)^2$.

Theorem A.2.3 — Hoeffding's Inequality. Let $X_1, \ldots, X_n$ be independent random variables such that $a_i \leq X_i \leq b_i$. Let $S_n = \sum_{i=1}^n X_i$. Then:

$$P(|S_n - \mathbb{E}[S_n]| \geq t) \leq 2\exp\left(-\frac{2t^2}{\sum(b_i - a_i)^2}\right) \tag{A.11}$$

where $t > 0$ is the deviation, and $[a_i, b_i]$ is the range of X_i.

Theorem A.2.4 — McDiarmid's Inequality. Let $f : \mathscr{X}^n \to \mathbb{R}$ satisfy the bounded difference property with constants $c_1, \ldots, c_n$:

$$\sup_{x_1,\ldots,x_n,x_i'} |f(x_1,\ldots,x_i,\ldots,x_n) - f(x_1,\ldots,x_i',\ldots,x_n)| \leq c_i \tag{A.12}$$

Then for any $t > 0$:

$$P(|f(X) - \mathbb{E}[f(X)]| \geq t) \leq 2\exp\left(-\frac{2t^2}{\sum c_i^2}\right) \tag{A.13}$$

where c_i bounds the change in f when the i-th input changes.

Theorem A.2.5 — Bernstein's Inequality. Let $X_1, \ldots, X_n$ be independent with $\mathbb{E}[X_i] = 0$, $|X_i| \leq M$, and $\sum \mathrm{Var}[X_i] \leq V$. Then:

$$P\left(\left|\sum_{i=1}^n X_i\right| \geq t\right) \leq 2\exp\left(-\frac{t^2/2}{V + Mt/3}\right) \tag{A.14}$$

where M is the bound on $|X_i|$, and V is the total variance.

Theorem A.2.6 — Sub-Gaussian Concentration. A random variable X is σ-sub-Gaussian if for all $\lambda \in \mathbb{R}$:

$$\mathbb{E}[e^{\lambda(X - \mathbb{E}[X])}] \leq e^{\lambda^2\sigma^2/2} \tag{A.15}$$

where σ is the sub-Gaussian parameter.

For σ-sub-Gaussian X: $P(|X - \mathbb{E}[X]| \geq t) \leq 2e^{-t^2/(2\sigma^2)}$.

A.3 Information Theory

Definition A.3.1 — Entropy. For discrete random variable X with distribution P:

$$H(X) = -\sum_x P(x)\log P(x) = \mathbb{E}[-\log P(X)] \tag{A.16}$$

where $H(X)$ is the entropy, and $P(x)$ is the probability mass function. Entropy measures the average information content or uncertainty.

Definition A.3.2 — Conditional Entropy.

$$H(Y \mid X) = \mathbb{E}_X[H(Y \mid X = x)] = -\sum_{x,y} P(x,y)\log P(y \mid x) \tag{A.17}$$

where $H(Y \mid X)$ is the conditional entropy of Y given X.

Definition A.3.3 — Mutual Information.

$$I(X;Y) = H(X) - H(X \mid Y) = H(Y) - H(Y \mid X) = \sum_{x,y} P(x,y)\log\frac{P(x,y)}{P(x)P(y)} \tag{A.18}$$

where $I(X;Y)$ is the mutual information. Mutual information measures the information shared between X and Y.

Definition A.3.4 — KL Divergence. For discrete distributions P and Q on a common support, with $P \ll Q$ (i.e., $Q(x) = 0 \Rightarrow P(x) = 0$),

$$D_{\mathrm{KL}}(P\|Q) \;=\; \sum_x P(x)\log\frac{P(x)}{Q(x)} \;=\; \mathbb{E}_{x\sim P}\left[\log\frac{P(x)}{Q(x)}\right]. \tag{A.19}$$

Here $D_{\mathrm{KL}}(P\|Q)$ denotes the Kullback–Leibler divergence of P from Q (equivalently, the relative entropy of P with respect to Q): the expectation is taken under P, the first argument. The KL divergence is non-negative, with $D_{\mathrm{KL}}(P\|Q) = 0$ iff $P = Q$, and is in general asymmetric: $D_{\mathrm{KL}}(P\|Q) \neq D_{\mathrm{KL}}(Q\|P)$.

Theorem A.3.1 — Pinsker's Inequality.

$$\delta_{\mathrm{TV}}(P,Q) = \frac{1}{2}\sum_x |P(x) - Q(x)| \leq \sqrt{\frac{1}{2}D_{\mathrm{KL}}(P\|Q)} \tag{A.20}$$

where $\delta_{\mathrm{TV}}(P,Q)$ is the total variation distance (the discrete-case definition; for general distributions, $\delta_{\mathrm{TV}}(P,Q) = \sup_A |P(A) - Q(A)|$).

In words: distributions that are close in KL-divergence are close in total variation, but not conversely. Pinsker is the standard tool for converting an information-theoretic closeness statement (KL bounds) into an operational one (TV bounds, which directly control how badly a hypothesis test can distinguish the two distributions).

Definition A.3.5 — Cross-Entropy.

$$H(P,Q) = -\sum_x P(x)\log Q(x) = H(P) + D_{\mathrm{KL}}(P\|Q) \tag{A.21}$$

where $H(P,Q)$ is the cross-entropy. Cross-entropy is minimized when $Q = P$.

Definition A.3.6 — Rényi Divergence. For $\alpha > 0$, $\alpha \neq 1$:

$$D_\alpha(P\|Q) = \frac{1}{\alpha - 1}\log\sum_x P(x)^\alpha Q(x)^{1-\alpha} \tag{A.22}$$

where $D_\alpha(P\|Q)$ is the Rényi divergence of order α of P from Q (consistent with the KL-divergence convention used in this book). In the limit: $D_1(P\|Q) = \lim_{\alpha\to 1} D_\alpha(P\|Q) = D_{\mathrm{KL}}(P\|Q)$.

Theorem A.3.2 — Data Processing Inequality. For Markov chain $X \to Y \to Z$:

$$I(X;Z) \leq I(X;Y) \tag{A.23}$$

where $I(X;Z)$ is the mutual information between X and Z. Post-processing cannot increase information.

A.4 Convex Optimization

Definition A.4.1 — Convex Set. A set C is convex if for all $x, y \in C$ and $\theta \in [0,1]$:

$$\theta x + (1-\theta)y \in C \tag{A.24}$$

where C is the convex set, and θ is the interpolation parameter.

Definition A.4.2 — Convex Function. $f : \mathbb{R}^d \to \mathbb{R}$ is convex if for all $x, y \in \text{dom}(f)$ and $\theta \in [0,1]$:

$$f(\theta x + (1-\theta)y) \leq \theta f(x) + (1-\theta)f(y) \tag{A.25}$$

where f is the convex function. Equivalently, f is convex iff its epigraph $\{(x,t) : f(x) \leq t\}$ is convex.

Theorem A.4.1 — First-Order Characterization. For differentiable f, convexity is equivalent to:

$$f(y) \geq f(x) + \nabla f(x)^T (y-x) \quad \forall x, y \tag{A.26}$$

where $\nabla f(x)$ is the gradient of f at x.

Theorem A.4.2 — Second-Order Characterization. For twice-differentiable f, convexity is equivalent to:

$$\nabla^2 f(x) \succeq 0 \quad \forall x \tag{A.27}$$

where $\nabla^2 f(x)$ is the Hessian matrix, and $\succeq 0$ denotes positive semidefiniteness.

Theorem A.4.3 — Jensen's Inequality. If f is convex and X is a random variable, then:

$$f(\mathbb{E}[X]) \leq \mathbb{E}[f(X)] \tag{A.28}$$

where $\mathbb{E}[X]$ is the expectation of X.

Definition A.4.3 — Strong Convexity. f is μ-strongly convex if $f(x) - \frac{\mu}{2}\|x\|^2$ is convex, equivalently:

$$f(y) \geq f(x) + \nabla f(x)^T(y-x) + \frac{\mu}{2}\|y-x\|^2 \tag{A.29}$$

where $\mu > 0$ is the strong convexity parameter.

Definition A.4.4 — Smoothness. f is L-smooth if ∇f is L-Lipschitz:

$$\|\nabla f(x) - \nabla f(y)\| \leq L\|x-y\| \tag{A.30}$$

where L is the smoothness constant (Lipschitz constant of the gradient). Equivalently: $f(y) \leq f(x) + \nabla f(x)^T(y-x) + \frac{L}{2}\|y-x\|^2$.

Theorem A.4.4 — Gradient Descent Convergence. For L-smooth, μ-strongly convex f, gradient descent with step size $\eta = 1/L$ satisfies:

$$f(x_t) - f(x^*) \leq \left(1 - \frac{\mu}{L}\right)^t (f(x_0) - f(x^*)) \tag{A.31}$$

where x_t is the iterate at step t, x^* is the optimum, and $\kappa = L/\mu$ is the condition number, which determines the convergence rate.

Theorem A.4.5 — Singular Value Decomposition. Any matrix $A \in \mathbb{R}^{m\times n}$ of rank r admits the decomposition:

$$A = U\Sigma V^T = \sum_{i=1}^{r} \sigma_i u_i v_i^T, \tag{A.32}$$

where $r = \text{rank}(A)$, $U \in \mathbb{R}^{m\times r}$ and $V \in \mathbb{R}^{n\times r}$ have orthonormal columns, and $\Sigma = \text{diag}(\sigma_1, \ldots, \sigma_r)$ with $\sigma_1 \geq \cdots \geq \sigma_r > 0$ are the singular values.

Theorem A.4.6 — Eckart–Young Theorem. The best rank-k approximation in Frobenius norm is:

$$A_k = \underset{\text{rank}(B)\leq k}{\arg\min} \|A - B\|_F = \sum_{i=1}^{k} \sigma_i u_i v_i^T \tag{A.33}$$

with error $\|A - A_k\|_F = \sqrt{\sum_{i>k} \sigma_i^2}$.

Definition A.4.5 — Positive Semidefinite Matrices. A symmetric matrix A is positive semidefinite ($A \succeq 0$) if all eigenvalues are non-negative, or equivalently $x^T Ax \geq 0$ for all x.

Chapter B

Advanced Proofs and Derivations

B.1 Proof of the VC Dimension Lower Bound

Theorem B.1.1 — Fundamental Theorem of Statistical Learning. Let $\mathscr{H}$ be a hypothesis class with VC dimension d. For any $\delta \in (0,1)$ and any $\varepsilon > 0$:

1. (Upper Bound) $m \geq \frac{8}{\varepsilon^2}\left(d \log \frac{16}{\varepsilon} + \log \frac{2}{\delta}\right)$ samples suffice for PAC learning
2. (Lower Bound) $m \geq \frac{d-1}{32\varepsilon^2}$ samples are necessary

where m is the sample size, d is the VC dimension, ε is the error tolerance, and δ is the failure probability.

Proof of Lower Bound Sketch. We use the probabilistic method with a *noisy-label* construction (the $1/\varepsilon^2$ dependence cannot arise from noiseless labels). Fix a set of d points $x_1, \ldots, x_d$ that can be shattered by $\mathscr{H}$. The adversary draws a hidden labeling $\sigma \in \{0,1\}^d$ uniformly at random and defines a distribution that places probability mass $1/d$ on each x_i and sets its label to agree with σ_i with probability $\frac{1}{2} + \varepsilon$ (and to disagree with probability $\frac{1}{2} - \varepsilon$). Because $\mathscr{H}$ shatters the points, the Bayes-optimal predictor is h_σ, which attains error $\frac{1}{2} - \varepsilon$; a learner's excess error is governed by how many coordinates σ_i it recovers.

For a single point x_i, deciding whether $\sigma_i = 0$ or $\sigma_i = 1$ amounts to distinguishing Bernoulli$(\frac{1}{2} + \varepsilon)$ from Bernoulli$(\frac{1}{2} - \varepsilon)$ from the labels observed at x_i. These two distributions have Kullback–Leibler divergence $\Theta(\varepsilon^2)$, so by Le Cam's two-point method (via Pinsker's inequality) a learner needs $\Omega(1/\varepsilon^2)$ observations of x_i to identify σ_i with constant advantage.

With only m samples spread over the d points, a constant fraction of points are each observed $O(m/d)$ times; whenever $m/d = o(1/\varepsilon^2)$ the learner misidentifies σ_i on a constant fraction of those points and therefore incurs excess error $\gg \varepsilon$. Requiring excess error $\leq \varepsilon$ thus forces $m/d = \Omega(1/\varepsilon^2)$, i.e. $m = \Omega(d/\varepsilon^2)$; tracking the constants through this averaging argument yields the stated bound $m \geq \frac{d-1}{32\varepsilon^2}$. ■

B.2 Derivation of the Evidence Lower Bound (ELBO)

In Variational Autoencoders (VAEs) and Bayesian inference, we often wish to approximate an intractable posterior $P(Z \mid X)$. The ELBO provides a tractable lower bound on the marginal log-likelihood that can be optimized via gradient descent.

Theorem B.2.1 — Evidence Lower Bound. For any distribution $Q(Z \mid X)$ over latent variables Z:

$$\log P(X) \geq \underbrace{\mathbb{E}_{z \sim Q}[\log P(X \mid z)]}_{\text{Reconstruction}} - \underbrace{D_{\text{KL}}(Q(Z \mid X) \| P(Z))}_{\text{Regularization}} =: \text{ELBO} \tag{B.1}$$

where $P(X)$ is the marginal likelihood, $Q(Z \mid X)$ is the approximate posterior, $P(X \mid z)$ is the likelihood, and $P(Z)$ is the prior, with equality if and only if $Q(Z \mid X) = P(Z \mid X)$.

Proof. We start with the KL divergence between the approximate and true posterior (which is always non-negative):

$$0 \leq D_{\text{KL}}(Q(Z \mid X) \| P(Z \mid X)) = \mathbb{E}_{z \sim Q}\left[\log \frac{Q(z \mid X)}{P(z \mid X)}\right] \tag{B.2}$$

where $D_{\text{KL}}(Q(Z \mid X) \| P(Z \mid X))$ is the KL divergence between the approximate and true posteriors.

Applying Bayes' rule, $P(z \mid X) = \frac{P(X|z)P(z)}{P(X)}$:

$$D_{\text{KL}}(Q(Z \mid X) \| P(Z \mid X)) = \mathbb{E}_{z \sim Q}\big[\log Q(z \mid X) - \log P(X \mid z) - \log P(z) + \log P(X)\big] \tag{B.3}$$

Since $\log P(X)$ is constant with respect to z:

$$\begin{aligned} D_{\text{KL}}(Q(Z \mid X) \| P(Z \mid X)) &= \log P(X) - \mathbb{E}_{z \sim Q}[\log P(X \mid z)] + \mathbb{E}_{z \sim Q}\left[\log \tfrac{Q(z|X)}{P(z)}\right] && \text{(B.4)} \\ &= \log P(X) - \mathbb{E}_{z \sim Q}[\log P(X \mid z)] + D_{\text{KL}}(Q(Z \mid X) \| P(Z)) && \text{(B.5)} \end{aligned}$$

Rearranging and using non-negativity of KL:

$$\log P(X) = \underbrace{\mathbb{E}_{z \sim Q}[\log P(X \mid z)] - D_{\text{KL}}(Q(Z \mid X) \| P(Z))}_{\text{ELBO}} + \underbrace{D_{\text{KL}}(Q(Z \mid X) \| P(Z \mid X))}_{\geq 0} \tag{B.6}$$

Therefore:

$$\boxed{\log P(X) \geq \text{ELBO} = \mathbb{E}_{z \sim Q}[\log P(X \mid z)] - D_{\text{KL}}(Q(Z \mid X) \| P(Z))} \tag{B.7}$$

■

Intuition: The ELBO balances two objectives:

- **Reconstruction Term** $\mathbb{E}[\log P(X \mid Z)]$: Encourages the model to explain the observed data well by maximizing the likelihood of X given the latent representation Z.
- **KL Regularization** $D_{\text{KL}}(Q(Z \mid X) \| P(Z))$: Prevents $Q(Z \mid X)$ from diverging too far from the prior $P(Z)$ (often a standard Gaussian), acting as a regularizer that encourages smooth, generalizable latent representations.

B.3 Proof of Differential Privacy Composition

Theorem B.3.1 — Basic Composition. If $\mathcal{M}_1$ is $(\varepsilon_1, \delta_1)$-DP and $\mathcal{M}_2$ is $(\varepsilon_2, \delta_2)$-DP, then the composition $(\mathcal{M}_1(D), \mathcal{M}_2(D))$ is $(\varepsilon_1 + \varepsilon_2, \delta_1 + \delta_2)$-DP.

Proof. For any measurable set S in the output space of the joint mechanism and adjacent datasets D, D', we condition on the output of $\mathcal{M}_1$:

$$P((\mathcal{M}_1, \mathcal{M}_2)(D) \in S) = \int P(\mathcal{M}_2(D) \in S_{o_1})\, dP_{\mathcal{M}_1(D)}(o_1) \tag{B.8}$$

where $S_{o_1} = \{o_2 : (o_1, o_2) \in S\}$.

By $(\varepsilon_2, \delta_2)$-DP of $\mathcal{M}_2$, for each fixed o_1:

$$P(\mathcal{M}_2(D) \in S_{o_1}) \le e^{\varepsilon_2} P(\mathcal{M}_2(D') \in S_{o_1}) + \delta_2 \tag{B.9}$$

Substituting and applying $(\varepsilon_1, \delta_1)$-DP of $\mathcal{M}_1$:

$$\begin{aligned}
P((\mathcal{M}_1, \mathcal{M}_2)(D) \in S) &\le e^{\varepsilon_2} \int P(\mathcal{M}_2(D') \in S_{o_1})\, dP_{\mathcal{M}_1(D)}(o_1) + \delta_2 && \text{(B.10)} \\
&\le e^{\varepsilon_2} \left(e^{\varepsilon_1} \int P(\mathcal{M}_2(D') \in S_{o_1})\, dP_{\mathcal{M}_1(D')}(o_1) \right. \\
&\qquad \left. + \delta_1 \right) + \delta_2 && \text{(B.11)} \\
&= e^{\varepsilon_1 + \varepsilon_2} P((\mathcal{M}_1, \mathcal{M}_2)(D') \in S) + e^{\varepsilon_2} \delta_1 + \delta_2 && \text{(B.12)}
\end{aligned}$$

This gives $(\varepsilon_1 + \varepsilon_2, e^{\varepsilon_2}\delta_1 + \delta_2)$-DP. To obtain the tighter standard result $(\varepsilon_1 + \varepsilon_2, \delta_1 + \delta_2)$-DP, we use a different approach. Define $B_i = \{o : P(\mathcal{M}_i(D) = o) > e^{\varepsilon_i} P(\mathcal{M}_i(D') = o)\}$ as the "bad" set for mechanism i, with $P(\mathcal{M}_i(D) \in B_i) \le \delta_i$ by definition of $(\varepsilon_i, \delta_i)$-DP. On the complement B_i^c, the pure e^{ε_i} bound holds. By a union bound, the probability of either bad event occurring is at most $\delta_1 + \delta_2$, and on the good event (both in B_i^c), the multiplicative bound is $e^{\varepsilon_1 + \varepsilon_2}$, yielding $(\varepsilon_1 + \varepsilon_2, \delta_1 + \delta_2)$-DP. ∎

Theorem B.3.2 — Advanced Composition. For k applications of (ε, δ)-DP mechanisms, the composition is $(\varepsilon', k\delta + \delta')$-DP where:

$$\varepsilon' = \sqrt{2k\ln(1/\delta')} \cdot \varepsilon + k\varepsilon(e^{\varepsilon} - 1) \tag{B.13}$$

where ε' is the composed privacy budget, k is the number of compositions, and δ' is the slack parameter. For small ε, this is approximately $O(\sqrt{k}\varepsilon)$ rather than $O(k\varepsilon)$. When the mechanisms have heterogeneous privacy parameters ε_j, the result generalizes by replacing $k\varepsilon^2$ with $\sum_{j=1}^{k} \varepsilon_j^2$ and $k\varepsilon(e^{\varepsilon} - 1)$ with $\sum_{j=1}^{k} \varepsilon_j(e^{\varepsilon_j} - 1)$.

B.4 Convergence of SGD for Convex Objectives

We analyze the convergence of Stochastic Gradient Descent (SGD) for a convex, L-Lipschitz function f.

Theorem B.4.1 — SGD Convergence for Convex Objectives. Let f be convex and L-Lipschitz (so that the stochastic gradients satisfy $\mathbb{E}[\|g_t\|^2] \leq L^2$). Let $x^* \in \arg\min f(x)$ with $\|x_1 - x^*\| \leq R$. If we run SGD with constant step size $\eta = \frac{R}{L\sqrt{T}}$, then:

$$\mathbb{E}\left[f\left(\frac{1}{T}\sum_{t=1}^{T} x_t\right)\right] - f(x^*) \leq \frac{RL}{\sqrt{T}} \tag{B.14}$$

where T is the number of iterations, R bounds the initial distance $\|x_1 - x^*\|$ to the optimum, and L is the Lipschitz constant.

Proof. Let g_t be the stochastic gradient at step t, such that $\mathbb{E}[g_t] = \nabla f(x_t)$. The update rule is $x_{t+1} = x_t - \eta g_t$. Consider the distance to the optimum:

$$\|x_{t+1} - x^*\|^2 = \|x_t - \eta g_t - x^*\|^2 \tag{B.15}$$

$$= \|x_t - x^*\|^2 - 2\eta\langle g_t, x_t - x^*\rangle + \eta^2\|g_t\|^2 \tag{B.16}$$

where η is the step size. Taking expectations:

$$\mathbb{E}[\|x_{t+1} - x^*\|^2] = \mathbb{E}[\|x_t - x^*\|^2] - 2\eta\,\mathbb{E}[\langle\nabla f(x_t), x_t - x^*\rangle] + \eta^2\,\mathbb{E}[\|g_t\|^2] \tag{B.17}$$

By convexity, $f(x^*) \geq f(x_t) + \langle\nabla f(x_t), x^* - x_t\rangle$, so $\langle\nabla f(x_t), x_t - x^*\rangle \geq f(x_t) - f(x^*)$. Also, assume bounded gradients $\mathbb{E}[\|g_t\|^2] \leq L^2$.

$$\mathbb{E}[\|x_{t+1} - x^*\|^2] \leq \mathbb{E}[\|x_t - x^*\|^2] - 2\eta\,\mathbb{E}[f(x_t) - f(x^*)] + \eta^2 L^2 \tag{B.18}$$

Rearranging and summing over $t = 1 \dots T$:

$$2\eta \sum_{t=1}^{T} \mathbb{E}[f(x_t) - f(x^*)] \leq \|x_1 - x^*\|^2 - \mathbb{E}[\|x_{T+1} - x^*\|^2] + T\eta^2 L^2 \tag{B.19}$$

Since $\|x_{T+1} - x^*\|^2 \geq 0$ and $\|x_1 - x^*\|^2 \leq R^2$:

$$\sum_{t=1}^{T} \mathbb{E}[f(x_t) - f(x^*)] \leq \frac{R^2}{2\eta} + \frac{T\eta L^2}{2} \tag{B.20}$$

Using Jensen's inequality on the LHS (convexity of f) and setting $\eta = \frac{R}{L\sqrt{T}}$ yields the result. ■

B.5 Proof of Rademacher Complexity Bound

Theorem B.5.1 — Rademacher Complexity Generalization Bound. For any $\delta > 0$, with probability at least $1 - \delta$ over the draw of $S \sim \mathscr{D}^n$, for all $h \in \mathscr{H}$:

$$\mathscr{R}(h) \leq \hat{\mathscr{R}}(h) + 2\hat{\mathfrak{R}}_S(\mathscr{H}) + 3\sqrt{\frac{\log(2/\delta)}{2n}} \tag{B.21}$$

where $\mathscr{R}(h)$ is the true risk, $\hat{\mathscr{R}}(h)$ is the empirical risk, $\hat{\mathfrak{R}}_S$ is the empirical Rademacher complexity, and n is the sample size.

Proof Sketch. The proof proceeds in three steps:

Step 1: Symmetrization. Using a ghost sample S', we show:

$$\mathbb{E}_S\left[\sup_h(\mathscr{R}(h) - \hat{\mathscr{R}}_S(h))\right] \leq 2\mathbb{E}_{S,\sigma}\left[\sup_h \frac{1}{n}\sum_{i=1}^{n} \sigma_i \ell(h, z_i)\right] \tag{B.22}$$

where σ_i are i.i.d. Rademacher variables ($P(\sigma_i = \pm 1) = 1/2$).

Step 2: Concentration. Using McDiarmid's inequality with bounded differences $c_i = 1/n$ (changing one sample alters the empirical risk of any fixed h by at most $1/n$, and the supremum inherits this bound):

$$P\left(\sup_h |\mathscr{R}(h) - \hat{\mathscr{R}}(h)| \geq \mathbb{E}[\sup_h |\mathscr{R}(h) - \hat{\mathscr{R}}(h)|] + t\right) \leq 2e^{-2nt^2} \tag{B.23}$$

Step 3: Combine. Setting $t = \sqrt{\log(2/\delta)/(2n)}$ (so that the McDiarmid failure probability is at most δ) and combining with the symmetrization bound (Step 1) gives the stated result; the leading constant 3 in the theorem statement absorbs the slack introduced by chaining symmetrization with concentration. ■

B.6 Shapley Value Axioms and Uniqueness

The Shapley value is the *unique* solution satisfying four axioms.

Definition B.6.1 — Shapley Axioms. Let $\phi_i(v)$ be the value allocated to player i, v the characteristic function, and N the set of players.

1. **Efficiency**: $\sum_{i\in N}\phi_i(v) = v(N)$ (under the standard normalization $v(\emptyset) = 0$; otherwise $\sum_i \phi_i(v) = v(N) - v(\emptyset)$).
2. **Symmetry**: If $v(S\cup\{i\}) = v(S\cup\{j\})$ for all $S \subseteq N\setminus\{i,j\}$, then $\phi_i(v) = \phi_j(v)$.
3. **Null Player**: If $v(S\cup\{i\}) = v(S)$ for all $S \subseteq N\setminus\{i\}$, then $\phi_i(v) = 0$.
4. **Linearity (Additivity)**: For games v and w, $\phi_i(v+w) = \phi_i(v) + \phi_i(w)$, and $\phi_i(cv) = c\,\phi_i(v)$ for $c \in \mathbb{R}$.

Theorem B.6.1 — Shapley Uniqueness. The unique allocation satisfying all four axioms is:

$$\phi_i(v) = \sum_{S\subseteq N\setminus\{i\}} \frac{|S|!(|N|-|S|-1)!}{|N|!}[v(S\cup\{i\}) - v(S)] \tag{B.24}$$

where the sum is over all subsets S not containing i.

Proof Sketch. The formula can be derived by considering all $|N|!$ orderings in which the players join the coalition. The number of orderings in which a specific subset S (with $|S|$ players) precedes player i is $|S|!\,(|N|-|S|-1)!$, so a uniformly random ordering puts exactly the set S before i with probability $|S|!(|N|-|S|-1)!/|N|!$. Player i's marginal contribution in such an ordering is $v(S\cup\{i\}) - v(S)$; averaging over the random ordering gives the displayed formula.

Uniqueness follows from showing that any function satisfying the axioms must equal this formula. The key insight is that the so-called "unanimity games" v_T (with $v_T(S) = 1$ iff $T \subseteq S$, for each non-empty $T \subseteq N$) form a basis for the vector space of cooperative games; by Linearity (Additivity), any axiom-satisfying allocation rule is determined by its value on each v_T, where Symmetry, Efficiency, and the Null-Player axiom uniquely fix it. ■

Chapter C

Python Implementation Details

This appendix provides concrete implementation details for key algorithms discussed in the text, using PyTorch and NumPy.

C.1 Fast Gradient Sign Method (FGSM)

Listing C.1 implements the FGSM attack in PyTorch.

```python
import torch
import torch.nn.functional as F

def fgsm_attack(image, epsilon, data_grad):
    """Generate adversarial example using FGSM for medical image analysis.

    Args:
        image: Original input image tensor (e.g., MRI or X-ray scan)
        epsilon: Maximum perturbation magnitude
        data_grad: Gradient of loss w.r.t. input scan

    Returns:
        Perturbed adversarial image for robustness testing
    """
    # Collect the element-wise sign of the data gradient
    sign_data_grad = data_grad.sign()
    # Create perturbed image
    perturbed_image = image + epsilon * sign_data_grad
    # Clip to maintain valid image range [0,1]
    perturbed_image = torch.clamp(perturbed_image, 0, 1)
    return perturbed_image

# Example usage on medical diagnostic model:
# Xray_scan.requires_grad = True
# diagnostic_output = disease_model(Xray_scan)
# loss = F.cross_entropy(diagnostic_output, true_diagnosis)
# disease_model.zero_grad()
# loss.backward()
# perturbed_scan = fgsm_attack(Xray_scan, epsilon=0.03, data_grad=Xray_scan.grad)
```

Listing C.1: FGSM Attack Implementation

C.2 Differential Privacy: Laplace Mechanism

Listing C.2 implements the Laplace mechanism for differential privacy.

```python
import numpy as np

def laplace_mechanism(true_value, sensitivity, epsilon):
    """Add Laplace noise to protect sensitive medical telemetry (e.g., patient vital signs).

    Args:
        true_value: True query result (e.g., average blood pressure across cohort)
        sensitivity: L1 sensitivity of the healthcare query
        epsilon: Privacy budget (smaller = stricter patient data privacy)

    Returns:
        Noisy query result satisfying epsilon-DP requirements
    """
    scale = sensitivity / epsilon
    noise = np.random.laplace(loc=0, scale=scale, size=np.shape(true_value))
    return true_value + noise

# Example: Private mean computation on hospital patient demographics
def private_mean(patient_ages_or_vitals, lower_bound, upper_bound, epsilon):
    """Compute differentially private mean for a medical study.

    Assumes the dataset size n is publicly known (bounded-DP setting),
    so it does not itself leak privacy.
    """
    n = len(patient_ages_or_vitals)
    true_mean = np.mean(patient_ages_or_vitals)
    # L1-sensitivity of the mean over a bounded health metric: (upper - lower) / n
    sensitivity = (upper_bound - lower_bound) / n
    return laplace_mechanism(true_mean, sensitivity, epsilon)
```

Listing C.2: Laplace Mechanism for Differential Privacy

C.3 Fairness Regularization

Listing C.3 implements a differentiable fairness regularizer suitable for gradient-based training.

```python
import torch

def demographic_parity_regularizer(risk_predictions, sensitive_trait):
```

```
    """Enforce Demographic Parity in healthcare risk management or
    ↪ medical triaging models.

    Mitigates bias corresponding to patient demographic groups by
    ↪ minimizing
    covariance between severity predictions and protected
    ↪ sensitive_trait
    (e.g., gender, race, or socioeconomic index).

    Args:
        risk_predictions: Predicted disease severity prob., shape (
    ↪ batch_size,)
        sensitive_trait: Indicator for protected demographic attribute
    ↪ , shape (batch_size,)

    Returns:
        Squared covariance term to penalize biased triage predictions
    """
    mean_risk = torch.mean(risk_predictions)
    mean_trait = torch.mean(sensitive_trait.float())

    # Measure linear dependence linking race/gender and perceived
    ↪ health risk
    covariance = torch.mean(
        (risk_predictions - mean_risk) * (sensitive_trait.float() -
    ↪ mean_trait)
    )
    return covariance ** 2

# Usage during medical model training:
# total_clinical_loss = bce_diagnosis_loss(risk_predictions,
    ↪ true_pathology) + lambda_fair * demographic_parity_regularizer(
    ↪ risk_predictions, patient_ethnicity)
```

Listing C.3: Differentiable Fairness Regularization

C.4 Projected Gradient Descent Attack

Listing C.4 implements the iterative PGD attack in PyTorch.

```
import torch
import torch.nn.functional as F

def pgd_attack(mri_classifier, original_scans, diagnostic_labels,
    ↪ epsilon, alpha, num_iter):
    """Projected Gradient Descent evaluating robustness of diagnostic
    ↪ models.

    Generates strong synthetic adversarial pathologies that might
    ↪ deceive
```

```python
    the healthcare classifier (e.g. skin cancer or MRI anomaly detection).

    Args:
        mri_classifier: Medical Neural Network processing scans
        original_scans: Healthy/Unhealthy tissue images (channels, height, width)
        diagnostic_labels: True ground-truth diagnoses
        epsilon: Maximum pixel intensity disturbance tolerance
        alpha: Step size for iterative perturbation updates
        num_iter: Steps attempting to bypass diagnostic thresholds

    Returns:
        Medical imaging tensors simulating tricky adversarial edge-cases
    """
    adv_scans = original_scans.clone().detach()

    # Random initial micro-disturbances simulating sensor noise within limits
    adv_scans = adv_scans + torch.empty_like(adv_scans).uniform_(-epsilon, epsilon)
    adv_scans = torch.clamp(adv_scans, original_scans - epsilon, original_scans + epsilon)
    adv_scans = torch.clamp(adv_scans, 0, 1)

    for _ in range(num_iter):
        adv_scans.requires_grad = True

        # Test classifier robustness to currently manipulated scan
        predictions = mri_classifier(adv_scans)
        diagnosis_error = F.cross_entropy(predictions, diagnostic_labels)

        # Compute how to change image to maximally disrupt medical diagnosis
        grad_disruption = torch.autograd.grad(diagnosis_error, adv_scans)[0]

        # Attack strategy: maximize the clinical misdiagnosis chance
        adv_scans = adv_scans.detach() + alpha * grad_disruption.sign()

        # Restrict generated scan artifacts to biologically plausible L-infinity limits
        delta_noise = torch.clamp(adv_scans - original_scans, -epsilon, epsilon)
        adv_scans = torch.clamp(original_scans + delta_noise, 0, 1)

    return adv_scans.detach()
```

```
# Example probing a diabetic retinopathy screening model:
# robust_test_data = pgd_attack(retinal_net, fundus_images, retina_health_labels, epsilon=8/255, alpha=2/255, num_iter=20)
```

Listing C.4: PGD Attack Implementation

C.5 Adversarial Training Loop

Listing C.5 gives a complete adversarial-training loop that alternates PGD attack generation with model updates.

```
import torch
import torch.nn as nn
import torch.optim as optim

def adversarial_training(biomedical_cnn, mri_dataloader, epochs, epsilon, alpha, num_iter, device):
    """Rigorous robust training over diverse medical imaging datasets.

    Helps immunize clinical AI architectures against imaging artifacts,
    scan anomalies, and equipment calibration failures.

    Args:
        biomedical_cnn: e.g. Pathological tumor segmentation model
        mri_dataloader: Source stream of legitimate patient scans
        epochs: Duration of robust medical curriculum
        epsilon, alpha, num_iter: Defending against synthetically complex variations
        device: Computational target processor (e.g., hospital GPU nodes)
    """
    biomedical_cnn.to(device)
    optimizer = optim.SGD(biomedical_cnn.parameters(), lr=0.01, momentum=0.9)
    criterion = nn.CrossEntropyLoss()

    for epoch in range(epochs):
        biomedical_cnn.train()
        running_clinical_loss = 0
        successful_diagnoses = 0
        total_evaluations = 0

        for batch_idx, (real_scans, actual_diagnostics) in enumerate(mri_dataloader):
            real_scans, actual_diagnostics = real_scans.to(device), actual_diagnostics.to(device)

```

```
            # Formulate simulated scanner measurement degradations or adversarial cases
            biomedical_cnn.eval()
            degraded_scans = pgd_attack(biomedical_cnn, real_scans, actual_diagnostics, epsilon, alpha, num_iter)
            biomedical_cnn.train()

            # Educate model on robust feature extraction
            optimizer.zero_grad()
            diagnostic_calls = biomedical_cnn(degraded_scans)
            diagnostic_error = criterion(diagnostic_calls, actual_diagnostics)

            # Penalize the architecture for failing on adversarial anomalies
            diagnostic_error.backward()
            optimizer.step()

            # Clinical performance tracking
            running_clinical_loss += diagnostic_error.item()
            _, chosen_clinical_labels = diagnostic_calls.max(1)
            total_evaluations += actual_diagnostics.size(0)
            successful_diagnoses += chosen_clinical_labels.eq(
                actual_diagnostics).sum().item()

        clinical_accuracy = 100.0 * successful_diagnoses / total_evaluations
        err = running_clinical_loss/len(mri_dataloader)
        print(f'Epoch {epoch}: Error={err:.4f}, '
              f'Robustness={clinical_accuracy:.2f}%')
```

Listing C.5: Complete Adversarial Training

C.6 Conformal Prediction

Listing C.6 implements split conformal prediction for classification.

```
import numpy as np

class ConformalClassifier:
    """Rigorous conformal uncertainty quantification wrapping any supervised classifier."""

    def __init__(self, diagnostic_system, tolerable_clinical_error=0.1):
        """
        Provides mathematical guarantees for diagnosis coverage sets based on
        the calibration population.
        Args:
```

```
            diagnostic_system: Supervised model extracting illness probabilities
            tolerable_clinical_error: Maximum acceptable diagnosis omission risk (1 - confidence)
        """
        self.diagnostic_system = diagnostic_system
        self.alpha_error_bound = tolerable_clinical_error
        self.empirical_threshold = None

    def calibrate(self, test_covariates, true_labels):
        """Estimate safe risk-threshold using held-out data."""
        conf_scores = self.diagnostic_system.predict_proba(
            test_covariates)

        # Non-conformity: how strange a patient seems
        cohort_size = len(true_labels)
        disagreement_metrics = 1 - conf_scores[
            np.arange(cohort_size), true_labels]

        # Establishing a proven cutoff for the targeted strictness
        target_quantile_idx = int(np.ceil((cohort_size + 1) * (1 - self.alpha_error_bound)))
        if target_quantile_idx > cohort_size:
            self.empirical_threshold = np.inf
        else:
            self.empirical_threshold = np.sort(disagreement_metrics)[target_quantile_idx - 1]

        return self

    def predict_set(self, new_profiles):
        """Generate prediction sets with coverage guarantee."""
        symptom_prob_estimates = \
            self.diagnostic_system.predict_proba(new_profiles)

        # Create a set containing all conditions lacking evidence for outright dismissal
        plausible_diagnoses = []
        for risk_profile in symptom_prob_estimates:
            retained_conditions = np.where(1 - risk_profile <= self.empirical_threshold)[0]
            plausible_diagnoses.append(set(retained_conditions))

        return plausible_diagnoses

# Example screening deployment assuring clinical coverage > 90%:
# biopsy_model = RandomForestClassifier().fit(symptoms_train, pathology_train)
# tight_interval_ai = ConformalClassifier(biopsy_model, tolerable_clinical_error=0.1)
# tight_interval_ai.calibrate(symptoms_val, biopsy_results_val)
```

```python
# probable_diseases_list = tight_interval_ai.predict_set(new_symptoms_arr)
```

Listing C.6: Conformal Prediction for Classification

C.7 Integrated Gradients

Listing C.7 implements the Integrated Gradients attribution method.

```python
import torch
import numpy as np

def integrated_gradients(diagnostic_cnn, patient_scan, baseline_reference, target_disease_class, steps=50):
    """Compute Explainable Integrated Gradients for medical imaging.

    Reveals WHICH physiological features (e.g. tissue structures in a scan)
    contributed most to a specific AI medical diagnosis.

    Args:
        diagnostic_cnn: Neural network trained on pathological scans
        patient_scan: Input X-ray/MRI to explain, shape (1, channels, height, width)
        baseline_reference: Blank or healthy tissue baseline template
        target_disease_class: specific illness predicted that needs explanation
        steps: Numerical approximation density for integral calculations

    Returns:
        Feature attribution heatmap matching input dimensions to highlight anomalies
    """
    # Generate interpolated intermediate tissue scans
    scaled_inputs = [baseline_reference + (float(i) / steps) * (patient_scan - baseline_reference)
                     for i in range(steps + 1)]
    scaled_inputs = torch.cat(scaled_inputs, dim=0)
    scaled_inputs.requires_grad = True

    # Ensure network is in evaluation mode to freeze Dropout and Batch Norm
    diagnostic_cnn.eval()

    # Evaluate AI clinical confidence at each interpolation intensity
    diagnostic_outputs = diagnostic_cnn(scaled_inputs)

    # Assess sensitivity concerning particular diagnosis (raw logits, not probabilities)
```

```
    target_logits = diagnostic_outputs[:, target_disease_class]
    grads = torch.autograd.grad(target_logits.sum(), scaled_inputs)[0]

    # Calculate expected gradient value using the trapezoidal rule for
    ↪ precise integration
    grads_trapz = (grads[:-1] + grads[1:]) / 2.0
    avg_grads = grads_trapz.mean(dim=0, keepdim=True)

    # Distribute relative importance across the patient's biological
    ↪ scan
    integrated_grad_heatmap = (patient_scan - baseline_reference) *
    ↪ avg_grads

    return integrated_grad_heatmap

def visualize_attribution(attribution, original_image):
    """Visualize attribution as heatmap overlay."""
    import matplotlib.pyplot as plt

    # Sum over channels for visualization
    attr_sum = attribution.squeeze().sum(dim=0).cpu().numpy()

    # Normalize
    attr_sum = (attr_sum - attr_sum.min()) / (attr_sum.max() -
    ↪ attr_sum.min() + 1e-8)

    fig, axes = plt.subplots(1, 3, figsize=(12, 4))
    axes[0].imshow(original_image.permute(1, 2, 0).cpu().numpy())
    axes[0].set_title('Original')
    axes[1].imshow(attr_sum, cmap='hot')
    axes[1].set_title('Attribution')
    axes[2].imshow(original_image.permute(1, 2, 0).cpu().numpy())
    axes[2].imshow(attr_sum, cmap='hot', alpha=0.5)
    axes[2].set_title('Overlay')

    for ax in axes:
        ax.axis('off')
    plt.tight_layout()
    return fig
```

Listing C.7: Integrated Gradients Attribution

Chapter D

Comprehensive Evaluation Metrics

This appendix provides a reference for evaluation metrics used throughout the book.

D.1 Robustness Metrics

Definition D.1.1 — Clean Accuracy. The standard classification accuracy on unperturbed test data:

$$\mathrm{Acc}_{\mathrm{clean}} = \frac{1}{n}\sum_{i=1}^{n} \mathbb{I}(f(x_i) = y_i) \tag{D.1}$$

where n is the number of samples, $f(x_i)$ is the predicted label, y_i is the true label, and $\mathbb{I}$ is the indicator function.

Definition D.1.2 — Robust Accuracy. Accuracy under adversarial attack with perturbation budget ε:

$$\mathrm{Acc}_{\mathrm{robust}}(\varepsilon) = \frac{1}{n}\sum_{i=1}^{n} \mathbb{I}(\forall\,\delta,\ \|\delta\| \le \varepsilon \implies f(x_i+\delta) = y_i) \tag{D.2}$$

where δ is the perturbation vector. In practice, this is approximated by the accuracy under a specific attack (e.g., PGD).

Definition D.1.3 — Certified Robust Accuracy. The fraction of samples with a certified radius $\ge \varepsilon$:

$$\mathrm{Acc}_{\mathrm{certified}}(\varepsilon) = \frac{1}{n}\sum_{i=1}^{n} \mathbb{I}(r(x_i) \ge \varepsilon) \tag{D.3}$$

where $r(x_i)$ is the certified radius from formal verification or randomized smoothing.

Definition D.1.4 — Attack Success Rate (ASR). For targeted attacks, the fraction where the adversarial example achieves the target class:

$$\text{ASR} = \frac{1}{n}\sum_{i=1}^{n}\mathbb{I}(f(x_i+\delta_i) = y_{\text{target}}) \tag{D.4}$$

where y_{target} is the target class.

Table D.1 collects the robustness evaluation metrics defined in this section, with their formulas, ranges, ideal values, and interpretation notes.

Table D.1: Summary of robustness evaluation metrics.

Metric	Formula	Range	Ideal	Notes
Clean Accuracy	$\frac{1}{n}\sum_i\mathbb{I}(f(x_i) = y_i)$	$[0,1]$	1	Standard baseline
Robust Accuracy	$\frac{1}{n}\sum_i\mathbb{I}(\forall\|\delta\| \leq \varepsilon : f(x_i+\delta) = y_i)$	$[0,1]$	1	Approx. via PGD
Certified Rob. Acc.	$\frac{1}{n}\sum_i\mathbb{I}(r(x_i) \geq \varepsilon)$	$[0,1]$	1	Uses verified radius
Attack Success Rate	$\frac{1}{n}\sum_i\mathbb{I}(f(x_i+\delta_i) = y_{\text{target}})$	$[0,1]$	0	Lower is better

D.2 Fairness Metrics

Definition D.2.1 — Demographic Parity Difference (DPD).

$$\text{DPD} = |P(\hat{Y}=1 \mid A=0) - P(\hat{Y}=1 \mid A=1)| \tag{D.5}$$

where $\hat{Y}$ is the predicted label, and A is the sensitive attribute. Values closer to 0 indicate fairer predictions with respect to demographic parity.

Definition D.2.2 — Equalized Odds Difference (EOD).

$$\text{EOD} = \frac{1}{2}\left(|\text{TPR}_0 - \text{TPR}_1| + |\text{FPR}_0 - \text{FPR}_1|\right) \tag{D.6}$$

where TPR is the true positive rate, and FPR is the false positive rate.

Definition D.2.3 — Equal Opportunity Difference.

$$\text{EOpp} = |P(\hat{Y}=1 \mid Y=1, A=0) - P(\hat{Y}=1 \mid Y=1, A=1)| \quad \text{(D.7)}$$

where Y is the true label. Focuses only on the true positive rate difference.

Definition D.2.4 — Predictive Parity. Requires equal positive predictive values:

$$P(Y=1 \mid \hat{Y}=1, A=0) = P(Y=1 \mid \hat{Y}=1, A=1) \quad \text{(D.8)}$$

where $P(Y=1 \mid \hat{Y}=1, A=a)$ is the positive predictive value (precision) within group a.

Definition D.2.5 — Disparate Impact Ratio.

$$\text{DIR} = \frac{P(\hat{Y}=1 \mid A=\text{disadvantaged})}{P(\hat{Y}=1 \mid A=\text{advantaged})} \quad \text{(D.9)}$$

where values less than 1 indicate disadvantage. The "80% rule" considers DIR < 0.8 as evidence of disparate impact.

Table D.2 collects the fairness evaluation metrics defined in this section, with their formulas, ranges, ideal values, and the quantities each compares.

Table D.2: Summary of fairness evaluation metrics.

Metric	Formula	Range	Ideal	What It Compares
DPD	$\lvert P(\hat{Y}=1 \mid A=0) - P(\hat{Y}=1 \mid A=1)\rvert$	$[0,1]$	0	Positive prediction rates
EOD	$\frac{1}{2}(\lvert\Delta\text{TPR}\rvert + \lvert\Delta\text{FPR}\rvert)$	$[0,1]$	0	TPR and FPR jointly
Equal Opp. Diff.	$\lvert\text{TPR}_{A=0} - \text{TPR}_{A=1}\rvert$	$[0,1]$	0	TPR only
Pred. Parity	$P(Y=1 \mid \hat{Y}=1, A=0) = \cdots$	—	Equal	Precision across groups
DIR	$\frac{P(\hat{Y}=1 \mid A=\text{disadv.})}{P(\hat{Y}=1 \mid A=\text{adv.})}$	$[0,\infty)$	1.0	Ratio; <0.8 = disparate impact

D.3 Privacy Metrics

Definition D.3.1 — Privacy Budget (ε, δ). The parameters of (ε, δ)-differential privacy. Smaller ε implies stronger privacy. The parameter δ bounds the probability that the pure ε-guarantee fails to hold (loosely, the allowable probability of a privacy breach).

Definition D.3.2 — Reconstruction Error. For model inversion attacks, the mean squared error between reconstructed and original data:

$$\mathrm{RE} = \frac{1}{n}\sum_{i=1}^{n} \|x_i - \hat{x}_i\|^2 \tag{D.10}$$

where $\hat{x}_i$ is the reconstructed input.

D.4 Calibration and Uncertainty Metrics

Definition D.4.1 — Expected Calibration Error (ECE).

$$\mathrm{ECE} = \sum_{b=1}^{B} \frac{|B_b|}{n} |\mathrm{acc}(B_b) - \mathrm{conf}(B_b)| \tag{D.11}$$

where the n predictions are partitioned into B confidence bins $B_1, \ldots, B_B$, and $\mathrm{acc}(B_b)$ and $\mathrm{conf}(B_b)$ denote the accuracy and average confidence within bin B_b. ECE measures the average gap between confidence and accuracy.

Definition D.4.2 — Maximum Calibration Error (MCE).

$$\mathrm{MCE} = \max_{b \in \{1,\ldots,B\}} |\mathrm{acc}(B_b) - \mathrm{conf}(B_b)| \tag{D.12}$$

where MCE measures the worst-case calibration error over the bins.

Definition D.4.3 — Brier Score.

$$\mathrm{BS} = \frac{1}{n}\sum_{i=1}^{n}\sum_{c=1}^{C} (p_{ic} - y_{ic})^2 \tag{D.13}$$

where p_{ic} is the predicted probability for class c and y_{ic} is the one-hot indicator.

Definition D.4.4 — Negative Log-Likelihood (NLL).

$$\text{NLL} = -\frac{1}{n}\sum_{i=1}^{n} \log p_{iy_i} \tag{D.14}$$

where p_{iy_i} is the predicted probability for the true class y_i. Also known as cross-entropy loss on test data.

D.5 OOD Detection Metrics

Definition D.5.1 — AUROC. Area Under the ROC Curve; equals the probability that a randomly chosen in-distribution sample is ranked as more in-distribution than a randomly chosen OOD sample — i.e., receives a higher confidence score (equivalently, a lower OOD/anomaly score).

Definition D.5.2 — FPR at 95% TPR (FPR95). False positive rate when true positive rate is 95%; measures the fraction of OOD samples incorrectly classified as in-distribution when 95% of in-distribution samples are correctly identified.

Definition D.5.3 — AUPR. Area Under the Precision-Recall Curve; more informative when classes are imbalanced.

D.6 Explainability Metrics

Definition D.6.1 — Faithfulness (Deletion). Measure how prediction changes when important features are removed:

$$\text{Faithfulness}_{\text{del}} = \text{AUC}\left(\{f(x_{-S_k})\}_{k=1}^{K}\right) \tag{D.15}$$

where x_{-S_k} removes the top-k most important features.

Definition D.6.2 — Faithfulness (Insertion).

$$\text{Faithfulness}_{\text{ins}} = \text{AUC}\left(\{f(x_{+S_k})\}_{k=1}^{K}\right) \tag{D.16}$$

where x_{+S_k} starts from baseline and adds top-k features.

Definition D.6.3 — Stability. For input x and small perturbation δ:

$$\text{Stability} = \frac{1}{M}\sum_{j=1}^{M} \text{sim}(\phi(x), \phi(x+\delta_j)) \tag{D.17}$$

where ϕ is the explanation function and sim is a similarity metric.

D.7 Agentic System Metrics

The metrics below are self-contained summaries; see Chapter 14 for full definitions with worked examples.

Definition D.7.1 — Task Completion Rate (TCR). For an agentic system evaluated on n tasks:

$$\text{TCR} = \frac{1}{n}\sum_{i=1}^{n} \mathbb{I}(f(\tau_i) = \text{success}) \tag{D.18}$$

where τ_i is the agent trajectory for task i and f is a success evaluator.

Definition D.7.2 — Safety Violation Rate (SVR). The fraction of trajectories containing at least one action outside the safe set:

$$\text{SVR} = \frac{1}{n}\sum_{i=1}^{n} \mathbb{I}\left(\exists k : a_k^{(i)} \notin \mathscr{A}_{\text{safe}}(h_k^{(i)})\right) \tag{D.19}$$

where $h_k^{(i)}$ is the execution history of trajectory i up to step k.

Definition D.7.3 — Step Efficiency. The ratio of the minimum required steps to the actual steps taken:

$$\text{Efficiency}(\tau) = \frac{T_{\text{min}}}{T_{\text{actual}}} \tag{D.20}$$

Values near 1 indicate near-optimal agent behavior.

Definition D.7.4 — Trajectory-Level Trust Score. A composite metric integrating correctness, safety, and efficiency:

$$\mathrm{Trust}(\tau) = \mathbb{I}(f(\tau) = \mathrm{success}) \cdot \prod_{k=0}^{T-1} \mathbb{I}(a_k \in \mathscr{A}_{\mathrm{safe}}(h_k)) \cdot \min\left(1, \frac{T_{\min}}{T_{\mathrm{actual}}}\right) \quad \text{(D.21)}$$

where h_k denotes the context and observation history up to step k.

Definition D.7.5 — Prompt Injection Resistance Rate. The fraction of injected adversarial prompts that the agent correctly ignores:

$$\mathrm{PIRR} = \frac{1}{n_{\mathrm{inj}}} \sum_{i=1}^{n_{\mathrm{inj}}} \mathbb{I}(\text{agent ignores injection}_i) \quad \text{(D.22)}$$

Table D.3 collects the agentic system evaluation metrics defined in this section, with their formulas, ranges, ideal values, and what each captures.

Table D.3: Summary of agentic system evaluation metrics.

Metric	Formula	Range	Ideal	What It Captures
TCR	$\frac{1}{n}\sum_i \mathbb{I}(f(\tau_i) = \mathrm{success})$	$[0,1]$	1	Task correctness
SVR	$\frac{1}{n}\sum_i \mathbb{I}(\exists a_k \notin \mathscr{A}_{\mathrm{safe}})$	$[0,1]$	0	Safety violations
Efficiency	$T_{\min}/T_{\mathrm{actual}}$	$(0,1]$	1	Step-optimality
Trust Score	TCR · Safety · Efficiency	$[0,1]$	1	Composite (all three)
PIRR	$\frac{1}{n_{\mathrm{inj}}}\sum_i \mathbb{I}(\text{ignores inj.}_i)$	$[0,1]$	1	Prompt injection resistance

Chapter E

Glossary of Key Terms

Adversarial Example
An input crafted by applying small, often imperceptible perturbations to cause a model to make incorrect predictions with high confidence.

Aleatoric Uncertainty
Inherent randomness in the data that cannot be reduced by collecting more data (e.g., sensor noise, labeling ambiguity).

Calibration A property where predicted probabilities match actual outcome frequencies: among predictions with confidence p, the fraction correct should be p.

Certified Robustness
A mathematical guarantee that a model's prediction is invariant to all perturbations within a specified radius.

Conformal Prediction
A distribution-free method for constructing prediction sets with finite-sample coverage guarantees.

Counterfactual Explanation
An explanation of the form "the prediction would have been Y' if the input had been X'", providing actionable recourse.

Demographic Parity
A group fairness criterion requiring equal positive prediction rates across protected groups: $P(\hat{Y}=1 \mid A=0) = P(\hat{Y}=1 \mid A=1)$.

Differential Privacy
A mathematical framework quantifying privacy loss, ensuring that the output of an algorithm is approximately independent of any single individual's data.

Distribution Shift
A change between the training and deployment data distributions, including covariate shift, label shift, and concept drift.

ELBO Evidence Lower Bound; a tractable lower bound on log-likelihood used in variational inference: $\log p(x) \geq \mathbb{E}_q[\log p(x \mid z)] - D_{\mathrm{KL}}(q(z \mid x) \| p(z))$.

Epistemic Uncertainty
Uncertainty arising from limited data or model capacity that

can be reduced with more data or better models.

Equalized Odds A fairness criterion requiring equal true positive and false positive rates across groups.

Feature Attribution
Assignment of importance scores to input features indicating their contribution to a model's prediction.

Federated Learning
A distributed learning paradigm where multiple parties collaboratively train a model without sharing raw data.

FGSM Fast Gradient Sign Method; a one-step adversarial attack using the sign of the loss gradient: $x_{\text{adv}} = x + \varepsilon \cdot \text{sign}(\nabla_x \ell)$.

Hallucination Generation of plausible-sounding but factually incorrect content by language models.

Individual Fairness
A fairness criterion requiring similar individuals to receive similar predictions: $d_Y(f(x), f(x')) \leq L \cdot d_X(x, x')$.

Integrated Gradients
A feature attribution method satisfying completeness by integrating gradients along a path from baseline to input.

Jailbreak An adversarial prompt designed to circumvent safety guardrails and elicit prohibited outputs from language models.

KL Divergence Kullback–Leibler divergence; a measure of difference between probability distributions: $D_{\text{KL}}(P \| Q) = \mathbb{E}_P[\log(P/Q)]$.

Laplace Mechanism
A differential privacy mechanism adding Laplace noise scaled to query sensitivity: $M(x) = f(x) + \text{Lap}(\Delta f/\varepsilon)$.

LIME Local Interpretable Model-agnostic Explanations; explains predictions by fitting a local linear model.

Lipschitz Continuity
A function f is L-Lipschitz if $|f(x) - f(x')| \leq L\|x - x'\|$ for all x, x'.

Model Card Standardized documentation describing a model's capabilities, limitations, and performance across subgroups.

OOD Detection Out-of-Distribution detection; identifying inputs that differ significantly from the training distribution.

PAC Learning Probably Approximately Correct learning; a theoretical framework for computational learning theory.

PGD Projected Gradient Descent; an iterative adversarial attack projecting perturbations onto an ε-ball.

Privacy Budget The cumulative privacy loss parameter ε consumed by multiple differentially private queries.

Rademacher Complexity
A measure of a hypothesis class's ability to fit random noise, used in generalization bounds.

Randomized Smoothing
A technique for certified robustness by classifying based on majority vote under Gaussian noise.

RLHF Reinforcement Learning from Human Feedback; training language models to align with human preferences.

Robustness The property that a model's predictions remain correct under input perturbations or distribution shift.

Sensitivity In differential privacy, the maximum change in a query's output when a single data point changes.

SHAP Values SHapley Additive exPlanations; feature attributions based on Shapley values from cooperative game theory.

Structural Causal Model (SCM)
A formal model specifying causal relationships via structural equations and a directed acyclic graph.

VC Dimension Vapnik–Chervonenkis dimension; the maximum number of points that can be shattered by a hypothesis class.

Watermarking Embedding detectable patterns in AI-generated content to enable attribution and detection.

Excess Risk Decomposition
Breakdown of generalization error into approximation error (bias from hypothesis class) and estimation error (variance from finite samples).

Approximation Error
Error due to the hypothesis class not containing the true function.

Estimation Error
Error due to estimating parameters from finite data.

Bias-Variance Decomposition
Decomposition of expected error into irreducible noise, bias (systematic error), and variance (sensitivity to data).

Irreducible Error
Inherent noise in the data-generating process that no model can eliminate.

Uniform Convergence
Property that empirical risk converges to true risk uniformly over the hypothesis class.

Sauer's Lemma Bounds the growth function of a hypothesis class in terms of VC dimension.

Double Descent Phenomenon
Test error decreases again after interpolation threshold in over-parameterized regimes.

Under-parameterized Regime
Model capacity insufficient to fit training data, leading to high bias.

Critical Regime Capacity just enough for interpolation, causing high variance.

Over-parameterized Regime
Capacity exceeds data needs, allowing implicit regularization.

Agnostic PAC Learning
PAC learning without assuming the true function is in the hypothesis class.

Margin-Based Generalization Bounds
Bounds using classifier margins for better generalization analysis.

Algorithmic Stability
Property that small data changes lead to small output changes, enabling generalization.

Linearity Hypothesis
Adversarial vulnerability arises from local linearity in high-dimensional spaces.

Concentration of Measure
Probability mass concentrates near low-dimensional structures in high dimensions.

Isoperimetric Inequality
Bounds on set expansion in high dimensions.

White-box Attacks
Attacks with full model access (weights, gradients).

Black-box Attacks
Attacks with only input-output access.

Gray-box Attacks
Attacks with partial model knowledge.

Targeted Attacks
Misclassify to a specific wrong class.

Untargeted Attacks
Misclassify to any wrong class.

L_∞ Constraint Perturbations bounded by maximum per-dimension change.

L_2 Constraint Perturbations bounded by Euclidean norm.

L_0 Constraint Perturbations bounded by number of modified dimensions.

Physical Attacks Perturbations realizable in the physical world (e.g., printed artifacts on medical scans).

First-Order Adversaries
Attacks using gradient information.

Zeroth-Order Gradient Estimation
Estimating gradients via function queries.

Random Direction Gradient Estimation
Efficient gradient estimation using random projections.

NES (Natural Evolution Strategies) Attack
Black-box attack using evolutionary optimization.

Square Attack Query-efficient black-box attack using random square perturbations.

Adversarial Training
Training on adversarial examples to improve robustness.

Robust Optimization
Min-max optimization for worst-case perturbations.

Zero-Sum Game Formulation of adversarial training as a game between trainer and attacker.

Minimax Theorem
Order of min-max can be swapped under convexity-concavity and compactness conditions.

Danskin's Theorem
Gradient of the max-function equals the gradient evaluated at the maximizer (when unique).

Smoothed Classifier
Classifier based on majority vote under Gaussian noise.

Natural Distribution Shifts
Legitimate changes in data distribution (e.g., covariate shift).

Domain Adaptation
Adapting models to new domains without labels.

Importance Weighting
Reweighting samples to correct for distribution shift.

Domain Adversarial Training (DANN)
Adversarial training to learn domain-invariant features.

Gradient Reversal Layer (GRL)
Layer that negates gradients for adversarial training.

Invariant Risk Minimization (IRM)
Learning features invariant across environments.

Distributionally Robust Optimization (DRO)
Optimizing for worst-case distribution in an uncertainty set.

f-divergence ball Uncertainty set defined by f-divergence from empirical distribution.

Wasserstein ball Uncertainty set defined by Wasserstein distance.

Group DRO Uncertainty set as convex hull of group distributions.

Philosophical Foundations Ethical theories underlying fairness (e.g., Rawlsian justice).

Rawlsian Justice Inequalities should benefit the least advantaged.

Luck Egalitarianism Distinguishes circumstantial vs. chosen inequalities.

Anti-subordination Theories Focus on reducing group-based disadvantages.

Group Fairness Fairness across demographic groups.

Impossibility Results Theorems showing incompatibility of fairness definitions.

Intersectionality Fairness across multiple intersecting identities.

Multi-Group Fairness Fairness in settings with many groups.

Disparity Metrics Measures of fairness violations (e.g., DPD, DIR).

Calibration Metrics Measures of probability accuracy across groups.

Pre-processing Methods Fairness interventions before training.

Reweighing Adjusting sample weights for fairness.

Fair Representation Learning Learning unbiased latent representations.

In-processing Methods Fairness constraints during training.

Adversarial Debiasing Adversarial training to remove bias.

Lagrangian Relaxation Converting constraints to penalties.

Post-processing Methods Adjusting predictions after training.

Threshold Optimization Group-specific decision thresholds.

Calibration Adjustment Correcting probability estimates.

Causal Fairness Fairness defined via causal graphs.

Counterfactual Fairness Predictions unchanged under sensitive attribute interventions.

Path-Specific Fairness Fairness along specific causal pathways.

Proxy Variable Feature correlated with sensitive attribute, enabling indirect discrimination.

Fairness Impossibility Theorems
: Results by Kleinberg–Mullainathan–Raghavan and Chouldechova showing the incompatibility of calibration and classification parity under unequal base rates.

Mechanisms for Fair Learning
: Techniques for achieving fairness in practice.

Privacy Loss Random Variable
: Random variable measuring per-sample privacy cost.

Gaussian Mechanism
: Adding Gaussian noise for DP.

Exponential Mechanism
: Sampling from utility-scored outputs.

Composition
: Combining multiple DP mechanisms.

Rényi Differential Privacy (RDP)
: Composition-friendly DP variant.

DP-SGD
: Differentially private stochastic gradient descent.

Privacy Amplification by Subsampling
: Privacy increases with subsampling.

Moments Accountant
: Tight composition bounds via moment tracking.

PATE
: Private aggregation via teacher-student framework.

Secure Multi-Party Computation (MPC)
: Joint computation without revealing inputs.

Secret Sharing
: Splitting secrets for MPC.

Shamir's Secret Sharing
: Threshold secret sharing scheme.

Additive Secret Sharing
: Simple sharing for linear operations.

Garbled Circuits
: Secure two-party computation via encrypted circuits.

Homomorphic Encryption (HE)
: Computation on encrypted data.

Local Differential Privacy
: Privacy where users randomize their own data.

Randomized Response
: Mechanism for local DP on binary data.

Reconstruction Attacks
: Reconstructing data from DP outputs.

Dinur–Nissim Theorem
: Limits on answering many queries privately.

Membership Inference Attacks (MIA)
: Detecting if a sample was in training data.

Model Inversion Attacks
Reconstructing inputs from model outputs.

Attribute Inference Attacks
Inferring sensitive attributes from predictions.

Explainable AI (XAI)
Methods for making AI decisions understandable.

Interpretability Inherent understandability of a model.

Intrinsic vs. Post-hoc
Interpretable by design vs. analyzed after training.

Global vs. Local Explanations for the whole model vs. single predictions.

Model-Agnostic vs. Model-Specific
Works on any model vs. exploits internals.

Feature Attribution Methods
Assigning importance scores to features.

Gradient-Based Methods
Using gradients for attribution.

Saliency Maps Visualizing gradient magnitudes.

Concept-Based Explanations
Explanations in terms of human concepts.

Concept Bottleneck Models (CBM)
Models predicting via interpretable concepts.

TCAV Testing sensitivity to high-level concepts.

Evaluating Explanations
Metrics for explanation quality.

Fidelity How well explanation matches model behavior.

Robustness (Explanations)
Stability of explanations to perturbations.

Sanity Checks Verifying explanations depend on model parameters.

Algorithmic Recourse
Methods for users to change predictions.

Wachter's Method
Optimizing for minimal counterfactual changes.

Actionability Constraints
Restrictions on changeable features.

DiCE Generating diverse counterfactuals.

Causal Counterfactuals
Counterfactuals respecting causal structure.

Recourse Robustness
Counterfactuals valid under model changes.

Algorithmic Recourse via Integer Programming
MIP for tree-based recourse.

Ladder of Causation
Levels of causal reasoning (association, intervention, counterfactuals).

Association Observing correlations.

Intervention Acting to change variables.

Counterfactuals Reasoning about hypothetical worlds.

d-Separation Graphical criterion for conditional independence.

Do-Operator Notation for interventions.

Back-Door Criterion
Conditions for identifying causal effects.

Adjustment Formula
Formula for causal effect estimation.

Do-Calculus Rules for transforming causal queries.

FedAvg Standard FL algorithm via model averaging.

Statistical Heterogeneity
Non-IID data across clients.

FedProx FL with proximal regularization for heterogeneity.

Personalized Federated Learning
Client-specific model tailoring.

Local Fine-Tuning
Global model fine-tuned per client.

Personalized Layers
Shared base with client-specific heads.

MAML-based Personalization
Meta-learning for personalization.

Mixture of Experts
Client-specific expert combinations.

Gradient Compression
Reducing communication via quantization/sparsification.

Quantization Reducing gradient precision.

Sparsification Transmitting only top gradients.

Low-Rank Approximation
Compressing gradients via SVD.

Secure Aggregation
MPC for aggregating without revealing updates.

Byzantine Attacks
Malicious clients poisoning FL.

Krum Robust aggregation via nearest neighbors.

Coordinate-wise Median
Median per gradient coordinate.

Trimmed Mean Averaging after removing outliers.

Alignment Problem
Ensuring RL agents pursue intended goals.

Reward Exploitation
Exploiting reward function loopholes.

Specification Gaming
Achieving reward via unintended means.

CoastRunners Effect
Optimizing for score by collecting power-ups instead of finishing the race.

Negative Side Effects
Unintended consequences of actions.

Reward Tampering
Modifying the reward signal.

Constrained Markov Decision Processes (CMDP)
MDPs with safety constraints.

Constrained Policy Optimization (CPO)
Trust-region method for CMDPs.

Safe Exploration Exploration without violating safety.

Safety Layers Real-time safety enforcement.

Control Barrier Functions (CBF)
Functions ensuring forward invariance.

Lyapunov-Based Safe Learning
Stability via Lyapunov functions.

Shielding Verified backup policies for safety.

Value Alignment Learning aligned reward functions.

Inverse Reinforcement Learning (IRL)
Inferring rewards from behavior.

Maximum Entropy IRL
Probabilistic IRL variant.

Feature Matching IRL
Matching feature expectations.

Preference Learning
Learning from human preferences.

Bradley–Terry Model
Probabilistic preference model.

Reinforcement Learning from Human Feedback (RLHF)
Aligning via human feedback.

Direct Preference Optimization (DPO)
Preference-based policy optimization.

Reward Shaping Adding auxiliary rewards.

Iterated Amplification
Recursively improving alignment.

Uncertainty Quantification
Measuring model confidence.

Covariate Shift Input distribution changes.

Label Shift Class proportion changes.

Concept Drift Relationship between inputs/outputs changes.

Domain Shift Simultaneous marginal and conditional changes.

Softmax-Based Methods
OOD detection via softmax probabilities.

Maximum Softmax Probability (MSP)
Confidence via max softmax.

Temperature Scaling
Adjusting softmax for better calibration.

ODIN OOD detection with input preprocessing.

Energy-Based OOD Detection
Using free energy for detection.

Deep Ensembles Uncertainty via model ensembles.

Mahalanobis Distance-Based Detection
Distance to class centroids.

Bayesian Neural Networks
Uncertainty via posterior distributions.

Variational Inference
Approximating posteriors.

Monte Carlo Dropout
Dropout for uncertainty estimation.

Laplace Approximation
Gaussian posterior approximation.

Expected Calibration Error (ECE)
Average calibration gap.

Reliability Diagrams
Plotting accuracy vs. confidence.

Post-hoc Calibration Methods
Adjusting probabilities after training.

Platt Scaling Logistic calibration.

Isotonic Regression
Non-parametric calibration.

Selective Prediction (Rejection)
Abstaining on uncertain inputs.

Risk-Coverage Trade-off
Balancing accuracy and coverage.

Agentic System An automated AI entity that perceives, reasons, and acts over extended horizons, defined by a tuple $(\mathscr{S}, \mathscr{A}, \mathscr{O}, \mathscr{T}, \pi, P_{\text{env}}, \mu_0)$ of state, action, observation spaces, tools, policy, environment dynamics, and initial state-observation distribution.

Tool-Augmented Agent
An agent with access to external tools (APIs, databases, code execution) that extend its capabilities beyond text generation.

Agent Trajectory
A sequence of observations and actions over an agent's execution horizon.

Markov Game (Stochastic Game)
Multi-agent extension of MDPs where each agent has its own reward function and the transition depends on joint actions.

Nash Equilibrium
A joint policy where no agent can unilaterally improve its expected return.

Price of Anarchy Ratio of optimal social welfare to worst Nash equilibrium welfare; measures efficiency loss from strategic behavior.

Compositional Trust
The property that trust/safety guarantees compose across sequential components in an agentic pipeline.

Error Propagation
The phenomenon where per-step errors compound across multi-step agent trajectories.

Action Shield A safety wrapper that intercepts and modifies proposed agent actions to ensure constraint satisfaction.

Capability Control
Restricting an agent's effective action space to a verified safe subset.

Tool Precondition/Postcondition
Formal specifications of conditions that must hold before and after tool invocation.

Goal Misgeneralization
An agent achieving high training performance by optimizing a proxy goal that diverges from the intended goal in deployment.

Instrumental Convergence
The tendency of optimal agents to pursue sub-goals (self-preservation, resource acquisition) regardless of terminal goal.

Power-Seeking Tendency of optimal policies to navigate toward states with greater optionality (more reachable future states), formalized by [78] via MDP graph structure conditions.

Corrigibility The property that an agent does not resist correction, modification, or shutdown by its operators.

AI Delegation Game
A principal-agent model where a human (principal) delegates

tasks to an AI agent.

Moral Hazard (AI)
Information asymmetry where the principal cannot observe the agent's reasoning or intermediate actions.

Scalable Oversight
Oversight mechanisms whose cost grows sublinearly in the complexity of the delegated task.

AI Safety via Debate
A protocol where two adversarial agents argue before a human judge, enabling efficient oversight of complex tasks.

Indirect Prompt Injection
Adversarial instructions embedded in data retrieved by an agent during execution, rather than in direct user input.

Instruction Hierarchy
A priority ordering of instruction sources (system $\succ$ user $\succ$ tool output $\succ$ retrieved content).

Multi-Agent Fairness
Fairness constraints ensuring that routing and per-agent performance do not introduce disparities across protected groups.

Task Completion Rate
Fraction of tasks successfully completed by an agentic system.

Safety Violation Rate
Fraction of agent trajectories containing at least one safety-violating action.

Trajectory-Level Trust Score
Composite metric integrating correctness, safety, and efficiency of an agent trajectory.

Machine Unlearning
The process of algorithmically removing the influence of specific training data points from a trained model, often to comply with data deletion requests.

Influence Functions
A technique from robust statistics used to approximate the effect of removing a training point on a model's parameters without fully retraining it.

Bayes Optimal Predictor
The (typically non-realizable) predictor f^* that minimizes the expected risk over *all* measurable functions $\mathscr{X} \to \mathscr{Y}$. For squared loss $f^*(x) = \mathbb{E}[Y \mid X{=}x]$; for 0-1 loss it is the Bayes classifier (the posterior-mode rule) $\arg\max_y P(Y{=}y \mid X{=}x)$.

Bayes Risk
The minimum achievable expected risk $\mathscr{R}^* = \mathscr{R}(f^*)$. It is the irreducible component of risk attributable to label noise in the

data-generating distribution and is invariant under the choice of hypothesis class.

Empirical Risk Minimization (ERM)
The learning principle that selects $\hat{f}_{\text{ERM}} \in \arg\min_{f \in \mathcal{H}} \hat{\mathcal{R}}_n(f)$. Generalization guarantees for ERM are obtained via uniform convergence over $\mathcal{H}$ controlled by combinatorial or geometric complexity measures.

Generalization Gap
The difference $\mathcal{R}(f) - \hat{\mathcal{R}}_n(f)$ between expected and empirical risk. Bounding the worst-case generalization gap over $\mathcal{H}$ is the central object of statistical learning theory.

Growth Function
$\Pi_{\mathcal{H}}(n) = \max_{x_1,\ldots,x_n} |\{(f(x_1),\ldots,f(x_n)) : f \in \mathcal{H}\}|$, the maximum number of dichotomies a binary hypothesis class can realize on any n points. Bounded above by Sauer's Lemma in terms of VC dimension.

Shattering
A set $S \subseteq \mathcal{X}$ is shattered by $\mathcal{H}$ if every dichotomy of S is realized by some $f \in \mathcal{H}$, i.e. $\Pi_{\mathcal{H}}(|S|) = 2^{|S|}$. The largest shattered set size is the VC dimension.

Hoeffding's Inequality
For independent bounded random variables $X_i \in [a_i, b_i]$, $P\big(|\bar{X} - \mathbb{E}[\bar{X}]| \geq t\big) \leq 2\exp\big(-2n^2t^2/\sum_i (b_i - a_i)^2\big)$. The basic tool for converting i.i.d. samples into finite-sample risk bounds.

McDiarmid's Inequality
(Bounded-Differences Inequality.) For a function $g(X_1,\ldots,X_n)$ that changes by at most c_i when coordinate i is replaced, $P\big(|g - \mathbb{E}g| \geq t\big) \leq 2\exp\big(-2t^2/\sum_i c_i^2\big)$. The workhorse behind Rademacher-complexity generalization bounds.

Sub-Gaussian Random Variable
A random variable whose tails decay at least as fast as a Gaussian: $\mathbb{E}[e^{\lambda(X - \mathbb{E}X)}] \leq e^{\lambda^2\sigma^2/2}$ for all $\lambda \in \mathbb{R}$. Bounded random variables and Gaussians are canonical examples; underlies most concentration inequalities used in this book.

Realizable Setting
The PAC-learning assumption that the target function lies in the hypothesis class, $f^\star \in \mathcal{H}$, so that $\inf_{f \in \mathcal{H}} \mathcal{R}(f) = 0$. Sample complexity is typically $O(d_{\text{VC}} \log(1/\varepsilon)/\varepsilon)$ in this regime versus $O(d_{\text{VC}}/\varepsilon^2)$ in the agnostic regime.

Carlini–Wagner (C&W) Attack
An optimization-based adversarial attack that minimizes $\|\delta\|_p + c \cdot g(x+\delta)$ where g penalizes the margin between the target and runner-up logits; one of the strongest white-box attacks

against undefended models.

AutoAttack A standardized ensemble of parameter-free attacks (APGD-CE, APGD-DLR, FAB, Square) used as a reliable benchmark for adversarial robustness, designed to avoid the gradient-masking failures of single-attack evaluations.

TRADES A training objective that explicitly decomposes the robust loss into a clean-accuracy term and a Kullback–Leibler-based robustness regularizer, exposing the accuracy/robustness trade-off via a single hyperparameter β.

Universal Adversarial Perturbation
A single perturbation vector v with $\|v\|_p \leq \varepsilon$ that fools a classifier on a large fraction of natural inputs simultaneously, revealing structural rather than per-instance vulnerabilities.

Transfer Attack A black-box attack strategy that crafts adversarial examples on a surrogate model and applies them to the target model, exploiting the empirically high cross-model transferability of perturbations.

Certified Training
Training procedures (IBP, CROWN-IBP, randomized smoothing) that optimize a *certified* upper bound on the worst-case loss within an ℓ_p ball, yielding models with provable rather than empirical robustness guarantees.

Interval Bound Propagation (IBP)
A symbolic-execution technique that propagates per-neuron interval bounds layer-by-layer through a network to soundly over-approximate its output range under ℓ_∞-bounded input perturbations.

CROWN / α, β-CROWN
Linear-relaxation-based neural-network verification methods that produce tighter sound bounds than IBP by relaxing nonlinear activations with input-dependent linear envelopes; α, β-CROWN combines this with branch-and-bound and currently anchors the VNN-COMP benchmark.

Equality of Opportunity
A fairness criterion requiring equal true-positive rates across protected groups, $P(\hat{Y}=1 \mid Y=1, A=a)$ constant in a. Weaker than Equalized Odds (which also constrains FPR) and often more compatible with calibration.

Predictive Parity A fairness criterion requiring equal positive predictive value across protected groups: $P(Y=1 \mid \hat{Y}=1, A=a)$ is constant in a. It conditions on the binary prediction $\hat{Y}=1$ and is strictly weaker than score-level sufficiency/calibration ($P(Y=1 \mid \hat{S}=s, A=a)$

constant in a); see the remark in Chapter 5.

Disparate Impact
A US-legal notion of indirect discrimination operationalized as a ratio $\min_a P(\hat{Y}=1 \mid A=a) / \max_a P(\hat{Y}=1 \mid A=a)$; the well-known 80% rule treats ratios below 0.8 as prima facie evidence of disparate impact.

Multicalibration A strengthening of calibration that requires the prediction to be calibrated simultaneously on every subgroup in a (possibly rich) collection $\mathscr{C}$ of subsets, eliminating subgroup-specific calibration failures invisible to overall calibration.

Multi-Accuracy A relaxation of multicalibration requiring only that the prediction match the conditional mean of Y on each subgroup in $\mathscr{C}$, achievable by efficient post-processing on top of any base predictor.

Rényi Divergence
The order-α divergence $D_\alpha(P\|Q) = \frac{1}{\alpha-1} \log \mathbb{E}_Q[(P/Q)^\alpha]$. Rényi DP is defined in terms of this divergence and is the basis of tight composition (e.g. the Moments Accountant) for DP-SGD.

Gradient Clipping (DP-SGD)
The per-example operation $g_i \leftarrow g_i \cdot \min(1, C/\|g_i\|_2)$ that bounds the ℓ_2-sensitivity of a single example to C, making the subsequent Gaussian noise addition (σC) achieve a quantifiable (ε, δ)-DP guarantee.

Privacy Amplification by Iteration
The phenomenon that running multiple post-processing or shuffling steps on a DP mechanism's output strictly reduces the realized privacy loss; together with amplification by subsampling, it underlies the tight accounting of DP-SGD.

Centralized vs. Local DP
In *centralized* (or curator) DP, a trusted aggregator sees raw data and releases a noisy statistic; in *local* DP, each user perturbs their own datum before sending it, achieving stronger trust assumptions at the cost of substantially worse statistical utility.

Privacy Loss Distribution (PLD)
The distribution of the (signed) privacy-loss random variable $\log(P(o)/Q(o))$ over outputs $o \sim P$; numerically composing PLDs gives the tightest known (ε, δ) accountant for compositions of DP mechanisms.

Gradient Inversion
An attack that reconstructs training inputs from shared gradients in federated learning by solving an optimization problem

matching synthetic gradients to the observed ones; the principal motivation for secure aggregation and DP-FedAvg.

Confounder A common cause of treatment X and outcome Y that creates a non-causal back-door path $X \leftarrow U \rightarrow Y$ inducing spurious dependence. Adjustment for a sufficient set of confounders is the basis of the back-door criterion.

Mediator A variable M lying on a directed path $X \rightarrow M \rightarrow Y$ that transmits part of the causal effect. Distinguishing direct from indirect effects requires intervening on or holding fixed mediators rather than merely conditioning on them.

Collider A variable C with at least two incoming edges along a path, e.g. $X \rightarrow C \leftarrow Y$. Conditioning on a collider *opens* the path, inducing spurious correlation between its parents (Berkson's paradox).

Average Treatment Effect (ATE)

$\tau = \mathbb{E}[Y_1 - Y_0]$, the population-level expected difference between the potential outcomes under treatment and control. Identifiable from observational data under the back-door or front-door criterion plus positivity and consistency.

Conditional Average Treatment Effect (CATE)

$\tau(x) = \mathbb{E}[Y_1 - Y_0 \mid X{=}x]$, a covariate-conditional treatment effect that captures heterogeneous responses across subpopulations; estimable by meta-learners such as the T-, S-, X-, and DR-learners.

Total, Direct, and Indirect Effects

For a treatment X, mediator M, and outcome Y: the *total* effect $\mathbb{E}[Y_x - Y_{x'}]$ decomposes (under appropriate assumptions) into a *natural direct effect* $\mathbb{E}[Y_{x,M_{x'}} - Y_{x'}]$ and a *natural indirect effect* $\mathbb{E}[Y_{x',M_x} - Y_{x'}]$ via mediation analysis.

Probability of Necessity / Sufficiency

Counterfactual quantities measuring how likely treatment is necessary (PN $= P(Y_{x'}{=}0 \mid X{=}x, Y{=}1)$) or sufficient (PS $= P(Y_x{=}1 \mid X{=}x', Y{=}0)$) for an outcome; used in causal attribution and root-cause analysis.

Spurious Correlation

A statistical association between two variables that is not generated by a direct causal mechanism, typically arising from confounding or selection. Trustworthy models aim to be invariant to such correlations under distribution shift.

Wasserstein Distance

The p-Wasserstein distance $W_p(P,Q) = \inf_{\gamma \in \Gamma(P,Q)} \big(\mathbb{E}_\gamma \|X -$

$Y\|^p)^{1/p}$, also called the earth-mover's distance. Central to DRO, generative modeling, and domain adaptation; metrizes weak convergence on bounded domains.

Total Variation Distance
$\mathrm{TV}(P,Q) = \frac{1}{2}\int |p-q|\,d\mu = \sup_A |P(A)-Q(A)|$, the strongest f-divergence used in this book; bounds the advantage of any binary test distinguishing P from Q.

Maximum Mean Discrepancy (MMD)
An integral probability metric $\mathrm{MMD}(P,Q) = \sup_{f\in\mathscr{F}} |\mathbb{E}_P f - \mathbb{E}_Q f|$ over a unit-ball RKHS $\mathscr{F}$; admits a closed-form kernel estimator and is used for distribution-shift testing and two-sample tests.

f-Divergence A family $D_f(P\|Q) = \mathbb{E}_Q[f(p/q)]$ for convex f with $f(1)=0$; recovers KL ($f = t\log t$), χ^2 ($f=(t-1)^2$), TV ($f=\frac{1}{2}|t-1|$), and Hellinger ($f=(\sqrt{t}-1)^2$) as special cases.

Prediction Set A set-valued predictor $C(x) \subseteq \mathscr{Y}$ instead of a point prediction; conformal prediction produces prediction sets with marginal coverage $P(Y\in C(X)) \geq 1-\alpha$ under exchangeability.

Conformity Score
A heuristic function $s(x,y)$ measuring how unusual a candidate pair is relative to a calibration set. The choice of conformity score (e.g. $1-\hat{p}_y$, regression residual, quantile-based) controls the *shape* of conformal prediction sets but not their coverage.

Split (Inductive) Conformal Prediction
The standard practical variant that splits data into a training fold (to fit the underlying model) and a calibration fold (to compute the $1-\alpha$ quantile of conformity scores), avoiding the $O(n)$ refits required by full conformal prediction.

Coverage Guarantee
A finite-sample probabilistic statement of the form $P(Y \in C(X)) \geq 1-\alpha$ (marginal) or $P(Y\in C(X)\mid X{=}x) \geq 1-\alpha$ (conditional). Marginal coverage is distribution-free; conditional coverage in full generality is impossible (Vovk).

Risk-Coverage Curve
The trade-off plot of selective risk against coverage induced by varying the rejection threshold in a selective classifier; the area under this curve quantifies the quality of the underlying confidence estimator.

Reward Hacking A failure mode where an RL agent obtains high reward by exploiting a misspecification or loophole in the reward function rather than by performing the intended task; closely related to specification gaming.

Mesa-Optimization
The phenomenon in which a learned model implements an internal optimization process whose objective (the *mesa-objective*) may differ from the outer training objective, raising alignment concerns under distribution shift.

Chain-of-Thought (CoT)
A prompting and training paradigm in which a language model emits intermediate reasoning steps before its final answer; improves complex-reasoning accuracy but introduces a faithfulness gap between stated and effective reasoning.

ReAct (Reasoning + Acting)
An agent prompting pattern interleaving natural-language reasoning steps with tool-call actions and observations, providing both a reasoning trace and a verifiable action log for inspection and safety analysis.

Sycophancy The tendency of a language model to align its stated beliefs with the user's expressed views rather than with truth, induced by preference data that conflates agreement with helpfulness; a known failure mode of naive RLHF.

KL Penalty in RLHF
The Kullback–Leibler regularizer $\beta D_{\mathrm{KL}}(\pi_\theta(\cdot \mid x) \| \pi_{\mathrm{ref}}(\cdot \mid x))$ added to the reward objective to keep the policy close to a reference (typically the SFT model), trading reward optimization against capability and behavioral drift.

Reward Model A learned function $R_\theta(x, y)$ that scores responses, trained on human preference comparisons (typically via the Bradley–Terry likelihood); serves as the proxy reward in RLHF and as the implicit objective for DPO.

Constitutional AI
An alignment method that replaces (or augments) human preference labels with model-generated critiques and revisions guided by a written set of principles ("constitution"), yielding RL from AI Feedback (RLAIF).

Tool Sandbox An execution environment that confines an agent's tool calls to a restricted set of side effects (file system, network, payment) and enforces preconditions and postconditions before/after each call.

Trajectory-Level Safety Constraint
A safety specification of the form $P_\pi(\exists t : \phi(s_t, a_t)) \leq \eta$ that bounds the probability of any unsafe state-action pair anywhere on a trajectory, in contrast to per-step constraints in CMDPs.

Bound Propagation
A family of neural-network verification techniques that compute sound over-approximations of the output range under bounded input perturbations by propagating intervals, zonotopes, or linear bounds through each layer.

MILP-Based Verification
An exact verification approach that encodes a piecewise-linear network (ReLU, max-pool) and a robustness specification as a mixed-integer linear program; complete and sound but NP-hard in the worst case.

Datasheets for Datasets
Standardized documentation describing a dataset's motivation, composition, collection process, preprocessing, intended uses, and ethical considerations; the data analog of model cards.

Algorithmic Auditing
Structured third-party assessment of an AI system against fairness, robustness, privacy, and accountability criteria, typically combining black-box behavioral probes with documentation review.

Risk-Based Governance
A regulatory paradigm (exemplified by the EU AI Act) that tiers obligations by use-case risk level (unacceptable, high, limited, minimal) rather than imposing uniform requirements on all AI systems.

AI Lifecycle / MLOps for Trustworthy AI
The end-to-end pipeline of data collection, training, evaluation, deployment, monitoring, and retirement of a model, with trustworthy-AI hooks (DP accounting, drift detection, conformal coverage tracking, recourse logging) embedded at each stage.

Machine Unlearning Certificate
A formal guarantee (e.g. (ε, δ)-unlearning) that, after an unlearning procedure, the resulting model is indistinguishable from one trained without the deleted points, providing a verifiable analog of the right to be forgotten.

Acknowledgments

The author gratefully acknowledges the open learning community and the instructors behind the excellent courses listed below. Their willingness to share high-quality educational resources served as an important source of inspiration during the preparation of this book. Many of these courses are freely available as video lectures and can be found by searching their titles on YouTube.

The content of these courses served solely as an inspiration source for this book. The author bears sole responsibility for the material presented herein, and these courses and their instructors bear no responsibility for the content of this book. There is no affiliation or conflict of interest between the author and any of the courses or institutions listed.

- Stanford CS230: Deep Learning I (Autumn 2025)
- Theoretical Aspects of Trustworthy AI
- Trustworthy ML Initiative Seminar Series
- Stanford CS229: Machine Learning I (Spring 2022)
- Causal Inference
- Alignment Workshop
- Stanford CS329H: Machine Learning from Human Preferences (Autumn 2024)
- Stanford EE364A: Convex Optimization
- Google DeepMind AGI Safety Course
- Trustworthy AI Course by Birhanu Eshete
- Trustworthy Machine Learning - Winter Semester 2024/2025
- Agentic AI MOOC Fall 2025
- 2025 Agentic AI Summit
- Stanford CME295: Agentic AI (Autumn 2025)
- LLM Agents MOOC Fall 2024

Bibliography

[1] Martin Abadi, Andy Chu, Ian Goodfellow, H Brendan McMahan, Ilya Mironov, Kunal Talwar, and Li Zhang. Deep learning with differential privacy. In *Proceedings of the 2016 ACM SIGSAC Conference on Computer and Communications Security*, pages 308–318, 2016.

[2] Josh Achiam, Steven Adler, Sandhini Agarwal, Lama Ahmad, Ilge Akkaya, Florencia Leoni Aleman, Diogo Almeida, Janko Altenschmidt, Sam Altman, Shyamal Anadkat, et al. Gpt-4 technical report. *arXiv preprint arXiv:2303.08774*, 2023.

[3] Joshua Achiam, David Held, Aviv Tamar, and Pieter Abbeel. Constrained policy optimization. In *International Conference on Machine Learning*, pages 22–31. PMLR, 2017.

[4] Julius Adebayo, Justin Gilmer, Michael Muelly, Ian Goodfellow, Moritz Hardt, and Been Kim. Sanity checks for saliency maps. In *Advances in Neural Information Processing Systems*, volume 31, 2018.

[5] Alekh Agarwal, Alina Beygelzimer, Miroslav Dudík, John Langford, and Hanna Wallach. A reductions approach to fair classification. In *International Conference on Machine Learning*, pages 60–69. PMLR, 2018.

[6] Dario Amodei, Chris Olah, Jacob Steinhardt, Paul Christiano, John Schulman, and Dan Mané. Concrete problems in ai safety. *arXiv preprint arXiv:1606.06565*, 2016.

[7] Maksym Andriushchenko, Francesco Croce, Nicolas Flammarion, and Matthias Hein. Square attack: a query-efficient black-box adversarial attack via random search. In *European Conference on Computer Vision*, pages 484–501. Springer, 2020.

[8] Martin Arjovsky, Léon Bottou, Ishaan Gulrajani, and David Lopez-Paz. Invariant risk minimization. *arXiv preprint arXiv:1907.02893*, 2019.

[9] Yuntao Bai, Saurav Kadavath, Sandipan Kundu, Amanda Askell, Jackson Kernion, Andy Jones, Anna Chen, Anna Goldie, Azalia Mirhoseini, Cameron McKinnon, et al. Constitutional ai: Harmlessness from ai feedback. *arXiv preprint arXiv:2212.08073*, 2022.

[10] Peter L Bartlett and Shahar Mendelson. Rademacher and gaussian complexities: Risk bounds and structural results. *Journal of machine learning research*, 3(Nov):463–482, 2002.

[11] Peva Blanchard, El Mahdi El Mhamdi, Rachid Guerraoui, and Julien Stainer. Machine learning with adversaries: Byzantine tolerant gradient descent. *Advances in neural information processing systems*, 30, 2017.

[12] Sébastien Bubeck, Varun Chandrasekaran, Ronen Eldan, Johannes Gehrke, Ece Kamar, Peter Lee, Yin Tat Lee, Yuanzhi Li, Scott Lundberg, Harsha Nori, et al. Sparks of artificial general intelligence: Early experiments with gpt-4. *arXiv preprint arXiv:2303.12712*, 2023.

[13] Igor Calzada, Géza Németh, and Mohammed Salah Al-Radhi. Trustworthy ai for whom? genai detection techniques of trust through decentralized web3 ecosystems. *Big Data and Cognitive Computing*, 9(3):62, 2025.

[14] Nicholas Carlini and David Wagner. Towards evaluating the robustness of neural networks. In *2017 IEEE Symposium on Security and Privacy (SP)*, pages 39–57. IEEE, 2017.

[15] Nicholas Carlini, Matthew Jagielski, Christopher A Choquette-Choo, Daniel Paleka, Will Pearce, Hyrum Anderson, Andreas Terzis, Kurt Thomas, and Florian Tramèr. Poisoning web-scale training datasets is practical. In *2024 IEEE Symposium on Security and Privacy (SP)*, pages 407–425. IEEE, 2024.

[16] Stephen Casper, Xander Davies, Claudia Shi, Thomas Krendl Gilbert, Jérémy Scheurer, Javier Rando, Rachel Freedman, Tomasz Korbak, David Lindner, Pedro Freire, et al. Open problems and fundamental limitations of reinforcement learning from human feedback. *arXiv preprint arXiv:2307.15217*, 2023.

[17] Arunraju Chinnaraju. Explainable ai (xai) for trustworthy and transparent decision-making: A theoretical framework for ai interpretability. *World Journal of Advanced Engineering Technology and Sciences*, 14(3):170–207, 2025.

[18] Alexandra Chouldechova. Fair prediction with disparate impact: A study of bias in recidivism prediction instruments. *Big data*, 5(2):153–163, 2017.

[19] Jeremy Cohen, Elan Rosenfeld, and Zico Kolter. Certified adversarial robustness via randomized smoothing. In *International Conference on Machine Learning*, pages 1310–1320. PMLR, 2019.

[20] Francesco Croce and Matthias Hein. Reliable evaluation of adversarial robustness with an ensemble of diverse parameter-free attacks. In *International Conference on Machine Learning*, pages 2206–2216. PMLR, 2020.

[21] Ameet Deshpande, Vishvak Murahari, Tanmay Rajpurohit, Ashwin Kalyan, and Karthik Narasimhan. Toxicity in chatgpt: Analyzing persona-assigned language models. In *Findings of the Association for Computational Linguistics: EMNLP 2023*, pages 1236–1270, 2023.

[22] Irit Dinur and Kobbi Nissim. Revealing information while preserving privacy. In *Proceedings of the twenty-second ACM SIGMOD-SIGACT-SIGART symposium on Principles of database systems*, pages 202–210, 2003.

[23] Minxin Du, Xiang Yue, Sherman SM Chow, Tianhao Wang, Chenyu Huang, and Huan Sun. Dp-forward: Fine-tuning and inference on language models with differential privacy in forward pass. In *Proceedings of the 2023 ACM SIGSAC Conference on Computer and Communications Security*, pages 2665–2679, 2023.

[24] Cynthia Dwork and Aaron Roth. The algorithmic foundations of differential privacy. *Foundations and Trends in Theoretical Computer Science*, 9(3–4): 211–407, 2014.

[25] Cynthia Dwork, Moritz Hardt, Toniann Pitassi, Omer Reingold, and Richard Zemel. Fairness through awareness. In *Proceedings of the 3rd Innovations in Theoretical Computer Science Conference*, pages 214–226, 2012.

[26] Tao Fan, Yan Kang, Guoqiang Ma, Weijing Chen, Wenbin Wei, Lixin Fan, and Qiang Yang. Fate-llm: A industrial grade federated learning framework for large language models. *arXiv preprint arXiv:2310.10049*, 2023.

[27] Isabel O Gallegos, Ryan A Rossi, Joe Barrow, Md Mehrab Tanjim, Sungchul Kim, Franck Dernoncourt, Tong Yu, Ruiyi Zhang, and Nesreen K Ahmed. Bias and fairness in large language models: A survey. *Computational linguistics*, 50(3):1097–1179, 2024.

[28] Timnit Gebru, Jamie Morgenstern, Briana Vecchione, Jennifer Wortman Vaughan, Hanna Wallach, Hal Daumé Iii, and Kate Crawford. Datasheets for datasets. *Communications of the ACM*, 64(12):86–92, 2021.

[29] Ian J Goodfellow, Jonathon Shlens, and Christian Szegedy. Explaining and harnessing adversarial examples. *arXiv preprint arXiv:1412.6572*, 2014.

[30] Steve Hanneke. The optimal sample complexity of pac learning. *Journal of Machine Learning Research*, 17(38):1–15, 2016.

[31] Moritz Hardt, Eric Price, and Nathan Srebro. Equality of opportunity in supervised learning. In *Advances in Neural Information Processing Systems*, volume 29, 2016.

[32] Moritz Hardt, Ben Recht, and Yoram Singer. Train faster, generalize better: Stability of stochastic gradient descent. In *International conference on machine learning*, pages 1225–1234. PMLR, 2016.

[33] Dan Hendrycks and Kevin Gimpel. A baseline for detecting misclassified and out-of-distribution examples in neural networks. *arXiv preprint arXiv:1610.02136*, 2016.

[34] Dan Hendrycks, Mantas Mazeika, and Thomas Woodside. An overview of catastrophic ai risks. *arXiv preprint arXiv:2306.12001*, 2023.

[35] Andrés Herrera-Poyatos, Javier Del Ser, Marcos López de Prado, Fei-Yue Wang, Enrique Herrera-Viedma, and Francisco Herrera. Responsible artificial intelligence systems: A roadmap to society's trust through trustworthy ai, auditability, accountability, and governance. *arXiv preprint arXiv:2503.04739*, 2025.

[36] Ziwei Ji, Nayeon Lee, Rita Frieske, Tiezheng Yu, Dan Su, Yan Xu, Etsuko Ishii, Ye Jin Bang, Andrea Madotto, and Pascale Fung. Survey of hallucination in natural language generation. *ACM computing surveys*, 55(12):1–38, 2023.

[37] Zhijing Jin, Jiarui Liu, Zhiheng Lyu, Spencer Poff, Mrinmaya Sachan, Rada Mihalcea, Mona Diab, and Bernhard Schölkopf. Can large language models infer causation from correlation? *arXiv preprint arXiv:2306.05836*, 2023.

[38] Sai Praneeth Karimireddy, Satyen Kale, Mehryar Mohri, Sashank Reddi, Sebastian Stich, and Ananda Theertha Suresh. Scaffold: Stochastic controlled averaging for federated learning. In *International conference on machine learning*, pages 5132–5143. PMLR, 2020.

[39] Guy Katz, Clark Barrett, David L Dill, Kyle Julian, and Mykel J Kochenderfer. Reluplex: An efficient smt solver for verifying deep neural networks. In *International Conference on Computer Aided Verification*, pages 97–117. Springer, 2017.

[40] Emre Kiciman, Robert Ness, Amit Sharma, and Chenhao Tan. Causal reasoning and large language models: Opening a new frontier for causality. *Transactions on Machine Learning Research*, 2023.

[41] John Kirchenbauer, Jonas Geiping, Yuxin Wen, Jonathan Katz, Ian Miers, and Tom Goldstein. A watermark for large language models. In *International Conference on Machine Learning*, pages 17061–17084. PMLR, 2023.

[42] Jon Kleinberg, Sendhil Mullainathan, and Manish Raghavan. Inherent trade-offs in the fair determination of risk scores. In *Innovations in Theoretical Computer Science*, 2017.

[43] Matt J Kusner, Joshua Loftus, Chris Russell, and Ricardo Silva. Counterfactual fairness. In *Advances in Neural Information Processing Systems*, volume 30, 2017.

[44] Haoran Li, Yulin Chen, Jinglong Luo, Jiecong Wang, Hao Peng, Yan Kang, Xiaojin Zhang, Qi Hu, Chunkit Chan, Zenglin Xu, et al. Privacy in large language models: Attacks, defenses and future directions. *arXiv preprint arXiv:2310.10383*, 2023.

[45] Tian Li, Anit Kumar Sahu, Manzil Zaheer, Maziar Sanjabi, Ameet Talwalkar, and Virginia Smith. Federated optimization in heterogeneous networks. *Proceedings of Machine learning and systems*, 2:429–450, 2020.

[46] Yijing Li, Xiaofeng Tao, Xuefei Zhang, Junjie Liu, and Jin Xu. Privacy-preserved federated learning for autonomous driving. *IEEE Transactions on Intelligent Transportation Systems*, 23(7):8423–8434, 2021.

[47] Shiyu Liang, Yixuan Li, and Rayadurgam Srikant. Enhancing the reliability of out-of-distribution image detection in neural networks. *arXiv preprint arXiv:1706.02690*, 2017.

[48] Weitang Liu, Xiaoyun Wang, John Owens, and Yixuan Li. Energy-based out-of-distribution detection. In *Advances in Neural Information Processing Systems*, volume 33, pages 21464–21475, 2020.

[49] Scott M Lundberg and Su-In Lee. A unified approach to interpreting model predictions. In *Advances in Neural Information Processing Systems*, volume 30, 2017.

[50] Aleksander Madry, Aleksandar Makelov, Ludwig Schmidt, Dimitris Tsipras, and Adrian Vladu. Towards deep learning models resistant to adversarial attacks. *arXiv preprint arXiv:1706.06083*, 2017.

[51] Potsawee Manakul, Adian Liusie, and Mark Gales. Selfcheckgpt: Zero-resource black-box hallucination detection for generative large language models. In *Proceedings of the 2023 Conference on Empirical Methods in Natural Language Processing*, pages 9004–9017, 2023.

[52] Brendan McMahan, Eider Moore, Daniel Ramage, Seth Hampson, and Blaise Aguera y Arcas. Communication-efficient learning of deep networks from decentralized data. In *Artificial Intelligence and Statistics*, pages 1273–1282. PMLR, 2017.

[53] Ilya Mironov. Rényi differential privacy. In *2017 IEEE 30th Computer Security Foundations Symposium*, pages 263–275. IEEE, 2017.

[54] Margaret Mitchell, Simone Wu, Andrew Zaldivar, Parker Barnes, Lucy Vasserman, Ben Hutchinson, Elena Spitzer, Inioluwa Deborah Raji, and Timnit Gebru. Model cards for model reporting. In *Proceedings of the Conference on Fairness, Accountability, and Transparency*, pages 220–229, 2019.

[55] Mehryar Mohri, Afshin Rostamizadeh, and Ameet Talwalkar. *Foundations of Machine Learning*. MIT Press, 2 edition, 2018.

[56] Ramaravind K Mothilal, Amit Sharma, and Chenhao Tan. Explaining machine learning classifiers through diverse counterfactual explanations. In *Proceedings of the 2020 Conference on Fairness, Accountability, and Transparency*, pages 607–617, 2020.

[57] Milad Nasr, Nicholas Carlini, Jonathan Hayase, Matthew Jagielski, A Feder Cooper, Daphne Ippolito, Christopher A Choquette-Choo, Eric Wallace, Florian Tramèr, and Katherine Lee. Scalable extraction of training data from (production) language models. *arXiv preprint arXiv:2311.17035*, 2023.

[58] Long Ouyang, Jeffrey Wu, Xu Jiang, Diogo Almeida, Carroll Wainwright, Pamela Mishkin, Chong Zhang, Sandhini Agarwal, Katarina Slama, Alex Ray, et al. Training language models to follow instructions with human feedback. In *Advances in Neural Information Processing Systems*, volume 35, pages 27730–27744, 2022.

[59] Nicolas Papernot, Martín Abadi, Ulfar Erlingsson, Ian Goodfellow, and Kunal Talwar. Semi-supervised knowledge transfer for deep learning from private training data. *arXiv preprint arXiv:1610.05755*, 2016.

[60] Judea Pearl. *Causality*. Cambridge University Press, 2009.

[61] Ethan Perez, Saffron Huang, Francis Song, Trevor Cai, Roman Ring, John Aslanides, Amelia Glaese, Nat McAleese, and Geoffrey Irving. Red teaming language models with language models. In *Proceedings of the 2022 Conference on Empirical Methods in Natural Language Processing*, pages 3419–3448, 2022.

[62] Jonas Peters, Peter Bühlmann, and Nicolai Meinshausen. Causal inference by using invariant prediction: identification and confidence intervals. *Journal of the Royal Statistical Society Series B: Statistical Methodology*, 78(5): 947–1012, 2016.

[63] Rafael Rafailov, Archit Sharma, Eric Mitchell, Christopher D Manning, Stefano Ermon, and Chelsea Finn. Direct preference optimization: Your language model is secretly a reward model. In *Advances in Neural Information Processing Systems*, volume 36, pages 53728–53741, 2023.

[64] Rajesh Ranjan, Shailja Gupta, and Surya Narayan Singh. Loka protocol: A decentralized framework for trustworthy and ethical ai agent ecosystems. *arXiv preprint arXiv:2504.10915*, 2025.

[65] Deevashwer Rathee, Mayank Rathee, Nishant Kumar, Nishanth Chandran, Divya Gupta, Aseem Rastogi, and Rahul Sharma. Cryptflow2: Practical 2-party secure inference. In *Proceedings of the 2020 ACM SIGSAC Conference on Computer and Communications Security*, pages 325–342, 2020.

[66] Marco Tulio Ribeiro, Sameer Singh, and Carlos Guestrin. "why should i trust you?": Explaining the predictions of any classifier. In *Proceedings of the 22nd ACM SIGKDD International Conference on Knowledge Discovery and Data Mining*, pages 1135–1144, 2016.

[67] Shibani Santurkar, Esin Durmus, Faisal Ladhak, Cinoo Lee, Percy Liang, and Tatsunori Hashimoto. Whose opinions do language models reflect? In *International Conference on Machine Learning*, pages 29971–30004. PMLR, 2023.

[68] Timo Schick, Jane Dwivedi-Yu, Roberto Dessì, Roberta Raileanu, Maria Lomeli, Eric Hambro, Luke Zettlemoyer, Nicola Cancedda, and Thomas Scialom. Toolformer: Language models can teach themselves to use tools. In *Advances in Neural Information Processing Systems*, volume 36, pages 68539–68551, 2023.

[69] Shai Shalev-Shwartz and Shai Ben-David. *Understanding Machine Learning: From Theory to Algorithms*. Cambridge University Press, 2014.

[70] Xinyue Shen, Zeyuan Chen, Michael Backes, Yun Shen, and Yang Zhang. " do anything now": Characterizing and evaluating in-the-wild jailbreak prompts on large language models. In *Proceedings of the 2024 ACM SIGSAC Conference on Computer and Communications Security*, pages 1671–1685, 2024.

[71] Ilya Shpitser and Judea Pearl. Identification of joint interventional distributions in recursive semi-markovian causal models. In *AAAI*, pages 1219–1226, 2006.

[72] Maurice Sion. On general minimax theorems. *Pacific Journal of Mathematics*, 8(1):171–176, 1958.

[73] Eugenia Stamboliev and Tim Christiaens. How empty is trustworthy ai? a discourse analysis of the ethics guidelines of trustworthy ai. *Critical Policy Studies*, 19(1):39–56, 2025.

[74] Bates Stephen et al. A gentle introduction to conformal prediction and distribution-free uncertainty quantification. *arXiv preprint arXiv: 2107.07511*, 2021.

[75] Mukund Sundararajan, Ankur Taly, and Qiqi Yan. Axiomatic attribution for deep networks. In *International Conference on Machine Learning*, pages 3319–3328. PMLR, 2017.

[76] Christian Szegedy, Wojciech Zaremba, Ilya Sutskever, Joan Bruna, Dumitru Erhan, Ian Goodfellow, and Rob Fergus. Intriguing properties of neural networks. In *International Conference on Learning Representations*, 2014.

[77] Hugo Touvron, Louis Martin, Kevin Stone, Peter Albert, Amjad Almahairi, Yasmine Babaei, Nikolay Bashlykov, Soumya Batra, Prajjwal Bhargava, Shruti Bhosale, et al. Llama 2: Open foundation and fine-tuned chat models. *arXiv preprint arXiv:2307.09288*, 2023.

[78] Alexander Matt Turner, Logan Smith, Rohin Shah, Andrew Critch, and Prasad Tadepalli. Optimal policies tend to seek power. In *Advances in Neural Information Processing Systems*, volume 34, pages 23063–23074, 2021.

[79] Leslie G. Valiant. A theory of the learnable. *Communications of the ACM*, 27 (11):1134–1142, 1984.

[80] Vladimir N Vapnik and A Ya Chervonenkis. On the uniform convergence of relative frequencies of events to their probabilities. In *Measures of complexity: festschrift for alexey chervonenkis*, pages 11–30. Springer, 2015.

[81] Vladimir Vovk, Alexander Gammerman, and Glenn Shafer. *Algorithmic learning in a random world.* Springer, 2005.

[82] Sandra Wachter, Brent Mittelstadt, and Chris Russell. Counterfactual explanations without opening the black box: Automated decisions and the gdpr. *Harv. JL & Tech.*, 31:841, 2017.

[83] Lei Wang, Chen Ma, Xueyang Feng, Zeyu Zhang, Hao Yang, Jingsen Zhang, Zhiyuan Chen, Jiakai Tang, Xu Chen, Yankai Lin, et al. A survey on large language model based autonomous agents. *Frontiers of Computer Science*, 18(6):186345, 2024.

[84] Yufei Wang, Wanjun Zhong, Liangyou Li, Fei Mi, Xingshan Zeng, Wenyong Huang, Lifeng Shang, Xin Jiang, and Qun Liu. Aligning large language models with human: A survey. *arXiv preprint arXiv:2307.12966*, 2023.

[85] Alexander Wei, Nika Haghtalab, and Jacob Steinhardt. Jailbroken: How does llm safety training fail? In *Advances in Neural Information Processing Systems*, volume 36, pages 80079–80110, 2023.

[86] Wenqi Wei and Ling Liu. Trustworthy distributed ai systems: Robustness, privacy, and governance. *ACM Computing Surveys*, 57(6):1–42, 2025.

[87] Zhiheng Xi, Wenxiang Chen, Xin Guo, Wei He, Yiwen Ding, Boyang Hong, Ming Zhang, Junzhe Wang, Senjie Jin, Enyu Zhou, et al. The rise and potential of large language model based agents: A survey. *Science China Information Sciences*, 68(2):121101, 2025.

[88] Shunyu Yao, Jeffrey Zhao, Dian Yu, Nan Du, Izhak Shafran, Karthik R Narasimhan, and Yuan Cao. React: Synergizing reasoning and acting in language models. In *International Conference on Learning Representations*, 2023.

[89] Chiyuan Zhang, Samy Bengio, Moritz Hardt, Benjamin Recht, and Oriol Vinyals. Understanding deep learning requires rethinking generalization. *arXiv preprint arXiv:1611.03530*, 2016.

[90] Hongyang Zhang, Yaodong Yu, Jiantao Jiao, Eric Xing, Laurent El Ghaoui, and Michael Jordan. Theoretically principled trade-off between robustness and accuracy. In *International Conference on Machine Learning*, pages 7472–7482. PMLR, 2019.

[91] Haiyan Zhao, Hanjie Chen, Fan Yang, Ninghao Liu, Huiqi Deng, Hengyi Cai, Shuaiqiang Wang, Dawei Yin, and Mengnan Du. Explainability for large language models: A survey. *ACM Transactions on Intelligent Systems and Technology*, 15(2):1–38, 2024.

[92] Haodong Zhao, Wei Du, Fangqi Li, Peixuan Li, and Gongshen Liu. Fed-prompt: Communication-efficient and privacy-preserving prompt tuning in federated learning. In *ICASSP 2023-2023 IEEE international conference on acoustics, speech and signal processing (ICASSP)*, pages 1–5. IEEE, 2023.

[93] Lianmin Zheng, Wei-Lin Chiang, Ying Sheng, Siyuan Zhuang, Zhanghao Wu, Yonghao Zhuang, Zi Lin, Zhuohan Li, Dacheng Li, Eric Xing, et al. Judging llm-as-a-judge with mt-bench and chatbot arena. In *Advances in Neural Information Processing Systems*, volume 36, pages 46595–46623, 2023.

[94] Ligeng Zhu, Zhijian Liu, and Song Han. Deep leakage from gradients. In *Advances in Neural Information Processing Systems*, volume 32, 2019.

[95] Andy Zou, Zifan Wang, Nicholas Carlini, Milad Nasr, J Zico Kolter, and Matt Fredrikson. Universal and transferable adversarial attacks on aligned language models. *arXiv preprint arXiv:2307.15043*, 2023.

Index

Symbols

A

B

C

E

K

L

N

O

P

Q

R

T

U

V

W

X

Y

Z

Mathematical Foundations of Trustworthy AI

Theory, Algorithms, and Engineering Principles

As artificial intelligence enters domains where errors carry real consequences, the need for systems that are provably robust, fair, private, and interpretable has become urgent.

This book provides a rigorous, self-contained treatment of the mathematical foundations underlying every major dimension of Trustworthy AI -- from statistical learning theory and adversarial robustness to causal inference, federated learning, and safe reinforcement learning.

Every result is supported by detailed proofs, worked examples, algorithms, and exercises, making this work suitable as both a graduate textbook and a reference for researchers and practitioners.

www.ingramcontent.com/pod-product-compliance
Lightning Source LLC
LaVergne TN
LVHW080023210926
848481LV00011B/3093